WORK AND JOB SATISFACTION IN THE PUBLIC SECTOR

This book takes a humanistic approach to the problem of improving the worklife of employees. Using data from a survey of randomly selected state public employees working in five state capitals, the author proposes a new model of job satisfaction that incorporates both job environment factors and job characteristics, and for the first time examines the impact of unionization on job satisfaction. The resulting "best fit" model challenges the appropriateness of the recent emphasis on job redesign by organizational psychologists.

WORK AND JOB SATISFACTION IN THE PUBLIC SECTOR

Anne H. Hopkins

ROWMAN & ALLANHELD
Totowa, New Jersey

ROWMAN & ALLANHELD

Published in the United States of America in 1983
by Rowman & Allanheld
(A division of Littlefield, Adams & Company)
81 Adams Drive, Totowa, New Jersey 07512

Library of Congress Cataloging in Publication Data

Hopkins, Anne H.
   Work and job satisfaction in the public sector.

   Bibliography: p.
   Includes index.
   1. Job satisfaction.   2. Job enrichment.
3. Public administration.   I. Title.
HF5549.5.J63H577   1983   350.1'47   82-24356
ISBN 0-86598-111-6

83 84 85/10 9 8 7 6 5 4 3 2 1

Printed in the United States of America

For my late parents,
Marian Cadle Houghton and
William Emmett Houghton,
and for my mentor,
the late Professor Frank J. Munger

CONTENTS

LIST OF TABLES AND FIGURES

TABLES

ACKNOWLEDGMENTS

A number of people have provided enormous assistance to me in conducting the research reported in this volume and in the preparation of this manuscript. The original stimulus to design and execute this research was provided by Professor Russel Smith, then a graduate student at the University of Tennessee. Smith and another graduate student, Professor George Rawson, worked jointly with me in designing the questionnaire and collecting the data. The University of Tennessee provided assistance in three ways: through its Bureau of Public Administration, by awarding me a Faculty Development Grant, and through its support of the University Computing Center. Support, intellectual and otherwise, was provided by Professors Michael Fitzgerald, Thomas Ungs, Paul Schulman, and Ms. Floydette C. Cory. The manuscript would not have been completed without the prodding and encouragement of Dr. Charles P. Cohen. Diane Kosier did a superior job in typing the manuscript, as did my good friend Martha G. Lindsay in editing the copy. My husband, Ward, tolerated with grace my preoccupations for the last several years.

The responsibility for any shortcomings or misinterpretations in this work remains mine alone.

CHAPTER 1

PERSPECTIVES ON WORK

Work occupies almost half of the waking hours of most Americans. The quality of life of most workers is dramatically influenced by the nature of that employment. The reactions of workers to their jobs alter their basic self-perceptions and self-esteem. To most individuals, work is one of the key elements of their lives. Rapidly changing technologies and an economic environment less oriented to growth have placed the worker in an increasingly stressful environment. In order to promote higher quality lives for workers, humanistically oriented scholars have focused considerable energy on understanding the complexities of work. The level and determinants of job satisfaction have in consequence been a central emphasis in such research.

Scholarly attention to the quality of worklife may arise not only from a concern with the well-being of the individual but from one's perspective about the nature of a "good" society. A society composed of a significant minority of dissatisfied or demoralized workers is not likely to be a healthy society either economically or socially. Reactions to work in the public sector have the added effect of influencing the style of delivery as well as the quality of services available to the public. Current budgetary cutbacks in the public sector, with accompanying reductions in government employees at all levels, raise important issues about the future quality of government services. Thus, whether one is concerned about the quality of individual life or the state of the larger society, the nature of workers' responses to their employment is critical.

This study examines work from the perspective of the individuals in a public sector setting. An individual's response to their work is effected primarily by the work environment, both in terms of its structure and the nature of the other individuals in that environment. Most studies of work identify only some of these components of the work setting and consistently do not consider the influence of unionization. The purpose of this book is to explore the interrelationships among the individual and the working environment including unions in a more comprehensive manner and in the context of the public sector. Specifically the setting for this study of work is state government, with samples of state employees in five states with varying employment and union practices.

This work builds on the recent humanistic orientations of both public administration and industrial psychology in their concern for the individual and individual fulfillment. The findings in this book challenge the current emphasis on job redesign, and an improved model of the individual's response to their work is developed. The implications and ultimate usefulness of such an improved model are strongly linked to the possible improvement of the quality of both the individual's working life and governmental operations.

To frame this study of public sector work, a model frequently used in the study of job satisfaction is examined. Basically, this model links the individual's response to their work (job satisfaction) with the nature of their jobs, the larger working environment, and broadly based individual orientations. Three modifications of the dominant pattern of previous research in this area are included in this study. The first difference, a potentially important modification of the model, is the addition of unionization as an aspect of the work environment. Second, more comprehensive indicators of the nature of the job and the job environment are developed. Finally, a multivariate analysis strategy is employed. Before the initial model is discussed, the research perspectives utilized in previous studies in this area are examined in general terms and the basic research problem is outlined.

Research Perspectives

Workers' responses to their jobs have long been a major focus of research in the various public and private management-oriented fields of study, such as industrial and organizational psychology and public administration. Although the research is voluminous, it seems fair to characterize this stream of research as having experienced a basic reorientation. Initially those who studied job satisfaction sought to relate it to productivity. Such research tended to have industrial sponsors who sought improved productivity as a direct outgrowth of the research. As is often the case, immediate results did not occur. In general, such research produced weak or mixed findings on the relationship between job satisfaction and productivity (Vroom, 1964; Ronan, 1970; Katzell and Yankelovich, 1975).

Despite the limited impact of this research in altering productivity, researchers were still substantially interested in the concept of job satisfaction. Studies of job satisfaction continued to flourish as part of an increasing concern by scholars with the role of the individual in organizations. This more recent humanistic approach (Gibson and Teasley, 1973), instead of focusing on productivity, seeks to improve the quality of workers' lives by increasing job satisfaction. Building on to the humanistic approach, some scholars have also made a strong case for job satisfaction as a social indicator (Kahn, 1972).[1]

This evolution in the reasons or motivations for studying job satisfaction has been accompanied by other changes in the model used to predict job satisfaction. One important variation is the extent to which Maslow's view of individual needs (Maslow, 1943, 1954) is followed. According to this view, job satisfaction is said to exist when an individual's needs are met by the job and its environment. Maslow asserted that these individual needs are uniform and hierarchically arranged. More recently, others have assumed that individual needs vary both across time and across individuals (Hackman and Lawler, 1971; Turner and Lawrence, 1965; Hulin and Blood, 1968).

Another pronounced change in the model used to predict job satisfaction has been in the amount of attention given to varying aspects of the job and its environment. As studies of job satisfaction shifted to a more humanistic focus, there was also a shift in emphasis toward an examination of job characteristics. The earlier studies of job satisfaction considered as important potential determinants both the nature of the job itself and the immediate environment within which the job takes place. With the advent of the humanistic approach, however, there was a shift away from the consideration of the job environment as a potential determinant of job satisfaction.

Numerous recent studies focus on job redesign or enlargement as a means of increasing satisfaction (Alderfer, 1969b; Lawler, 1969; Hackman and Oldham, 1980). The redesign approach sees job characteristics as the prime determinant of job satisfaction, moderated by the nature of the workers' needs. It seems likely that there has been a greater focus on job characteristics, at least partly, because researchers feel it may be easier to redesign jobs than to alter their environments (Hackman, 1969). Consistent with this perspective is a concern with the impact of organizational structure (Oldham and Hackman, 1981), defined variously as size, hierarchical levels, formalization, and centralization (James and Jones, 1976). Although in one sense these structural factors may be considered part of the job environment, they are also consistent with the focus on redesigning jobs since they are more subject to manipulation than are most job environment factors. The focus on job redesign has also led to the development of a number of applied projects on quality of worklife in which the potential negative or facilitative role of unions has been of some concern (Holley, Field and Crowley, 1981; Nadler, Hanlon and Lawler, 1980).

The Research Problem

The development of an expanded understanding of workers' reactions to their jobs is important for several reasons. Improvement in the quality of worklife is directly dependent upon understanding those factors that affect employees' reactions (satisfaction). For humanistic reasons, such an improvement, as defined by individual workers, is desirable. Values as to what is desired from work may vary across individuals, but if we can understand (predict) variations in job satisfaction, we have taken the first step in potentially altering those factors most apt to suppress satisfaction. The last twenty-five years in American society have frequently been characterized as the age of alienation. Alienation in the work place is common. Rapid social and technological changes, the increasing size of organizations, and the increasing complexity of work-based problems that most workers face daily have placed alienation and its effect on the quality of life among our society's most pressing problems.

If one considers the quality of worklife to be an important topic, then it becomes essential to explore how and why workers respond as they do to their jobs. Workers' responses to their employment are essentially attitudinal and may or may not have behavioral manifestations in the work setting. As with many attitudes, they may have multiple origins, as well as variations in intensity and durability, and the task of understanding how and why workers respond to their jobs thus becomes exceedingly complex, though all the more important if one values maximizing individual life quality.

If, for a moment, previous research in this area is put aside, perhaps a clearer picture of what may be involved in expanding this understanding of worklife responses can be drawn. All jobs have a context within which workers perform their tasks. Undoubtedly that context, as well as the nature of the tasks' requirements, affects the worker. Thus the most obvious potential determinant of job responses is the nature of the work situation and the primary issues to be dealt with are conceptual and measurement ones. But it is equally obvious that the work situation may not be the *only* important determinant of worker attitudes. Attitudes held by workers occupying virtually the same jobs in the same context may be widely different. Timing may be an issue here because an individual's attitudes are not always stable over time and there are certainly fluctuations in the intensity of even long-held attitudes.

A potentially very important factor in why workers respond as they do to their jobs is those attitudes, values, and behaviors that individuals bring with them into their employment. For example, individual workers may vary in terms of their expectations about their jobs, the importance of work in their lives, or the manner in which they relate to other people. Unlike the work situation, major theoretical issues dominate the consideration of the nature of the factors that individuals bring with them to their job. Conceptual and measurement problems also exist in this area, but major theoretical issues predominate.

If the reader now returns to a consideration of the brief research perspectives discussed above, a sense of the contribution of this study may be seen. The objective of the investigation is to enhance our understanding of worker responses to their jobs (job satisfaction), and this needs careful conceptual definition and measurement. Previous research that paid considerable attention to the measurement issues is drawn on in this study.

Two types of determinants of job satisfaction are posited: the nature of the work situation and the orientation brought by the individual to the work setting. In considering the work situation, the most crucial issue concerns what factors are included as a component of the work situation. Recent reorientations of the research efforts in this area of study toward job redesign have ignored the importance of the job environment. Another crucial dimension of the work situation, unionization, has rarely been studied.

Figure 1.1 A Model of Work and Job Satisfaction

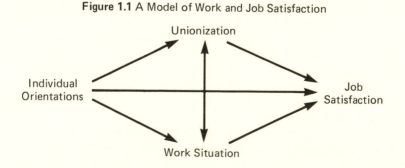

Important theoretical issues dominate the consideration of the nature of the factors that individuals bring with them to their jobs. These issues revolve around the implicit or explicit reliance on Maslow's needs-hierarchy or some variation on it as the theory to explain human motivation and, in this instance, to link the nature of the work situation to job satisfaction. There are substantial problems with the way human needs are treated in this literature. Although resolution of this theoretical issue is not possible here, adaptations are made to ameliorate some of the problems.

Theoretical Framework

To provide a point of departure for our analysis of work in the public sector, a job satisfaction model has been adapted from previous research. The model focuses on job satisfaction as an effect rather than a cause of the other factors and thus the dependent variable.[2] There are four basic components of the model: job satisfaction, unionization, the work situation, and individual orientations. Figure 1.1 presents the model with arrows indicating the linkages hypothesized to exist among the components. To elaborate the model each of the four components is defined and a discussion of the linkages follows.

Job satisfaction can be simply defined as the fulfillment or gratification of certain needs of the individual that are associated with one's work. Although utilized in research since the 1930s (Hoppock, 1935; Roethlisberger and Dickson, 1939), job satisfaction has only rarely been treated theoretically. Most often job satisfaction is defined only by its measurement. Locke, in one of the more interesting discussions of the concept of job satisfaction, defines job satisfaction as the "pleasurable emotional state resulting from the appraisal of one's job as achieving or facilitating the achievement of one's job values" (Locke, 1969: 316). Most definitions assume the existence of the individual's needs and see satisfaction as resulting from the fit between these needs and the job and its environment.

The second major component of the model is the work situation. Although there have been considerable changes in emphasis, most studies distinguish between the nature of the job and the environment within which the work takes place. This distinction has its origins in the work of Herzberg, Mausner and Synderman (1959) in which they distinguished intrinsic and extrinsic job-related factors and is employed in most job satisfaction studies in some form. For our purposes the work situation is divided into job characteristics and the job environment. Three dimensions of job characteristics are considered: job quality, effort, and resources. The job environment is the immediate context within which the job is performed and in general is defined and designed by individuals other than the employee. Considered as environmental factors are: supervision, job mobility, working conditions, discrimination, pay, promotions, size of work place, and civil service status.

Both job characteristics and the job environment are measured by workers' perceptions rather than by more objective observational techniques. In one sense employee's perceptions of the work situation may be superior to more objective measurements because the phenomena we are seeking to explain, job satisfaction, is highly personalized and subjective. If one defines job satisfaction as an emotional response to—or evaluation of—one's job, then the process of evaluation must involve the employees' subjective perceptions of the job and their immediate job environment. Studies that have included both subjective and objective measurement of the work situation confirm that subjective perceptions are closely correlated with job satisfaction (Seashore and Taber, 1975: 356; Stone and Porter, 1978). Additionally, practical considerations of data acquisition prevented the collection of individual-level objective measures.

Our conceptualization of the work situation encompasses unionization, since it clearly exists within the immediate job environment. Individual employees may be union members and may engage in union activities on the job. Additionally, being in a unionized environment may affect both perceptions of one's job and its environment as well as one's satisfaction with it. In these ways unions are very much a part of the job environment. It is also possible, however, to consider unions as external to the job environment. Unions exist as organizations operating outside the immediate context of an employee's job. Etzioni (1964) sees unions as external to the job but at the same time likely to affect both the work situation and individuals' satisfaction with their jobs. Our two prime indicators of unions, membership and the contractual context of the individual's work setting, are both clearly descriptive of the individual in the job environment. Thus, in this study, unions are considered conceptually as part of the work situation. As unions have not been treated in previous studies of job satisfaction and in order to provide added focus, unions are separated from the work situation in the graphic presentation of the model and in our discussion.

The fourth and final component of the model is individual orientations and attributes. Individuals bring attitudes and orientations with them to their jobs, and these orientations may affect an individual's expectations of work and unions. These "person variables," as termed by Seashore and Taber (1975), play a critical role in affecting the relationship between the work situation and job satisfaction. Three kinds of individual orientations and attributes are examined: psychological orientations, job orientations, and personal attributes. The first of these, psychological orientations, have been studied by a variety of researchers (Maslow, 1954; McGregor, 1960; Likert, 1967; Katz and Kahn, 1978). Psychological orientations, as viewed by these researchers, were concerned with individual need structures. Instead, we conceptualize psychological orientations as acting as a frame of reference that individuals use in evaluating other phenomena. The two psychological orientations examined are the workers' view of their ability to control, direct, or influence their lives, and the relative priority placed upon one's job among such competing priorities as family and religion.

The second type of individual orientations, job orientations, are characteristics derived from previous or current experiences, involving, for example, job training and family experiences. Job orientation factors considered include: occupational status, mobility, length of service, education, and attitudes toward working. The third kind of individual orientations are personal attributes, such as age, sex, and race, that may predispose an individual's responses to the work situation and job satisfaction.

Although many of these work-related concepts have been utilized in previous research, they are usually linked together in a piecemeal way. By relying on bivariate hypotheses and first-order correlations, an overall model has not been tested. Virtually all scholars in this area agree with Seashore and Taber (1975: 361–66) on the need for multivariate research designs and analytical strategies. Some research has already moved in this direction (Oldham and Hackman, 1981). Our model is clearly multivariate and is evaluated using multivariate statistical techniques. For such an analysis to be most fruitful, it is necessary to examine the theoretical underpinnings of the linkages among the components in the model.

The major linkage in the model, which has been the subject of most research, is that between perceptions of the work situation and job satisfaction. If job satisfaction is the state of mind resulting from the achievement of one's job values, then the major and most immediate impact on that state of mind would seem to be the perceptions of one's job. Most of the studies that examine the work situation—job satisfaction linkage do so by examining only a few components of the work situation (Ingham, 1970; Katzell, Ewen and Korman, 1970) or a certain type of worker or organization (Levine and Weitz, 1968; Korman, 1968). Studies of this nature number in the hundreds, if not thousands, with their usefulness being restricted by either the testing of narrow hypotheses or the use of a narrow data base.

Attempts have been made, however, to broaden the focus of such studies. Centers and Bugental (1966), for example, surveyed a cross section of workers in the greater Los Angeles area in an attept to determine if blue collar workers derived satisfaction from different aspects of the work situation than white collar workers. Quinn and others *(The Survey of Working Conditions,* 1971) examined job satisfaction, as well as a wide range of other work-related perceptions, in a national survey conducted by the Institute for Social Research at the University of Michigan.[3] Oldham and Hackman (1981) studied almost three thousand employees in thirty-six governmental, service, and industrial organizations. Several researchers have also attempted to enlarge the conceptualization of the work situation by increasing the number of variables considered simultaneously and using factor analysis to search for underlying dimensions (Friedlander, 1963; Ewen, 1964). These factor-analytical studies have been fairly successful in relating the dimensions of the work situation to job satisfaction (Ronan and Marks, 1973), but have not always found the same underlying dimensions. Also factor-analytic structures are very difficult to interpret substantively.

Another linkage in the model is between individual orientations and the work situation and is also the first part of the three-variable relationship between individual orientations, work situation, and job satisfaction. Individual attributes, whether psychological orientations, job orientations, or individual characteristics, may predispose individuals in the way they perceive the work situation, and thus indirectly affect the degree of job satisfaction.

The third linkage in the model from individual orientations is to job satisfaction. Ordinarily one would expect that the effect of individual orientations on job satisfaction would be mediated by the individual's perceptions of the work situation. However, if particular individual orientations, such as attitudes toward working, are very dominant, they may impact job satisfaction levels independently of perceptions of the work situation.

Unionization, the fourth component of the model, adds several additional linkages to the model. Of particular interest here is that no studies, either public or private, have incorporated unionization into studies of the work situation or job satisfaction. This omission may be due partly to some degree of management bias in these studies, or it may partially result from the fact that multivariate studies have been so rare. By incorporating unionization into our model, we are wedding two quite different streams of research (job satisfaction and labor relations) into one model.

The most important union linkage in the model is expected to be its direct relationship to other aspects of the work situation, which then affects job satisfaction. It is also expected that the perceptions of other aspects of the work situation will affect the nature and degree of unionization. For example, at time 1, negative perceptions of the work situation may lead an individual to join unions and seek collective bargaining agreements. However, at time 2, after unions are the bargaining agent and employees are working under a union contract, the nature of unionization may influence the way in which individuals perceive their work situation. The use of the double-headed arrow in Figure 1.1 is because both of these scenarios are possible. Unfortunately, since we have cross sectional rather than longitudinal data, these variations cannot be explored in this study.

Another arrow in the model links unions directly to job satisfaction. Although it is expected that most union influence on job satisfaction will be indirect (mediated by perceptions of the work situation), some degree of direct linkage is also anticipated. This seems most likely to occur when union attachments are deep and union leadership particularly strong. The model also indicates that individual orientations may be related to unionization. Individuals may be predisposed toward or against unions regardless of their perceptions of the work situation.

In the last few pages we have briefly defined the four primary components of the model and hypothesized about the general anticipated nature of the linkages involved. This model of work and job satisfaction is operationalized, tested, and modified in the remainder of this book. Both the quality of the operationalization and testing of the model is dependent upon the quality of the data. The nature of the data used in this study is discussed below.

Data

The data used in this study are derived from a five-state survey of a sample of state public employees. A mail questionnaire was sent to a random sample of state employees working in the state capitals of five states: Nebraska, New York, Oregon, Tennessee, and Wisconsin. The ten-page questionnaire included an array of questions dealing with unions, the nature of work situation, job satisfaction, and individual orientations.[4]

The five states were selected on the basis of three criteria: the strength of unionization, data-base availability, and geographic spread. Since an important goal of the study is to consider unionization as an aspect of the work situation, states were selected that had a variety of union practices, ranging from little union activity to extensive bargaining. The practical consideration of which states had inclusive telephone directories for their capital city was the second criterion. In several cases, more than one state with a given union intensity also had available an appropriate telephone directory. In these cases the states that provided the best geographical spread to the other states studied were selected.

The universe from which the sample was drawn within each state included all state employees, from heads of departments to secretaries and road workers, who either worked in the state capital or in close proximity to it. A full range of employee types were sampled to expand the narrow occupational scope of previous job satisfaction studies. The samples were drawn from state employee telephone directories with an initial sample of four hundred being drawn from each of the five states. There is some bias in drawing samples from state capitals since people there are less apt to be involved in the delivery of services and more in administration. However, a list of employees was necessary in order to draw a sample and virtually no states had complete rosters of state employees.[5]

A method suggested by Dillman, Carpenter, Christenson, and Brooks (1974) and Dillman (1978) was followed in distributing the questionnaire. As Dillman et al. urge, four contacts were made with each respondent. The only major deviation from their procedure was that the last mailing was not sent by certified mail. The four contacts consisted of an initial mailing of the questionnaire and a cover letter explaining the purpose of the study, a post card reminder, and two further mailings of the questionnaire each with different cover letters.

Response rates were fairly high, 64.7 percent across all five states. Table 1.1 presents the flow of responses and response rates for each of the five states. Since the survey was conducted from Tennessee, it is not surprising that the largest proportion of the Tennessee sample returned questionnaires. Nebraska had the lowest response for no apparent reason. The distribution of returns across time was relatively uneven. Tennessee and Wisconsin respondents returned the questionnaires more quickly

Table 1.1   Flow of Responses and Response Rates (by Percent)

	Tennessee	Nebraska	Oregon	Wisconsin	New York	Total
Mailing 1	33.4	13.5	0.0	24.7	9.9	16.4
	(123)	(46)	(0)	(90)	(38)	(297)
Mailing 2	17.1	19.7	35.7	20.8	22.7	23.3
(postcard)	(63)	(67)	(128)	(76)	(87)	(422)
Mailing 3	15.2	16.8	24.6	17.8	23.0	19.4
	(56)	(57)	(88)	(65)	(88)	(353)
Mailing 4	6.0	2.9	8.1	3.8	7.1	5.6
	(22)	(10)	(29)	(14)	(27)	(102)
Total	71.7	52.9	68.4	67.1	62.7	64.7
response	(264)	(180)	(245)	(245)	(240)	(1,174)
Non-response	28.3	47.1	31.6	32.9	37.3	35.3
	(104)	(160)	(113)	(120)	(143)	(640)
Total sample	368	340	358	365	383	1,814
Inappro-priate*	32	60	42	35	17	186

*This category includes those who were originally included in the sample errone-ously such as those who are no longer employed by state government, those who worked for the federal government, retired employees, and part-time employees.

Note: Number of respondents in parentheses.

than those in Nebraska, Oregon, or New York. All the mailings were sent bulk rate and this may have affected the timing of the returns. It is known that in the case of the farthest state geographically, Oregon, none of the questionnaires were received by the respondents for over two weeks after mailing, thus overlapping with the period when the post card reminder would otherwise have been sent.

Although our 65 percent response would generally be considered fairly substantial, it did fall 7 percent below that attained by Dillman, Carpenter, Christenson and Brooks (1974). The differences in the response rate between the two studies are difficult to explain. Primarily it seems that Dillman, et al.'s overall response rate of 72 percent was reached because of the use of certified mail on the last mailing. This permitted identification of households originally selected in their sample but no longer available (i.e., deceased, moved), thus reducing the size of their N. We did not realize the importance of this aspect of certified mail until the last wave of our questionnaire. At that time we included a request in our cover letter that the questionnaire be returned for those individuals who fell into our inappropriate category. Although some were then returned, we believe this would have been much more effective if the request had been included in our first mailing instead of our last.

One of the primary concerns with the use of mail questionnaires versus direct survey techniques is the amount of non-random bias introduced by the relatively high non-response rates. Ideally, checks for non-response bias should compare several key attributes of respondents and non-respondents, testing for no difference. The idea is to ensure that those who respond to the questionnaire are not materially different from those who did not return the questionnaire. As a compromise with direct comparisons of respondents and non-respondents, two steps were taken to check for response bias. First, the only variable that is available for all respondents and non-respondents within the sample, sex, was subjected to the chi square test for significant difference. Checking each state and the total sample, it was found that in four of the five states and in the total, there was no significant difference on sex between respondents and non-respondents. The one exception was in Nebraska where the differences were significant at just the .05 level.

A second check for response bias was made by comparing the response to the survey items by dividing the sample into early and late returns. The idea behind this comparison is that the late returners are those who responded only on prodding from the researchers and should be similar to non-respondents. It would obviously be preferable to have a sample of non-respondents, however, in its absence, the late returners may be considered a sample of non-respondents.[6] Chi square was used to test for significant differences in each of the seven hundred tables generated (five states by 140 survey items). Of the seven hundred tables, only 5.4 percent were significant at .05 or greater.[7] A careful examination of the direction of the differences between early and late returners indicated no discernable patterning or bias in particular questions.

On the basis of these checks for non-random bias, we can be confident that the results obtained from the survey have not been substantially biased.[8] The data, however, are not without limitations, which should be borne in mind as the discussion proceeds. A possible bias toward administrative rather than service-delivery personnel has already been noted, and the data are cross sectional and thus cannot be used to respond to developmental or change-oriented issues; the five states may not be representative of the other forty-five, therefore, caution should be exercised in making inferences beyond these states.

One additional reservation should be noted about our reliance on a single-survey instrument as the data source. At best, multiple indicators should be drawn from varying data sources. In this instance an independent measurement of the nature of the work situation would have been desirable; however, because of the wide geographical range of the states studied and the multiple job settings, this was impossible. When research is based on a single instrument, common-method variance may be a problem as respondents tend to seek consistency within their replies on a single questionnaire. This problem has been noted in a variety of survey research, and has been particularly criticized in studies of job reactions (Roberts and Glick, 1981). Common-method variance is more pronounced when questions supposedly tapping different variables are similarly worded. This is the case with many previously used indicators of the work situation and job satisfaction. Particular care was taken in this study to minimize this problem by using a variety of question formats and approaches.

Even with these reservations in mind, we have a substantial data base of state employees in a wide range of union and work settings. We have a fairly high degree of confidence in the representativeness of our sample, and we have taken steps to counteract common-method variance by varying the format and placement of related questions.

Study Outline

The remainder of this study is organized around the testing of the model of work and job satisfaction presented above. The following chapters deal with the four primary components of the model: job satisfaction, the work situation, unionization, and individual orientations. In these chapters, the relevant literature is reviewed, concepts defined and operationalized, and bivariate relationships examined.[9] Chapter 6 provides the multivariate test of the model. Finally, Chapter 7 summarizes the key findings, iterates the strengths and weaknesses of the study, and makes suggestions for further research. Additionally, the policy implications of the research findings are discussed from the perspective of the public manager seeking the enhancement of job satisfaction.

Notes

1. In this vein some have argued for using job satisfaction as a means of "monitoring the quality of employment on a societal scale . . ." (Seashore and Taber, 1975: 333). This is one of a number of articles in a symposium on "The Quality of Employment Indicators," edited by Albert D. Biderman and Thomas F. Drury in *American Behavioral Scientist* 18 (1975).
2. Much of the early research dealt with job satisfaction as a consequence rather than a cause. The productivity/job satisfaction literature is the major exception. Other studies that view job satisfaction as a cause are reviewed by Seashore and Taber (1975: 359-60).
3. Two subsequent national surveys were also conducted by ISR in 1973 and 1977. The 1977 survey included a number of questions about labor unions (Staines and Quinn, 1979).
4. A copy of the full questionnaire appears in the Appendix. *The Survey of Working Conditions* (1971) and Robinson, Athanasiou and Head (1969) were especially helpful in the formulation of the questionnaire.
5. Although payroll listings might have been used to identify state employees working throughout a given state, such listings were not possible to obtain.
6. For an explication of this position, see Feber (1948) and Goode and Hatt (1963).
7. For individual states the percentage significant were: Tennessee, 3.6 percent; Nebraska, 5 percent; Wisconsin, 4.3 percent; New York, 7.1 percent; Oregon, 7.1 percent.
8. As Moser (1958:139) has noted, such checks for non-random bias "can never prove the *absence* of bias; at best, they can assure the researcher that the final sample is not too badly out of line."
9. Bivariate relationships are examined in these early chapters to provide some simplicity to a complex model and to provide comparability to previous studies.

CHAPTER 2
JOB SATISFACTION

For over fifty years, job satisfaction has been the focus of repeated study. In 1935, Hoppock could already point to and review thirty-two prior studies of job satisfaction. By 1972, Kahn estimated there were over two thousand studies of job satisfaction, and the number today is certainly substantially larger. Job satisfaction remains the most common topic studied relative to work. It has been treated as both independent and dependent variables. As an independent variable, job satisfaction is seen as the cause of other phenomena such as productivity and motivation. As the dependent variable, job satisfaction is seen as being caused by other conditions such as the nature of the job and individual characteristics.

Previous Studies

There has been considerable change in the reasons for studying job satisfaction, while at the same time there has been a refocusing of research designed to expand our understanding of job satisfaction (Salancik and Pfeffer, 1977: 433). Manipulative goals, such as seeking to understand job satisfaction so that productivity can be increased, have underlaid most studies of job satisfaction. The motives for seeking the enhancement of job satisfaction have changed. In earlier research efforts, job satisfaction was most often linked to productivity, turnover, and absences.[1] Funding for these studies was often provided by industrial firms that sought to increase their productivity; however, as time went on, researchers had mixed results in establishing a linkage between productivity and job satisfaction (Katzell and Yankelovick, 1975; Ronan, 1970; Vroom, 1964), and the direction of job satisfaction research altered as well its source of funding. It is difficult to tell whether a change in funding source caused the reorientation in the study of job satisfaction or whether the reorientation led researchers to seek other funding.[2] In either case, change in funding to predominately governmental sources was accompanied by a change to studying job satisfaction as a dependent variable rather than as an independent variable (Salanick and Pfeffer, 1977). In the public sector, the focus on job satisfaction was justified on humanistic grounds (Gibson and Teasley, 1973) as a promoter of the community's mental health and as an indicator of the quality of working life (Kahn, 1972).

Until recently, in most of the studies of job satisfaction, researchers did little to acknowledge that their research efforts had manipulative goals and did not discuss the ethical dimensions of such manipulative goals. One of the early exceptions is Herzberg, Mausner and Synderman (1959), who in their preface acknowledge manipulative goals and see them as a potential cause of certain ethical problems. The authors, however, state without elaboration that the social usefulness of such studies far outweighs the potential for manipulation, which contrasts with the explicit approach to value questions in more recent treatments of job satisfaction. For example, when job satisfaction is seen as a social indicator (Seashore, and Taber, 1975), then, as Kahn (1972) aptly points out, social action is the desired end and presumably planned social change is advocated. Also, the recent focus on job redesign (Hackman and Oldham, 1980) has expressly acknowledged manipulative goals.

Critique

Given the high number of job satisfaction studies, no attempt will be made to review their findings. It is important, however, to assess the quality and direction of this research. Some would argue that the improvements and advances in knowledge resulting from this research stream do not justify the quantity of research effort. In any case, there are a number of important criticisms to consider, among which the most important is that job satisfaction is rarely dealt with conceptually (Locke, 1969). Instead, the definition of job satisfaction is most often implied from its measurement. With so much reliance placed on measurement, it is important to note that the measurement of job satisfaction has been somewhat haphazard. Also of importance is that most studies of job satisfaction were geographically restricted and occupationally confined to single plants and often to single occupations (Kahn, 1972: 169; Kalleberg, 1974: 299; Kalleberg and Griffin, 1978: 374). Some recent exceptions to this narrow focus are evident (see *Survey of Working Conditions*, 1971; *Quality of Employment Survey*, 1973, 1977; Oldham and Hackman, 1981). Finally, most studies have been highly descriptive rather than explanatory (Kahn, 1972). Bivariate analysis (correlations) predominate even when multivariate designs have on occasion guided the collection of the data.[3] Explanatory studies are essential to expand our understanding of the multiple causes and consequences of job satisfaction.

With the exception of some recent literature on job satisfaction as an indicator of the quality of life, most studies have relied either implicitly or explicitly on a need-satisfaction model.[4] Basically, the need-satisfaction model assumes that individuals have stable needs that are identifiable and that jobs have stable and identifiable characteristics; however, some have argued that these basic assumptions of the need-satisfaction model are questionable (Salancik and Pfeffer, 1977). The most important problem with the model arises from its dual assumptions that needs are relatively stable across individuals and across time and that jobs have fixed characteristics.[5] This universality of individuals' needs is derived from the work of Maslow (1943, 1954) and has remained central to much of the need-satisfaction research, despite its lack of empirical verification (Hall and Nougaim, 1968; Wahba and Bridwell, 1976; Roberts and Glick, 1981). Gibson and Teasley (1973: 92), in reviewing various tests of Maslow's theory, found "little empirical justification for adopting it, to explain organizational behavior." Roberts and Glick (1981) criticize the use of growth-need measures because no account is taken of the expected job responses to those with low-growth needs.

In response to such criticism, modifications have been made in the need-satisfaction model that acknowledge different strengths of needs in individuals (Vroom, 1964; Hackman and Lawler, 1971) and different individual expectations from jobs (Argyris, 1973).[6] The persistence of the need-satisfaction model, despite its modification and its varying uses of the concept of needs, seems to result, at least partly, because of its consistency with other models of human behavior that presume human rationality. Such psychological models are particularly attractive to researchers. The need-satisfaction model as modified in terms of variable needs and/or expectations and the subjectivity of job characteristics leaves a model that lacks the simplicity of its earlier version. No research to date has provided a comprehensive test of such a multivariate need-satisfaction model operationalized in this modified way. Given these problems with the use of the need-satisfaction model, it is important to consider and develop a definition and conceptualization of job satisfaction that takes these problems into account.

Defining Job Satisfaction

Among the voluminous studies that incorporate job satisfaction, few scholars attempt its definition apart from its measurement. Hoppock (1935: 47) reflects the approach of definition through measurement by viewing job satisfaction as "any combination of physiological, psychological, and environmental circumstances that causes a person truthfully to say, 'I am satisfied with my job.' " The most common definitions are those that assume the existence of needs (in varying forms) and generally view job satisfaction as resulting from the fit between these individual needs and the job and its environment. Issues of how to define job satisfaction arise primarily because of the implications of such definitions in terms of causes of satisfaction, particularly the nature of individual needs. This may also be why many researchers have avoided explicit definitions of job satisfaction.

Locke (1969), in one of the more interesting treatments of job satisfaction, rejects the concept of needs. Job satisfaction instead is defined as the pleasurable emotional state resulting from gratification or satisfaction about one's job. Locke views job satisfaction as being caused primarily by the interaction of one's values and one's perceptions of the job and its environment. Whether one employs the concept of needs or values, these approaches are consistent in viewing that there is something within individuals that conditions their reactions to their jobs. It is not our purpose to define the nature of that preconditioner or its origins (although this question is discussed in greater detail in Chapter 5). Rather we will focus primarily on the nature of the interrelationships among the four components of the model: the work situation, unionization, individual characteristics, and job satisfaction.

In this study, job satisfaction is seen as an individual's response to their work place, which includes unionization and its impact on perceptions of the work setting. Viewing job satisfaction in this way is consistent with both the views of those who seek to use job satisfaction as a social indicator (Kahn, 1972; Seashore and Taber, 1975), as well as those who see job satisfaction resulting when an individual's needs or values are met by the job and its environment. Like other researchers we rely on a need-satisfaction model in a *modified* form, which views needs as *variable* in strength across different individuals and across time within the same individuals (Hackman and Lawler, 1971). Therefore, job satisfaction results from the interaction of variable individual needs and variable individual perceptions of the job and its environment, including unionization.

The Measurement of Job Satisfaction

There are a large number of ways to measure job satisfaction and it is clear that many studies are not measuring the same phenomena (Wanous and Lawler, 1972). Recently a number of studies have utilized portions of the Job Diagnostic Survey developed by Hackman and Oldham in 1974 to measure job satisfaction and other employee reactions to their jobs. It is still accurate to say, as have Seashore and Taber (1975: 344), that no single desirable measurement exists. There are two basic ways of measuring job satisfaction. Most common are facet-free measures of job satisfaction. Using this approach, the employee is asked directly, "All in all, how satisfied would you say you are with your job? . . . (1) very satisfied; (2) somewhat satisfied; (3) not too satisfied; (4) not at all satisfied."[7] This common sense approach to measuring job satisfaction has the benefit of being easy to administer and understand (Kalleberg, 1974: 301), and it correlates highly with more complex measurements of job satisfaction (Robinson, Athanasious, and Head, 1969: 100). In the process of responding to facet-free questions, individuals are likely to consider a variety of different aspects of their job and provide their own means of summarizing these into a single response (Seashore and Taber, 1975: 335; Johns, 1980).

Despite these advantages, facet-free job satisfaction has been severely criticized for a number of reasons. Most importantly, the direct measure assumes that job satisfaction is unidimensional, when job satisfaction seems very likely to be multidimensional (Kalleberg, 1974: 301; Seashore and Taber, 1975). For example, an individual might be satisfied with the content of the tasks required on his/her job and dissatisfied with pay or the social interrelationships in the work environment. The facet-free measure is also of questionable utility in asking individuals to provide a single answer to a concept that may be vague or complex (Blauner, 1966). Evidence exists that responses to facet-free measures tend to overestimate the degree of job satisfaction (Kahn, 1972; Kalleberg, 1974) when compared with more complex job satisfaction indicators.[8]

The second general means of measuring job satisfaction is through the use of facet-specific measures (Hackman and Oldham, 1975). Essentially faceted job satisfaction measures ask the respondent to assess his/her satisfaction with a series of job facets. The responses are then combined in one of a number of ways as specified by the researcher. As Seashore and Taber (1975: 335-336) note, the specification of facets can never be complete so the difference between facet-free and faceted measures of job satisfaction is one of degree rather than of kind. Faceted measurement is advantageous in that it coincides with the multidimensional character of job satisfaction, provides comparability across the respondents, and permits a degree of control and direction by the researcher (Seashore and Taber, 1975: 336).

Once one concedes that job satisfaction is multidimentional or multifaceted, two major measurement issues remain: which facets to incorporate and how to combine the responses to a number of facets of job satisfaction? The first of these issues— which facets to study?—is ultimately unresolvable. Research studies differ widely in both the number of facets of job satisfaction investigated and the kinds of facets included (Wanous and Lawler, 1972). Most investigations that are reliant on the need-satisfaction model employ facets that reflect various areas of individual needs (Porter, 1961; Hackman and Oldham, 1975), such as self-esteem or a feeling of security. Others ignore needs by having the various facets represent specific aspects of the job, such as pay or working conditions. We have combined both approaches by studying twenty-three facets, some corresponding roughly to *potential areas* of individual need fulfillment from a job and some representing *specific aspects* of jobs. Given the problems associated with the concept of needs, the choice to use a number of facets representing potential needs is not without its limitations and difficulties.

The facets selected for investigation here are not unique to this study but follow questions originally used by the Survey Research Center in the *Survey of Working Conditions* (1971). Many scholars have criticized the lack of replication of varying measurements of job satisfaction (Seashore and Taber, 1975; Kahn, 1972: 169) on different populations at different times. Thus, the use of questions from a previous study should facilitate evaluation of the measurement of job satisfaction. The twenty-three facets studied are:

1. Chance to make friends
2. Chance for promotions
3. Friendliness and helpfulness of co-workers
4. Opportunity to develop special abilities
5. Convenience of travel to and from work
6. Enough help and equipment to get the job done
7. Proper amount of work
8. Enough information to get the job done
9. Work is interesting
10. Adequate pay
11. Freedom to decide how to get the work done
12. Chance to do the things I do best
13. Job security
14. Challenging problems to solve
15. Competence of supervisor
16. Responsibilities clearly defined
17. Authority to do my job
18. Adequate fringe benefits
19. Pleasant physical surroundings
20. Seeing the results of my work
21. Enough time to get the job done
22. Freedom from conflicting demands
23. Reasonable working hours.

In assessing this list of job facets, one of the problems with the faceted measurement of job satisfaction that was mentioned above is evident. It is not possible to specify what an appropriate list of job facets is since needs and values vary by individuals and across time. When the researcher specifies a list of potential need facets, regardless of what the facets are, they suffer the common problem of incompleteness. Also, if the respondent is only asked to respond to a list of facets provided by the researcher, then the researcher is either implicitly defining the values or needs of the individual (Blauner, 1966; Kalleberg, 1974) or specifying which job factors are relevant to the individual.

In relation to the twenty-three facets, state employees were asked two questions about each:

> Below are two sets of questions about selected aspects of jobs. First, we'd like to know how important to *you* each of these things are in any job you might have. Secondly, does *your* present job actually provide these things?

For the "how important" questions, responses were: (1) very important; (2) fairly important; and (3) not important. Responses for the "actually provides" questions were: (1) quite a bit; (2) in some ways; and (3) not at all.[9]

Studies vary in the kinds of questions asked about the various facets of job satisfaction. Our second question, "actually provides," is similar to what is commonly called the "is now" question and asked the respondent to express their degree of satisfaction with the facets of their current job. "Is now" questions are part of virtually every faceted measurement of job satisfaction, although question wording may vary somewhat. In most investigations of faceted job satisfaction, at least one question, in addition to the "is now" question, is asked about the job facets. In this study, the additional question, "how important," was asked. The most common second questions asked are "would be" questions; that is, how much would they like to have of a given facet (Wanous and Lawler, 1972)? The format and wording of these questions have very important consequences in terms of the meaning of job satisfaction. These are considered below in the context of how to combine the raw responses to faceted job satisfaction questions.

The second major measurement issue in regard to job satisfaction is how to combine responses to the various job satisfaction facets. There are at least three different kinds of treatments of raw responses that have been commonly used: weighting, clustering, and discrepancy scoring (Seashore and Taber, 1975: 337–39). The first of these treatments, weighting, utilizes the relative importance to the individual (or the researcher) of the given job facets as weights in a summated "is now" scale of job satisfaction

(Vroom, 1964). In other words, the respondents are asked to assess the relative importance to them of each of the job facets. Relative importance is then used to weight their responses as to how satisfied they are with their current job ("is now"). These weighted faces are then summed across facets to provide an overall job satisfaction score for each individual.

The weighting of facets by their relative importance was conceived as a means of taking into account individual differences in need structures. Locke (1969) objects to this weighting of job facets as redundant. He believes individuals weight their own responses in the course of providing their satisfaction with job facets. Others have pointed out that in a summated index, even powerful weights are unlikely to significantly influence composite scores (Seashore and Taber, 1975: 338). In their empirical assessment of nine faceted indicators of job satisfaction, Wanous and Lawler (1972: 103) found that, in general, faceted satisfaction measures weighted by importance were not an improvement over other methods and at times were worse. Seashore and Taber (1975: 337) conclude that there is "an emerging consensus that differential item weighting seldom offers a significant gain in construct validity, measurement reliability, or predictive power."

The second type of treatment given to the raw responses to faceted job satisfaction questions is clustering. Although there is agreement on the multidimensional character of job satisfaction, the best way of clustering or dimensioning job satisfaction is still unresolved (Seashore and Taber, 1975: 338). Clustering can be done on either rational or empirical grounds, with factor analysis being the most common empirical technique employed. Despite problems arising from the lack of comparable job facets and varying populations, there is considerable agreement on at least the nature of the largest of the major dimensions. Whether or not to use some dimensioning in the treatment of job satisfaction depends largely on the purpose of the research involved. In this study a single measure of job satisfaction is desirable in order not to make the testing of the model presented in Chapter 1 overly complex.

The third and now most common treatment of raw responses to faceted job satisfaction involves discrepancy or differences scoring (Johns, 1981). Basically, discrepancy scoring involves the calculation for each facet of the discrepancy between two satisfaction-based questions, such as the "is now," "should be," or "would be" questions discussed above. The discrepancies across facets are then summed to yield an overall job satisfaction score. The logic of discrepancy scoring is that the degree of job satisfaction depends upon the relationship between one's satisfaction with a given facet and either the importance assigned to it by the individual or one's sense of equity or values relative to an ideal job. First used by Porter (1962), discrepancy scorings is viewed as having conceptual elegance, given its link to psychological theories (Seashore and Taber, 1975: 339). Discrepancy scoring implies a subjective theory of values (Kalleberg, 1974) since the respondent's own standards of what is satisfied are used by the researcher, rather than the researchers' own standards. There is no proof, however, that this method is more valid or reliable than non-faceted measures of job satisfaction. There are also several potential drawbacks to discrepancy scoring (Wall and Payne, 1973): they may be redundant as has been argued with weighting; the scores themselves may be somewhat ambiguous in meaning; and measurement errors and bias may be additive rather than random and offsetting.[10] There are, however, empirical grounds, in addition to the argument of conceptual elegance, that favor the use of discrepancy scoring. Discrepancy scores have been shown to act well as measures of job satisfaction in previous research (Porter and Lawler, 1968; Locke, 1969; Tolliver, Wanous, Lawler and Zenisek, 1980), and in their study of nine measures of faceted job satisfaction, Wanous and Lawler (1972) found that discrepancy scores worked better than non-discrepancy scores.

Because of its fit with psychological theory and its past track record, the discrepancy scoring technique was selected for this study. Before elaborating how it was used, it is important to consider in greater detail what the range of options are in terms of discrepancy scoring and the implications of each approach. In almost all instances one of the components of discrepancy scoring is some form of an "is now" question, where the respondent assesses the satisfaction provided by the current job in its various facets. The most common discrepancy scoring options are a comparison of "is now" responses with either "should be" or "would be" questions. The "should be" questions ask the respondent how much of a particular facet of a job there should be. Implicit in this is the notion of equity or fairness (Porter and Lawler, 1968). The "would be" questions ask the respondent how much of a particular facet they would like to have in their ideal or desired job (Locke, 1969). Thus, in the first instance the respondents are asked how their current job compares to their sense of job equity and in the second instance how their job compares with their ideal. Although this may seem like splitting hairs, as Wanous and Lawler (1972: 97) point out, "It is not difficult to imagine people who believe their job is not 'right for them' because it is quite different from their desires, but who also believe that the job provides fair or equitable outputs for the inputs required."

A variation of the "would be" question utilizes the concept of importance. The respondent is asked how important a given facet is to them in any job, not just their current job. This wording is similar to the "would be" question in asking the respondent to consider their personal job desires in a broader context than just their immediate job. This question form is utilized in this study.

In order to calculate the discrepancy between our "actually provides" question and "how important" question, each pair of responses were compared and then assigned a discrepancy score on the following basis:

Discrepancy Score	Discrepancy	
	Provide	Importance
1	Not at all	Very important
2	In some	
	ways	Very important
	Not at all	Fairly important
3	Quite a bit	Very important
	In some	
	ways	Fairly important
	Not at all	Not important
4	Quite a bit	Fairly important
	In some	
	ways	Not important

The scoring thereby takes into account the direction of the differences between the items (Johns, 1981). The discrepancy scores for each pair of questions were then summed for each employee and divided by the number of sets of questions answered, thus providing comparability of scores across individuals.[11] A score with no discrepancy (3–4) means that there is no negative discrepancy between the importance of various facets of the job and the degree to which the employee feels the job supplies his/her needs. A low discrepancy score (2) means that in some of the facets covered, the job does not fulfill all of the individual's needs, yet in other areas the individual's needs are fulfilled. Employees with a high discrepancy score (1) report a large gap between things they value in a job and the degree to which their job supplies these things. Simply put, the greater the discrepancy, the higher the level of dissatisfaction.

How Satisfied Are State Employees?

One of our interests in studying job satisfaction is to examine the satisfaction levels of state employees. The distribution of job satisfaction is of particular interest if one views job satisfaction as a social indicator of the quality of employment (Kahn, 1972; Seashore and Taber, 1975). Job satisfaction's distribution is also of importance since, in this study, it is the variance in job satisfaction that the multivariate model presented in Chapter 1 is designed to explain.

Virtually all previous studies report the distributions of job satisfaction. Reviewing job satisfaction studies in 1935, Hoppock found approximately one-third of the workers dissatisfied, although the populations studied were not broadly representative. In his own job satisfaction study in New Hope, Pennsylvania, Hoppock found 15 percent of all employed persons in his survey were dissatisfied with their jobs. Writing thirty-five years later, Kahn (1972: 174), although roughly agreeing with the findings of Hoppock's New Hope study in terms of numbers, felt that adequate generalizations about the distribution of job satisfaction were inappropriate given differences in time, sample populations, data collection, and statistical treatment. In one of the

Table 2.1   Job Satisfaction by State (in Percentages)

	Tennessee	Nebraska	Wisconsin	New York	Oregon
High discrepancy (1)	11.6	17.3	18.2	16.1	14.7
Low discrepancy (2)	61.0	58.0	59.5	55.5	59.7
No discrepancy (3-4)	27.4	24.7	22.3	28.4	25.6
	100.0	100.0	100.0	100.0	100.0
N =	(249)	(174)	(242)	(236)	(238)

earliest national surveys, Robinson, Athanasious and Head
(1969) reported that 89 percent of the employees surveyed were
"completely" or "somewhat" satisfied. Other broad studies (*Survey of Working Conditions*, 1971, 1977) have found similar levels
of satisfaction among employees.

In addition to comparing our findings on levels of job satisfaction with other studies, it is interesting to examine job satisfaction levels across our five survey states. The five states represent
a variety of social, economic, and political environments. Despite
these differences it seemed likely that the distribution of job
satisfaction would not differ significantly across the states. State
distributions for the discrepancy measure of job satisfaction are
shown in Table 2.1. For ease of presentation the discrepancy
scores were grouped into categories of no discrepancy, low
discrepancy, and high discrepancy.[12] Over 70 percent of the
employees in each state report some discrepancy between what
they value in a job and what their job supplies them. Less than 20
percent, however, have high discrepancy scores, which is
roughly equivalent to high levels of job dissatisfaction. There is
little variation across the states.[13]

The discrepancy measure of job satisfaction indicates a marginally larger proportion of employees more dissatisfied with their
jobs than do other non-discrepancy measurements. The nature of
the discrepancy scoring method seems the probable cause of the
slightly higher dissatisfaction levels since, by using twenty-three
facets, the measure encourages individuals to report some dissatisfaction. It seems unlikely that a large percentage of employees

would be completely satisfied with a wide range of aspects of their jobs and job environments. That it is the nature of the discrepancy measure, rather than the satisfaction levels of state employees, that has led to the higher proportions of dissatisfaction is substantiated by the distribution of job satisfaction among the same respondents when the question was a single, direct question of the level of satisfaction. In this instance, overall levels of job satisfaction were within the ranges reported in other such studies, showing between 10 and 15 percent dissatisfied.

An Overview of Job Satisfaction

A concern for the place of the individual in today's society, and particularly in the world of work, has led us to the study of job satisfaction. The pains and pleasures of job tasks, the dreams of material success met and unmet, and the sense of self derived from work are likely to dramatically effect the nature of individual lives. Although our focus is on the quality of individual life, the well-being of individuals in an aggregate sense is critical to the quality of the larger society.

Job satisfaction has been the focus of an enormous amount of previous research. Much of this research is thin conceptually and narrow occupationally and geographically. Given the new interest in job satisfaction as a measure of the quality of employment, there has been some improvement in both conceptualization and measurement. For the most part, the study of job satisfaction remains a part of a stream of research that is dependent upon a theory of human needs, although the view of needs has been modified substantially. Job satisfaction, for our purposes, is defined as the state of mind that results from an individual's needs or values being met by the job and its environment.

Individuals bring different values and needs with them to the world of work. Individuals' personality structures differ, as do their perceptual abilities. Values and needs may also vary for given individuals across time. The current objective is to define and understand job satisfaction sufficiently so that the process of how individuals' perceptions of their work interact with their values to produce job satisfaction can be understood. Only then can informed suggestions be made about ways in which worklife might be improved.

Individuals respond to, and their lives are affected by, common factors in the job setting, such as the task environment and the nature of supervision. It is the perceptions of those common multiple factors that are most salient in influencing the level of job satisfaction. Since there are so many dimensions of work and a variety of individual values, job satisfaction measurement must be designed to tap a variety of aspects of the job and the individual.

Thus, in selecting an appropriate measurement device to tap this book's conceptualization of job satisfaction, a faceted measure was employed that reflects a wide range of both potential areas of need fulfillment from a job and specific aspects of jobs. The questions asked were of the general form of "is now" and "would be," and were scored on the basis of the discrepancies between the two questions across the twenty-three facets. Discrepancy scoring, although somewhat criticized, has the advantage of conceptual elegance in its fit with psychological theories, and of a fairly strong record of usefulness in previous studies.

On the whole, state employees are fairly satisfied with their jobs, with little variation across the states. The level of satisfaction, although somewhat lowered by the nature of discrepancy scoring, is relatively consistent with research in the private sector.

The next chapter defines the nature of the work situation including unionization. Chapter 4 examines the bivariate linkages between the work situation and job satisfaction.

Notes

1. It is interesting to note that the orientation of Hoppock's *Job Satisfaction* (1935), one of the earliest job satisfaction studies, is toward improving vocational counseling. Job satisfaction is viewed as a goal of vocational counseling. Considerable discussion is provided on whether the most feasible way of providing counseling is to counsel all individuals or only those who suffer job dissatisfaction since these are the individuals who have trouble adjusting to their work life. This argument is similar to much later discussions of job redesign.

2. For an interesting discussion of the impact of funding sources, see Useem (1976).
3. This point is also made by Roberts and Glick (1981).
4. See Blauner (1960), Vroom (1964), Kahn (1972), Salanick and Pfeffer (1977), and Robinson, Athanasiou and Head (1969). Much of the following discussion of the need-satisfaction model draws from the arguments of Salancik and Pfeffer (1977).
5. The problems with the conceptualization of job characteristics utilized in the need-satisfaction model are discussed in Chapter 3 on the work situation and relate to viewing job characteristics as fixed and objectively defined as opposed to being the socially constructed reality of the perceiver.
6. Most job satisfaction research prior to 1970 presumed individual needs were taken into account through the measurement of job satisfaction. More recently, separate indicators of needs have been incorporated as mediators of the job-satisfaction linkage. For a description of these indicators, see Roberts and Glick (1981).
7. This is not the only facet-free measure of job satisfaction. Kalleberg (1974) discusses the use of another work indicator ("rather do some other kind of work"), and the Survey of Working Conditions (1971) and the Quality of Employment Survey (1973, 1977) have used other direct facet-free measures, such as "How often do you get wrapped up in your work?" and "How often do you leave feeling you've done something well?"
8. Several facet-free job satisfaction questions were asked in our survey of state employees; however, because of the limitations of this kind of measurement, they were not used in this analysis.
9. This question format was originally used by Duane Marvick (1954) for a quite different purpose than to measure job satisfaction. Marvick wanted to distinguish among different career types in government. This question format is advocated by Kahn (1972: 197–203) because of its value component.
10. In a critique of difference scoring, Johns (1981) argues that such scores may be unreliable and produce spurious correlations with other variables.
11. Each employee had to answer at least fifteen of the twenty-three sets of questions in order to have their scores computed and used in subsequent analysis.
12. In our subsequent analysis, job satisfaction is not grouped but treated as a continuous variable.
13. Because there is little variance across the states in job satisfaction, subsequent analysis is not conducted separately within the state samples. Where characteristics differ substantially by state, this is noted.

CHAPTER 3

THE WORK SITUATION

The nature of the physical, social, and psychological environment within which individuals work, and the nature of the work itself, are critical components of the model of work and job satisfaction developed in Chapter 1. All individuals exist within overlapping environments, one of which is the work situation. The average American spends almost one quarter of each week within this work environment. In this chapter individual perceptions of the work situation are isolated in order to define the nature of the working environment from the employee's perspective. This will also permit an examination in Chapter 4 of the relationship between workers' perceptions of their job and job satisfaction.

Previous Studies

DEFINING THE WORK SITUATION

Studies that incorporate aspects of the work situation abound in the field of industrial and organizational psychology, as well as in public administration. Almost all of these studies seek to define the work situation by identifying components of the work environment that may affect something else, usually the level of job satisfaction or productivity.[1] Since the nature of the research on the work situation has altered over time, a brief review of these changes seems an important preliminary to definitional refinement. Implicit or explicit in most studies involving the work situation is a need-satisfaction model (Gibson and Teasley, 1973; Salancik and Pfeffer, 1977; Hackman and Lawler, 1971). Job attitudes are portrayed by the degree of satisfaction and are causally linked to individual needs (Maslow, 1943, 1954), the nature of the job, and at times to the larger work environment. Satisfaction is seen as resulting when an individual's needs are met by the job and its environment.[2] Aspects of this need-satisfaction model were discussed in Chapters 1 and 2; our concern here is with the conceptualization and measurement of the work situation.

With some variations of emphasis over time, most studies distinguish between the nature of the job itself and the environment within which the work takes place. This distinction has its origins in the work of Herzberg, Mausner and Snyderman (1959), in which they distinguish motivators and hygiene factors in the work situation. Motivators refer to those things intrinsic to the job, while hygiene factors are extrinsic to the job but defined by the job's environment. Although Herzberg's hypotheses about differential correlations for motivation and hygiene aspects of work have been largely refuted (Vroom, 1964; Hinton, 1968; Dunette, Campbell, and Hakel, 1967; Waters and Waters, 1972; King, 1970; and Schneider and Locke, 1971), the distinction between the job itself and its context remains an important one in the literature.

As the focus of job attitude research has changed to a more humanistic approach (Gibson and Teasley, 1973), that is, from seeking increased productivity to seeking improvement of the quality of the worker's life, there has also been a shift in emphasis in the study of the work situation. This is reflected in numerous studies that focus on job redesign or job enlargement in order to maximize satisfaction or motivation (Lawler, 1969; Hackman and Oldham, 1980). This emphasis on the nature of the job has tended to ignore the immediate job environment or context (Hackman and Lawler, 1971). The change in focus in studying the work situation may be accounted for by a perception that it is easier to redesign jobs than to alter environments.[3] Recent research has also examined the impact of the organization structure on job satisfaction (James and Jones, 1976; Oldham and Hackman, 1981). Such structural characteristics as size, hierarchy, formalization, and centralization are implicitly part of the job environment, but are more subject to manipulation than many other job environment factors. Implicit in these newer job-redesign studies is the assumption that job redesign or structural change is likely to be more effective in altering satisfaction levels. This assumption derives from the nature of the need-satisfaction model utilized by most of the researchers in this area of study (Salancik and Pfeffer, 1977: 434). There are also important implications to a focus on job redesign and organizational structure that seem to deny the ability of individuals to adapt and cope with their environment. Additionally, someone other than the individual worker is thus the primary agent manipulating the job to increase satisfaction (Salancik and Pfeffer, 1977: 440).

A CRITIQUE

A number of problems exist with current conceptualizations of the work situation. First, it seems to be assumed in much of the previous research that the characteristics of jobs and their environment are both stable over time and relevent to the needs of individual workers.[4] Contrary to Maslow's original formulation, which assumes that individual needs are uniform and hierarchically arranged (Maslow, 1943, 1954, 1970; Alderfer, 1969a; Argyris, 1957; Herzberg, Mausner and Snyderman, 1959), some studies now assume that individual needs vary both across time and across individuals (Hackman and Lawler, 1971; Turner and Lawrence, 1965; Hulin and Blood, 1968; Porter and Steers, 1973). More importantly for the purposes of this chapter, the relevance of the components of the work situation to the worker are seen to vary by individual and by time.[5] If either job characteristics or their context vary in importance to individuals over time or across indivduals, then general job redesign may have limited utility in maximizing individual levels of job satisfaction. After all, jobs that are expanded in scope and depth may appeal only to either certain workers or workers at certain times.

Another problem with conceptualizations of the work situation is that the researchers seem to believe that they are studying the characteristics inherent in the jobs or in their context. Of course some studies do measure the nature of the work situation apart from the perceptions of the employees (Hulin and Blood, 1968; Turner and Lawrence, 1965); however, the dominant mode is to measure the work situation through workers' perceptions (Roberts and Glick, 1981). These researchers do not seem to realize that they are studying the work situation as a social construct of the individual(s) viewing it (Salancik and Pfeffer, 1977: 431), rather than an objective reality.

Using workers' perceptions to measure the nature of the work situation raises questions about the relationship between perceptions and the phenomena under study, the job. This has been addressed in the work of several researchers. For example, Hackman and Lawler (1971), who used workers' perceptions as the primary measure of job satisfaction, also employ measures of the work situation based on objective job characteristics (as defined by supervisors and researchers). They find substantial correspondence between the subjective and objective measures of job satisfaction. Other studies have also found substantial correspondence between employee perceptions of their jobs and ratings by both supervisors and outside researchers (Hackman and Oldham, 1975; Stone and Porter, 1978). Additionally, research has shown that such independent assessments explain approximately the same amount of variance in job satisfaction as do employers' descriptions of job characteristics (Oldham, Hackman and Pearce, 1976; Stone and Porter, 1978).[6] Although caution seems appropriate when using such perceptually based measurements, these studies suggest that employee descriptors of the work situation are not too far off the mark in characterizing the nature of jobs and their environment (Oldham and Hackman, 1981: 72).

If the researcher is to investigate the work situation through employees' perceptions, then relevant factors in the work situation had to be identified and defined by either the researchers, employees, or supervisors. After a certain point in time, researchers tended to borrow other researchers' lists of job and contextual characteristics to thereby appear to grant a certain legitimacy to the choices. There is no solution to this problem of the relevance of varying work situation factors since someone must identify the characteristics for study. It does, however, seem possible to derive a view of the work situation first conceptually and then measure these phenomena in the best way possible while recognizing and ackowledging the limitation that the factors so identified are not inherent in the phenomena under study.

A related problem is that in most of this research, the employees who define the work situation and/or their reaction to it, are usually prompted by the researcher in one way or another. When the researcher preselects the aspects of the work situation about which to question the employee, there is a serious potential problem of priming. The respondent is directed toward the phenomena under study by the researcher, whose stimulus of the question may or may not be of importance to the respondent. Alternatively, a few researchers have followed a strategy that seems, on its face, to obviate some of these problems by having the respondents react, without prompting, to how they feel about their jobs. This process, however, leads to substantial interviewing problems and perhaps even more substantial coding and evaluation problems.

Since the components of the work situation have been derived and measured largely in response to the definitions of the researcher and have been based on an expected relationship with productivity and/or job satisfaction, a serious question can be raised about the comprehensiveness of past measurements. The omission of unionization as a component of the work situation illustrates this problem. To a certain extent each author has his or her own list of relevant job and contextual factors,[7] and most recent research has focused almost exclusively on the nature of the job, rather than the social context or environment within which the job is located. This approach clearly omits the probability that the immediate environment of the work substantially affects how people both define the nature of their jobs and how they feel about their work (Salancik and Pfeffer, 1977: 446).

There is no ideal way to define the nature of the work situation. To a certain degree, both definition and measurement must be arbitrary and affected by the researcher. A number of improvements, however, can be made by clearly understanding and elaborating the assumptions made in the research process and the limitations of the results.

Defining and Measuring the Work Situation

For our purposes the work situation will be viewed as having two principle components: job characteristics and the job environment (including unioninzation).[8] All jobs have certain characteristics associated with them. Job characteristics include such factors as the repetitiveness and variety of the work, and the degree of autonomy or freedom to execute the tasks associated with the work. The job environment provides the immediate context within which the job is performed. Much of the nature of the job environment is determined by the attitudes and actions of others. The job environment includes such factors as compensation, supervision, promotions, working conditions, and unionization. In our survey of state public employees, a number of questions were asked to tap the workers' perceptions of both aspects of the work situation. Following the dominant mode in this stream of research, we utilize these perceptions to measure the nature of the work situation.[9]

Current measurement of job characteristics has its origins in the work of Turner and Lawrence (1965). Two measurement instruments have been frequently used: the Job Diagnostic Survey (Hackman and Lawler, 1971; Hackman and Oldham, 1975) and, to a lesser extent, the Job Characteristics Inventory (Sims, Szilagyi and Keller, 1976). Although both sets of measurements have advantages, both have been criticized (Alday, Barr and Brief, 1981). Roberts and Glick (1981:211) are particularly critical of the use of the Job Diagnostic Survey and the four or five task dimensions derived from it. They argue: "The question of what tasks are and how they should be measured is still a major issue. . . ."

Table 3.1   The Work Situation

Job characteristics	Job environment
Job quality:	Supervision:
learning new things	personal interest in employees
planning ahead	high standards in supervisors own
freedom	work
decisional discretion	requires hard work
variety	leaves employees alone unless they
level of skill	need help
Job effort:	Job mobility:
work fast	within state government
work hard	outside state government
physical effort	Work conditions:
repetitiveness	healthful
use of hands	comfortable
Job resources:	Discrimination
co-worker help	Other:
authority	income
time	fairness of promotions
information	size of work place
equipment	civil service
	Unionization:
	membership
	working under contract

Note: See Appendix for a sample of the questionnaire.

Given that part of the purpose of this research is to expand the scope of the definition of the work situation, a somewhat analogous but different measurement strategy was followed. One major measurement difference exists and should be noted. Summary unidimensional indicators of job characteristics are most often utilized despite arguments of the multimensionality of the concepts involved; however, this practice has been criticized (Roberts and Glick, 1981) and is not followed in this study. Instead a number of separate indicators of components of the work situation are developed and used.

Table 3.1 presents a listing of the varying aspects of the work situation explored in our questionnaire along its two major dimensions—job characteristics and the job environment. Three major aspects of job characteristics are investigated: job quality, the nature of the job effort required, and the resources available to facilitate doing the job. The quality of a job is measured by answers to questions pertaining to the following: the degree to which jobs require learning new things, planning ahead, decisional discretion, variety of tasks, freedom to execute tasks, and the level of skill. Job effort is measured by the speed, hardness, and physical effort required to do the job, as well as by the repetitiveness of the job and the skill in using one's hands. The third aspect of job characteristics, job resources, is basically those things which are available to the worker on the job to facilitate the execution of the job. Respondents were asked about whether their job provided enough of five resources: co-worker help, authority, time, information, and equipment.

The second dimension of the work situation is the job environment. Supervision, job mobility, working conditions, income, promotions, and size of work place are all commonly studied components of the job environment. Three additional and related aspects of the job environment are also investigated. Workers' perceptions of their being discriminated against in their work seems an important aspect of the job environment. In addition, since we are studying public employees who may or may not be covered by civil service, such coverage is included as an aspect of the job environment. Finally, unionization in terms of both membership and working under a union contract is added as a component of the job environment.

In order to facilitate an examination of the nature of the work situation and its relationship to job satisfaction, a series of additive indices relative to the work situation were created. Such index construction was undertaken to search for underlying common dimensions that would reduce the complexity of the analysis by lowering the number of discrete variables to be considered.[10] For this purpose, job characteristics and the job environment were considered separately. In each instance, indices were created based upon explicit scaleability criteria involving the use of factor analysis and the standardized Alpha coefficient of reliability.[11] The indices are all additive in nature, meaning that individual answers to the included questions are summed across the questions and divided by the number of questions answered, thus providing an index score for each respondent on each index.[12]

Among the sixteen questions utilized to tap the nature of workers' perceptions of job characteristics, two indices were created. First and largest is the job quality index, composed of six questions relating to varying aspects of job tasks that, when a job requires these aspects, seem to indicate a job with both depth and scope. Each respondent was asked how much each of the six job characteristics is like their job.[13] Those features of jobs included in the job quality index incude: requires that you learn new things, requires that you do a lot of planning ahead, allows a lot of freedom as to how you do your work, allows you to make a lot of decisions on your own, allows you to do a variety of different things, and requires a high degree of skill.

The second job characteristic index is the job speed/hardness index. This index is simply the summation of the two job effort questions, requires that you work fast and requires that you work hard, which met our scaleability criteria.[14] The remaining three job effort measures and the five job resources measures did not meet the scaleability criteria and thus are treated as separate items in later analysis.

Table 3.2 presents the distribution of responses in regard to the task characteristics associated by workers with their jobs. The distributions of the job quality index indicate that almost 90 percent of the surveyed state employees have jobs with at least some of the factors associated with greater depth and scope. The modal responses indicate job requirements of some speed and hardness, little or no physical effort, and little use of hands. A wide variety exists in the degree of repetitiveness associated with the state employee's job. The five job resources seem to be in fairly adequate supply, although it should be remembered that the distribution of these resources are not highly related to each other. As was expected, the distribution of job characteristics varies very little across the five survey states.

Indices were also created among job environment indicators where appropriate. Unlike the responses to questions relating to job characteristics, however, no large grouping of job environ-

Table 3.2   Job Characteristics Distribution (by Percent)

	a lot	somewhat	a little	not at all
Job quality index	32.1	55.4	11.7	0.8
Job speed/hardness index	15.4	51.4	27.0	6.2
Physical effort	7.3	19.5	33.5	39.7
Repetitiveness	20.0	32.2	35.3	12.5
Using your hands	16.7	19.9	21.9	41.5

	enough	not enough		
Co-worker help	80.3	19.7		
Authority	74.8	25.5		
Time	69.9	30.1		
Information	69.7	30.3		
Equipment	78.5	21.5		

ment questions was found.[15] Instead, only two, two-item indices were created. The first index is a measure of the quality of supervision, combining responses to two questions relating to the employees' immediate supervisor: the extent to which they take a personal interest in those they supervise and maintain high standards of performance in their own work. The second two-item job environment scale relates to working conditions and sums responses on the comfort and health of the respondent's working conditions.

Note should be taken of the measure of job discrimination. Each respondent was asked if they felt discriminated against on the job because of age, sex, or race. Previous research (Hopkins, 1980) has shown that the correlates of discrimination vary to some degree with the type of discrimination (age, sex, or race) and whether it is "normal" discrimination (as perceived by older workers, women, or non-whites) as opposed to "reverse" discrimination (as perceived by younger workers, men, or whites). Because of the small number of individuals perceiving each of these individual types of discrimination, however, it was decided to employ only a simple dichotomous discrimination variable, did or did not perceive job discrimination.[16]

This measure of discrimination, two supervision variables and job mobility, as well as income, promotions, size of work place, and civil service did not meet our scaleability criteria. Each are thus considered as separate components of the job environment in subsequent analyses.

Two primary aspects of unionization are investigated as aspects of the job environment: union membership and union contracts. The reasons workers in both the public and private sectors join unions has been found to be related to the nature of the work situation (Bakke, 1945; Warner, Chisholm and Munzenrider, 1978; Imundo, 1973, 1975; Christrup, 1966; Smith and Hopkins, 1979). Public sector unions are defined here as including both unions and employee associations.[17] Working under a union contract is an additional contextual factor that defines the nature of the working environment. Union contracts, to varying degrees, may influence working conditions, pay, civil service structures, and supervisor-employee relationships. Membership and working under a union contract are both self-defined by the respondents.

The distributions of state employees' perceptions of their job environment are shown in Table 3.3. On the whole, employees are fairly pleased with their supervisor, feel it would be somewhat hard to secure another job, have favorable views of their working conditions, have somewhat mixed views regarding promotion, are covered by civil service, and have a range of incomes and sizes of work places. In addition, approximately 18 percent of the surveyed state employees feel discriminated against on the basis of either age, sex, or race. In terms of unionization, approximately one-third of the respondents are union members and one-third of the respondents work in a job environment that is partly defined by a union contract.

It was expected that, in some cases, aspects of the job environment would vary by the state of the respondent. Differences by state were evident in job mobility, income, civil service, and uninization. No state differences were found in supervision, working conditions, discrimination, promotions, or size of work place.

Perceptions of job mobility seem likely to be affected by the

Table 3.3 Job Environment Distribution (by Percent)

	very true	somewhat true	not too true	not at all true
Quality of supervision index	38.3	40.1	16.5	5.1
Supervisor requires hard work	32.5	47.2	15.8	4.5
Supervisor leaves employees alone unless they need help	51.3	35.4	8.7	4.6

	hard	somewhat hard	somewhat easy	very easy
Job mobility within state government	17.2	43.5	33.0	6.3
Job mobility outside state government	15.7	44.4	28.7	11.3

	adequate	inadequate
Working conditions index	84.5	15.5

	yes	no
Discrimination	17.7	81.1

	completely fairly	somewhat fairly	not too fairly
Fairness of promotions	26.3	51.2	22.6

	yes	no
Civil service	68.7	31.3

	to $7,999	$8,000– 9,999	$10,000– 14,999	$15,000+
Income	22.4	17.6	31.1	29.0

	1–24	25–99	100–499	500+
Size of work place	27.6	32.2	27.9	12.3

	yes	no
Union membership	31.2	68.8
Work under union contracts	30.6	69.4

N = 1,177

economic climate in the employee's state, as well as by the nature of the particular employment picture existing within state government. In this study, job mobility is examined both in terms of mobility *within* and *outside* the state government. In three states, New York, Tennessee, and Wisconsin, to change jobs within the state government is seen as more difficult by a substantial proportion of state employees than in either Nebraska or Oregon. In New York and Wisconsin, state employees feel it would be almost as difficult to change jobs outside of state government as within state government. In Tennessee, however, state employees view the job environment as much more favorable outside of state government than within it. In both Oregon and Nebraska, there is only a small variance between perceptions of ease or difficulty in changing jobs within or outside of state government.

It was also expected that the distribution of incomes would be substantially different depending upon the state examined. On opposite ends of the income spectrum are Tennessee (low) and New York (high), with salaries of employees in Nebraska, Wisconsin, and Oregon in between these extremes.[18] The average New York employee earned more than twice the salary of the average employee in Tennessee.

The civil service status of state employees was also expected to vary by state. Virtually complete coverage (90 percent and above) exists in Wisconsin, Oregon, and New York, with low coverage (under 35 percent) in both Tennessee and Nebraska.

Unionization was also expected to differ substantially by state. Indeed, the states included in the study were selected to ensure wide variation in union practices. Table 3.4 presents the number and percentages of our sample respondents who are union members by state and for the total sample. New York and Oregon have the largest number of their state employees as union members, while the other three states, Wisconsin, Nebraska, and Tennessee, have smaller proportions of members.

Although proportions for union members and workers under union contract are approximately similar (see Table 3.5), the distribution of union membership and workers under union contract differs among the states. In only three of our five states,

Table 3.4   Respondent Union Membership by State (in Percentages)

	Tennessee	Nebraska	Wisconsin	New York	Oregon	Total
Union members	4.6	18.3	21.8	50.6	59.6	31.2
Non-members	95.4	81.7	78.2	49.4	40.4	68.8
	100.0	100.0	100.0	100.0	100.0	100.0
N =	260	180	238	239	240	1,157

Wisconsin, New York, and Oregon, do significant number of employees have bargaining rights guaranteed by contract.[19] It should also be noted that an employee may work under a union contract without being a union member, as well as that many union members do not work in settings in which collective bargaining contracts have been established.[20]

Measurement Limitations

The work situation has been defined conceptually to include both job characteristics and the job environment. The distributions of the indicators of the work situation have been examined and some variations noted across the five survey states. Predominately, however, individual-level differences in the work situation far exceed state variations.

Our elaboration of the nature of the work situation is potentially limited in two ways by the nature of our data base. The first limitation relates to our reliance on workers' perceptions as measures of the nature of the work situation (Kahn, 1972; Seashore and Taber, 1975: 356–57). Such perceptions are, by nature, subjective definitions and will differ dependent upon the perceptual apparatus of the worker. It is clearly possible that a worker's perception of the work situation might differ from a more objective view provided by an outside observer, based on some agreed-upon standards of judgment. Given the number and geographic scope of the workers studied in this project, external

Table 3.5 Respondent Union Contracts by State (in Percentages)

	Tennessee	Nebraska	Wisconsin	New York	Oregon	Total
Employees under union contract	0.4	2.8	26.2	66.5	52.1	30.6
Employees not under union contract	99.6	97.2	73.8	33.5	47.9	69.4
	100.0	100.0	100.0	100.0	100.0	100.0
N =	260	180	237	233	234	1,144

observation of this kind was impossible. It should be borne in mind, however, that the work situation discussed here is only as the worker *perceives* it to be. Perceptually based measurements seem to make sense when they are used, as in this study, to explain variations in another highly subjective phenomenon, such as job satisfaction.

A related potential limitation of our measurement of the work situation is the process by which aspects of job characteristics and job environments were selected for study. We have criticized previous research on the work situation for presuming that characteristics identified in association with jobs and their environment are inherent in them. We follow a strategy similar to previous studies in identifying aspects of the work situation appropriate for study. For the most part, workers were asked about aspects of the work situation that were found to be of importance in previous studies, and it is clearly possible that this approach may overlook other important aspects. In order to decrease this possibility, considerable, although unsystematic, attempts were made to identify additional factors that might be of importance in characterizing the work situation, such as unionization, civil service coverage, and job discrimination.

Somewhat troublesome is that our descriptions of the work situation lack a certain vitality or texture. An irritating supervisor or lack of adequate time to perform one's job are not abstractions to individuals. Work can be compelling, pleasing, or frustrating for workers. Such abstraction is, unfortunately, the price one pays when research and measurement are made systematic. Others, such as Studs Terkel (1972), have vividly described work. Both types of knowledge are necessary for a full comprehension of the nature of work.

Having operationalized the work situation and noted its limitations, Chapter 4 turns to the question of the nature of the relationship among the varying components of the work situation and job satisfaction. Previous studies are reviewed, and hypotheses are stated and tested. The nature of these linkages is the most important aspect of the model presented in Chapter 1.

Notes

1. Absenteeism and turnover are, to a lesser extent, a focus of analysis. For an excellent review of this literature, see Porter and Steers (1973).
2. Expectancy theory has been employed by some of these researchers (Porter and Steers, 1973). In expectancy theory, job satisfaction is viewed as the summation of expectations that have been satisfactorily met on the job. Numerous facets of the work situation and its environment are seen as phenomena about which individuals may or may not have their expectations met. Roberts and Glick (1981) argue that expectancy theory underlies most of the recent task characteristics approach to explaining workers responses to their jobs. For a recent analysis of expectancy theory, see Pecstich and Churchhill (1981).
3. This is consistent with the changes that have been made in the past in this stream of research; that is, altering design to maximize that phenomena—productivity, now satisfaction—which is the justification for external research support. Thus Hackman asserts that to understand and affect the nature of the job or task "may be an especially efficient strategy both for increasing our understanding of performance in work situations—and for developing the ability to influence effectively its directions" (Hackman, 1969: 443). In a recent critique of this literature, Roberts and Glick (1981: 209) argue that this research "provides little evidence about how to change tasks" to alter job responses.
4. Salancik and Pfeffer (1977:428) make this point as well.
5. For example, Argyris (1973) has argued that, given uniform needs, workers may come to expect different things from their jobs. Thus, both instrumental or expressive orientations toward one's job might lead to quite different expectations and thus perhaps different correlates of satisfaction. Hackman (1969) discusses individual strategies for adaptation to the task environment, while Porter and Steers see work situation variables as not having "uniform impact on withdrawal decisions" (1973:152).

6. Roberts and Glick (1981) are severely critical of these findings, arguing that these are inadequate tests of the congruence between objective and perceptual measurements of task characteristics. Indeed their broader argument is that both objective and perceptual measures of job characteristics should be incorporated in the same studies to permit testing of the extent to which job responses (satisfaction) are influenced by perceptions or the characteristics themselves.

7. For a most complete and interesting discussion of varying aspects and impacts of work, see Terkel (1972).

8. This is the most common conceptual distinction utilized in defining the work situation (Herzberg, Mausner and Synderman, 1959; Porter and Steers, 1973).

9. Some of these perceptions are more evaluative than others. For example, judging the adequacy of resources is more evaluative than describing whether one's job exists in a setting covered by a union contract.

10. This strategy is similar to that used by Hackman and Lawler (1971) and Hackman and Oldham (1975) in the development and use of the Job Diagnostic Survey (Hackman and Oldham, 1980).

11. Factor analysis is utilized to group questions on dimensions. In general the criteria for the development of an index required that all questions load highly (above ± .4) on the same factor and that there is little or no overlap with other factors. The second criteria for index creation is the commonly employed standardized Alpha coefficient of reliability which measures the scaleability of the items tested. In general for an index to be created, Alpha exceeded .75. Although we would prefer to have larger Alpha scores, given the large sample size, it is extremely difficult to obtain high scaleability scores.

12. The varying indices also employ a minimum number of questions to be answered by the respondent to have index scores calculated.

13. To be scaled, employees must have responded to four of the six questions.

14. For all two-item indices, each respondent must have responded to both questions to be scaled.

15. In creating indices, union indicators were not included in order to preserve its separateness for subsequent analysis.

16. The impact of utilizing the simplified discrimination variable should, in general, be to depress the strength of the relationships found with other variables but not to change their direction.

17. As the labor movement has grown in the public sector, employee associations have tended to take on the characteristics of unions. In a review of the public sector union literature, Estey (1976) sees the difference between unions and employee associations as unions having collective bargaining as its primary function while employee associations have only recently begun to collectively bargain. Steiber (1973) discusses the evolving nature of both types of organizations in the public sector, including the increasingly common jurisdictional disputes among organizations. Although for some purposes it may be useful to distinguish unions and employee associations, it seemed unnecessary for our purposes and was not done here.

18. It should be noted that these salary variances are not a function of occupational variance within the state samples, but rather a reflection primarily of different pay scales across the states.

19. It should be noted that we did not seek information about the bargaining unit. Working under a union contract is different from exclusive recognition. In the federal government and in many states and localities, unions have sought exclusive recognition and do not necessarily seek negotiation of contracts.

20. The proportions of union members who do not work in a job environment covered by a collective bargaining agreement vary by state. Virtually no employees work under a union contract in either Tennessee or Nebraska. In Wisconsin, 23 percent of union members are not covered by a union contract. The comparable figures for New York and Oregon are 5 and 31 percent respectively.

CHAPTER 4
THE WORK SITUATION AND JOB SATISFACTION

Virtually all studies of job satisfaction see the work situation as a primary component of a model seeking to explain job satisfaction because it is individuals' views of the interaction between their own job values and their working environment that produces job satisfaction. Implicit in this study's model is that the work situation exists in a causal sense prior to job satisfaction. This assumption, however, ignores the very real possibility that a worker's satisfaction may affect the nature of the work environment or the worker's perception of it.[1] For example, a supervisor, seeing that an individual is highly satisfied, might treat that worker more favorably than other workers (Gibson and Teasley, 1973:93). Additionally, individuals who are satisfied with their job, for whatever reason, might tend to see the characteristics of their job or its environment more favorably (Salancik and Pfeffer, 1977:428). Although these types of feedback are probable, it still seems plausible to assume that the predominate direction of the work situation-job satisfaction relationship is from the former to the latter.

The Work Situation and Job Satisfaction

EXPECTED RELATIONSHIPS

Many of the work situation variables included in this study have been examined previously in relation to job satisfaction. These studies were utilized to develop Table 4.1, which presents the expected relationships between the varying components of the work situation and job satisfaction. For each work situation variable, the supporting literature and the expected direction of the relationship is discussed below.

Job characteristics, those phenonmena associated with the nature of job tasks, are considered first. Our measurement of job characteristics includes a six-item scale of job quality. Questions included in this index relate to employee discretion, variety, scope, and skill. Although the measurement differs, these factors roughly coincide with the concerns expressed in the upsurge of interest in job redesign (Alderfer, 1969b; Hackman and Lawler, 1971; Gibson and Teasley, 1973; Pierce and Dunham, 1976; Hackman and Oldham, 1980). Those studying job redesign argue that when the nature of jobs are expanded in their depth and scope, increased job satisfaction results (Hackman and Oldham, 1980). As most job redesign studies have taken place in a factory or production setting (Salancik and Pfeffer, 1977), it has been assumed by most scholars that as job quality increases, so too does job satisfaction, regardless of the setting. The job quality index also seems consistent with Kahn's (1972:184) notion of job challenge. Although it is clearly possible that public sector employment is different or that some workers might not respond as favorably to jobs with expanded scope and depth, we hypothesize that as job quality increases, job satisfaction increases.[2]

In our consideration of job characteristics, the degree of effort required to do a job is measured in four different ways: the speed/hardness index, physical effort, repetition, and skill in the use of hands. Of these four measures, only repetition has received

Table 4.1   Work Situation and Job Satisfaction: Expected Relationships

Job characteristics	Expected direction	Job environment	Expected direction
Job quality index	+	Supervision:	
Job effort:		Quality of supervision	
Speed/hardness index	−	index	+
Physical effort	−	Supervisor required	
Repetitiveness	−	hard work	+
Skilled use of hands	+	Supervisor leaves	
Job resources:		employees alone to	
Co-worker help	+	do their own work	+
Authority	+	Job mobility:	
Time	+	Within state government	+
Information	+	Outside state government	+
Equipment	+	Working conditions index	+
		Discrimination	−
		Other:	
		Income	+
		Fairness of promotions	+
		Size of work place	−
		Civil service	+
		Unionization	
		Membership	−
		Union contract	−

considerable attention in previous studies, which have found that the repetitiveness of the job is inversely related to job satisfaction, or as the repetitiveness of jobs increases, levels of job satisfaction decline and turnover increases (Guest, 1955; Kahn, 1972: 184–85; Katz and Kahn, 1966; Vroom, 1964; Hackman and Lawler, 1971). Since physical effort and working both hard and fast seem somewhat similar to repetition conceptually, it is expected that as repetition, speed/hardness, and physical effort increases, job satisfaction decreases.

The fourth aspect of job effort, skill in the use of hands, seems likely to be related to job satisfaction in a different way. The requirement of manual skill on the job may be a type of job quality to particular kinds of workers. Some research indicates an inverse relationship between the opportunity to utilize one's abilities on the job and turnover. Since we would expect an inverse relationship between turnover and job satisfaction, we hypothesize that as the requirement for skill in the use of hands increases, job satisfaction increases.

The third aspect of job characteristics considered in this study are the resources available to employees to do their jobs. Availability of resources is not commonly dealt with in job satisfaction studies, with the exception of co-worker help. In their survey of these studies, Porter and Steers (1973) report mixed results, but have found a general trend toward an inverse relationship between supportive co-worker relationships and employee turnover; therefore, we might expect a positive relationship between co-worker help and job satisfaction. It also seems likely that persons hampered in the performance of their job by a lack of other resources would become frustrated and perhaps eventually dissatisfied. The ability to adequately perform is seldom considered as a partial determinant of satisfaction (Kirchner, 1967). In addition to co-worker help, a range of other resources are considered, including authority, time, information, and equipment. In general, as the adequacy of resources increases, job satisfaction is expected to increase.

In addition to job characteristics, the environmental context of the job is of critical importance in understanding job satisfaction. Although ignored in more recent research because of its emphasis on job redesign, the job environment is conceptually central to our model of job satisfaction. Working is not simply task oriented because jobs exist in a context that interacts with both the tasks involved and individual values or needs so as to produce job satisfaction. Aspects of the job environment may produce either negative or positive effects on job satisfaction, and our consideration of the job environment extends to supervision, job mobility, working conditions, discrimination, income, promotions, size of work place, civil service status, and unionization.

The nature of supervision is defined by the relationship between the individual employee and the immediate supervisor. Supervision has been seen as a function of both the personality of the supervisor and their behavior in the job environment (Hoppock, 1935; Vroom, 1964). For example, research indicates that high turnover is related to authoritarian ratings for foreman (Ley, 1966), and recognition and feedback from the supervisor is significantly related to employee participation (Ross and Zander, 1957). In his review of the job satisfaction literature, Kahn (1972:185–89) found virtually all studies agree that supervision had an important impact on job satisfaction. We measure supervision from the employees' perspective in three ways: the quality of supervision index and responses to two single questions on supervision—the degree to which supervisors require hard work and leave employees alone to do their work unless they need help. It is expected that most employees would prefer supervisors who leave them alone, require hard work, take a personal interest in employees and maintain high personal standards in their own work. Thus, it is hypothesized that as the quality of supervision increases, job satisfaction increases.

Our second indicator of the job environment relates to employees' perceptions of their own potential job mobility, both within and outside of state government. Although not dealt with frequently in the job satisfaction literature, mobility is treated relative to concepts such as absenteeism and job turnover (Porter and Steers, 1973; Michaels and Spector, 1982). These studies are based on the idea that people who are dissatisfied with their jobs may avoid their work through absenteeism or, if dissatisfied enough, quit (Tallachi, 1960; Water and Roach, 1971).[3] Our measure of job mobility taps individuals' perceptions of the possibility of their changing jobs. Potential job mobility is not seen as a result of satisfaction or dissatisfaction, as are absenteeism or turnover, but as a potential cause of satisfaction. Individuals who believe they could move out of their jobs, either within or outside of state government, could use this as a frustration relief mechanism, thereby becoming more satisfied than those who feel they do not have this option. Whether or not the individuals' assessments are accurate or not should not alter their effect on the level of job satisfaction. Therefore, it is hypothesized that as the perception of the ease of job mobility increases, job satisfaction increases.

Adequate working conditions are also expected to be positively related to job satisfaction. It is not that plush surroundings are likely to yield proportionate increases in satisfaction, but rather that very poor conditions seem likely to increase job dissatisfaction (Herzberg, Mausner, and Snyderman, 1959). Thus, working conditions are expected to operate only at the negative extreme (Kahn, 1972:191). Our working conditions index measures the adequacy of the health and comfort of working conditions. Therefore, we hypothesize that as the adequacy of working conditions increases, job satisfaction increases.

The fifth aspect of the job environment, discrimination, is expected to be inversely related to job satisfaction. Somewhat surprisingly, discrimination is not considered in the job satisfaction literature. Individuals who feel discriminated against on their job whether on the basis of age, sex, or race seem likely to be less satisfied with their jobs (Hopkins, 1980). Thus it is hypothesized that as discrimination increases, job satisfaction decreases.

One of the most frequently studied determinants of job satisfaction is the level of income. Despite considerable attention, the literature evidences somewhat mixed findings about its importance (Kahn, 1972:190). When people are asked to rank order aspects of their work as it relates to satisfaction, wages tend to the middle of the listing (Vroom, 1964). Hoppock (1935) found income unrelated to job satisfaction. Herzberg (1968), pursuing his notion of separate satisfiers and dissatisfiers, reports that while adequate salaries may promote dissatisfaction, high salaries will not lead to satisfaction. Other studies report positive relationships betwen pay and job satisfaction but fairly low correlations (Seashore and Taber, 1975:350). Despite the doubts raised by these researchers about the nature and strength of the relationship, it is hypothesized that as income increases, job satisfaction increases.

Promotion as an aspect of the job environment has been largely concerned with individuals' perception of the opportunity for their own promotion. Viewing promotion in this way complicates an examination of its linkage with job satisfaction. Promotional opportunities may be a strong determinant of job satisfaction for an ambitious, upwardly mobile person. On the other hand, promotion may be something to be avoided by a person with either strong work group attachments or strong family relations that such a change might disrupt. A promotion has, after all, the potential to change a person's job tasks, salary, work group, and even physical location (Vroom, 1964). In order to avoid some of these problems, we deal not with the individual's opportunity for promotion but their perception of the fairness of promotions (Kahn, 1972). This is consistent with Patchen (1960), who found that the fairness of promotions, rather than their number or rapidity, was crucial in influencing satisfaction. It is expected that the fairness of the job environment as it relates to promotions should be positively related to job satisfaction because this would promote both a sense of individual and group well-being (Hulin, 1968). Thus, it is hypothesized that as the fairness of promotions increases, job satisfaction increases.[4]

Another aspect of the job environment is the size of the work place. Size has been studied numerous times as a potential determinant of job satisfaction (Tallachi, 1960; Kerr, Koppelmeier and Sullivan, 1951; Indik and Seashore, 1961) and as a correlate of absenteeism and turnover (Ingham, 1970), although it has been studied less in studies of job redesign (Kahn, 1972:192). Size is generally one of the few systemic variables considered (Seashore and Taber, 1975:350) and has received increased attention recently as a component of organizational structure (James and Jones, 1976; Oldham and Hackman, 1981). These studies generally anticipate that individuals would prefer smaller unit sizes, perhaps because so many of the job environments studied are large industrial plants. The results of these studies have been mixed. Nonetheless, we hypothesize, with limited expectations, that as size of the work place increases, job satisfaction decreases.

Another component of the job environment is the civil service status of state employees. Since public employees have rarely been the subject of job satisfaction studies (Grupp and Richards, 1975), this variable has not been included in previous research. There is, however, a large literature in public administration that describes and promotes civil service as a means of ensuring fair treatment of employees and job security. As with promotions and supervision, fair treatment in the job environment protected by a civil service system seems likely to promote satisfaction. In addition, the lack of security in a job, which might exist without civil service coverage, seems likely to produce a degree of apprehension and perhaps dissatisfaction. It is thus expected that the presence of a civil service system covering a given employee would tend to increase job satisfaction.

The theoretical framework of work and satisfaction proposed in Chapter 1 posits a direct relationship between unionization and job satisfaction. In addition, the model hypothesizes an indirect linkage between unionization and job satisfaction through unionization's relationship to perceptions of the work situation. The linkages between unionization and job satisfaction are examined below, along with other components of the work situation. The interrelationships among unionization and other aspects of the work situation are treated later in this chapter.

Scholars of union activities have given some attention to employee attitudes toward unions and why workers join unions (Smith and Hopkins, 1979:485-488; Gordon and Long, 1981). These studies provide a number of interesting suggestions about unionization. Those who join unions have been found to be from lower socioeconomic backgrounds (Seidman, London and Karsh, 1951; Kornhauser, 1965), blue collar workers in the private sector (Blum, 1971; Troy, 1971; Imundo, 1973; Thompson and Weinstock, 1967), in the lower educational ranks (Kornhauser, 1965; Thompson and Weinstock, 1967; Hellriegel, French and Peterson, 1970), more independent with the opportunity to exercise some control over their lives (Bakke, 1945), and be dissatisfied with employee participation and decision making (Alutto and Belasco, 1972). Union scholars have also found that negative perceptions of certain aspects of work, such as supervision, leave, promotions, and work resources, are related to favorable union attitudes (Imundo, 1973; and Warner, Chisholm and Munzenrider, 1978). In addition, the relationship of the individual to the work organization is correlated with union attitudes. Larger organizations (Ingham, 1969; Porter, Lawler, and Hackman, 1975), with accompanying feelings by individuals of separation from the organization (Tannebaum, 1959:750) and of frustration, tend to lead to more favorable attitudes by workers toward unions.

In the studies of unionization cited above, there is virtually no research on the direct relationship between job satisfaction and unionization. This direct relationship is the object of investigation here, but several limitations should be borne in mind. First, it is important to note that one's attitudes toward unions, which is the primary focus of the investigations cited above, may not be the same thing as joining a union. A second limitation arises, as noted earlier, from the fact that our data is cross-sectional rather than longitudinal. As a consequence, we may discern a covariance between union membership or union contracts and job satisfaction, but we cannot tell whether dissatisfaction leads to joining a union or whether union membership encourages job dissatisfaction. Despite these limitations, it is expected that unionization will be related inversely to job satisfaction in terms of union membership and working under a union contract.

In summary, job characteristics seen as promoting job satisfaction include job quality, skill in the use of hands, and the adequacy of job resources. The nature of the job effort as measured by repetitiveness, physical effort, speed, and difficulty have been viewed as depressants of job satisfaction. In the job environment many aspects have been viewed as promoters of job satisfaction, including supervision, mobility, working conditions, income, promotions, and civil service. In contrast, discrimination, size of work place, union membership, and working under a union contract have been seen as factors that seem likely to reduce job satisfaction. We turn now to a testing of these hypotheses.

FINDINGS

We have hypothesized a series of relationships between the varying aspects of the work situation and the extent of satisfaction. Although, at this point in our analysis, the purpose is simply to examine the strength and direction of a series of bivariate relationships, later we will pursue multivariate analysis. Since our independent variables (the work situation indicators) are measured at the nominal and ordinal levels, and our dependent variable (job satisfaction) is measured at the interval level, Multiple Classification Analysis (MCA) was selected as the most appropriate statistical technique (*see* Andrews, Morgan, Sonquist and Klem, 1973). For each category of an independent variable, MCA calculates an unadjusted deviation from the grand mean of the dependent variable. If multiple independent variables are employed, MCA also calculates an adjusted deviation, which controls for the effects of other independent variables. Additionally, MCA provides a measure of bivariate association between each independent variable and the dependent variable. With multiple independent variables, MCA provides a measure analogous to the Beta coefficient in regression analysis, which indicates the importance of each predictor relative to the other predictors in explaining the variation in the dependent variable. Eta squared represents the total variance in the dependent variable explained by a single independent variable or the combined effects of multiple independent variables.[5]

It should be remembered that each of these variables is related to job satisfaction separately, thus no inferences can be made about the total impact of the work situation on job satisfaction. An examination of the unadjusted deviations in Table 4.2 indicates that virtually all the relationships between the work situation indicators and job satisfaction are in the hypothesized direction. The only exception is physical effort, which is positively related to job satisfaction (we hypothesized an inverse relationship). These relationships vary in strength, even though they are in the hypothesized direction.

Among the job characteristics, eight of the ten indicators are significantly related to job satisfaction, including all five job resource measures, repetitiveness, use of hands, and the job quality index. The job quality index is the most powerful predictor of job satisfaction among the job characteristics, explaining 7.8 percent of the variance in job satisfaction, with co-worker help and authority each explaining 5.8 percent of the variance.[6]

Ten of the thirteen job environment variables are significantly related to job satisfaction.[7] Differences in state employees' perceptions of job mobility outside state government, income, size of work place, and civil service status are not significantly related to job satisfaction. However, the three supervision variables, job mobility within state government, working conditions, discrimination, the fairness of promotions, union membership, and working under a union contract are significantly related to job satisfaction. The two strongest work situation predictors of job satisfaction, whether job characteristics or measures of the job environment, are the quality of supervision index and the fairness of promotions. Both supervision and promotions explain in excess of 10 percent of the variance in job satisfaction. The importance of these two job environment factors in explaining job satisfaction points to the substantial limit of recent studies in focusing almost exclusively on job characteristics.

A preliminary picture thus emerges of the work situation of state employees who are most satisfied with their jobs. Their jobs are characterized by scope and depth, adequate co-worker help, authority, and information, as well as, to a lesser extent, adequate equipment and time and a lack of repetitiveness. In terms of their job environment, a favorable supervisor and fair promotions are most important, with adequate working conditions, job mobility within state government, and the lack of discrimination also found to be significant. These findings are basically consistent with previous research on the bivariate relationships between aspects of the work situation and job satisfaction. Recent research, however, in focusing on job redesign and thus job characteristics, appears to be missing at least two critical enviromental factors—supervision and promotions. Additionally, job resources appear to be an important aspect of job characteristics that are often not considered. Finally although unionization is not a very important predictor of job satisfaction directly, it may still be of importance as a mediator of perceptions of the work situation and thus indirectly affect job satisfaction.[8]

The Work Situation and Unionization

EXPECTED RELATIONSHIPS

We have defined and measured the nature of the work situation from the employee's perspective, and examined as well the relationships between the various indicators of the work situation and job satisfaction. To conclude the bivariate analysis of the

Table 4.2   The Work Situation and Job Satisfaction: MCA

Predictor	N	Unadjusted deviations	Eta^2
Job characteristics			
Job quality index:			
High	369	.19	
Medium	619	−.04	
Low	143	−.33	.078*
Job speed/hardness:			
High	168	−.05	
Medium-high	571	.04	
Medium	293	−.03	
Low	69	−.12	.006
Physical effort:			
A lot	81	.15	
Somewhat	215	.04	
A little	377	−.03	
Not at all	446	−.02	.008
Repetitiveness:			
A lot	222	−.10	
Somewhat	361	.02	
A little	402	.03	
Not at all	139	.04	.008*
Use of hands:			
A lot	183	.09	
Somewhat	221	.03	
A little	247	.00	
Not at all	464	−.05	.008*
Co-worker help:			
Enough	910	.07	
Not enough	223	−.29	.058*
Authority:			
Enough	836	.08	.058*
Not enough	285	−.24	
Time:			
Enough	785	.06	
Not enough	344	−.13	.023*
Information:			
Enough	787	.10	
Not enough	346	−.22	.063*
Equipment:			
Enough	886	.06	
Not enough	242	−.21	.036*
Job Environment			
Quality of supervision:			
High	424	.22	
Medium-high	457	−.04	
Medium	188	−.28	
Low	56	−.43	.123*
Supervisor requires hard work:			
Very true	359	.10	
Somewhat true	528	.00	
Not too true	180	−.16	
Not at all true	52	−.12	.023*
Supervisor leaves employees alone to work:			
Very true	575	.13	
Somewhat true	400	−.09	
Not too true	99	−.24	
Not at all true	51	−.34	.063*

Table 4.2 Continued

Predictor	N	Unadjusted deviations	Eta²
Job mobility within state government:			
Very hard	190	−.12	
Somewhat hard	494	−.06	
Somewhat easy	375	.10	
Very easy	70	.16	.026*
Job mobility outside state government:			
Very hard	177	−.02	
Somewhat hard	499	−.03	
Somewhat easy	328	.04	
Very easy	128	.05	.004
Working conditions index:			
Adequate	950	.05	
Inadequate	170	−.30	.048*
Discrimination:			
Yes	199	−.16	
No	933	.03	.017*
Income:			
to $7,999	252	.03	
8,000–9,999	195	.04	
10,000–14,999	353	−.04	
15,000+	333	.00	.004
Fairness of promotions:			
Completely fairly	267	.28	
Somewhat fairly	522	−.03	
Not too fairly	227	−.26	.102*
Size of work place:			
1–24	311	.00	
25–99	361	.02	
100–499	318	−.01	
500+	140	−.02	.000
Civil service:			
Yes	779	−.00	
No	349	.01	.000
Union membership:			
Member	355	−.06	
Non-member	772	.03	.005*
Union contracts:			
Under contract	336	−.06	
Not under union contract	774	.03	.005*

*Significant at .05 or greater

65

work situation, we turn our attention to the relationships between unionization and other aspects of the work situation. This
permits a partial examination of the impact of unionization and
indirectly of its effect on job satisfaction.

For the most part, union organizations in the private sector
have been hostile to efforts toward job redesign or job enlargement. Indeed, almost all of the attempts to redesign jobs that are
reported in the job satisfaction literature have taken place in
non-union organizations (Schlesinger and Walton, 1977). Because
of this, most previous research on the relationship between the
work situation and job satisfaction may be biased. Our interest at
this initial stage, however, is simply in the two variable relationships between unionization and other aspects of the work situation.

Whether or not a state employee is a member of a union or
whether or not they work under a union contract, act to define
the context within which individuals perform their jobs and thus
may be viewed as part of the job environment.[9] If we view
unionization as acting within the work situation, there is a
problem in examining the relationship between unionization and
the work situation. One might argue that perceptions of the work
situation at t_1 lead to joining unions or establishing union contracts at t_2. It is also plausible to argue that having joined a union
or working under a union contract at t_1 (for whatever reason)
leads to a reshaping of individual perceptions of the work situation in a negative direction at t_2. Unfortunately, our data are not
longitudinal in nature but rather a cross section of state employees' perceptions about work and unions at one point in time.
Since it is possible that unionization may affect perceptions of the
work situation and/or that perceptions of the work situation may
lead to unionization, it is important to note that this analysis
cannot untangle the issues of the direction of causality involved.

Table 4.3 summarizes the direction of the relationships hypothesized between the twenty-one indicators of the work situation
and the two indicators of unionization. Basically, negative perceptions of the work situation are expected to be related to
increased unionization. If the work situation contains enough
negative features, individuals may turn to unions in an attempt

Table 4.3   The Work Situation and Unionization: Expected Relationships

Job characteristics	Expected direction	Job environment	Expected direction
Job quality index:	−	Supervision:	
Job effort:		Quality of supervision	
Speed/hardness	+	index	−
Physical effort	+	Supervisor requires	
Repetitiveness	+	hard work	−
Use of hands	+	Supervisor leaves	
Job resources:		employees alone to	
Co-worker help	−	do their own work	−
Authority	−	Job mobility:	
Time	−	Within state government	+
Information	−	Outside state government	+
Equipment	−	Working conditions index	−
		Discrimination	+
		Other:	
		Income	−
		Fairness of promotions	−
		Size of work place	−
		Civil service	−

to ameliorate these problems. It is unclear at this stage how negative the job environment or the nature of the job must be before a significant number of employees turn to unions as a possible solution. And, of course, the threshold level for a turn to unions may vary among individuals. The culture and larger values of the society within which the work takes place may also encourage or discourage viewing unions as possible solutions to negative work situations. Being a member of a union and/or working in an environment containing a union contract may lead to more negative perceptions of the work situation than would exist without unionization. In either instance, an inverse relationship between unionization and perceptions of the work situation is anticipated.

Among the ten job characteristics, those individuals or groups of employees with lower scores on the job quality index and less adequate job resources are expected to be more unionized. Those workers whose jobs require higher levels of job effort are also expected to be more unionized. This expectation is consistent with the commonly held view that unions are more attractive to people with more routine jobs that may also require more physical effort or dexterity.

It is also anticipated that most of the job environment variables are negatively related to unionization. Employees with less favorable views of their supervision, mobility, working conditions, income, fairness of promotions, and with less civil service coverage, seem more apt to be unionized. Those employees who feel discriminated against on their jobs or who work in larger work places seem more apt to be unionized. Since unions are more likely to influence the environment of jobs than the nature of job tasks, it seems reasonable to expect that the relationships between job environment variables and unionization might be somewhat stronger than between job characteristics and unionization. Whether this is correct is dependent upon workers' views of the most positive role for unions in the work place.

Analysis of the 1977 Quality of Employment Survey confirmed that employees seek union activities primarily to affect the job environment (Kochan, 1979; Staines and and Quinn, 1979). A national sample of workers was asked to assess the quality of union activities. On the whole, union members, whether white or blue collar employees, gave high marks to unions in performing relatively traditional functions such as improving wages, fringe benefits, working conditions, and job security. Union members were not nearly as satisfied in terms of union activities aimed at improving job quality or worker participation in job redesign. Interestingly, most union members wanted unions to focus more on the traditional areas of union activity (Kochan, 1979). Two other studies found dissatisfaction with these more traditional issues is a pertinent reason for workers joining a union (Gutman, Goldberg and Herman, 1977; Schreisheim, 1978).

FINDINGS

Table 4.4 presents the results of our analysis of the relationship among job characteristics and the job environment on the one

Table 4.4   The Work Situation and Unionization

	Union Membership	Union Contract
Job Characteristics		
Job quality index	−.081	−.137*
Job speed/hardness index	−.096	−.167*
Physical effort	.007	−.098
Repetitiveness	.109*	−.013
Use of hands	−.037	−.120
Co-worker help	−.106	.026
Authority	−.082	−.054
Time	−.083	.091
Information	−.094	.006
Equipment	−.033	.012
Job Environment		
Supervision quality index	−.078	−.051
Supervisor requires hard work	−.108	−.044
Supervisor leaves workers alone	−.096	−.058
Job mobility within state govt.	.231*	.186*
Job mobility outside state govt.	.104	.188*
Working conditions index	.069	.085
Discrimination	−.110	.012
Income	−.261*	−.334*
Fairness of promotions	−.132	−.161*
Size of work place	−.066	−.201*
Civil service	.623*	.885*

*Significant at .05 or greater.

Note: Strength of association is indicated with gamma values. Chi square is used to test for significant differences.

hand and unionization on the other. Since none of the data is interval in character, MCA is an inappropriate method of analysis. Instead, bivariate relationships are tested using gamma as a measure of the strength of the association. In this analysis, states are not treated separately, despite variations in unionization across the states. This may tend to depress (lower) the strength of the association, but, in general, the patterns are similar to those found when the state of the respondent is controlled for.

The data in Table 4.4 indicates that job characteristics are much less apt to be significantly related to unionization than are indicators of the job environment. Among the job characteristics, only repetitiveness is significantly related to union membership, while the job quality index and the job speed/hardness index are significantly related only to working under a union contract. None of these three relationships are very strong, although all three are in the expected direction and the remaining relationships among our unionization indicators and job characteristics also tend in the anticipated direction; they are, however, very weak and the relationships seen are apt to be due to chance distributions. It is notable that none of the job resources are significantly related to unionization.

Certain aspects of the job environment are significantly related to union membership and/or working under a union contract. The strongest of these relationships is between civil service and unionization. Contrary to this finding, an inverse relationship was hypothesized assuming that the lack of civil sevice status would be viewed by employees as one of a number of negative job environment factors that would tend to promote unionization. The positive relationship is understandable when viewed at the aggregate rather than individual level since civil service tends to be most comprehensive in coverage in those states that are most unionized. Given this positive relationship, it seems likely that employees are more likely to turn to unions if they find the protection and benefits of the civil service system inadequate, whereas those employees who have not experienced a civil service system first are more reticent about joining unions. An alternative explanation for the positive relationship between civil service and unionization is that there may be similar forces promoting both unionization and civil service coverage.

Both indicators of unionization are also moderately related to income with lower income workers being more apt to be unionized. This finding is consistent with the general union literature about association with unions, although the strength of the relationship is somewhat lower than found elsewhere. Job mobility within state government is also related to unionization. As was expected, greater inability to change jobs tends to increase unionization. Weak but significant relationships also exist between perceptions of the fairness of promotions, the size of the work place, and working under a union contract. It is not clear whether unionization promotes the perception of unfair promotional practices, or whether employees join unions or enter into union contracts to try to combat such perceived unfairness. Finally, a moderate relationship exists between size of work place and union contracts, with employees working in larger work settings being more apt to work under a union contract.

Summary and Implications

The focus of this chapter has been the nature of the relationship between the work situation and job satisfaction, as well as the linkage between unionization and other aspects of the work situation. The work situation is defined as having two components, the job itself (job characteristics) and the context of the job (job environment). Although a large body of literature exists that examines the work situation, research in recent years has placed its emphasis on job characteristics primarily as a means to redesign jobs and, as the researchers believe, enhance job satisfaction.

The findings of our research in this chapter raise tentative doubts about this strategy. Among our sample of state employees, the largest predictors of job satisfaction are job environment variables, although some of the job characteristics are also of importance. It is important to remember that our examination of the relationships between the work situation variables and job satisfaction is bivariate in nature. When the work situation is examined in a multivariate model, with appropriate controls and all work situation variables predicting job satisfaction simultaneously, the relative importance of the predictors may be different. This task will be undertaken in Chapter 6.[10] Our model hypothesizes a relationship between unionization and the work situation. Although it is not possible with our data to examine the causal direction of this relationship, a test of the interrelationships was made. An examination of union memberships and union contracts indicates that the job environment is somewhat more related to unionization than are job characteristics. With the exception of civil service coverage, none of the relationship is very strong. It is possible, of course, that this may mean that unionization does not play an important role in understanding job satisfaction; however, it is more likely that unionization mediates the work situation-job satisfaction linkage. This possibility is examined in detail in Chapter 6.

Thus far we have examined the relationships between the work situation (including unionization) and job satisfaction. One more component needs to be added to our model—individual characteristics—which is reported in Chapter 5. The model of work and job satisfaction will be tested in a multivariate setting in Chapter 6 and conclusions drawn in Chapter 7.

Notes

1. Some recent works also suggest that reciprocal causation may be indicated (Kohn, 1976; Seeborg, 1978; James and Jones, 1980).
2. It seems highly likely that this relationship is mediated by some combination of individual needs, values, or characteristics, but at this point in our analysis, only the bivariate relationship is examined. In the job redesign model, the mediating variable is seen as individual orientations.
3. There is some dispute about the impact of perceived opportunities for alternatives on turnover. See Mobley, Griffeth, Hand and Meglino (1979) and Michaels and Spector (1982).
4. It is interesting to note that Telly, French and Scott (1971) found equity in promotions unrelated to absenteeism while indicating that the unionization of the workers studied might have disrupted the commonly found relationship.
5. One of the limitations of MCA is that it is not sensitive to interaction among the independent variables. Thus, when employing multiple independent variables, it is necessary to check for interaction.
6. Explained variance cannot be summed across the predictors since the relationship between each work situation variable and job satisfaction are calculated separately.
7. In our discussion of the job environment we saw how certain environmental variables (income, mobility, civil service, and unionization) were distributed differently across the five states. However, in our analysis of the relationship between the job environment and job satisfaction, the relationship among these variables did not differ by state.
8. See Chapter 6 for the multivariate analysis incorporating unionization.
9. It is also possible to view unions as organizations external to the work environment acting in other arenas (i.e., the state legislature) promoting

member interests. This view is held by Etzioni (1964) and others. This perspective of unions is not possible to investigate here given our individual level data on employees' perceptions of the work place.

10. In the course of developing indices to measure the work situation, the interrelationships among job characteristics and the job environment were each examined. The lack of substantial interrelationships within each of these two groups of variables suggest that multivariate analysis will not substantially alter the relative importance of the predictors within the groups in relation to job satisfaction. However, since job characteristics were not related to the job environment, and there is some reason to believe some fairly strong relationships exist, it is expected that in a multivariate model the relative importance of the job characteristic and job environment predictors may be somewhat different.

CHAPTER 5
THE INDIVIDUAL

This chapter adds the fourth and final component, individual orientations and attributes and their relationship to job satisfaction and the work situation, to our model of work and job satisfaction. In one way or another, all individual orientation factors are phenomena that reflect the kinds of predispositions and expectations individuals have toward their work and unions. No one looks through a perfectly clear glass; the glass is distorted by the combination of life experiences unique to that individual (Smith, 1968; Brousseau, 1978). Individuals do not enter the work world with a clean slate. The purpose here is not to examine the antecedents of such predispositions and expectations, but to examine their relationship to and impact on more immediate attitudes (toward jobs), as well as on perceptions of the immediate environment (the work situation).

It should be noted that this treatment of individual orientations and attributes is substantially different from that utilized in most previous job satisfaction research. Relying on Maslow's (1943) hierarchy of needs, previous research has most commonly used indicators of individual growth needs as mediators of the relationship between job characteristics and job satisfaction (Hackman and Lawler, 1971). This approach has been attacked because of its reliance on Maslow's hierarchy and its lack of attention to both situational and social influences on perceptions (Salancik and Pfeffer, 1977; Roberts and Glick, 1981: 196). Our approach to individual orientations is, in a sense, one step removed from the motivational psychology used in other research efforts. Such approaches are based on causal theories about the reasons underlying an individual's predispositions and expectations. Instead, we seek to define the predispositional factors themselves.

Linkages: Individual Orientations and Attributes

The three dimensions of salient individual orientations that may affect work include: psychological orientations, job orientations, and personal attributes. Two components of psychological orientations seem particularly relevant to our concern—an individual's general view of their ability to control, direct, or influence their own lives (including their jobs), and the relative importance of their job or their employer to their own lives. Individuals who have a positive life view seem more likely to feel positively about their job and its environment than those who have a negative or pessimistic life view. Identification with, or commitment to, one's job seems likely to predispose an individual to greater job satisfaction. Ranking one's job highly also seems likely to promote joining a union, other pro-union forces being equal.

In addition to psychological orientations, individuals also possess certain job orientations, characteristics, or attitudes. These orientations derive from previous training as well as current or past jobs. They may impact to varying degrees and ways individuals' perception of their entire work millieu. The job orientations considered in this study include occupational status, occupational mobility,[1] length of service, education, and attitudes toward working.

The third kind of orientation of possible importance in affecting work satisfaction is individual attributes. It seems likely that certain personal attributes such as age, sex, and race may predispose an individual's response to the work situation and thus indirectly affect job satisfaction.

Neither the literature on job satisfaction nor unionization provide much guidance for our examination of individual orientations, so such limited studies and the model developed in Chapter 1 provide the primary basis for our consideration of individual orientations here. Specifically, the model indicates that individual orientations and attributes are linked in five different ways to other components of the model involving three two-variable linkages and two three-variable linkages.

The three two-variable direct linkages in the model are the relationships between individual orientations and each of the other three components of the model—unionization, the work situation, and job satisfaction. Unionization may be influenced by individual orientations affecting attitudes toward unions as well as behavior in relation to them (i.e., joining). Perceptions of the work situation may be affected by one's psychological orientations, job orientations, or personal attributes. Individual orientations may also predispose individuals to be more or less satisfied with their job regardless of their work setting. The two three-variable linkages involve individual orientations and attributes affecting job satisfaction indirectly. Individual orientations may affect job satisfaction indirectly by means of their influence on perceptions of the work situation or by their affecting unionization. Thus, by not specifying the impact of individual orientations on unionization and the work environment, a quite faulty picture may emerge of the interrelationships among the factors involved in the work setting.

Definition and Measurement

The first component of individual psychological orientations, life view, may be thought of as conceptually akin to personality characteristics.[2] Although personality is a complex multidimensional concept, we will only explore one limited aspect of personality, a person's life view. Life view is the extent to which individuals feel they can control their lives and thus it acts as a "frame of reference" for individuals in evaluating unions and their job as well as other events and objects. Life view is a subjective rather than objective indicator in the sense that it is measured by individuals' own assessment of their ability to control their lives.

To measure life view, employees were asked two questions about planning ahead and the outcome of those plans and running their own lives.[3] An additive index of these two questions was created yielding a classification of respondents as having either a pessimistic life view (felt they could not successfully plan and run their lives) or an optimistic life view (felt some ability to either plan or run their lives or both). Table 5.1 presents the distributions of employee responses on life view as well as the other nine individual orientations indicators. Most employees (75 percent) are at least somewhat optimistic about their lives and their ability to plan and run them. The almost 25 percent who feel pessimistic about their lives make up a fairly large minority who would tend to be negatively predisposed toward life in general, including work. As might be expected in examining a psychological indicator, there is no significant variation in the distribution of life views across the five surveyed states.

The second component of psychological orientations is organizational commitment. The degree of commitment by individuals to their jobs and/or their employer varies considerably. Individuals may differently map the relative priorities in their lives of job, family, religion, and other factors. If greater organizational commitment is present, it seems likely to promote greater intensity of response to all phases of the work environment.

Organizational commitment is measured by employee responses to a question rating a series of phrases as self-descriptors, including both one's occupation and employer.[4] Those judged to have a high degree of commitment identify both employer and occupation as either first and second choices; medium commitment is a response of first choice to either one's employer or occupation; and none means neither occupation nor employer rated as a first or second choice. Although Table 5.1 indicates that each of the possible degrees of organizational commitment have some respondents, it is particularly interesting to note that 15 percent of the employees clearly put occupation/employer in less than a secondary position in their own lives.

Table 5.1 Distribution of Individual Orientations (by Percent)

Psychological

Life view	Optimistic	Pessimistic		
	75.5	24.5		

	High	Medium	Low	None
Organizational commitment	36.3	25.6	22.4	15.7

Job orientation

Occupational status	Professionals, officials	Technical, managerial	Clerical, craft, service	
	37.5	30.8	31.7	

	Upward	Same	Downward	
Occupational mobility	48.4	35.2	16.5	

	High school or less	Some college	College graduate	Grad. school
Education	30.2	27.5	17.0	25.2

	0–5 yrs.	6–10 yrs.	11+ yrs.	
Length of service	69.8	20.0	10.1	

	Prefer not work	Prefer work		
Not work	34.1	65.9		

Personal attributes

	to 29	30–39	40–49	50+
Age	24.7	23.2	20.4	31.7

	Male	Female		
Sex	54.4	43.6		

	White	Non-white		
Race	94.9	5.1		

Unlike life view, there is some variation of organizational commitment across the states. In Tennessee distributions of individuals among the categories from high to none are virtually even, evidencing less organizational commitment than in other states. In contrast, both Oregon and New York had over 45 percent of all respondents rated high on organizational commitment. These differences by state seem to be partial descriptors of the states' political culture and, in particular, of the relative importance of religion.

In addition to the two kinds of individual psychological orientations discussed above, five individual job orientation characteristics are examined including occupational status, occupational mobility, length of service, education, and working preference. Each characteristic reflects the individual's past interaction with some other factor, such as family, schooling, or job, that potentially may condition or predispose the individual toward his/her current work and union environment.

Occupational status is just one of many ways to group occupations. Alternatives include grouping occupations on the basis of skill requirements, training, social responsibility, or societal assessments. Occupational status is one of the few individual characteristics that has been frequently studied in relation to unionization, the work situation, and job satisfaction, and has been found to be fairly strongly related to these factors. Even though it arises from the nature of the job and its environment, occupational status is considered here as an individual characteristic because it becomes, in time, a part of the individual and his/her self-identification.

The classification used to measure occupational status is the Duncan Socioeconomic Status Index of Occupation (Duncan, 1961). This index was created to classify census data on occupations, and it originally used education and income in addition to occupation to determine the socioeconomic status of occupations. For purposes of our analysis we have aggregated the occupation classification into three categories: professionals and officials; technical and managerial; and clerical, crafts, and service workers.[5] Table 5.1 indicates a fairly even distribution of employees among occupational categories. Although there are some differences in the distribution of occupational types across the five states, there seems to be no particular pattern to these variations. Occupational mobility is another job orientation factor. Occupational mobility is the attainment by an individual of an occupation level that is higher or lower (in a prestige or status sense) than his or her father's occupational level. An individual who is a professional chemist and whose father was a laborer would be upwardly mobile. An individual who is a highway construction worker, but whose father was a teacher, would be considered downwardly mobile. Likewise, an individual could be at the same occupational level as his/her father.

Often occupational mobility is measured by using subjective measures or self-identification (Form and Geschwender, 1962; Bonjean, Bruce and Williams, 1967). Because it is common for subjects to misidentify themselves, it was decided to use a more objective measure of occupational mobility. Our measure of mobility is based on a comparison of the employee's occupational status with the father's occupational status. Examination of Table 5.1 shows that almost half of all state employees experienced some degree of upward mobility, whereas only 16 percent experienced downward mobility. There is little significant variation across the states in the distribution of occupational mobility.

The third job orientation characteristic is length of service. How long an employee has been on the job has been a frequent item of study in previous research. Note should be made of the large number of state employees (70 percent) who have worked on their state jobs for five years or less. When length of service is normally so short there are undoubtedly consequences of considerable importance.

Education is rarely seen as a job orientation factor but is more often, if studied at all, considered with occupation and income as a status measure. Education may, however, provide the individual with a way of viewing the world around them, helping them to frame personal expectations and aspirations. Our measure of education as a quantity may or may not be sensitive enough to pick up these potential linkages between personal orientations and work. Table 5.1 indicates that 70 percent of all state employees have at least some college education, while fully 25 percent have attended graduate school. These relatively high levels of education suggest high aspirations. When coupled with the short tenures found for most state employees, it suggests that employment in state government may not be meeting these expectations.

The final job orientation factor, work preference, has not been examined, to our knowledge, in any previous union or work environment study. It seems likely that a certain proportion of the work force would prefer not to be working. Initially it seemed as if women forced by family economics into the work place might fit this category disproportionally. If individuals prefer not to work it seems likely to affect their responsiveness and response to their jobs. Employees were asked simply "If you were financially able, would you prefer not to work?" Fully 34 percent expressed a preference for not working; however, there were not significant differences in sex, age, or occupation.

The third dimension of individual orientations is personal attributes. Many past studies of job satisfaction and the work situation have relied heavily upon personal attributes as rough surrogates for individual personality and life experience characteristics (Seashore and Taber, 1975: 353). As a partial alternative to the use of personal attributes, we have identified two psychological orientations and five job orientations that may be of importance. In addition to this improvement, age, sex, and race are also examined.

Aging is a process that impinges upon many of the activities of individuals and affects our performance in the work place and our evaluation and treatment by others. The roles we play and the status we enjoy are often determined at least partially by age. The sex and race of an employee may also affect aspirations and performances as well as evaluation by others. Although sex and race are not commonly studied personal attributes in the work setting, there is some evidence to suggest that they should be (Hopkins, 1980). The distributions of age, sex, and race are shown in Table 5.1.

We have identified and defined ten individual orientations and attributes that may affect unionization, the work situation, or job satisfaction. The remainder of this chapter is devoted to elaborating hypotheses about the expected nature of the relationships involved, based upon previous research and our model, and testing these hypotheses with our state employee data.

Individual Orientations and Job Satisfaction

EXPECTED RELATIONSHIPS

Most studies of job satisfaction seek its antecedent causes and focus on growth needs rather than individual orientations. The primary exception to this is the attention given to personal attributes as surrogates for these individual orientations. The most common expression of this is tests of the attraction-selection framework for explaining job satisfaction (Oldham and Hackman, 1981). Table 5.2 indicates the direction of the expected relationships between the ten individual orientations and job satisfaction.

Both psychological orientations—life view and organizational commitment—are expected to be related positively to job satisfaction. It is anticipated that as life view is more optimistic or organizational commitment increases, job satisfaction will also increase. Individual life views, whether optimistic or pessimistic, seem likely to spill over into predispositions toward the work environment. As early as 1935 Hoppock found emotional maladjustment related to job dissatisfaction. Hypothesizing a positive relationship between job satisfaction and life view is consistent with the assertion by Argyris (1973) that only individuals who show a high degree of self-direction in setting their own goals and following through on them feel successful on their jobs.

There is also an expectation of a positive relationship between organizational commitment and job satisfaction. This is consistent with the findings that as self-identification with a job increases, turnover is likely to decrease (Porter and Steers, 1973). Those who give a high priority to job and/or occupation seem likely to do so for a prolonged period of time only if their job is relatively satisfying or has the hope of becoming more so. Otherwise, if job and occupation is rated highly and job satisfaction is

Table 5.2   Individual Orientations and Job
Satisfaction: Expected Relationships

Psychological orientations	Direction
Organizational commitment	+
Life view	+
Personal attributes	
Age	+
Sex	+
Race	−
Job orientation	
Occupational status	+
Occupation mobility	+
Length of service	+
Education	+
Not work	−

low, too much tension and dissonance might result. This is consistent with the findings of Morris and Steers (1979) that organizational commitment is positively associated with age. It also seems likely that if job and occupation are important in an overall self-view, then individuals would be more likely to adjust their expectations to their job reality as they see it. Contrawise, people who have a particularly satisfying job tend to raise job orientation in their life priorities.

Table 5.2 indicates that three of the five job orientation factors (occupational status, mobility, length of service) are expected to be positively related to job satisfaction, while education and work preferences are expected to be inversely related to job satisfaction. Occupational status is the most frequently studied of the individual orientations and has been found to be positively related to job satisfaction (Litterer, 1965: 66-81; Hoppock, 1935). Herzberg (1959) found in seventeen of eighteen studies that occupational status was positively related to job satisfaction. In another survey of the job satisfaction literature, Vroom (1964) noted that consistently occupational status is positively related to job satisfaction. This is to be expected because higher status jobs generally carry with them greater job freedom, wider responsibilities, and greater variety, all of which have been found to promote greater satisfaction.

The second of our job orientation characteristics, occupational mobility, it is also expected to be positively related to job satisfaction. Unlike occupational status, mobility has not received a great deal of attention in previous job satisfaction studies.[6] If an employee is downwardly mobile, the individual may well be experiencing unmet aspirations, greater frustrations, and consequently lower levels of job satisfaction. The converse seems likely to hold for those who are upwardly mobile or at the same level. An individual's expectations are at least partially derived from his/her family experiences. If upward mobility occurs, then an individual would seem more apt to be satisfied. Form and Geschwender (1962), in a survey of manual workers, found that individuals who felt they had achieved an occupational level equal or higher than that of their parents exhibited higher job satisfaction scores. In a related test, Bonjean, Bruce and Williams (1967) attempted to extend the Form and Geschwender analysis to middle-class, managerial workers. Their findings support the Form and Geschwender conclusions for blue collar workers but not for the white collar sample.

A third job orientation factor also expected to be positively related to job satisfaction is length of service. Previous findings relating length of service to job satisfaction have been somewhat conflicting. Herzberg (1959) found that in the seventeen studies that looked at length of service, eight found that as job tenure increased job satisfaction also increased. Seven of the studies, however, could not reach any conclusion as to the relationship between length of service and job satisfaction, and two studies concluded that length of service and job satisfaction were related inversely. Because of the ambiguity of these early studies, many of the more recent studies of job satisfaction have not examined the length of service.

Those more recent studies that incorporate length of service have tended to find that new employees have higher job satisfaction levels; those in the middle periods exhibited low satisfaction; and those in the long-service category display high levels of satisfaction, presumably because of the weeding out of dissatisfied employees at earlier times. Kilpatrick, Cummings and Jennings (1964) suggest an alternative explanation for this curvilinear relationship by noting that job security, which has long been viewed as an important benefit of governmental jobs, decreases in importance to the employee as tenure increases. As job security becomes less important to the long-term government employee because of attainment, there is an erosion of the perceived benefit and subsequently job satisfaction. Satisfaction may also be greater among long-term employees as they adjust their expectations downward to meet that which is possible for them.

Education is the fourth job orientation characteristic and is expected to be negatively related to job satisfaction. Although Herzberg (1959) reports mixed findings on the relationship between education and job satisfaction, there is some tendency for education levels to be inversely related to job satisfaction. In other words higher education levels tend to decrease the likelihood of job satisfaction. This presumably results from the impact of increased education in heightening job expectations. Some contrary evidence comes from a recent study of over four thousand employees by Weaver (1980), which found a positive relationship between education and satisfaction.

The final job orientation factor, work preference, is also expected to be inversely related to job satisfaction. It seems likely that those who would prefer not to work will be apt to be less satisfied with their jobs. Like a negative life view, preferring not to work seems likely to establish a basic predisposition that would then negatively affect job satisfaction.

Three final individual orientations—age, sex, and race—seemingly act as surrogates for attitudes and predispositions not tapped elsewhere. Previous research consistently indicates that age is positively related to job satisfaction (Herzberg, 1959; Rousseau, 1978; Weaver, 1980). As an individual ages, his or her likelihood of being satisfied is greater than at a younger age. This relationship may be the result of the individual adjusting to the increased difficulty of alternative employment or it may be that one's expectations alter with maturity. Traditional wisdom suggests that being female may be positively related to job satisfaction while being non-white may be inversely related. Women might be expected to be more satisfied with their jobs than men because their lower expectations are consistent with the female role in the home. It has also been found that sex differences exist on those work situation factors most related to job satisfaction (Miller, 1980). In contrast to gender differences, non-whites might be expected to be less satisfied than whites since previously low expectations seem to have risen since the civil rights movement. These increased expectations by non-whites, coupled with employment discrimination, might produce lower levels of job satisfaction (Konar, 1981).

All ten individual orientation factors have been reviewed in terms of how they are expected to be related to job satisfaction. Before turning to the relationships between individual orientations and the work situation, the nature of our findings on the relationship between individual orientations and job satisfaction are discussed below.

FINDINGS

Hypotheses were developed above relating the ten individual orientations and attributes to job satisfaction. Table 5.3 presents the results of the MCA for the ten bivariate relationships, including the unadjusted deviations and the Eta squared values. A quick perusal indicates that none of the individual variables are related very strongly to job satisfaction and, importantly, many of the individual variables are not related to job satisfaction in the expected direction.

Both of the psychological orientations, life view and organizational commitment, are weakly positively related to job satisfaction in the expected direction. The deviations across predictor categories are relatively small; however, the E^2 (Eta squared) indicate that each of the psychological orientations—life view and organizational commitment—explain only just over 1 percent of the variance in job satisfaction.

Table 5.3   Individual Orientations and Job Satisfaction: MCA

Predictor	N	Unadjusted deviations	Eta^2
Psychological orientations			
Life view:			
Optimistic	824	.04	
Pessimistic	265	.11	.012*
Organizational commitment:			
High	423	.07	
Medium	291	−.00	
Low	257	−.06	
None	174	−.08	.012*
Job orientations			
Occupational status:			
Professional, officials	433	−.03	
Tech., mgr.	350	−.02	
Clerical, craft, service	360	.06	.005
Occupational mobility:			
Upward	487	−.03	
Same	353	.02	
Downward	165	.05	.004
Length of service:			
0–5 years	789	.00	
6–10 years	232	.00	
11+ years	112	.02	.000
Education:			
H.S. or less	338	.06	
Some college	310	.03	
College graduate	192	−.10	
Grad. school	289	−.03	.010*
Work preference:			
Not work	381	−.02	
work	736	.01	.000
Personal attributes			
Age:			
to 29	281	−.08	
30–39	264	−.07	
40–49	229	.01	
50+	352	.11	.020*
Sex:			
Male	644	−.04	
Female	489	.05	.006*
Race:			
White	1,073	.00	
Non-white	53	.07	.000

*Significant at .05 or greater

Job orientations fare even less well than psychological orientations in explaining job satisfaction. Of the five variables investigated, only education is significantly related, and then only weakly, to job satisfaction. As expected, education was found to be inversely related to job satisfaction. Occupational status and mobility are not significantly related to job satisfaction, and the very weak relationships that do exist are the reverse of the hypothesized direction. Finally, both length of service and work preference are unrelated to job satisfaction.

The final group of individual characteristics, personal attributes, show mixed results. Only age is significantly related to job satisfaction in the hypothesized direction. There is no evidence of a curvilinear relationship as in some studies. Our findings indicate a positive linear relationship between age and job satisfaction. Sex is related to job satisfaction, with females being slightly more satisfied with their jobs. Race is unrelated to job satisfaction, although the small number of non-whites sampled may have affected this finding.

On the basis of this examination of the bivariate relationships between individual orientations and job satisfaction, direct linkage does not appear to be a very promising line of inquiry. Individual orientations, however, may have an indirect impact on perceptions of the work situation and may be indirectly important as part of a chain of linkages explaining job satisfaction. This latter possibility will be examined in Chapter 6.

Individual Orientations and the Work Situation

EXPECTED RELATIONSHIPS

In varying ways, the individual orientation factors may affect the work situation. It seems likely that individual orientations will influence perceptions of both jobs and their environment, including unionization.[7] Few of the individual orientations have been examined in previous studies of the work situation in relation to job satisfaction and organizational structure.[8] Thus, there is little literature to directly guide our investigation about the particular relationships between individual orientations and most of the work situation factors. Instead, we hypothesize based upon the logic of the conceptual linkages involved. The situation is slightly different in regard to the relationship between unionization and individual orientations. The union literature has examined some of what we define here as individual orientations in its quest to understand both why employees join unions and attitudes toward unions. This literature informs the hypothesized relationships between individual orientations and unionization.

We have identified two psychological orientations, life view and organizational commmitment. Whether an individual is generally optimistic or pessimistic about his/her life seems likely to color their perception of work. The optimist might see through rose-colored glasses and perceive a job that is more interesting and an environment more pleasant and supportive than an outside, more objective observer might see. Of course, since we do not have data on the "objective" work situation, we cannot judge the degree of distortion. Although we are positing that life view affects perceptions of the work situation, it is clearly possible that the process may also be operating in the reverse direction. In other words, it may be that perceptions of the work situation cause individuals to partially readjust their life views.

It is expected that organizational commitment will relate to the work situation in much the same way as life view. Those who are more committed seem likely to have more favorable views of their job and its environment. The degree of commitment may produce these perceptions or the perceptions may lead to an adjustment in level of organizational commitment.

In terms of unionization, a positive life view and stronger organizational commitment would seem likely to predispose an individual against joining a union. Contrawise, pessimism and the lack of organizational commitment would seem to promote joining unions. The anticipation of an inverse relationship between life view and unionization is consistent with the notion that life view is essentially a personal assessment of one's life expectations, and thus seems to encompass the need or lack of need for additional psychologically supportive organizational networks such as unions. This anticipated inverse relationship between organizational commitment and unionization is consistent with the findings of previous studies (Tannenbaum, 1965: 750; Glick, Mirvis and Harder, 1977: 149). A feeling that one's job or employer is important may be, in part, a reflection of satisfaction with the individual's job, but it is likely also a statement about whether the employee feels he or she can cope with the work organization. Both in seeking new members and in operation, unions attempt to improve the quality of the work situation and thus may affect employee's attitudes toward their jobs and their environment.

The five individual factors indicating job orientations (occupational status, occupational mobility, length of service, education, and work preference) may also be related to perceptions of the work situation, although the direction of the relationship is not always clear. Higher level occupations, more upward occupational mobility, and higher degrees of education seem most likely to be associated with perceptions of jobs of higher quality and more favorable job environments. These relationships would be consistent with the expected relationship among objective indicators of the nature of jobs and their associated occupational status and educational requirements. It is also possible, however, that the relationship is in the reverse direction; higher education, mobility, and occupational status increases expectations and in so doing leads to more negative perceptions of jobs and their environment than might be seen by an outsider observer.

The two other job orientation factors—work preference and length of service—seem likely to act in opposite directions in relation to perceptions of the work situation. Longer length of service seems to positively affect perceptions of the work situation and suggests a more static job environment, which, in turn, implies an adjustment of expectations and perhaps perceptions to cope with that continuing reality. Work preference, on the other hand, seems likely to negatively affect perceptions of the work situation because individuals who would prefer not to work may be more apt to view their jobs and the environment of their jobs more negatively.

One's job orientations may also be related to unionization. A number of researchers have examined the relationship of socioeconomic status and education to unionization. Studies in the private sector have found that, in general, employees from lower socioeconomic backgrounds are more favorable to unionization than employees from families who have higher socioeconomic backgrounds (Seidman, London, Karsh, 1951: 76-77; Kornhauser, 1965: 224–25). The frustrations and disadvantages often associated with low socioeconomic status have been offered as one explanation for these more pro-union stances (Kornhauser, 1965: 224–25; Thompson and Weinstock, 1967: 17; Blum et al., 1971). Researchers have also found that those employees with lower education levels are the most pro-union, with the more highly educated employees being less favorable toward unionism.

Consistent with the findings in regard to education, occupational status has been found to be strongly related to unionization.[9] These relationships between unionism and education may be a result of the process of education increasing loyalty to more professional criteria of employment. In general, more highly educated and white collar employees have been ignored by most union organizing efforts (Bakke, 1945; Seidman, London and Karsh, 1951; Thompson and Weinstock, 1967) and thus white collar employees may continue to identify more with management.

Such research, concerned primarily with the private sector, suggests that unionization will be most pronounced in lower occupational and educational levels and, by inference, among those with lesser occupational mobility. It is important to note, however, that there is some evidence that unions organizing among public employees has been much more directed toward white collar and professional employees (for example, teachers) than private sector union organizing activity (Smith and Hopkins, 1979).

Three additional individual orientation factors—the personal attributes of age, sex, and race—may also affect perceptions of the work situation. Rather than a generalized impact for age, sex, and race on perceptions of the work situation, some more particularized relationships seem likely. For example, these personal attributes seem highly likely to be related to perceptions of discrimination (Hopkins, 1980). It also seems plausible that if discrimination exists, then perceptions of job quality, promotions, and income may also vary by age, sex, and race. It seems unlikely that any of the personal attributes are associated with unionization.

The expected relationships discussed above between individual orientations and the work situation are primarily speculative, with the exception of some of hypotheses about unionization. The actual relationships found in our five survey states are discussed below.

FINDINGS

Table 5.4 presents the degree of association and significance for the bivariate relationships between the ten individual orientation factors and the twenty-three work situation variables. Life view and organizational commitment, the two psychological orientations, are related to the work situation in somewhat similar ways. As was expected, optimism and higher commitment are related to perceptions of higher quality jobs with adequate resources, better working conditions, less discrimination, and fairer promotions. Somewhat surprisingly, those with more positive life views and stronger organizational commitments tend to have lower incomes. Perhaps this is a reflection of the need to adjust one's psychological orientations toward the future rather than current existence. Although it was expected that a positive life view and stronger organizational commitment would be negatively related to unionization, instead these factors tend to promote unionization. These relationships involving unionization, with one exception, are not statistically significant.

Three of the job orientation factors—occupational status, occupational mobility, and education—are similarly related to perceptions of the work situation.[10] In general, status, mobility, and education are positively related to job quality and unrelated to most job resources and environment factors, with the exception of income and unionization. Length of service was expected to be positively related to perceptions of the work situation. Instead, length of service is unrelated to job characteristics and related only to higher income, less mobility, and very weakly to promotions and working conditions. Longer service is also negatively associated with unionization. Although related to a few of the work situation factors, work preference evidences no patterned relationship to either job characteristics or the job environment.

Several interesting relationships exist between individual attributes and perceptions of the work situation. Older employees tend to perceive their jobs as higher in quality, see themselves as less mobile, promotions as less fair, and have higher incomes. Younger employees are more apt to be unionized. Females have perceptions of lower quality jobs, inadequate working conditions, less fair promotions, have lower incomes, and are more apt to be unionized. Finally, non-whites have perceptions of somewhat lower quality jobs, less mobility, more discrimination, less fairness of promotion, have lower incomes, and are more apt to be unionized.

These findings suggest a number of ways in which individual orientations may have an indirect impact on job satisfaction by altering perceptions of the work situation. Of particular importance seem to be life view, organizational commitment, and education, although several other factors were also related significantly to certain aspects of the work situation.

The Direct Impact of Individual Orientations

In this chapter we have defined and measured the nature of the individual orientations of our state employees. The relationships between the ten individual orientations and job satisfaction and between individual orientations and the work situation have been examined. We found little relationship between individual orientations and job satisfaction. Among the job characteristics, job quality, physical effort, repetitiousness, and using your hands were all related significantly to a number of the individual orientations. The remaining job characteristics were much less related to individual orientations. Certain of the job environment factors were also related strongly to individual orientations. The most strongly related job environment factors were income, the fairness of promotions, job mobility within state government,

Table 5.4 Individual Orientations and the Work Situation

	Life View	Organ. Comm.	Occup. Mob.	Occup. Status	Work Pref.	Length of Service	Education	Age	Sex	Race
Job characteristics										
Job quality index	.166*	.238*	.164*	.215	-.165	-.057	-.328*	-.256*	.264*	.212*
Job speed/hard index	-.083*	.121*	-.087	-.093*	-.023	.067	-.036	.054	-.163*	.022
Physical effort	-.081	-.086	-.114*	-.210*	-.108*	-.141*	.339*	-.039	-.243*	-.200
Repetitiveness	-.138*	-.191*	-.115	-.176*	.149*	-.025	.240*	.144*	-.125	-.207
Using your hands	-.081	-.138*	-.279*	-.373*	.008	-.111	.482*	.086*	-.410*	-.136
Co-worker help	.167	.086	.047	.077	-.021	.082	.088	.007	-.097	.243
Authority	.151	.106*	-.034	-.069	-.029	.087	-.012	-.055	-.130	-.221
Time	.260*	-.061	-.031	-.037	-.063	.073	.109	.054	-.024	-.102
Information	.306*	.026	-.042	-.053	-.059	.066	.094	.042	-.117	.039
Equipment	.109	.005	-.071	-.138*	-.029	.116	.149*	.053	-.287*	.288

Job environment

Quality of supervision	.116	.056	-.109	-.088	-.131	.005	.042	-.075	-.103*	.074
Super. reqs. hard work	-.040	-.023	-.064*	-.109*	-.065	.081	.083	.009	-.085	.299*
Super. leaves emp. alone	.103	.063	-.087	-.011	-.030	.033	-.017	-.031	-.118	.029
Job mobility within	-.076*	.034	.117	.158*	-.054*	-.149*	-.093*	-.128*	.159*	.037
Job mobility outside	-.085	-.003	.045	.045	.121	-.110	-.002	-.124*	-.017	.120*
Working conditions index	.265*	.143*	-.001	.030	-.103	-.025	-.119	-.123	.111	.051
Discrimination	-.277*	-.149*	-.067	.059	.199*	-.048	-.124	.067	-.311*	.633*
Fairness of promotions	.229*	.174*	.040	.012*	-.120	.048*	-.098	-.161*	.142*	.164*
Civil service	.104	.164	.036	.028	.259*	-.033	-.222	-.075*	-.073	.413*
Income	-.213*	.289*	-.503*	-.539*	.202*	.185*	.627*	.350*	-.798*	.415*
Size of work place	-.070*	-.048	-.055	-.030	-.075	.052	.040*	.086*	.032	.143*

Unionization

Union membership	.059	.122	.149*	.256*	.108	-.245*	-.085	-.220*	.200*	.275
Under union contract	.094	.160*	.181*	.282*	.032	-.130	-.139*	-.057*	.224*	.355*

*Significant at .05 or greater.

Note: Strength of association is indicated with gamma values. Chi Square is used to test for significant differences.

and perceptions of discrimination. Unionization was significantly related to occupational mobility, occupational status and, in terms of membership, to length of service, age, and sex.

That individual orientations are not strongly related to job satisfaction and related unevenly to work situation factors does not necessarily mean that individual factors are not important in our model. Examination of only bivariate relationships can easily be misleading since variables often act in combination in significant ways that can be suppressed when the study is of only two variables at a time (Seashore and Taber, 1975: 356). Thus far our study has been bivariate in nature, as have been most prior studies of work and job satisfaction. In order to test fully our model of job satisfaction and work, it is necessary to do so with a multivariate model that permits a study of the *cumulative* impact of all the independent variables (unions, the work situation, individual orientations) acting on the dependent variable (job satisfaction), as well as assessing the independent effects of each of the predictor variables. A testing of the multivariate model presented in Chapter 1 is the topic of Chapter 6.

Notes

1. Occupational mobility refers to upward and downward occupational movement from parental status. This contrasts to job mobility (the ease or difficulty of changing jobs) discussed in Chapter 3.
2. The most widely cited studies of employee personality characteristics utilize varying approaches to motivational psychology. For example, see Maslow (1954), McGregor (1960), Likert (1967), and Katz and Kahn (1978). Our use of life view here as a frame of reference or predisposing agent represents a quite different approach from that of motivational psychologists.
3. A third life view question was initially asked of state employees; however, since the responses were not highly correlated with the other two questions, it was dropped from the analysis. That question asked "Have you usually felt pretty sure your life would work out the way you want it to or do you usually feel unsure your life will work out the way you want it to?" To be scored, each employee must have answered both of the following questions: "When you make plans ahead, do you usually get to carry things out the way you expected to or do things usually come up to make you change your plans?" and "Some people feel they can run their lives pretty much the way they want to; others feel the problems of life are sometimes too big for them. Which ones are you most like?"

4. The question used to measure organizational commitment is "If someone asked you to describe yourself, and you could tell only one thing about yourself, which of the following answers would you be most likely to give—I come from (my home state); I work for (my employer); I am a (my occupation or type of work); I am a (my church membership or preference); or I am a graduate of (my school)." First and second choice responses to either employer or occupation were used to indicate potential organizational commitment.

5. These three occupational categories are the same as those used by the United States Bureau of Census except that we have made several changes in combining the numerous categories. Officials have been combined with professionals because the state officials were, without exception, closer in occupational status to our professionals than to our managers. Likewise, technical employees were grouped with managerial employees rather than with professional employees as the Census does. Finally, the number of workers that were classified as operatives, laborers, crafts, or service workers was so small (N = 59) that we combined them with the next closest occupational category—clerical workers.

6. A good discussion of mobility is contained in Presthus (1962).

7. Rousseau (1978) examines the possibility that the nature of the work experience may shape individual personalities. This has important implications for job redesign since an essentially dynamic rather than static personality would respond quite differently to altered job stimuli.

8. The so-called attraction-selection framework argues that certain kinds of organizations (structurally) may either attract or select employees with particular individual characteristics. Employee reactions (satisfaction) to their jobs are seen as a result of organizational structural characteristics mediated by individual characteristics (Kohn, 1971; Oldham and Hackman, 1981).

9. This is supported over a number of years by membership figures. For studies involving the blue/white collar distinction, see Blum (1971) and Troy (1971).

10. The direction of the relationship indicated in Table 5.4 between education and the work situation is reversed from that for the relationship with status and mobility because of the direction of the coding.

CHAPTER 6

TOWARD A MODEL OF JOB SATISFACTION

Whether studying job satisfaction as either an independent or dependent variable, virtually all studies involving job satisfaction have relied primarily on bivariate correlational analysis. Job satisfaction is a multifaceted psychological concept that clearly demands a multivariate explanation (Vroom, 1964; Locke, 1969; Seashore and Taber, 1977). One of several multivariate models, the need-satisfaction model (Salancik and Pfeffer, 1977) and its kin, the job redesign model (Alderfer, 1969; Hackman and Oldham, 1980), has been either implicit or explicit in much of the job satisfaction research. These models inform the analysis that follows.

An important potential danger exists in partitioning the examination of multivariate relationships into a series of bivariate relationships as we have done in earlier chapters. In stastistical terms, distortion can occur through judging relationships as "real" when they are spurious. In spurious relationships the effects of third variables are ignored, causing either an inflation or suppression of the associational relationship involved. This distortion occurs because of the nature of the relationships among the independent variables, or some untapped variable, and the dependent variable. The only way to protect against this problem is to employ a multivariate approach incorporating all potentially important independent variables and utilizing appropriate statistical controls.[1]

Once it is agreed that a multivariate approach is essential to expanding our understanding of job satisfaction and work, a discussion of alternative explanatory models is necessary. In Chapter 1, a fairly simple four-variable model is elaborated to explain variations in job satisfaction. Individual characteristics, unionization, and the work situation are all portrayed as potentially important determinants of job satisfaction. Prior chapters define these determinants of job satisfaction conceptually, review alternative definitional and measurement approaches used in previous research, and elaborate the measurement selected for this study of job satisfaction among state government employees. Because the work situation and individual characteristics are both broad conceptually and have been measured in a variety of ways in previous research, a number of aspects or dimensions of these concepts have been operationalized in this study. Specifically, twenty-three aspects of the work situation—ten job characteristics, eleven job environment features, and two union characteristics—are considered, as well as ten individual characteristics tapping psychological orientations, job orientations, and personal factors.

A model with this many independent variables (33) obviously errs in having too much complexity; some degree of parsimony is desirable in attempts to explicate social relationships. To this end, two strategies are employed. The first strategy involves reducing the total number of independent variables to a more manageable size. This is done on the basis of the findings of previous research and, to a lesser extent, on the bivariate relationships discussed in earlier chapters. Both empirical evidence and the logical strength of the arguments for a potential predictor's impact on job satisfaction are considered. The second strategy involves testing two alternative models of job satisfaction, a job redesign model and a job environment model. The

Figure 6.1 Stages of Analysis in Developing a Model of Job Satisfaction

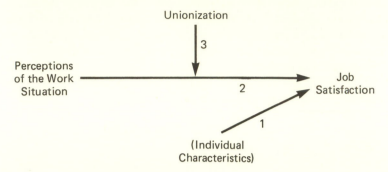

results of these analyses are then synthesized to develop a more complete model of job satisfaction.[2]

Before proceeding to the explication and testing of the alternative models, it is necessary to explain the general treatments applied to all three models. In each the primary interest is the nature of the relationship between the work situation (or some selected aspect of it) and job satisfaction. Unionization, an aspect of the job environment, is seen as an important differentiator in the general work situation-job satisfaction relationship, potentially altering levels of satisfaction and/or perceptions of work. Thus, the impact of unionization is examined after looking at the relationship between the work situation and job satisfaction. Although individual characteristics have been examined in some detail in Chapter 5 relative to their potential bivariate impact on the work situation and job satisfaction, the results, with some exceptions, are relatively weak and in the models discussed here are considered primarily as *potential* conditioners of job satisfaction. This is accomplished by treating individual characteristics as covariates in the Multiple Classification Analysis (MCA) so that the variance in the dependent variable (job satisfaction), which is attributable to variance in individual characteristics, is removed prior to an examination of the linkage between the work situation and job satisfaction.

Graphically, the analysis proceeds in three steps, as presented in Figure 6.1. The first step is to remove the variance in job satisfaction attributable to individual characteristics. The second step is to examine the relationship between the work situation factors and job satisfaction by assessing the relative importance of the work situation predictors in explaining job satisfaction. The third and final stage is to assess the impact of unionization, specifically union membership or non-membership, on the relationship between the work situation and job satisfaction. This control is introduced by running a separate MCA for union members and non-members.

A Job Redesign Model

The first model to be examined that purports to explain job satisfaction is the job redesign model. This has been the dominant model in job satisfaction research for the last twelve to fifteen years (Hackman and Oldham, 1980). It reflects both the common conceptual division of the work situation into job characteristics and the job environment as well as the recent humanistic approach and its concern with the quality of work life. The main thrust of job redesign proponents is that the enhancement of job characteristics will promote increased job satisfaction (Lawler, 1969). Heavily dependent upon the need-satisfaction model (Salancik and Pfeffer, 1977), the model assumes that with higher quality work (i.e., greater work autonomy and variety) satisfaction of higher order needs will result (Maslow, 1943).

In the job redesign model, job characteristics are seen as the major determinant of job satisfaction. As the quality of jobs increases, individual satisfaction with work should also increase. The nature of this relationship, however, may be affected by whether or not unionization exists in the work place. Although not part of the original job redesign model as proposed by industrial psychologists and public administrators, we will explore this variation below.[3] Individual characteristics will be treated as covariates, or as prior conditioners, of job satisfaction.

Our definition of job characteristics is somewhat broader than most previous studies involving job redesign, and includes three components. First, and most important in the job redesign literature, is job quality. The job quality index is composed of

Table 6.1 Job Redesign Model: MCA

Covariates: life view, organizational commitment, and education*

Predictors	Total Employees			Union members			Non-members		
	N	Adjusted deviations	Beta	N	Adjusted deviations	Beta	N	Adjusted deviations	Beta
Job Quality Index									
1	344	.20		88	.29		247	.18	
2	564	-.05		186	-.06		371	-.04	
3	128	-.32	.28*	38	-.39	.33*	89	-.32	.29*
Skill in the use of ones hands									
1	162	.12		38	.12		119	.10	
2	202	.03		65	.03		134	.02	
3	234	-.02		76	-.03		155	.01	
4	438	-.05	.10*	133	-.03	.08	299	-.05	.09
Resources: co-worker help									
1	836	.05		247	.09		577	.03	
2	200	-.20	.17*	65	-.33	.27*	130	-.14	.12*
Resources: authority									
1	771	.05		222	.03		536	.06	
2	265	-.15	.15*	90	-.08	.08	171	-.17	.18*
	$R^2 = 18.9\%$			$R^2 = 24.8\%$			$R^2 = 17.8\%$		

*Significant at .05 or greater. No interaction effects.

responses to six questions dealing with job freedom, variety of skills, learning new things, planning ahead, and decisional independence. The second and third components of job characteristics in this study involve indicators of the nature of the job effort required, such as speed and skill in the use of hands, and indicators of the nature of the resources available for doing the job, such as equipment and co-worker help. For the purposes of testing the job redesign model, four of the ten job characteristics were selected: the job quality index, one of the effort measures (skill in the use of hands), and two job resources indicators—co-worker help and authority.

Three individual characteristics were selected for use as co-variates in testing the job redesign model. Originally three kinds of individual characteristics were conceptualized: psychological orientations, job orientations, and personal factors. For the multivariate analysis only three indicators—life view, organizational commitment, and educational level—are used. These three factors were found to be either somewhat more related to job satisfaction and the work situation or to have stronger arguments relative to their importance in explaining job satisfaction.

Table 6.1 presents the results of the Multiple Classification Analysis for the job redesign model, both with and without unionization incorporated. Considering first the simple job redesign model (excluding unionization) presented in the left portion of Table 6.1, all three individual characteristics are significantly related to job satisfaction. The four indicators of job characteristics acting together explain just under 20 percent of the variance (R^2) in job satisfaction.[4] All four job characteristics are significantly related to job satisfaction and act in the expected direction. Those with more ample resources, having jobs requiring less skill in the use of their hands and more job quality, tend to be more satisfied with their jobs.

An examination of the Betas for this model indicates that the job quality index is clearly the strongest of the predictors of job satisfaction. Both job resources also have fairly substantial Betas. Skill in the use of ones hands is the least important of the four job characteristic indicators in explaining job satisfaction. The finding that job quality is the strongest predictor of job satisfaction is consistent with the expectations of the proponents of job redesign. The importance of the two job resources, co-worker help and authority, indicates, however, that perhaps a broader view of the nature of job characteristics might enhance the understanding of job satisfaction. The relatively low R^2 may discourage some job redesign proponents and clearly suggests the need to look beyond job characteristics in explaining job satisfaction.

Given that the presence or absence of unionization may affect the nature of the work situation, or employees' perceptions of it, and thus indirectly, the level of job satisfaction, Table 6.1 presents a modification of the job redesign model. This modification considers the relationship between job characteristics and job satisfaction among two kinds of workers—those who are union members and those who are not. Among union members, almost 25 percent of the variance of job satisfaction is explained by the four job characteristics acting together. This contrasts to an R^2 of 18 percent among non-members. Further comparison of union members and non-members reveals additional differences as well as several similarities. Regardless of unionization, job quality is the most important predictor of job satisfaction. Among union members, however, only the job resource of co-worker help is also a significant predictor of job satisfaction. In contrast, among non-members, both the job resources are significantly related to job satisfaction with the resource of adequate authority being the stronger of the two. The importance of co-worker help suggests a potential problem with efforts to redesign jobs to enhance satisfaction. Like some job environment factors, the ability to alter or manipulate co-worker help is probably limited.

This analysis suggests, in addition to the usefulness of a broader definition of job characteristics, the importance of taking into account the union context. It is evident that something about union membership enhances the importance of some job characteristics, in particular job quality and co-worker help. The absence of union membership lowers the importance of co-worker help and advances the relative significance of authority as a resource. Given the lack of a longitudinal data base, it is impossible to tell whether individuals join unions because of the greater importance of co-worker help and job quality or whether being a member of a union creates more negative perceptions and enhances the position of job quality and co-worker help relative to their levels of job satisfaction.

The job redesign model examines only one-half of what is defined in Chapter 3 as the work situation and ignores the impact of the nature of the job environment on job satisfaction. A job environment model that excludes job characteristics is tested below, following which a combined model is examined.

A Job Environment Model

The focus on job redesign in most recent research on job satisfaction has clearly ignored an important component of the work situation, the job environment. All jobs have certain characteristics associated with them, and the job environment provides the immediate context within which the job is performed. In general, the environment or context of the job is defined by individuals and groups other than the employees; the environment then acquires meaning to the employees as it filters through their own perceptual apparatus. As elaborated in Chapter 4, variations in the job environment are closely linked to job satisfaction. Negative perception of the job environment by state employees are associated with lower levels of job satisfaction.

The conceptualization and measurement of the job environment in this study is much broader than in most previous studies. Supervision, promotions, income, size of the work place, and working conditions have been analyzed in a number of previous studies. Discrimination, job mobility, civil service status, and unionization are essentially new components of the job environment.

In order to simplify our analysis of the job environment model, five of the thirteen indicators of the job environment (excluding unionization) were selected based, as was the case with the job redesign model, on their bivariate relationship to job satisfaction and the strength of the theoretical arguments about the relationship between job satisfaction and the particular environmental

Table 6.2 Job Environment Model: MCA

Covariates: life view, organizational commitment, and education*

Predictors	Total Employees			Union members			Non-members		
	N	Adjusted deviations	Beta	N	Adjusted deviations	Beta	N	Adjusted deviations	Beta
		Covariates significant			Life view and education not significant			Covariates significant	
Fairness of promotions									
1	241	.17		61	.23		176	.14	
2	480	-.04		149	-.02		322	-.05	
3	210	-.11	.18*	71	-.17	.22*	134	-.07	.16*
Working conditions index									
1	798	.03		245	.02		538	.03	
2	133	-.16	.11*	36	-.12	.07	94	-.17	.13*
Job mobility									
1	133	-.02		56	-.07		72	.04	
2	417	-.05		135	-.02		276	-.07	
3	315	.05		74	.04		234	.05	
4	66	.11	.10*	16	.23	.11	50	.08	.11*
Quality of supervision									
1	369	.14		109	.12		255	.16	
2	373	-.03		102	.01		262	-.05	
3	142	-.19		54	-.24		85	-.16	
4	47	-.30	.23*	16	-.02	.20*	30	-.44	.27*
Lets alone									
1	483	.07		131	.11		342	.05	
2	321	-.06		106	-.09		209	-.04	
3	84	-.08		27	-.06		56	-.09	
4	43	-.16	.12*	17	-.20	.18*	25	-.15	.10*
	$R^2 = 23.6\%$			$R^2 = 23.8\%$			$R^2 = 22.3\%$		

*Significant at .05 or greater. No interaction effects.

feature. The five indicators are: (1) the fairness of promotions; (2) an index of working conditions; (3) job mobility within state government; (4) an index of the quality of supervision combining answers to questions on the extent of personal interest supervisors take in employees and the standards the supervisors set in their own work; and (5) a single question on the extent to which supervisors leave employees alone to do their work unless they need help.[5] It is expected that a job environment with fairer promotions, better working conditions, greater job mobility, and higher quality supervision will be associated with higher degrees of job satisfaction. As with the analysis of the job redesign model, three individual characteristics are used as covariates.

Table 6.2 presents the results of the MCA for the job environment model and incorporates a sub-analysis that distinguishes union members from non-members. In the simple job environment model (excluding unionization), the three covariates are significant and the five job environment features explain approximately 24 percent of the variance (R^2) in job satisfaction. All five of the job environment features act in the expected direction and are significant predictors of job satisfaction. An examination of the Betas for the job environment model indicates that the quality of supervision index and the fairness of promotions are substantially more important than the other job environment features in predicting job satisfaction. Nonetheless, working conditions, job mobility, and the other supervision indicator are also of importance.

Table 6.2 also indicates the relationships between perceptions of the job environment and job satisfaction that are important for union membership. Among union members, neither the life view nor education are significantly related to job satisfaction, whereas among non-members both factors as well as organizational commitment are significantly related to satisfaction. Only the fairness of promotions and the two indicators of the nature of supervision are significantly linked to job satisfaction among union members. In contrast, among non-members, job mobility and working conditions are also significant. Interestingly, the relative importance (Beta) of supervision is more substantial among non-members while among union members the fairness of promotions is slightly more important than supervision.

Our examination of the job redesign and job environment models indicates that both are useful in understanding variations in job satisfaction. Both models work slightly differently for union members and non-members. Although the job redesign literature would lead one to expect otherwise, the job environment model works slightly better (R^2 higher) than the job redesign model. Since the work setting includes both job characteristics and the job environment, it is necessary to expand our model of job satisfaction to incorporate both kinds of factors.

An Expanded Model of Job Satisfaction

Although our examination of both the job redesign and job environment models has enhanced our understanding of job satisfaction substantially over the previous bivariate and limited multivariate models, further specification is desirable. Previously conceptually distinguished, the job environment and job characteristics together compose what we have termed the work situation. Utilizing the same procedures as with the job redesign and job environment models, a work situation model of job satisfaction is examined below. As before, individual characteristics are employed as covariates so that the variance in job satisfaction attributable to the life view, organizational commitment, and education is first removed from the analysis. From our analysis of the job redesign model, the job quality index and the two job resource indicators—co-worker help and authority—are selected for inclusion in the expanded version of the job satisfaction model. The quality of supervision index and fairness of promotions are selected from the job environment model. The impact of union membership on the work situation-job satisfaction linkage is also considered.

Table 6.3 presents the MCA for the expanded model of job satisfaction. The first predictor of job satisfaction listed is a combination of the job quality index and fairness of promotions, both of which were found to be substantial predictors of job satisfaction in earlier analysis. Job quality and promotions are combined because their impact on job satisfaction is significantly interactive in nature. This simply means that the presence of both job quality and fairness of promotions impact job satisfaction in ways different from the summation (or addition) of the impact of each separately. MCA assumes an additive model. Thus, in order to portray more accurately the impact of these two variables, a new variable was created whose categories are simply each combination of the categories of the original variables. This new variable can then be utilized in the MCA with no distortion resulting from its additive assumptions.

The expanded work situation model (excluding unionization) on the left side of Table 6.3 is substantially more effective in explaining variations in job satisfaction than either the job redesign or job environment models alone.[6] The R^2 for the work situation model is 10 percent higher than the job redesign model and 5 percent higher than the R^2 for the job environment model. As might be expected from the earlier analysis, job quality from the redesign model and fairness of promotions and the quality of supervision from the job environment model are the most important predictors of job satisfaction. Job resources, although significantly related to job satisfaction, are much less substantial in their relative importance to understanding variations in job satisfaction.

A most interesting contrast is provided when union membership is controlled. The most striking difference between union members and non-members is that a substantially larger proportion of the variance in job satisfaction is explained by the expanded work situation model among union members (37 percent) than among non-members (28 percent). It may be that being a union member heightens one's awareness of both job characteristics and the job environment, or it may be that people who join unions already are more aware of their jobs and its environment. The cross sectional nature of the data examined here does not permit a systematic treatment of this issue.

The importance of the various predictors (Betas) also varies somewhat among union members and non-members. In both groups, job quality and promotions are the most important predictors, but they have greater relative magnitude among

Table 6.3 Expanded Work Situation Model: MCA

Covariates: life view, organizational commitment, and education*

Predictors	Total employees			Union members			Non-members		
	N	Adjusted deviations	Beta	N	Adjusted deviations	Beta	N	Adjusted deviations	Beta
		Covariates significant			Life view and education not significant			Covariates significant	
Job quality and fairness of promotions†									
1	101	.27		20	.52		80	.21	
2	162	.15		43	.26		117	.13	
3	127	.20		36	.23		89	.17	
4	265	-.13		89	-.13		175	-.13	
5	51	.08		15	.10		32	.08	
6	12	-.22		5	-.82		7	.20	
7	118	-.10		46	-.16		71	-.06	
8	53	-.19		17	-.07		35	-.25	
9	45	-.49	.33*	11	-.69	.44*	34	-.42	.31*
Resources: co-worker help									
1	758	.03		233	.05		526	.02	
2	176	-.12	.10*	59	-.20	.16*	114	-.08	.07

Resources: authority								
1	698	.03		200	.01		490	.03
2	236	-.09	.09*	82	-.02	.03	150	-.11	.11*
Quality of supervision								
1	372	.13		109	.11		259	.14
2	366	-.03		100	.02		260	-.05
3	148	-.15		55	-.21		91	-.11
4	48	-.27	.20*	18	-.10	.19*	30	-.38	.23*
		$R^2 = 28.3\%$			$R^2 = 37.0\%$			$R^2 = 28.1\%$

*Significant at .05 or greater

†The categories below are a combination of the responses to the job quality index and fairness of promotions. Each numerical category is composed in the following way: 1 = 1 on job quality (a lot) and 1 on fairness of promotions (completely fair); 2 = 1 on job quality (a lot) and 2 on fairness of promotions (somewhat fairly); 3 = 2 on job quality (some) and 1 on fairness of promotions (completely fairly); 4 = 2 on job quality (some) and 2 on fairness of promotions (somewhat); 5 = 1 on job quality (a lot) and 3 on fairness of promotions (not too fairly); 6 = 3 on job quality (a little, not at all) and 1 on fairness of promotions (completely fairly); 7 = 2 on job quality (some) and 3 on fairness of promotions (not too fairly); 8 = 3 on job quality (a little, not at all) and 2 on fairness of promotions (somewhat fairly); 9 = 3 on job quality (a little, not at all) and a 3 on fairness of promotions (not too fairly).

union members. The quality of supervision index is the second most important predictor of job satisfaction with little difference between the union members and non-members. Differences are apparent in the relative importance of the two job resource variables, co-worker help and authority. Among union members, co-worker help is significantly related to job satisfaction while authority is only very weakly related to job satisfaction. In contrast, among non-members authority is significantly related to job satisfaction, whereas co-worker help is not significantly related to satisfaction. Thus, in addition to the substantial differences in the amount of job satisfaction variance explained (R^2) among members and non-members, there is also some variance in the relative importance of the predictors (Betas) in explaining job satisfaction. Most notable is the heightened importance of job quality and promotions to union members and the variance in the importance in job resources to union members and non-members.

The Work Situation Model of Job Satisfaction

The expanded work situation model of job satisfaction adds considerably to our understanding of job attitudes and the role of unions in the work setting. Both job characteristics *and* the job environment are important determinants of job satisfaction. In particular, job quality, supervision, and promotions are of most importance. Individual characteristics are significant factors in a prior sense, and union membership clearly intervenes to enhance the linkage between the perceived work situation and job satisfaction. The development of a job satisfaction model including individual characteristics, features of job characteristics, and the job environment, as well as unionization, has moved our understanding a long way from a series of bivariate relationships. The next chapter will summarize the major findings of this research, raising questions about the most productive direction for future research, and discuss the implications of this research for public policymakers.

Notes

1. A related issue, but one of considerable importance, is the problem of multicolinearity. This occurs when two or more independent variables are related to each other at such substantial levels that it is not possible to statistically disentangle them and thus judge their independent effects on the dependent variable. The potential of this problem must be examined throughout one's analysis.

2. This analysis strategy is similar to that followed by Oldham and Hackman (1981) in their study of the impact of organizational structures on satisfaction in which they initially utilized two competing models subsequently synthesizing the two models into a third, improved model.

3. The potential mediating effects of unions in job redesign is now an acknowledged part of projects to improve the quality of worklife (Holley, Field and Crowley, 1981; Nadler, Hanlow and Lawler, 1980).

4. It should be noted that neither this R^2 nor the other two presented in Table 6.1 are particularly large. This is not surprising given the fact that these models are basically attitudinal. A high degree of predictability of attitudes has been found to be difficult to achieve in a large number of inquiries. Explained variance in the 20 to 25 percent range is not unusual.

5. In terms of both selection criteria, perceptions of discrimination should have been included in the job environment model. It was not included in the analysis because of the small Ns caused partly by the large proportion of perceptions of reverse discrimination. For a discussion of the nature and correlates of this discrimination, see Hopkins (1980).

6. For an excellent discussion of interaction, MCA, and appropriate treatments, see Andrews, Morgan, Sonquist and Klem (1973:17–22).

CHAPTER 7

WORK AND UNIONS: IMPLICATIONS FOR FUTURE RESEARCH AND POLICYMAKERS

This study explores the relationship between employees and their work in the public sector at the individual level. To define the relationship between employees and their work, the analysis is focused on the employees' response to their own job as indicated by their degree of job satisfaction. Job satisfaction in the private sector has been the focus of an enormous amount of research; it has only occasionally been investigated in the public sector. There have been literally hundreds of publications on job satisfaction that seek a definition and determination of its correlates and causes. It is interesting to note that, despite this voluminous research stream, there have been only scattered attempts to develop a multivariate model to explain job satisfaction. Most analysis has instead proceeded in a bivariate way, or created models incorporating only selected types of variables. Recently, the work situation has been defined by job characteristics, ignoring the potential importance of the job environment. Another major deficiency of these job satisfaction studies is that a critical component of the job environment, unionization, is rarely explored in relation to job satisfaction. Thus, this study departs from previous investigations of job satisfaction in four principal ways: (1) in dealing with the public sector, (2) in testing a multivariate model, (3) in reincorporating the job environment, and (4) in incorporating unionization as part of the work setting.

In terms of its relationship to previous work in this area, this study clearly builds upon the evolving humanistic approach to work (Gibson and Teasley, 1973; Hackman and Oldham, 1980). Basically, we examine three kinds of factors in our search for a better understanding of job satisfaction: individual orientations, the work situation, and unionization. These factors and their potential linkages are explored in Chapter 1 and an abbreviated model set forth to explain job satisfaction. Early chapters explored the four major components of the model and their interrelationships in a bivariate analysis mode. Having explored the relevant bivariate relationships, Chapter 6 examines, two models of job satisfaction using multivariate analysis: job redesign and job environment. The results of these two analyses are then used to build a synthesized work situation model of job satisfaction. Since a large number of relationships are investigated, it seems appropriate to briefly summarize the major findings. This summary supports a discussion of future research as well as a consideration of the implications of these findings for policymakers.

Findings: Summary

The analysis begins with an exploration of the nature of the dependent variable, job satisfaction, among state employees. Job satisfaction is viewed from an individual's perspective as a descriptor of the work place resulting from the interaction of variable individual values and variable individual perceptions of the job and its environment. A faceted measurement scheme is employed to reflect the multidimensional nature of job satisfaction. For each of the twenty-three facets, employees were asked how important the facet is to the individual (value component) and the extent to which their current job provides such a facet ("is now"). Discrepancy scoring, comparing the "is now" and "importance" responses summed across facets, is used to develop an indicator of job satisfaction. The overall distribution of job satisfaction among state employees indicates that the ranges are comparable to previous private sector studies with approximately 15 percent revealing a high discrepancy (low satisfaction). As was expected, job satisfaction does not vary substantially across the states.

Chapter 3 examines the nature of the work situation from the employees' perspective. The nature of the job is distinguished from the environment or context within which the work takes place. The focus of analysis is on both components of the work situation, despite the tendency of those who share the so-called humanistic orientation to focus on the job itself and not its environment. All jobs have certain characteristics associated with their work or tasks. Three major aspects of job characteristics are studied: job quality, job effort, and job resources. The job environment is the proximate context within which the job is performed. The major components of the job environment are supervision, mobility, working conditions, discrimination, promotions, income, size, civil service, and unionization.

Overall, state employees see their jobs as having some degree of depth or scope, little physical effort, and fairly adequate resources. The state employee's job environment includes fairly favorable reactions to his/her supervisor and working conditions, mobility as somewhat of a problem, mixed feelings about promotions, and a variety of responses on income and size of the work place. Almost 20 percent feel discriminated against and approximately one-third are union members and a comparable number work under union contracts. Although many of the job environment features were not expected to vary by state, several were expected to be variable. Perceptions of job mobility, income levels, civil service coverage, and unionization vary considerably by state.

The central linkage in this study of job satisfaction and work is between perceptions of the work situation and job satisfaction (Chapter 4). This is so because it is individuals' views of their working environment that will interact with their own job values or needs to produce varying levels of job satisfaction. Relating each of the twenty-three indicators of the work situation (various indices plus individual questions) to job satisfaction results in most interesting findings. Employees who are more satisfied with their jobs tend to have jobs that are characterized by scope and depth, as well as adequate resources. Favorable perceptions of one's supervisor and fairness of promotions, as well as adequate working conditions, job mobility, a lack of discrimination, and not being union members or working under a union contract are the job environment features consistent with more satisfied workers. This preliminary bivariate analysis suggests that the job environment may be even more important than job characteristics in explaining variations in job satisfaction.

Because unionization may mediate the work situation-job satisfaction linkage, Chapter 4 also examines the relation between perceptions of the work situation and unionization. Unionization is viewed as part of the job environment and also as operating separately from it. Since the goal of unions is to affect workers and their job environments, it is expected that unionization is strongly related to perceptions of the work situation. Unionization tends to be related predominately to indicators of the job environment rather than to job characteristics. Supervision, mobility, income, and civil service coverage are all linked to unionization.

The fourth component of the job satisfaction model, individual orientations, is discussed in Chapter 5. Individuals bring prior orientations and experiences to their jobs that may affect their expectations or predispositions to their work. Without attempting to uncover the antecedents for such expectations, individual orientations are identified and related to perceptions of the work situation (including unionization) and to job satisfaction. Three kinds of individual orientations are explored: psychological orientations (life view and organizational commitment), job orientations (occupational status, mobility, length of service, education, and attitudes toward working), and personal attributes (age, sex, and race). Generally, these ten individual orientations are not very related to job satisfaction, which suggests that individual orientations may be influential further back in the causal chain. Individual orientations are related to the varying aspects of the work situation with some success. In terms of job characteristics, individual orientations are most frequently significantly related to indicators of job quality. Among the job environment factors, promotions, mobility, and discrimination all are significantly related in varying degrees to individual orientations. It was expected that individual orientations might predispose an individual in relation to unionism. The union-individual orientation relationships are somewhat mixed, but unionization is associated with occupational mobility and status as well as age and sex.

These mixed findings about the linkages between individual orientations and the other components of the job satisfaction model do not necessarily mean that individual orientations are not important in the model. It does seem likely, however, that individual orientations act as predispositional factors or as conditioners of job attitudes.

Having examined the four components of the job satisfaction model and the interrelationships of these components, Chapter 6 attempts to develop a more fully specified model of job satisfaction. Using a multivariate approach, two alternative models are tested initially: a job redesign model and a job environment model. Each of these models focuses on the linkage between one aspect of the work situation, either job characteristics or the job environment, in relation to job satisfaction. In both models, individual orientations are treated as conditioners of job satisfaction. Unionization is treated as a control variable whose nature may alter the work situation-job satisfaction linkage.

The job redesign model focuses on selected aspects of job characteristics in relation to job satisfaction. The four job characteristics included in the model—job quality, skill in the use of one's hands, the resources of co-worker help, and authority—are all significantly related to job satisfaction, as are the three individual characteristics of the life view, organizational commitment and education. Job quality and co-worker help are most important in predicting satisfaction. Whether one is a union member or not alters these relationships somewhat but not substantially.

The second model of job satisfaction, the job environment model, performs somewhat better (higher R^2s) than the job redesign model in predicting job satisfaction. Promotions, working conditions, mobility, and the two indicators of supervision are included in the job environment model. All are significantly related to job satisfaction as are the three individual orientations. Supervision and promotions are the strongest predictors of job satisfaction. Controlling for union membership makes more difference with the job environment model than with the job redesign model. Among union members, the importance of promotions is enhanced, whereas among non-members the importance of supervision is enhanced. In addition, of the individual orientations only organizational commitment is significantly related to job satisfaction among union members, whereas among non-members all three individual orientations are significant.

After testing the job environment and job redesign models, a combined model is developed to examine the interaction of both the components of the work situation (including unionization), relative to job satisfaction. Three job characteristics—the job quality index, the resources of co-worker help, and authority—are included in the new model, as well as two of the job environment factors—supervision quality and promotions. The expanded model is substantially more effective in explaining variations in job satisfaction than the other two models. The interactive effect of job quality and promotions is the most important predictor of job satisfaction. Supervision is also a major predictor while the two job resource variables, although significant, are of less importance. Also of substantial importance is the fairly wide difference in the variance in job satisfaction explained among union members and non-members, suggesting a heightened awareness of the work situation by union members. Finally the resource of co-worker help is of greater importance to union members, whereas authority as a resource is of more importance to non-members.

Future Research

The development of this multivariate model of job satisfaction is an advance over previous research in this area in several ways. First, an essentially complex set of interrelationships relative to job attitudes is examined in a multivariate rather than bivariate model. Secondly, job environment factors are reintroduced as predictors of job satisfaction. Third, a major aspect of the work situation and the job environment, unionization, is incorporated in this research. Finally, the study of job attitudes and unionization is extended to the public sector.

A number of limitations exist relative to this research, the review of which should both place the research findings discussed above in an appropriate context and suggest the direction for future research. This study focuses on employee's attitudes in state government in five states at one point in time. State employees may or may not be typical of other public sector employees, thus it would seem highly appropriate to explore some of these same questions among national and local government employees. Considerable care was taken in the selection of the five states studied, although those interested in particular state governments may want to conduct investigations within their own states.

In one sense, this study is bound by the particular time context of the data. Events have occurred in each of the states, particularly with regard to union activities that might alter employee attitudes; however there is no reason to believe that job attitudes and their determinants should in the aggregate vary across time. If this is a correct assumption, then the findings should hold across time.

A related issue is that this study is based on a cross-sectional research design, while some of the research interests addressed demand longitudinal data. The focus of recent work in this area on job redesign makes longitudinal data particularly desirable. If change is the desired end, then the analysis of change and change agents over time and their impact on the same individuals, rather than cross-sectional analysis, is the preferred research strategy (Roberts and Glick, 1981). There is a tendency to think of such issues as if one were working with longitudinal data. Clearly, the practical considerations of time and money precluded a longitudinal study when such a large number of employees (1,177) were studied. Future research on work and unions would seem likely to be substantially enriched by longitudinal studies of smaller samples of employees.

Finally, a question must be raised about the quality of the measurement of job attitudes, unions, individual characteristics, and the work situation. Much of the job attitude research has been conducted by industrial psychologists who place a premium on the development and validation of testing instruments. Partially as a result of this focus, much of the job satisfaction research has been conducted on small groups of workers in particular work settings. Although considerable care was taken in the design of this questionnaire, substantive interests required modifications of existing measurement strategies as well as the addition of areas not usually studied (especially unionization). Further testing of instruments designed with broader research interests in mind is essential.

Implications for Policy and Practice

It is usually easy to explain the contribution and limitations of a given piece of scholarship and its fit with an evolving and expanding understanding of some phenomena such as work and unions. What is far more difficult is to portray such research to the policymaker in such a way as to be understandable and, at the same time, consistent with the nature of the research. The implications of research are even more difficult to elaborate than the findings because, by their nature, implications are inferences from findings and thus slightly removed from them. It is somewhat personally painful to develop such a statement of implications and to offer "advice" because of the responsibilities attendant to that task. Nonetheless, there seem to be important implications to the research reported here that demand discussion.

The most obvious issues and the most important to address relative to the implications of this research are the ways in which job satisfaction can be enhanced. There are important differences as to why one might wish to increase satisfaction, i.e., humanistic values or some potential to increase productivity, but regardless of the motivation more positive job attitudes is an often-sought goal. If one posits such an increase in job satisfaction as the goal, the advice that can reasonably be provided to the manager or policymaker is limited in several ways. First, not all factors that determine the level and nature of job satisfaction are subject to alteration in the work setting. For example, if an individual's family background is an important determinant of job satisfaction, there is nothing the manager or policymaker can do to change it and thus alter job satisfaction.[1] Therefore, all aspects of our study are not equally relevant to the immediate concerns of the manager.

A related issue, and one rarely considered, is that not all factors that influence job satisfaction may be equally morally desirable to manipulate. For example, if verbal threats by a supervisor lead indirectly to increased satisfaction (by inducing faster work that leads to a sense of accomplishment), then one might appropriately question whether promoting such fear is consistent morally with enhanced human values.

Finally, it should be remembered that the data utilized in this study is based on workers' perceptions of the work situation. Since the purpose of this research is to enhance our understanding of a subjective phenomenon, subjective indicators are also used of the nature of the work situation. From the perspective of the manager or policymaker who wants to attempt to enhance job satisfaction, this presents certain problems. For one thing, the manager has no direct way of knowing how his/her particular employees perceive and react to their jobs and its environment. Although attempts probably should be made to ascertain this information, there is the additional problem that employees may not wish to provide such information to their own superiors. Even if we assume that such perceptual information is available, there is the flip side of this perceptual issue. Managers, like employees, do not see work objectively, but operate within their own personal frameworks in examining their work organizations. In a sense, this is the dilemma of all problems in communication. For research such as this study to have a direct application, it is necessary for these perceptual issues to be confronted. If they are not addressed, then considerable efforts may be expended to enhance job satisfaction with little or no change ensuing.[2]

With these cautions in mind, it is appropriate to examine the implications of this research for the public manager and policymaker. Recent research on job satisfaction has focused on job redesign as the primary means of increasing satisfaction. The main argument is that if jobs are redesigned to provide more desirable characteristics, such as greater autonomy or variety, then increases in job satisfaction will result. The assumption of this line of argument is that by implication the enhancement of job characteristics is desired by most employees. By its omission, the job environment is inferred to be an unimportant factor.

The major findings of this research are not consistent with these assumptions. On the whole, a much broader approach to increasing job satisfaction than job redesign seems warranted. Job characteristics, especially job quality, are important in predicting job satisfaction; however, other factors are also of substantial importance, in particular the job environment. Indeed when job redesign and job environment models were both tested, the job environment model was stronger, explaining more of the variance in job satisfaction than in job redesign model. There are also indications that unionization influences job satisfaction indirectly through affecting perceptions of the work situation. Thus, from the perspective of the manager seeking to enhance job satisfaction, a number of avenues are possible.

This research suggests that the approach most likely to impact job satisfaction is to alter several key aspects of the environment within which the job takes place, particularly promotional procedures and supervision. In settings where unions were important, the fairness of promotional policies takes on added importance, whereas if unions are less important, the quality of supervision is more critical. In either case, however, fairness in the handling of promotions and supervisor-employee relations are the two most critical job environment factors in impacting job satisfaction. It is, of course, one thing to suggest that promotions and supervision need attention and quite another to suggest how to improve such matters. In this study the answers to the questions asked concerning promotion and supervision seem to point toward alterations in both procedures and style. Studies in greater depth about both employees' perceptions of practices, as well as expectations relative to promotions and supervision, may produce a fuller basis on which to elaborate the best ways to improve levels of job satisfaction.

The job redesign movement is only somewhat consistent with this data since the job environment is found to be more closely related to job satisfaction than job characteristics. In most recent research, job characteristics are related to job satisfaction without reference to the job environment and thus no comparison of relative importance has been possible. The findings for this sample of state employees suggest that job characteristics are somewhat lesser influences on job satisfaction than the job environment, but still of major importance.

By far the strongest predictor of job satisfaction among the job characteristics is the job quality index. This index generally taps the scope and depth of a job and is composed of indicators of variety, planning, skill, freedom, decision making, and learning new things. Although the measurement instrument differs from other job characteristic studies, factors conceptually similar to these are generally part of the focus on job redesign. The findings here are consistent with the direction of job redesign. The findings here are consistent with the direction of job redesign efforts in that increases in job quality seem likely to increase job satisfaction. As the job redesign movement has discovered in the industrial world, it is not easy to redesign job characteristics given the nature of the task requirements of varying industrial and commercial enterprises.

It is also important to remember that two predictors of job satisfaction—the fairness of promotions and the job quality index—had an interactive effect in explaining job satisfaction. The impact of altering both simultaneously is thus likely to maximimize the enhancement of job satisfaction. This kind of two-pronged management strategy makes sense substantively. Those whose jobs are expanded in scope and depth need to feel that promotions to even higher quality jobs are handled fairly in order for satisfaction levels to rise.

Given our interest in the impact of unions on work, it is interesting to note that industrial unions have from time to time opposed job redesign efforts. This opposition stems from the union's fear that job redesign efforts are veiled attempts to increase work loads or responsibilities without commensurate increases in salary and other benefits. Whether or not public sector unions would oppose job redesign efforts on the part of public management remains to be seen since almost all redesign efforts have taken place in industrial settings. It seems likely, however, that public and private union responses to job redesign would be fairly similar.

Unions and individual orientations, in addition to the job environment and job characteristics, are two factors important in understanding job satisfaction and should be of concern to managers. First of all this research found that unions are an important intermediary in the relationship between perceptions of the work situation and job satisfaction. Unionization seems to highlight or focus perceptions of work. If one examines the implications of these findings, two quite different perspectives are possible. One perspective, and the one that is most commonly espoused by managers, is that unions promote negativism among employees and in doing so promote job dissatisfaction. In one sense this conclusion is consistent with our finding that more negative job attitudes are associated with union membership as well as more negative perceptions of the work situation. An alternative perspective is that since unions tend to enhance worker awareness of their work environment, union members may be potentially impacted more than non-union employees by management-induced alterations of either job characteristics or the job environment.

Unions are an important part of the work setting regardless of their impact on job satisfaction. Enormous changes are underway with public sector employees producing the greatest increases in union strength. Few studies of public union impact exist. Unions are a relatively new ingredient in the public sector and one with which public managers must learn to cope. Much is unknown about the nature and impacts of public sector unions. As our understanding grows, it seems plausible that managers may find ways of working with unions to enhance the quality of work life.

This study has also found that certain individual orientations tend to act as predispositional factors relative to employees' perceptions of the work situation and levels of job satisfaction. The most important of these individual orientations are the life view, organizational commitment, and education. Individual orientations are the determinants of job satisfaction least subject to alteration by managers. Although over the long run these characteristics may be partially modified by work experiences, they are not likely to be influenced in the short run.

The implications of this study of public sector employees of state government differs from the job redesign focus of most recent studies of job satisfaction. Our findings suggest that managers should pay particular attention to two job environment features, promotions and supervisor-employee relations, as well as to job quality, the key job characteristic. Unions may be either an indirect benefit to managers in their potential enhancement of workers' responses to organizational changes or a promoter of negative job attitudes. Whether or not these findings are unique to the public sector or state employees remains to be tested in further studies. Clearly, public managers at the state level need to have a broad perspective on potential means of promoting job satisfaction.

Notes

1. It might be possible to take such factors into account in the hiring process. This is a major component of the attraction-selection framework discussed by Oldham and Hackman (1981).
2. Roberts and Glick (1981) go so far as to argue that objective changes in jobs should not be made unless based upon studies that incorporate more objectively defined, non-perceptally based indicators of the work situation.

APPENDIX

The Bureau of Public Administration
The University of Tennessee
Knoxville, Tennessee

No. _____

STATE NAME

STATE EMPLOYEE WORK ORIENTATIONS

CONFIDENTIAL

Directions

Below are questions dealing with state employee work orientations. Most require that you simply check the appropriate response. Space is provided at the end for any additional comments you may wish to make.

1. What is your job title? _____

2. What is the name of the department in which you work (for example, Department of Finance, Department of Public Works)?

   _____

3. In what division of the department do you work (for example, Division of Accounting in the Department of Finance, Division of Roads in the Department of Public Works)?

   _____

4. What do you do on this job? _____

   _____

5. All in all, how satisfied would you say you are with your job?

   _____ very satisfied   _____ not too satisfied
   _____ somewhat satisfied   _____ not at all satisfied

6. Knowing what you know now, if you had to decide all over again whether to take the job you now have, what would you decide? Would you

   _____ decide without hesitation to take the same job
   _____ have some second thoughts
   _____ decide definitely not to take the same job

7. How often do you get so wrapped up in your work that you lose track of time?

   _____ very often   _____ once in a while
   _____ pretty often   _____ never

8. How often do you leave work with a feeling that you've done something particularly well?

   _____ very often   _____ once in a while
   _____ pretty often   _____ never

9. How likely is it that you will make a genuine effort to find a new job with another employer within the next year?

_____ very likely   _____ not too likely
_____ somewhat likely   _____ not at all likely

10. If you were financially able, would you prefer not to work?

_____ yes
_____ no

11. About how many people work for the division of the department at the building where you work--in all types of work?

_____ 1-12   _____ 50-99
_____ 13-24   _____ 100-499
_____ 25-49   _____ 500 and over

12. How many years and months have you worked for state government?

_____ years and _____ months

13. For about how long have you had the job you have now, doing what you do now?

_____ years and _____ months

14. Have you worked outside state government?

_____ yes--how long? _____ years
_____ no

15. Was your first job in state government obtained on the basis of personal contacts, political contacts or civil service procedures?

_____ personal contacts
_____ political contacts
_____ civil service procedures
_____ other (specify) _____

16. Does your current job carry civil service status with it or not?

_____ yes
_____ no

17. Other than holidays like Christmas and Labor Day, how many working days are you allowed to take off with full pay as vacation days?

_____ none
_____ number of days

18. How many sick leave days are you allowed to take off with full pay each year?

_____ none
_____ number of days

19. Considering your work, are your working conditions comfortable?

_____ yes
_____ no

20. Considering your work, are your working conditions healthful?

_____ yes
_____ no

21. How much does your pay or income from your job figure out to be a year, before taxes and other deductions are made?

_____ Under 4,000	_____ 8,000-8,999
_____ 4,000-4,999	_____ 9,000-9,999
_____ 5,000-5,999	_____ 10,000-14,999
_____ 6,000-6,999	_____ 15,000-24,999
_____ 7,000-7,999	_____ 25,000 and over

22. Here is a list of some fringe benefits. Just check off whether or not these are available to you.

	yes	no
a. medical, surgical or hospital insurance	_____	_____
b. life insurance	_____	_____
c. a retirement program other than social security	_____	_____
d. (women only) maternity leave with pay	_____	_____
e. (women only) maternity leave with full re-employment rights	_____	_____

23. In your division how fairly are promotions generally handled?

_____ completely fairly   _____ not too fairly
_____ somewhat fairly   _____ no promotions have been given

24. Of the following reasons, which was the most important in your seeking state government employment?

_____ salary
_____ job security
_____ opportunity for advancement
_____ general preference for public service over private enterprise
_____ Other _____(specify)

25. How hard or easy do you think it would be for you to change your job within state government, if you didn't like it?

_____ very hard   _____ somewhat easy
_____ somewhat hard   _____ very easy

26. How hard or easy do you think it would be for you to get a new job outside of state government?

_____ very hard   _____ somewhat easy
_____ somewhat hard   _____ very easy

27. Below are two sets of questions about selected aspects of jobs. First, we'd like to know how important to you each of these things are in any job you might have. Secondly, does your present job actually provide these things?

	How Important to you?			Does Your Present Job Actually Provide This?		
	very important	fairly important	not important	quite a bit	in some ways	not at all
1. chance to make friends						
2. chance for promotion						
3. friendliness and helpfulness of co-workers						
4. opportunity to develop special abilities						
5. convenience of travel to and from work						
6. enough help and equipment to get the job done						
7. proper amount of work						
8. work is interesting						
9. enough information to get the job done						
10. adequate pay						
11. freedom to decide how to get the work done						
12. chance to do the things I do best						
13. job security						
14. challenging problems to solve						
15. competence of supervisor in doing his/her job						
16. responsibilities being clearly defined						
17. authority to do my job						
18. adequate fringe benefits						
19. pleasant physical surroundings						
20. seeing the results of my work						
21. enough time to get the job done						
22. freedom from the conflicting demands other people make of me						
23. reasonable working hours						

28. Below are a list of some resources you might receive from your employer or those people you work with that could help you work your best. For each, do you feel you are being given enough or not enough for you to work your best?

	enough	not enough
a. help or assistance from those you work with	_____	_____
b. the authority to tell certain people what to do	_____	_____
c. time in which to do what others expect of you	_____	_____
d. the facts and information you need	_____	_____
e. the machinery, tools, or other equipment you need	_____	_____

29. Through your previous experience and training, do you have some skills that you would like to be using in your work but can't use on your present job?

_____ yes
_____ no

30. What level of formal education do you feel is needed by a person in your job?

_____ no special level of education
_____ some grade school (grades 1-7)
_____ completion of grade school (grade 8)
_____ some high school (grades 9-11)
_____ complete high school (grade 12)
_____ some college
_____ complete college
_____ graduate or professional education beyond a college degree

31. Do you feel vocational or technical training is needed by a person in your job?

_____ yes
_____ no

32. Are there in-service training programs available for employees in your department?

_____ yes
_____ no

If yes

33. Have you ever participated in in-service training programs?

_____ yes--how many? _____ (specify approximate number)
_____ no

34. Below are some things which may or may not be true of your immediate supervisor. Check how true you think each is of him or her.

	Very true	Somewhat true	Not too true	Not at all true
a. takes a personal interest in those he/she supervises	___	___	___	___
b. insists that those under him/her work hard	___	___	___	___
c. maintains high standards of performance in his/her own work	___	___	___	___
d. lets those he/she supervises alone unless they want help	___	___	___	___

35. Here is a list of things that might describe a person's job. For each thing check how much this is like your job.

	A lot	Somewhat	A little	Not at all
a. requires that you have to learn new things	___	___	___	___
b. requires that you do a lot of planning ahead	___	___	___	___
c. requires that you work very fast	___	___	___	___
d. allows you a lot of freedom as to how you do your work	___	___	___	___
e. requires a high level of skill	___	___	___	___
f. requires that you work very hard	___	___	___	___
g. requires that you exert a lot of physical effort	___	___	___	___
h. allows you to make a lot of decisions on your own	___	___	___	___
i. allows you to do a variety of different things	___	___	___	___
j. requires that you do things that are very repetitious	___	___	___	___
k. requires that you be skilled in using your hands	___	___	___	___

36. Do you feel in any way discriminated against on your job because of your age, sex, or race?

_____ yes
_____ no

If yes

37. How much of a problem for you is this discrimination?

AGE	SEX	RACE
_____ A slight problem	_____ A slight problem	_____ A slight problem
_____ A sizable problem	_____ A sizable problem	_____ A sizable problem
_____ A great problem	_____ A great problem	_____ A great problem

Now, here are some questions dealing with unions. A union is any union or employee association that is attempting to gain bargaining rights or has them already.

38. As part of your present job do you belong to a union or employee's association?

_____ yes
_____ no (skip to question 45)

If yes answer questions 39-44

> If a union member answer questions 39-44
> If not a union member skip to question 45

39. Which one of the following unions or employee associations are you a member of?

    _____ American Federation of State, County, and Municipal Employees
    _____ Service Employees International Union
    _____ Laborer's International Union
    _____ International Brotherhood of Teamsters
    _____ Assembly of Governmental Employees Affiliate
    _____ Other (specify) _____

40. Do you attend the union's meetings?

    _____ no
    _____ yes, I attend regularly
    _____ yes, I attend most of the meetings
    _____ yes, but not very often

41. Members feel that it is worthwhile to belong to my union.

    ___ strongly agree ___ agree ___ undecided ___ disagree ___ strongly disagree

42. My union spends enough time telling members about its activities.

    ___ strongly agree ___ agree ___ undecided ___ disagree ___ strongly disagree

43. Union officers operate in the union member's best interest.

    ___ strongly agree ___ agree ___ undecided ___ disagree ___ strongly disagree

44. Many things are already decided before union meetings are held.

    ___ strongly agree ___ agree ___ undecided ___ disagree ___ strongly disagree

45. Do you work under a union contract with your employer?

    _____ yes
    _____ no

> If yes

46. Do you think that the union that represents you has affected working conditions in your department?

    _____ yes, for the better (specify) _____

    _____ yes, for the worse (specify) _____

    _____ no (specify) _____

Now, here are six general statements about unions. Please specify your agreement or disagreement, whether you belong to a union or not.

47. Unions provide protection against favoritism on the job.

_____ strongly agree _____ agree _____ disagree _____ strongly disagree

48. Wages and working conditions are better when all employees of a department belong to a union.

_____ strongly agree _____ agree _____ disagree _____ strongly disagree

49. The best person should be kept on the job regardless of seniority.

_____ strongly agree _____ agree _____ disagree _____ strongly disagree

50. Unions can fight the selfishness of employers.

_____ strongly agree _____ agree _____ disagree _____ strongly disagree

51. Local union meetings should be regularly attended by union members.

_____ strongly agree _____ agree _____ disagree _____ strongly disagree

52. Union dues are a good investment.

_____ strongly agree _____ agree _____ disagree _____ strongly disagree

53. Public employees should have the right to strike.

_____ strongly agree _____ agree· _____ disagree _____ strongly disagree

In this last section we would like to obtain some information on your background.

54. What is your marital status?

_____ Single   _____ Widowed
_____ Married   _____ Separated or divorced

55. How many children do you have?

_____ None   _____ 3-4
_____ 1-2   _____ 5 or more

56. How old were you on your last birthday?

_____ 19 or under   _____ 40-49
_____ 20-29   _____ 50-59
_____ 30-39   _____ 60 and over

57. What was the highest grade of school you completed?

_____ None
_____ Some grade school (grades 1-7)
_____ Completed grade school (grade 8)
_____ Some high school (grades 9-11)
_____ Completed high school (grade 12)
_____ Some college
_____ Completed college
_____ Graduate or professional training in excess of college degree

58. What is your sex?   _____ Male _____ Female

59. What is your race?   _____ White _____ Black _____ Other (specify) _____

60. How much is your total family income each year before taxes?

_____ Under 4,000   _____ 8,000-8,999
_____ 4,000-4,999   _____ 9,000-9,999
_____ 5,000-5,999   _____ 10,000-14,999
_____ 6,000-6,999   _____ 15,000-24,999
_____ 7,000-7,999   _____ 25,000 and over

61. What kind of work did your father do for a living while you were growing up?

_____

62. What kind of work did your mother do for a living while you were growing up?

_____

63. Do you remember when you were growing up whether your parents were very
much interested in politics, somewhat interested or didn't pay much attention
to politics?

_____ Very much interested
_____ Somewhat interested
_____ Not much attention

64. Would you say that you are very much interested in politics, somewhat
interested, or not much interested in politics?

_____ Very much interested
_____ Somewhat interested
_____ Not much interested

65. How would you best describe your political party affiliation?

_____ Democrat   _____ Independent
_____ Republican   _____ Other (specify) _____

66. When you make plans ahead, do you usually get to carry things out the way you
expect to or do things usually come up to make you change your plans?

_____ Things work out as expected
_____ Have to change plans

67. Have you usually felt pretty sure your life would work out the way you want it to or do you usually feel unsure your life will work out the way you want it to?

    _____ pretty sure
    _____ usually unsure

68. Some people feel they can run their lives pretty much the way they want to; others feel the problems of life are sometimes too big for them. Which ones are you most like?

    _____ can run own life
    _____ problems of life are too big

69. If someone asked you to describe yourself, and you could, tell only one thing about yourself, which of the following answers would you be most likely to give (Put a number 1 next to that item).

    _____ I come from (my home state)
    _____ I work for (my employer)
    _____ I am a (my occupation or type of work)
    _____ I am a (my church membership or preference)
    _____ I am a graduate of (my school)

    If you could give two answers, which of the items above would you choose second? (Put a number 2 next to that item)

If you wish to make any other comments about your job, union or this questionnaire, please do so below. Thank you for your assistance!

BIBLIOGRAPHY

Alderfer, C. P. 1969a. An empirical test of a new theory of human needs. *Organizational Behavior and Human Performance* 4: 142–75.
————. 1969b. Job enlargement and the organizational context. *Personnel Psychology* 22: 418–26.
Aldaq, R. J.; Barr, S. H.; and Brief, A. P. 1981. Measurement of perceived task characteristics. *Psychological Bulletin* 90: 415–31.
Alutto, J. A., and Belasco, J. A. 1972. A typology of participation in organizational decision making. *Administrative Science Quarterly* 17: 117–25.
Andrews, F. M.; Morgan, J. N.; Sonquist, J.; and Klem, L. 1973. *Multiple Classification Analysis*. Ann Arbor: Institute for Social Research.
Argyris, C. 1957. *Personality and Organization*. New York: Harper & Row.
————. 1973. Personality and Organization Theory Revisited. *Administrative Science Quarterly* 18: 147–67.
Bakke, E. W. 1945. Why workers join unions. *Personnel* 22: 2–11.
Barbash, J. 1967. *American Unions: Structure, Government and Politics*. New York: Random House.
Begin, J. P. 1971. The private grievance model in the public sector. *Industrial Relations* 10: 21–35.
Bent, A. E., and Noblito, G. W. 1976. Collective bargaining in local government: effects of urban political culture on public labor-management relations. In *Urban Administration*, eds. A. E. Bent, and R. A. Rossum, 46–61. New York: Kennikat Press.
Biderman, A. D., and Drury, T. F., eds. 1975. *American Behavorial Scientist* 18: 299–432.
Biles, G. E. 1974. Allegiances of unionized employees toward employee and union. *Public Personnel Management* 3: 165–69.
Blauner, R. 1960. Work satisfaction and industrial trends in modern society. In

Labor and Trade Unionism, eds. W. Galenson and S. M. Lipset, 339–60. New York: Wiley.

Blum, A. A. 1971. The office employee. In *White-Collar Workers*, eds. A. A. Blum et al., 3–45. New York: Random House.

Blume, N. 1973. Control and satisfaction and their relation to rank and file support for union political activity. *Western Political Quarterly* 26: 51–63.

Bonjean, C. M.; Bruce, G. D.; and Williams, A. Jr. 1967. Social mobility and job satisfaction: a replication and extension. *Social Forces* 45: 492–502.

Brousseau, K. R. 1978. Personality and job experience. *Organizational Behavior and Human Performance* 22: 235–52.

Centers, R., and Bugental, D. E. 1966. Intrinsic and extrinsic job motivation among different segments of the working population. *Journal of Applied Psychology* 50: 193–97.

Choi, Y. H. 1978. Collective Bargaining in the Public Sector. *State Government* 51: 225–29.

Christrup, H. J. 1966. Why do government employees join unions. *Personnel Administration* 29: 49–54.

Cohany, H. P., and Dewey, L. M. 1970. Union membership among government employees. *Monthly Labor Review* 93: 15–20.

Cook, A. 1965. *Union Democracy: Practice and Ideal*. Ithaca, NY: Cornell University Press.

Dillman, D. A.; Carpenter, E. H.; Christenson, J. A.; and Brooks, R. M. 1974. Increasing mail questionnaire response: a four state comparison. *American Sociological Review* 39: 744–56.

Dillman, D. A. 1978. *Mail and Telephone Surveys: The Total Design* New York: Wiley.

Directory of National Unions and Employee Associations. 1975. 1977. Washington, D. C.: U. S. Department of Labor, Bureau of Labor Statistics.

Duncan, O. D. 1961. A socioeconomic index for all occupations. In *Occupations and Social Status*, ed. A. J. Reiss Jr., 109–38. New York: Free Press.

Dunnett, M. D.; Campbell, J. P.; and Hakel, M. D. 1967. Factors contributing to job satisfaction and dissatisfaction in six occupational groups. *Organizational Behavior and Human Performance* 2: 143–74.

Etzioni, A. 1964. *Modern Organizations*. Englewood Cliffs, N. J.: Prentice-Hall.

Estey, M. 1976. *The Unions: Structure, Development and Management*. 2nd ed. New York: Harcourt Brace Jovanovich.

Ewen, R. B. 1964. Some determinants of job satisfaction: a study of the generality of Herzberg's theory. *Journal of Applied Psychology* 48: 161–63.

Ferber, R. 1948. The problem of bias in mail returns: a solution. *Public Opinion Quarterly* 12: 669–76.

Form, W., and Geschwender, J. 1962. Social reference bias of job satisfaction: the case of manual workers. *American Sociological Review* 27: 228–37.

Friedlander, F. 1963. Underlying sources of job satisfaction. *Journal of Applied Psychology* 47: 246–50.

Getman, J. G.; Goldberg, S.; and Herman, J. 1976. *Union Representation Elections: Law and Reality*. New York: Russell Sage Foundation.

Gibson, F. K., and Teasley, C. E. 1973. The humanistic model of organizational motivation: a review of research support. *Public Administration Review* 33: 89–96.

Glick, W.; Mirvis, P.; and Harder, D. 1977. Union satisfaction and participation. *Industrial Relations* 16: 145–51.

Goode, W. J., and Hatt, P. K. 1963. *Methods in Social Research.* New York: McGraw-Hill.

Gordon, M. E., and Long, L. N. 1981. Demographic and attitudinal correlates of union joining. *Industrial Relations* 20: 306–11.

Grupp, F. W. Jr., and Richards, A. R. 1975. Job satisfaction among state executives in the U. S. *Public Personnel Management* 4: 104–9.

Guest, R. H. 1955. A neglected factor in labor turnover. *Occupational Psychology* 29: 217–31.

Hackman, J. R. 1969. Nature of the task as a determiner of job behavior. *Personnel Psychology* 22: 435–44.

Hackman, J. R., and Lawler, E. E. III. 1971. Employee reactions to job characteristics. *Journal of Applied Psychology Monograph* 55.

Hackman, J. R., and Oldham, G. R. 1975. Development of Job Diagnostic Survey. *Journal of Applied Psychology* 60: 159–70.

————. 1980. *Work Redesign.* Reading, MA: Addison-Wesley.

Hall, D. T., and Nougaim, K. E. 1968. An examination of Maslow's need hierarchy in an organizational setting. *Organizational Behavior and Human Performance* 3: 12–35.

Hellriegel, D.; French, W.; and Peterson, R. B. 1970. Collective negotiations and teachers: a behavioral analysis. *Industrial and Labor Relations Review* 23: 380–96.

Herzberg, F. 1957. *Job Attitudes: Review of Research and Opinion.* Pittsburgh, PA: Psychological Service of Pittsburgh.

————. 1968. One more time: how do you motivate employees? *Harvard Business Review* 26: 53–62.

Herzberg, F.; Mausner, B.; and Snyderman, B. 1959. *The Motivation to Work.* 2nd ed. New York: Wiley.

Hinton, B. L. 1968. An empricial investigation of the Herzberg methodology and two-factor theory. *Organizational Behavior and Human Performance* 3: 286–309.

Hopkins, A. 1980. Perceptions of employment discrimination in the public sector. *Public Administration Review* 40: 131–37.

Hopkins, A.; Rawson, G. E.; and Smith, R. L. 1976. Public employee unionization in the states: a comparative analysis. *Administration and Society* 8: 319–41.

Holley, W. H.; Field, H. S.; and Crowley, J. C. 1981. Negotiating quality of worklife, productivity and traditional issues: union members' preferred roles of their unions. *Personnel Psychology* 34: 309–28.

Hoppock, R. 1935. *Job Satisfaction.* New York: Harper & Row.

Hulin, C. L. 1968. Effects of changes in job satisfaction levels on employee turnover. *Journal of Applied Psychology* 52: 122–26.

Hulin, C. L., and Blood, M. R. 1968. Job enlargement, individual differences and worker responses. *Psychological Bulletin* 74: 18–31.

Imundo, L. V. Jr. 1973. Why federal government employees join unions: a study of AFGE Local 916. *Public Personnel Management* 21: 23–38.

————. 1975. Why federal government employees join unions: a study of AFGE Local 1138. *Journal of Collective Negotiations* 4: 319–28.

Indik, B., and Seashore, S. 1961. *Effects of Organizational Size on Member Attitudes and Behavior.* Ann Arbor: Institute for Social Research.

Ingham, G. K. 1969. Plant size, political attitudes and behavior. *Sociological Review* 17: 235–49.

———. 1970. *Size of Industrial Organization and Worker Behavior.* Cambridge, U. K.: Cambridge University Press.

James, L. R., and Jones, A. P. 1976. Organizational structure: a review of structural dimensions and their conceptual relationship with individual attitudes and behavior. *Organizational Behavior and Human Performance* 16: 74–113.

Johns, G. 1981. Difference score measures of organizational behavior variables: a critique. *Organizational Behavior and Human Performance* 27: 443–63.

Kahn, R. L. 1972. The meaning of work: interpretation and proposals for measurement. In *The Human Meaning of Social Change,* eds. A. Campbell and P. E. Converse, 159–203. New York: Russell Sage Foundation.

Kalleberg, A. L. 1974. A causal approach to the measurement of job satisfaction. *Social Science Research* 3: 299–322.

Kalleberg, A. L., and Griffin, L. J. 1978. Positional sources of inequality in job satisfaction. *Sociology of Work and Occupations* 5: 371–401.

Katz, D., and Kahn, R. L. 1978. *The Social Psychology of Organizations.* 2nd ed. New York: Wiley.

Katzell, M. E. 1975. *Productivity, the Measure and the Myth.* AMACOM.

Katzell, R. A., and Yankelovich, D. 1975. *Work, Productivity and Job Satisfaction.* New York: The Psychological Corporation.

Katzell, R. A.; Ewen, R. B.; and Korman, A. 1970. *The Job Attitudes of Workers from Different Ethnic Backgrounds.* Washington, D. C.: U. S. Department of Labor.

Kerr, W.; Koppelmeir, G.; and Sullivan, J. 1951. Absenteeism, turnover and morale in a metal fabrication factory. *Occupational Psychology* 25: 50–55.

Kilpatrick, F. P.; Cummings, M. C.; and Jennings, M. K. 1964. *The Image of the Federal Service.* Washington, D. C.: Brookings Institution.

King, N. 1970. A clarification and evaluation of the two-factor theory of job satisfaction. *Psychological Bulletin* 74: 18–31.

Kirchner, W. K. 1967. Job attitudes and performance. *Personnel Administration* 30: 42–45.

Kochan, T. A. 1974. A theory of multilateral collective bargaining in city government. *Industrial and Labor Relations Review* 27: 525–42.

———. 1979. How American workers view labor unions. *Monthly Labor Review* 102: 23–31.

Kohn, M. L. 1971. Bureaucratic man: a portrait and interpretation. *American Sociological Review* 36: 461–74.

———1976. Occupational structure and alienation. *American Journal of Sociology* 82: 111–30.

Konar, E. 1981. Explaining racial differences in job satisfaction: a reexamination of the data. *Journal of Applied Psychology* 66: 522–24.

Kornhauser, A. 1965. *Mental Health of the Industrial Worker: A Detroit Study.* New York: Wiley.

Korman, A. K. 1968. Task success, task popularity and self-esteem as influences on task liking. *Journal of Applied Psychology* 52: 484–90.

Lawler, E. E. III. 1969. Job design and employee motivation. *Personnel Psychology* 22: 426–35.

Levine, E. L., and Weitz, J. 1968. Job satisfaction among graduate students: intrinsic versus extrinsic variables. *Journal of Applied Psychology* 52: 263–71.

Lewin, D. 1976. Collective bargaining impacts on personnel administration in the American public sector. *Labor Law Journal* 27: 426–36.

———. 1977. Public sector labor relations. *Labor History* 18: 133–44.

Ley, R. 1966. Labor turnover as a function of worker differences., work environment and authoritarianism of foremen. *Journal of Applied Psychology* 50: 497–500.

Likert, R. 1967. *The Human Organization*. New York: McGraw-Hill.

Litterer, J. A. 1965. *The Analysis of Organizations*. New York: Wiley.

Locke, E. A. 1969. What is job satisfaction? *Organizational Behavior and Human Performance* 4: 309–36.

Love, T. M., and Sulzner, G. T. Political implication of public employee bargaining. *Industrial Relations* 11: 18–33.

McGregor, D. 1960. *The Human Side of Enterprise*. New York: McGraw-Hill.

Manley, T. R., and McNichols, C. W. 1975. Attitudes of federal scientists and engineers toward unions. *Monthly Labor Review* 98: 57–60.

———. 1978. Scientists, engineers and unions revisited. *Monthly Labor Review* 101: 32–33.

Marvick, D. 1954. *Career Perspective in a Bureaucratic Setting*. Ann Arbor: University of Michigan Press.

Maslow, A. H. 1943. A theory of human motivation. *Psychological Review* 50: 370–96.

———. 1954. *Motivation and Personality*. New York: Harper & Row.

———. 1970. *Motivation and Personality*. 2nd ed. New York: Harper & Row.

Michaels, C. E., and Spector, P. E. 1981. Causes of employee turnover: a test of the Mobley, Griffeth, Hand and Meglino model. *Journal of Applied Psychology* 67: 53–59.

Miller, J. 1980. Individual and occupational determinants of job satisfaction. *Sociology of Work and Occupations* 7: 337–66.

Mobley, W. H.; Griffeth, R. W.; Head, R. W.; and Meglino, B. M. 1979. Review and conceptual analysis of employee turnover process. *Psychological Bulletin* 86: 493–522.

Morris, J. H., and Steers, R. M. 1979. Structural influences on organizational commitment. Working paper, Graduate School of Management, University of Oregon, Eugene.

Moser, C. A. 1958. *Survey Methods in Social Investigations*. London: W. Heinemann.

Nadler, D.; Hanlow, M.; and Lawler, E. E. III. 1980. Factors influencing the success of labor-management quality of life projects. *Journal of Occupational Behavior* 1: 53–67.

Oldham, G. R., and Hackman, J. R. 1981. Relationships between organizational structure and employee reactions: comparing alternative frameworks. *Administrative Science Quarterly* 36: 66–83.

Oldham, G. R.; Hackman, J. R.; and Pierce, J. L. 1976. Conditions under which employees respond positively to enriched work. *Journal of Applied Psychology* 61: 395–403.

Olson, M. 1965. *The Logic of Collective Action*. Cambridge: Harvard University Press.

Patchen, M. 1960. Absence and employee feelings about fair treatment. *Personnel Psychology.* 13: 349–60.

Pecotich, A., and Churchill, G. A. Jr. 1981. An examination of the anticipated satisfaction importance variance controversy. *Organizational Behavior and Human Performance.* 27: 213–26.

Pierce, J. L., and Dunham, R. B. Task design: a literature review. *Academy of Management Review.* 1: 83–97.

Porter, L. W. 1961. A study of perceived need satisfaction in bottom and middle management jobs. *Journal of Applied Psychology.* 45: 1–10.

————. 1962. Job attitudes in management: I. perceived deficiencies in need fulfilment as a function of job level. *Journal of Applied Psychology.* 46: 375–84.

Porter, L. W., and Lawler, E. E. III. 1968. *Managerial Attitudes and Performance.* Homewood, IL: Richard D. Irwine.

Porter, L. W.; Lawler, E. E. III; and Hackman, J. R. 1975. *Behavior in Organizations.* New York: McGraw-Hill.

Porter, L. W., and Steers, R. M. 1973. Organizational, work and personal factors in employee turnover and absenteeism. *Psychological Bulletin* 80: 152–76.

Presthus, R. 1962. *The Organizational Society.* New York: Knopf.

Quinn, R.; Mangione, T.; and Seashore, S. 1973. *Quality of Employment Survey, 1972–73.* Ann Arbor: Institute for Social Research.

Quinn, R., and Staines, G. 1977. *Quality of Employment Survey. 1977.* Ann Arbor: Institute for Social Research.

Roberts, K. H., and Glick, W. 1981. The job characteristics approach to task design: a critical review. *Journal of Applied Psychology* 66: 193–217.

Robinson, J. P.; Athanasious, R.; and Head, K. B. 1969. *Measures of Occupational Attitudes and Occupational Characteristics.* Ann Arbor: Institute for Social Research.

Roethlisberger, F. J., and Dickson, W. J. 1939. *Management and the Worker.* Cambridge: Harvard University Press.

Ronan, W. W. 1970. Individual and situational variables relating to job satisfaction. *Journal of Applied Psychology* 54: 1–31.

Ronan, W. W., and Marks, E. 1973. The structure and stability of various job satisfaction measures. *Studies in Personnel Psychology* 6: 2–27.

Ross, I. C., and Zander, A. 1957. Need satisfaction and employee turnover. *Personnel Psychology* 10: 327–38.

Rousseau, D. M. 1978. Characteristics of departments, positions and individuals: contexts for attitudes and behavior. *Administrative Science Quarterly* 23: 521–40.

Salancik, G. R., and Pfeffer, J. 1977. An examination of the need-satisfaction model of job attitudes. *Administrative Science Quarterly* 22: 427–56.

Schlesinger, L. A., and Walton, R. E. 1977. The process of work restructuring and its impact on collective bargaining. *Monthly Labor Review* 100: 52–55.

Schneider, J., and Locke, E. A. 1971. A critique of Herzberg's incident classification system and a suggested revision. *Organizational Behavior and Human Performance* 6: 441–57.

Schreisheim, C. A. 1978. Job satisfaction, attitudes toward unions, and voting in a union representation election. *Journal of Applied Psychology* 63: 548–52.

Seeborg, I. S. 1978. The influence of employee participation on job redesign. *Journal of Applied Behavioral Science* 14: 87–98.

Seashore, S. E., and Taber, T. D. 1975. Job satisfaction indicators and their correlates. *American Behavioral Scientist.* 18: 333–68.

Seidman, J., and Cain, G. G. 1964. Unionized engineers and chemists: a case study of a professional union. *Journal of Business* 37: 238–57.

Seidman, J.; London, J.; and Karsh, B. 1951. Why workers join unions. *The Annals of the American Academy of Political and Social Science* 274: 76–77.

Sims, H. P.; Szilaqyi, A. D.; and Keller, R. T. 1976. The measurement of job characteristics. *Academy of Management Journal* 19: 195–212.

Smith, M. B. 1968. A map for the analysis of personality and politics. *Journal of Social Issues* 24: 15–28.

Smith, R. L., and Hopkins, A. H. 1979. Public employee attitudes toward unions. *Industrial and Labor Relations Review.* 32: 484–95.

Spero, S. D., and Capozzola, J. M. 1973. *The Urban Community and Its Unionized Bureaucracies.* New York: Dunellen.

Staines, G. L., and Quinn, R. P. 1979. American workers evaluate the quality of their jobs. *Monthly Labor Review* 102: 2–12.

Stanley, D. T. 1971. *Managing Local Government Under Union Pressure.* Washington, D. C.: Brookings Institution.

Steiber, J. 1973. *Public Employee Unionism: Structure, Growth, Policy.* Washington, D. C.: Brookings Institution.

Stone, E. F., and Porter, L. W. 1978. On the use of incumbent-supplied job-characteristics data. *Perceptual and Motor Skills* 46: 751–58.

The Survey of Work Conditions. Final Report and Univariate and Bivariate Tables. 1973. U. S. Government Printing Office, Document No. 2916–0001.

Tallachi, S. 1960. Organizational size, individual attitudes and behavior: an empirical study. *Administrative Science Quarterly* 5: 398–420.

Tannenbaum, A. S. 1965. Unions. In *Handbook of Organizations.* ed. J. March. Chicago: Rand McNally.

Terkel, S. 1972. *Working.* New York: Random House.

Thompson, A., and Weinstock, I. 1967. White collar employees and unions at TVA. *Personnel Journal* 46: 14–21.

Tolliver, J. M.; Wanous, J. P.; Lawler, E. E. III; and Zenisek, T. 1980. Measuring job satisfaction. *Proceedings, Annual Conference of the Administrative Sciences Association of Canada, Organizational Behavior Division.* 121–30.

Troy, L. 1971. White collar organization in the federal service. In *White Collar Workers,* ed. A. A. Blum, 166–210. New York: Random House.

Turner, A. N., and Lawrence, P. R. 1965. *Industrial Jobs and the Worker.* Cambridge: Harvard Graduate School of Business Administration.

Useem, M. 1976. Government influence on the social science paradigm. *The Sociological Quarterly* 17: 146–61.

Vroom, V. 1964. *Work and Motivation.* New York: Wiley.

Wahba, M. A., and Bridwell, L. G. 1976. Maslow reconsidered: a review of research on the need hierarchy theory. *Organizational Behavior and Human Performance* 15: 212–40.

Wall, T. D., and Payne, R. 1973. Are difference scores deficient? *Journal of Applied Psychology* 58: 322–6.

Wanous, J. P., and Lawler, E. E. III. 1972. Measurement and meaning of job satisfaction. *Journal of Applied Psychology* 56: 95–105.

Warner, K. S.; Chisholm, R. F.; and Munzenrider, R. F. 1978. Motives for unionization among state social service employees. *Public Personnel Management* 7: 181–91.

Waters, L. K., and Waters, C. W. 1972. An empirical test of five versions of the two-factor theory of job satisfaction. *Organizational Behavior and Human Performance* 7: 18–24.

Weaver, C. N. 1980. Job satisfaction in the United States in the 1970s. *Journal of Applied Psychology* 65: 364–67.

Webb, E. J.; Campbell, D. T.; Schwartz, R. D.; and Sechrest, L. 1966. *Unobstrusive Measures: Nonreactive Research in the Social Sciences*. Chicago: Rand McNally.

Zagoria, S., ed. 1972. *Public Workers and Public Unions*. Englewood Cliffs, N.J.: Prentice-Hall.

INDEX

ABOUT THE AUTHOR

Anne H. Hopkins received her Ph.D. in Political Science from Syracuse University and is an Associate Professor at the University of Tennessee, Knoxville.

War and the
Soviet Union

WAR and the SOVIET UNION

NUCLEAR WEAPONS AND THE REVOLUTION IN SOVIET MILITARY AND POLITICAL THINKING

Revised Edition

BY H. S. DINERSTEIN
The RAND Corporation

FREDERICK A. PRAEGER, *Publisher*

New York • London

Published in the United States of America in 1962 by
Frederick A. Praeger, Inc., Publisher
64 University Place, New York 3, N. Y.

Published in the United Kingdom in 1962 by
Frederick A. Praeger, Ltd., Publisher
49 Great Ormond Street, London WC1

This is a revised edition of the book
first published in 1959 by Frederick A. Praeger, Inc.

© 1959, 1962 in the United States of America
by The RAND Corporation

Library of Congress Catalog Card Number: 62-20815
Printed in the United States of America

WAR AND THE SOVIET UNION is published in two editions:
    A Praeger Paperback (P-101)
    A clothbound edition

This book is Number 79 in the series
of *Praeger Publications in Russian History and World Communism.*

AUTHOR'S NOTE

The author owes more than the usual debt of gratitude to colleagues and friends. Military developments proceed so rapidly that even the few works of synthesis that have appeared have become rapidly outdated. The author, who brought some experience in work on Soviet problems to this task, could not have essayed or completed it without the instruction in military developments willingly furnished by some colleagues. Others with primary interest in the social sciences have in writing or conversation helped me think through many thorny problems. The following persons have all been of great assistance: James F. Digby, Raymond L. Garthoff, Alexander L. George, Jerzy Gliksman, Herbert Goldhamer, Leon Gouré, A. M. Halpern, L. J. Henderson, Jr., Victor M. Hunt, Anne M. Jonas, Herman Kahn, Paul Kecskemeti, Joseph E. Loftus, Andrew W. Marshall, Emmanuel G. Mesthene, Stefan Possony, Melville J. Ruggles, Myron Rush, Frederick M. Sallagar, Hans Speier, Allen S. Whiting, Eric Willenz, and Albert J. Wohlstetter. Probably none of these persons who have so generously helped me agrees with everything in the book; some would certainly dissent sharply on particular points. This variety of opinion, so common when large and contemporary subjects are treated, explains why individuals and not collectives write books on such subjects and why, as in this case, authors assume sole responsibility for the whole.

Ian C. C. Graham has brought to the editing of the manuscript a rare critical judgment that has contributed greatly to whatever merit this book may possess.

This study was prepared as part of the research undertaken for the U.S. Air Force by The RAND Corporation.

H. S. Dinerstein

Washington, D.C.
August 11, 1958

For my father and mother

CONTENTS

INTRODUCTION

Three years have passed since the first edition of this book was published. Although the character of the strategic relationship between the Soviet Union and other great powers remains essentially unchanged, some interesting developments have taken place.

From the Soviet point of view the most welcome change since World War II is the growing confidence that war with capitalism is not inevitable. Soviet leaders of an earlier period had no doubt that the capitalist countries would attack the Soviet Union sooner or later. Accordingly, they tried to postpone the fateful day until they would be relatively stronger. Their recent reappraisal of the future, expressed in theses solemnly promulgated at Communist Party congresses, postulates a major improvement in their position. But this new security is not absolute since, for Communists, capitalist hostility is axiomatic. The American failure to attack the Soviet Union when nuclear monopoly obviated effective retaliation is explained not by American forbearance, but by a transitory combination of circumstances that restrained American aggressiveness. It was expected that the capitalists, when they finally recognized that their doom had been decreed by "history," would have recourse to the most desperate remedies, not excluding nuclear war. In recent years, the acquisition of greatly improved nuclear weapons and delivery capabilities has given the Kremlin a new confidence that its enemies will avoid the extreme of war.

These new weapons, in the Soviet view, make a sizable

number of capitalists fearful of war and eager to avoid it. Moreover, many other elements of Western society, in their fear of the awesome consequences of nuclear war, are believed to be restraining "the warmongers." But capitalist restraint, the Soviet leaders think, might be replaced by bellicosity if the military balance shifted sharply. Only constant Soviet application to the problem and continued investment in defense development can prevent such a shift. Thus the enjoyment of a new feeling of security is tempered by the realization that it can only be maintained by heavy and probably increasing expenditures.

In addition to a new sense of security, the Soviet leaders have tried to extract the maximum political benefit from the priority they have accorded to rocket-missiles. The Soviet Union has tried to frighten Western European leaders and peoples with repeated reminders of how completely their countries would be devastated by a nuclear war. Presumably the expectation was that, in the face of such a generalized menace, the NATO countries could be forced to make political concessions, beginning with the status of West Berlin.

In this effort to frighten their opponents into yielding political positions, the Soviet leaders, by implication, have exaggerated their nuclear and missile strength. Since the Soviet Union was clearly first in the development of large rockets capable of carrying nuclear weapons, it was generally assumed that the Soviet Union would gain and maintain a lead over the United States in the procurement and development of such weapons. In public statements, the Soviet Union gave the impression that it was rapidly pursuing such a course. Belief that the Soviet Union was pulling ahead in nuclear-armed missiles varied widely and depended on the information available to particular countries and individuals.

The fear and respect inspired by the belief in Soviet missile superiority constituted a political asset, which, the Soviets hoped, could be converted into tangible gains. But along with the possibility of gains, the attempt to create a belief in Soviet missile superiority involved some costs in Soviet relations with the Chinese Communists and with the United States. The Soviet

Union seems not to have revealed to the Chinese Communists that their missile claims were greatly exaggerated. Apparently, in their efforts to mislead their opponents, the Soviet leaders deceived their allies. Proceeding on an incorrect assumption of what Soviet missile power was, the Chinese pressed for a more aggressive policy than the Soviets wanted to pursue. In the bitter polemics between the two, produced by this and other policy differences, the Soviet Union did not reveal that the military balance was not what the Chinese believed it to be.

The Soviet Union, therefore, in its polemic with the Chinese, had to confine the argument to the world-wide consequences of nuclear war and to statements that the Soviet Union, too, would suffer grievously. The conclusion was inescapable that Soviet military strength, if war came, was inadequate to avoid a disaster of unprecedented proportions. The Soviet Union insisted that nuclear war must be avoided, and the Chinese argued that it probably could not be avoided.

In addition to creating misunderstanding with allies, the Soviet Union has paid a price in relations with the United States because of its boasts about missile strength. Whatever opinions were about the true Soviet missile strength at any given moment, Soviet boasts about superiority, and attempts at blackmail, convinced most Americans that, sooner or later, the Soviet Union would acquire a formidable intercontinental missile force. As might have been expected, the United States tried to catch up with the Soviet Union, and as we shall see presently has evidently surpassed it in ICBM strength.

Since the Soviet failure to build ICBM's rapidly has surprised most observers, the evidence deserves careful examination.

After Joseph Alsop reported sharply reduced estimates of Soviet missile strength, Deputy Secretary of Defense R. L. Gilpatric in October, 1961, lent official support to the newspaper account by his public claim that the United States could take a Soviet first strike and retaliate with equal effectiveness. Thus, Mr. Gilpatric put a ceiling, as it were, on the intercontinental nuclear capability of the Soviet Union. In subsequent public statements, Secretary of Defense McNamara repeated and reinforced this claim.

The Soviet response strongly suggests that these authoritative challenges to their claims have probed a sensitive area. Soviet leaders, beginning with Khrushchev, insisted that the Soviet Union was ahead of the United States in the *development* of nuclear weapons, and that the Soviet Union had the forces necessary to destroy any nation which attacked her. In addition, the Soviet leaders claimed advances in other weapons: in the development of anti-missiles; in the possession of a global missile; in nuclear missile-equipped submarines and in aircraft with air-to-surface missiles. This last boast is of particular interest because at the time when the Soviet claim to missile superiority had been widely accepted. Khrushchev, in particular, had publicly minimized the importance of military aircraft and had denied it a future role. But in this long catalogue of Soviet claims to superiority one is conspicuously absent: the claim that the Soviet Union has more ICBM's than the United States. This silence speaks loudly.

Given the secrecy that the Soviet Union tries to maintain about military affairs, and especially about military inferiority, we cannot be certain that the Soviet Union built and deployed few ICBM's in 1960-61, but it seems likely enough to justify an examination of its implications, if true.

In analyzing the Soviet failure to expand a portion of its offensive forces, it is useful to establish the general Soviet policy governing its allocations for offense and defense. This policy has been framed to meet the needs of Soviet policy in Europe and of the United States-Soviet confrontation.

The American policy toward the Soviet Union was formulated in the years immediately following World War II and during the Korean War. At that time, Soviet conduct in Eastern Europe and the North Korean attack on South Korea created the firm conviction in the United States and in Western Europe that the Soviet Union would, when it could, employ its superior ground forces to threaten and even, on occasion, to attack weaker countries on its very long borders. The United States response to the threat, so conceived, was to build an impressive air-nuclear capability which, it was hoped, would deter the Soviet Union from such efforts at expansion. The weapons in this deterrent force were offensive weapons. In the earlier period they were largely nuclear bombs carried by aircraft, and more recently missiles carrying nuclear weapons have been added. Although the threshold of aggression over which the Soviet Union would have to step before this offensive force would be employed was never precisely defined, for good and obvious reasons, it clearly was not low. Some large and clear act of aggression would presumably be required to trigger retaliation.

The Soviet Union constructed its forces from other premises. It was reasonable for it to be unworried about an American attack unless it triggered the attack by its own behavior. Thus the inception of war was in its hands, and it did not need to match the American offensive forces even if it could have. To match American capability, before it possessed intercontinental vehicles, the Soviet Union would have had to build a large navy and then acquire bases as close to the United States as Western Europe and North Africa were to the Soviet Union. Then it could have hoped to make nuclear strikes against the United States. But acquiring such overseas bases would have risked precipitating a war long before the preparations for it would have been completed.

The case was just the opposite for Soviet offensive forces against Europe. From 1945 onward, Soviet forces in Western Europe have been preponderant. As technology has advanced, Soviet forces have been refitted and reorganized, and now they are large, mobile, and equipped with aircraft, missiles of different ranges, and nuclear weapons. A simple analogy might illustrate Soviet military policy toward the United States and Western Europe. In the immediate postwar period, the United States was armed with a very long spear, which could reach Soviet vitals, but the Soviet Union had a short spear, whose effectiveness was limited to Western Europe. The American involvement in the future of Western Europe made the Soviet capability against that area an important instrument in Soviet policy. As the United States improved its ability to strike the

Soviet Union, the latter developed its ability to strike Western Europe. At the present time, both these offensive capabilities are formidable.

The defensive arrangements, the shields to parry the spears fashioned by both sides, are consistent with the offensive arrangements. The Soviet Union, from 1945 onward, reasoned that without direct offensive capability against the United States, it required the best possible defenses and has expended no little effort to get them. Consistently and methodically, since 1945, the Soviet Union has built defense against aircraft and now talks confidently of creating defenses against missiles. The defensive system against aircraft has never been completed to the point of reliable defense against a serious attack, but it has always provided some defense, which was better than nothing. This heavy Soviet investment in defense was not inconsistent with its reappraisal of the likelihood of war. If the reappraisal was a mistake and the United States became more hostile, defenses were all the Soviets had to mitigate war's fury. Moreover, defenses could not be improvised; they had to be built bit by bit.

The United States requirement for defensive weapons has been quite different. The very success of the deterrent effect of superior American offensive forces has reduced the chances that defensive forces would have to be employed. This situation altered radically when the Soviet Union got intercontinental aircraft. Then, for the first time, the Soviet Union could strike directly at the United States. Yet the Soviet Union acquired far fewer such aircraft than the United States possessed. Although the Soviet Union has not revealed the reasons for this decision, retrospective analysis can uncover some of them.

First, the Soviet Union probably feared that if it increased the numbers of its intercontinental aircraft markedly, a corresponding increase in United States intercontinental aircraft would follow. In the late 1950's it was not attractive for the Soviet Union to start an expensive aircraft-procurement race in which their relative position would probably not improve, and in fact might even deteriorate.

Second, much evidence suggests that Khrushchev had become reasonably certain that the United States would not initiate war without extreme provocation. As long as the Soviet Union limited its policy to pressuring the West into making concessions and refrained from overt aggression, this confidence was justified. Besides, the Soviet leaders believed that United States policy could shift radically only after correspondingly radical internal political changes occurred, and that, therefore, ample notice of the need to expand offensive forces would be available.

The question of the optimum size for offensive forces must have arisen once more in the summer and fall of 1957, when the Soviet Union demonstrated a technological lead in missiles. The Soviet Union then had to decide, probably in stages, whether to try to gain and maintain a lead in ICBM's or whether to permit the United States to attain superiority. If they permitted, or were unable to prevent, the latter contingency, they would have to face the same hard choice that the imbalance in aircraft presented earlier: a procurement race against a superior opponent and one who had, to boot, a reputation for high efficiency in production.

Since we do not know the details of the formation of Soviet policy, we can provide no confident explanation of Soviet behavior on this important issue. We can only describe some of the major considerations that entered into Soviet decisions without assessing their relative weight or even being certain that some important factors have not been ignored. The major factors affecting the seemingly modest Soviet deployment of ICBM's in 1960-61 seem to be (1) military, (2) foreign political, and (3) internal political considerations.

1. *Military*. Even though the Soviet Union knew how to make weapons of the most modern design, her need for yesterday's weapons did not disappear. The Soviet offensive forces for the European theater continued to make their claims. Although the number of men in the Soviet armies was sharply reduced, new and improved equipment, including large numbers of medium-range missiles, continued to be made available to them. It seemed as if the maintenance of offensive superiority in the European theater had priority over offensive forces capable of striking the United States. Anti-air defense, always large, also continued to absorb resources. The offensive capacity of Amer-

ican aircraft had improved steadily, requiring new and expensive improvements in the Soviet defensive arrangements. The major American advance was the modification of its aircraft to deliver nuclear weapons by missiles outside the range of the Soviet defenses. Unless the Soviet air-defensive system can extend its range to cope with this and with the other advantages of the aerial offensive, air forces will continue to be formidable offensive weapons systems. Hence the Soviet leaders are constrained to salvage the enormous investment in defense against aircraft by still further investment, which, although large in its own right, is small by comparison with the total investment in air defense over the years. In addition to these two large claims on the military budget, expenditures were necessary, among other things, for submarines, civil defense, and research and development. Clearly, therefore, ICBM's are not the only contenders for shares of the Soviet military appropriations, and it may have been considered desirable on balance to allocate less of the over-all budget to ICBM's in order to support other costly military programs.

Even after one reconstructs the possible reasons for the small Soviet deployment of ICBM's in 1960 and 1961, it remains something of a puzzle, particularly in view of the political capital the Soviets saw in missile strength. Perhaps the tradition of heavy allocations to the European theater and to defense, established when the strategic balance was different, persisted beyond its time. Perhaps the Soviet Union preferred to wait for perfected later-generation missiles before procuring and deploying on a large scale.

In any case, whatever the reasons, Soviet procurement of missiles was deliberate rather than hasty, and the United States seems to have taken the lead. As with aircraft, a production race has evidently not seemed promising to the Soviet Union. The most hopeful avenue to Soviet over-all weapons parity with the United States, in view of the American lead, is probably in quality. If the Soviet Union makes good progress in anti-missile systems and improves its offensive weapons, it may match the United States' strategic capability without matching numbers of missiles. These considerations seem to have played a role in the

Soviet decision to resume weapon-testing, since Soviet accounts of these tests have emphasized large weapons and anti-missile systems.

2. *Foreign Political.* The Soviet Union now competes with the United States in seeking to influence neutral countries by loans and subvention. Although relatively modest by American standards, this program nevertheless represents a considerable burden. It has been estimated that since 1955, the Soviet allocation has been about $3 billion. Although this is a comparatively modest sum, it is probably hard to procure.

3. *Domestic Political.* The phrase "rising expectations," so aptly employed to characterize the political situation in many parts of the world, can also be used to describe the Soviet Union. Its population has been promised a great increase in the standard of living, only part of which has been accomplished. To meet this need, in addition to the pressing demands of an ambitious program of economic investment, is not easy.

If the picture here drawn of straitened Soviet economic circumstances and severe choices is valid, the question naturally arises: Why should not the Soviet Union try instead to end the arms race and make large-scale agreements on disarmament? One answer has already been suggested: Soviet leaders have not given up the hope of attaining military equality, and even superiority, by improvements in the quality of their strategic weapons. Moreover, Soviet inferiority in ICBM's, if this is indeed the case, reinforces Soviet reluctance to make a comprehensive disarmament agreement. Although the United States has successively brought its position closer to the Soviet position on disputed issues of disarmament, the Soviet Union has continued to avoid an agreement, perhaps because the American position has always retained one important feature. The United States has insisted on inspection not only of arms as they are destroyed, but of undestroyed arms as well. In view of American uncertainty about the numbers of Soviet weapons, this precaution is an elementary and irreducible safeguard. However, the Soviets would naturally be reluctant to accept a situation that would disclose to all the world their marked inferiority in ICBM's. Not only would they lose whatever prestige they derive from a general belief in their military strength, but they would face the prospect that the United States would break off the disarmament process in order to exploit politically the demonstrated Soviet inferiority. In trying to reconstruct Soviet calculations, it must always be borne in mind that they believe their opponents wish them ill, not well.

If this is indeed the Soviet view, alternative policies offer themselves for choice: either to build up to rough parity in order to disarm without embarrassment or to seek general equality, and perhaps superiority, by qualitative gains. The indications are that the second course is favored. But these alternatives are not exclusive, and both may be pursued.

The problem of allocation of resources is, of course, constant. But Soviet leaders have recently drawn attention to a problem on which they have focused their interest only once before, namely, pre-emption. As a result of this appraisal in 1955, Soviet military leaders (the political leaders maintaining silence) took the official position that the Soviet Union should have a pre-emptive capability. This resolution represented more than a mere restatement of the truism that it is better to be first than second. On the contrary, it followed from the realization that in nuclear war, a surprise attack could be decisive, and that, whether a nation was inferior or superior, priority of attack in nuclear war was not only advantageous but perhaps even critical.

Once this obvious principle had been established, it hardly seemed necessary to return to it again. Passing mention of pre-emption in the Soviet military press suggested that the military judgment of the validity of the principle of pre-emption had not changed and that further elaboration was not required. But recently the theme of pre-emption has been revived at the highest official level and in full view of the public, which suggests that new purposes are being served in addition to the old ones. The mere revalidation of the military principle of pre-emption hardly necessitates public discussion in -the most prominent media of communication.

The subject of pre-emption was first revived at a high level by the Minister of Defense, Marshal Malinovskii, when he spoke to the Twenty-second Congress of the Communist Party of the Soviet Union in October, 1961, just after U.S. Deputy Secretary of Defense Gilpatric had challenged Soviet claims to superiority. Malinovskii stated that the main task of the armed forces was the study of means of "exploding his [the enemy's] aggressive plans by a timely and devastating blow against him."

The Soviet position is an awkward one. Their spokesmen have not stated that the Soviet Union has larger number of ICBM's than the United States, and yet they want to deflate the American claim to superiority. From what they write, it appears that Soviet leaders fear that the United States will employ its military superiority in order to put political pressure on the Soviet Union by warnings of war if the Soviet Union should threaten American vital interests. By talking about pre-emption, the Soviet Union seeks to put the United States on notice that it might initiate war in such a situation and that, therefore, the United States should exercise restraint on the political use of its military superiority. On two occasions, Khrushchev has referred to pre-emption in connection with President Kennedy's statements printed in the *Saturday Evening Post* of March 31, 1962. There the President said, "in some circumstances, we must be prepared to use the nuclear weapon at the start, come what may —a clear attack on Western Europe, for example." Khrushchev has characterized this statement as "a sinister competition as to who will be the first to start such a [thermonuclear] war" (*Pravda*, May 19, 1962) and as a competition "in who will be the first to 'push the button'" (*Pravda*, July 11, 1962).

If it is believed that the United States has superior strategic forces, confidence in threatened areas is higher that the United States would defend her vital interests—the freedom of Western Europe, for example. If it is believed that the Soviet Union has superior strategic forces, confidence in the threatened areas that the United States would risk war to defend them is naturally lower. Thus in a period when the Soviet Union does not claim superiority in intercontinental missiles, Khrushchev's statements on pre-emption are framed in order to reduce the effect and incidence of American statements of intention to defend vital interests by the employment of nuclear weapons, if necessary. This obviously political purpose of the 1961-62 Soviet statements on pre-emption contrasts with the 1955 statements, which were made only by military leaders. However, the military implications have not disappeared. Marshal Malinovskii's statement on pre-emption in October, 1961, continues to be repeated in the military press, together with exhortations to improve the readiness of Soviet military forces.

This introduction has dealt in a general way with the most important new developments in the Soviet military position. Now the reader is invited to a more detailed examination of the basis upon which present Soviet military thinking is built.

H. S. Dinerstein

September, 1962

CHAPTER ONE

THE CHANGING SOVIET OUTLOOK*

Since Stalin's death the world has watched the Soviet Union intently in the expectation of great changes. Some expected that Stalin's heirs would founder on the problem of succession. Others believed that the long-suppressed bitterness of social groups hitherto silent and impotent might find violent expression. But important as the changes have been, the Soviet leaders have thus far coped with them. The problem of succession has been settled for the present, and with much less bloodshed than in previous Soviet political crises. The new oligarchy has maintained political control, making concessions here and there but preserving the old system in its broad essentials. Nevertheless, there have been some gradual but important transformations in the system. The Western world has looked for more dramatic and obvious reversals so that its attention has been somewhat distracted from such changes as have actually taken place. The transformation of the Soviet appraisal of their own power position and of Soviet military thinking, for example, has not been properly appreciated.

The Soviet leaders now believe that the world military balance of power has changed decisively in their favor. They believe the new Soviet military strength makes a war not of

* This introductory chapter sets the stage for the rest of the book, and anticipates many of its arguments. The evidence for these arguments is set forth in later chapters.

1

Soviet choosing less likely. Yet the Soviet Union must be always ready to wage a full-scale nuclear war. Moreover, the Soviet Union's new military strength furnishes her with opportunities for expansion without the actual employment of military force.

A confident mood has replaced the feeling of constant peril which pervaded Soviet life from the Revolution until very recently. Instead of worrying about forces of destruction beyond their control, the Soviet leaders now see themselves as masters of their own fate. So radical a change has naturally entailed a re-evaluation of the prospects for the future. In the past the Bolsheviks feared for the safety of their regime in the short run and clung to the vision of a distant utopia. Today, however, their powerful military forces so greatly enhance the security of the Soviet state that many policies once seemingly dictated by the need to preserve it have come up for re-examination. Is it possible, for example, to relax the furious effort to industrialize the country and expand the armed forces? Are the ferocious security measures of the later Stalin era still necessary? Is it possible to yield somewhat to the pressures within the Soviet Union for more abundant consumer goods? Can the Soviet Union be more flexible in its foreign policy? Is the Soviet Union now secure enough to make small concessions abroad in the expectation of making large political gains? These and similar questions flow from the new confidence in Soviet power.

The mood of re-evaluation that now permeates much of Soviet thought will be examined in more detail at a later stage. It is first necessary to recall as vividly as we can the sense of insecurity that recently prevailed in the Soviet Union.

It is already becoming difficult for the student of Russia to recapture the feeling of extreme vulnerability that pervaded Soviet life for a third of a century after the October Revolution. The constant communist fear of the outside world was no product of a disordered imagination. The Western European powers failed to crush the Soviet regime in 1917-1920 only because their leaders to some extent, and peoples to a greater extent, were too weary of fighting to prolong their intervention in the Russian Civil War. By and large, however, the Western powers continued openly to detest the Soviet regime. In the years following the Civil War the Soviet leaders were not unreasonable in suspecting that the "capitalist" nations might well try at some favorable juncture to dislodge the Soviet regime even by violent means. Obviously the Soviet Union in its early years would have lost any major war in which it became engaged. Indeed this might have occurred had not its enemies been divided. Historical speculation is usually unsafe, but it is not unlikely that between the two world wars Germany alone could have beaten the Soviet Union. The Soviet Union could hardly have survived attack by a major power or powers without the aid of one or another of the capitalist countries. Such allies were hard to come by and unlikely to be reliable.

During the Second World War disaster often seemed imminent. The German campaign of 1941 fell only a little short of complete victory. The first stages of World War II reinforced the Bolshevik conviction that annihilation was a distinct possibility. After the defeat of Germany the Soviet Union faced an awesome spectacle. A large part of the country had been devastated and population losses had been fearful. Had the United States chosen to make war upon the Soviet Union in 1945, the latter would probably have been defeated. While such a course never occurred to any American in a responsible position, the Soviet leaders, suspicious as ever, could not be sure of United States intentions. From the Soviet point of view, security now depended on America's foregoing her opportunity. The Russian leaders must have been considerably reassured by the rapid American demobilization of 1945.

In 1947-1948 the United States announced her intention to rebuild her military establishment, but the Soviet Union realized that years must elapse before the American force level of 1945 could be restored. Meanwhile the Soviet Union had already built up new strength and was steadily improving her military posture. The exclusive American possession of nuclear weapons, however, added a new element to the situation. Many Americans contended that their country's initial monopoly of the atom bomb and subsequent preponderance in nuclear weapons and air power made it possible for the United States to destroy the Soviet Union at will. Since this position would be transitory, some prominent Americans even urged that an early attack be made on the Soviet Union. However slight the chance that such a reckless policy would be adopted, the plain fact is that for a number of years the United States *could* have devastated the Soviet Union with a minimal likelihood of retaliation. Hence the Soviet leaders, even after the great territorial gains of World War II, could not rid themselves of the fear of annihilation.

These apprehensions have sometimes been described as irrational, even psychopathic. Had this been the whole truth, no change in the power balance could have elicited the self-confidence now displayed. by the Soviet leaders. Growing confidence has kept pace with expanding armaments, and this is one of several reasons for assuming the essential rationality of the Russian rulers.

The rise of the new spirit has coincided with the Soviet acquisition of nuclear weapons, so that one is tempted to ascribe the change *exclusively* to this phenomenon. It should not be forgotten, however, that the Soviet Union in recent years has made great advances in heavy industry and in the education of adequate numbers of recruits for a steadily expanding economy. The industrial strength of the Soviet Union is still far from matching that of the United States, but the gap is closing. Moreover, the Soviet Union is no longer the only communist country in the world. In recent years the Soviet leaders have boasted again and again of the accession of Eastern Europe and China to their camp. However doubtful the political and military value of the satellites at any given time, the expansion of international communism has raised official morale in the Soviet Union. The acquisition of nuclear weapons, then, has hastened the growth of Soviet power and self-confidence, but it is not the sole cause of that growth.

The change in the balance of power brought about by the Soviet development of atomic weapons differs in character from similar changes in the preatomic age. The increased destructiveness of weapons, coupled with their relatively even distribution between two hostile camps, seems to improve prospects for an extended peace. Their very destructiveness suggests that they will not be employed on a large scale, since the risks of retaliation are too high. In this thought there is an element of reassurance for both the Soviet Union and the United States.

Finally, the Soviet leaders must derive some satisfaction from the difficulties met by the West in present or former colonial areas. When we add together all the above factors, the new Soviet confidence is understandable. Some Soviet leaders, as we shall see later, have felt that peace is assured, while others, now dominant, have condemned this belief as reckless complacency. The official line now postulates that increasing Soviet military and industrial strength improves the prospects for peace but never guarantees it.

In the Soviet reappraisal of their situation, a careful examination of the implications of nuclear weapons has played a large role. As we shall see, the Soviet leaders adopted a strategy suited to the demands of the new situation. They did so, however, only after some waverings and backward glances.

Until the death of Stalin neither the Soviet specialist press nor the propaganda media assessed, with any care, the implications of the existence of nuclear weapons. The Soviet press usually confined itself to propagandistic charges that the presumptive enemy, the United States, falsely believed the atomic bomb to be an absolute weapon that could win wars by itself, and to charge that the United States tried to wring concessions in the cold war by threats to use the atomic bomb. But such verbiage did not meet the main issue at all. The fruitful question was not, Is the atom bomb an absolutely decisive weapon? It was rather, How, if at all, do nuclear weapons modify warfare?

Of the many important questions that cried out for analysis, none was discussed until after Stalin's death. In his last years Stalin became ever more rigid and unwilling to entertain any major proposals for change, unless he felt or was persuaded to feel that he had initiated them. Perhaps the picture that Khrushchev drew in his "secret" speech of a warped and tyrannical old man was somewhat overdrawn, but basically it was probably true. Such a man would doubtless insist that his leadership in the last war, and the principles on which it was based, should not be re-examined. The disasters of the initial period of that war made it all the more likely that he would insist that everything had been perfectly planned. Soviet military literature reflected this hypothesis. It presented the war as a series of Soviet successes, and explained the withdrawals of the initial period as a planned policy of "active defense." But Stalin, though old and intolerant of new ideas, was not a lunatic. He did not commit the cardinal error of neglecting the development of nuclear weapons. Nevertheless, he failed to understand their true importance, clung to dogmatic, old-fashioned theories, and prevented the emergence of a military doctrine suited to the nuclear age. Stalin's personal conception of the nature of warfare governed Soviet military planning and was presented in the Soviet military press without debate, variation, or development.

In 1942, when it became apparent that the Germans had fallen short of victory in their first campaign, Stalin promulgated a dictum that became the last and only word on the subject for more than ten years. Stalin's position was that war was a massive social phenomenon in which two or more societies were pitted against one another. In this contest all the strength and weakness of the societies came into play. It was not a gladiatorial contest in which the superior skill of one man, or the accident of, say, a man stumbling over a stone, could determine the outcome. Since war was a social phenomenon, the laws of society were applicable to it. In the special social context of warfare, what were known as the "permanently operating factors" would determine the outcome. These factors were "the stability of the rear, the morale of the army, the quantity and quality of divisions, the armament of the army, the organizational ability of the army commanders."

This formulation is so truistic as to be almost devoid of meaning. Obviously the country with the stronger economy, the better morale, superior equipment, larger forces, and abler commanders will win the war. The only really substantive point in Stalin's formula was his conclusion from the above premises: that transitory factors such as surprise could not determine the outcome of war. He argued that the Germans, who had already lost the advantages derived from surprise, would lose the war because they were inferior in the permanently operating factors.

Stalin's view was relevant chiefly to the world wars. Whereas earlier wars had been fought, for the most part, with forces in being at the outset of the war, the Napoleonic wars inaugurated the systematic replacement of men and materiel lost in the fighting, often with an actual increase in their numbers. In the popular phrase, Detroit won the last world war for the United States. Popular morale was more important than in previous wars because of the need for all-out industrial production and for masses of draftees to replenish units at the front.

Stalin's view of the permanently operating factors could readily be applied to a war in which nuclear weapons figured. In a nuclear war it was certainly important to have a stable rear, high morale, divisions adequate in quantity and quality, good weapons, and skillful command. These things might well continue to be prerequisites of victory, but they did not necessarily guarantee it. Stalin's dogma merely provided a general framework for the discussion of war. The true criterion of its usefulness as a basis of discussion was its ability to solve the problems raised by the existence of nuclear weapons. This capacity was lacking in the doctrine of the permanently operating factors, which debarred any discussion of the real issues.

The obvious innovation introduced by nuclear weapons was their enormous destructive power. The development of the hydrogen bomb meant that a successful nuclear campaign could achieve more in a day than old-fashioned attrition and blockade could in years. The new power of destruction raised a whole range of theoretical questions: Do the new weapons mean that air power will determine the final outcome of a future war? What kinds of delivery vehicles, and how many of each, are required for various purposes? Can active defense measures frustrate a nuclear blow, or can they so blunt it as to render it indecisive? Can civil defense save enough people and resources to justify the investment in it? Will the initial disruption of industry be so great that a country that suffers nuclear attack must plan on fighting the war with weapons and materiel in hand at the outset of the war? Is the effectiveness of surprise attack so certain that a potential victim must strike a forestalling blow, when convinced that the opponent means to strike, and thus start a war that might have been avoided? Assuming that sufficient damage can be inflicted on the enemy to make him "surrender," what will be the cost in destruction to one's own country? How important will the role of navies and armies be in nuclear warfare? Naturally, no positive answers can be given to these broad questions, but decisions have been taken on the basis of such tentative answers as have been forthcoming.

Until late in 1953 the Soviet discussions of Stalin's doctrine evaded these important questions. The Soviet press mechanically reiterated Stalin's few paragraphs on permanently operating and transitory factors and touched on the new issues only in polemics against Western statements. If some American commentators and spokesmen stressed the greater importance of air power, the Soviet press would point to the fallacy of the belief that any single arm could win the war. If Americans discussed the possible decisiveness of a nuclear blow, the Soviet press answered with the charge that the Americans sought to revive the discredited strategy of blitzkrieg. If any American talked of preventive war, the Soviet press warned that the United States would be beaten. Many of the American statements singled out by the Russians for propaganda rebuttal were carelessly framed or superficial, but the Soviet treatment of them was even less impressive.

Stalin's framing of basic military doctrine was obligatory for Soviet theoreticians, which meant in practice that many subjects could not be discussed. Failure to discuss the decisiveness of the nuclear blow, however, did not prevent the decision to develop nuclear weapons. To make that decision it was necessary only to assume that nuclear weapons were important, not that they were decisive. That Soviet military doctrine failed to take into account the likelihood of an aerial blitzkrieg did not detract from the Soviet desire to possess all the latest weapons, including radar, interceptors, antiaircraft, and missiles. Stagnant doctrinal development did not mean stagnant weapons development. It meant, rather, an absence of criteria for making the best decision as to the allocation of resources among various weapon systems. No government can afford to produce everything that the military would like to have or to prepare for every conceivable contingency. A choice must be made between alternatives, and a system of priorities created. Choice based on an up-to-date theory of warfare is usually, but not always, better than one based on obsolete principles or on no principle at all.

Even before Stalin's death some Soviet military leaders must surely have realized that his obsolete formula hampered the procurement of the best weapon systems. As long as Stalin was alive, however, no one dared suggest the desirability, much less the necessity, of a reappraisal of doctrine.

Some months after Stalin died, the chief theoretical organ of the Soviet Ministry of Defense, *Voennaia mysl'* (*Military Thought*), carried an article by Major General Talenskii that opened the first real discussion on military theory in the Soviet Union for twenty-five years. Since 1945 this journal has been intended only for Soviet military officers.

Talenskii rejected Stalin's formula concerning the permanently operating factors, asserting that it was not a basic law of war. He advanced a basic law that, he argued, was an improvement over Stalin's formula because it did "not exclude the possibility of a decisive defeat within a limited time . . . given the existence of certain conditions." For the first time since 1945 a Soviet publication had envisaged a possible war of the future essentially different from World Wars I and II. There could be decisive defeat in a limited time. This did not mean that a single campaign with nuclear weapons would be decisive or that measures could not be taken to reduce the likelihood that the nuclear phase would be decisive. The inconclusiveness of Talenskii's article was not important. What was important was the attention it focused on a new basic issue.

The discussion, initiated at least ostensibly by Talenskii, produced ten articles of comment and forty letters combined in a single article, together with a summation and an official resolution of the issues by the editors. These writings reveal how novel was the serious consideration of these theoretical issues. Obviously no official line on the subject existed. Some argued that Stalin's idea of the permanently operating factors was still perfectly satisfactory; others said that "surprise . . . might in certain conditions even determine the outcome of the war," a clear rejection of Stalin's view that transitory factors cannot be decisive. Such diversity of views on matters of basic importance had not been possible in the Soviet Union for a generation. There seems to be no doubt that this was a real, and not a staged, discussion, for there was considerable irrelevance and some of the disputants failed to discern the main issues, concentrating on peripheral ones.

Several major conclusions emerged and the editors of *Military Thought* established these, in a sense, as a new official line in an article of April, 1955, which closed the discussion. The new line characterized the doctrine of permanently operating factors as inadequate on the whole, although valid in some contexts. The formula first dropped out of sight and then, in 1957, was explicitly abandoned as more confusing than helpful.

Talenskii's chief verbal innovation was his emphasis on the *armed conflict* as the crucial aspect of warfare. A strange innovation! Surely a law of war ought to deal with war. But the number of objections raised by Soviet commentators to this simple proposition reveals the significance of Talenskii's approach in the Soviet context. Not only did he put the armed conflict in the forefront of his treatment, but he insisted that the same principles of war affected both parties in the armed conflict. His opponents complained that it was anti-Marxist, that is, theoretically and morally wrong, to apply the same social laws to two radically different social systems. Capitalist states organized differently and seeking different goals could not command the loyalty of their own peoples over an extended period and had perforce to try for quick conclusions. The wars conducted by a socialist state were just by definition and therefore enjoyed the enthusiastic support of the population, which besides worked within a more rational economic framework. Talenskii and his supporters accepted the importance of these differences but insisted on maintaining at the center of attention an armed conflict whose laws applied equally to both contending sides.

In emphasizing combat at the expense of economics and morale, Talenskii made it possible to assess justly the role of nuclear weapons. Once discussion was freed from the confines of the permanently-operating-factors formula, the obvious implications of the existence of nuclear weapons followed almost automatically. Plainly, if one country's nuclear campaign were successful in destroying a large proportion of the armed forces, industry, and cities of another country, the attacker might gain an irreversible advantage. The Soviet theorists did not follow some Western ones who have proceeded to argue that the initial nuclear campaign itself would end the war; they contended merely that the success of the nuclear campaign *could* mean ultimate victory. This view, now official doctrine, puts an unprecedented emphasis on the importance of surprise. As a corollary, the Russians argued that the advantages of surprise might be denied to the enemy if foreknowledge of his intentions were obtained and defensive action were taken to reduce the likelihood that his nuclear blow would decide the war. From a defensive as well as from an offensive standpoint, the importance of the factor of surprise had grown greatly in Soviet eyes.

If the advantages that the offense may gain from achieving surprise are so great, every power that recognizes this fact must experience a temptation to pre-empt the initiative when the outlook for peace is unpromising. Generally, Soviet writers have gone no further than to say, and only rarely, that surprise is a two-edged weapon, but in the more restricted columns of *Military Thought,* written for officers, we find the plain statement that the Soviet Union has to be prepared to deal a forestalling blow so as to deprive the enemy of the advantage of surprise. The image called up is that of a quick blow against the enemy, who is poised to strike, before he can launch his own attack. While the capacity to deliver such a blow is officially advocated, the writers who express official views hasten to add that this policy should not be confused with that of preventive war. In this context the term "preventive war" may be taken to indicate a war initiated in order to forestall a remote possibility of enemy attack at some indefinite time in the future. In this sense, the term may be distinguished from "pre-emptive war," defined as a war initiated in order to forestall an attack that is believed to be imminent. Whatever the intention of the Soviet leaders, in public statements they would automatically deny that preventive war could be their policy. Preventive war and warmongering have become identified with each other in Soviet propaganda, and consequently it cannot be admitted that a socialist government would even consider preventive war.

The professional discussion of these matters was subsequently reflected in the public press, and it was even more obvious that the realistic military thinkers had won the day. Changes in the Soviet military posture over the next two years seemed to reflect the changes in theory. The military consequences of the new theory will be treated in more detail at a later stage. Meanwhile, what of its political consequences?

The main political result of the reappraisal of nuclear weapons was the improved prospect that the Soviet Union would not have to fight a major war unless she chose to do so. In the past, nations had often been deterred from making war because they feared that they would lose more than they gained. The experience of France and Great Britain during and after the First World War strongly suggested that in modern wars the cost of victory might be so great as to bring about a relative decline in the power of the victors. This paradox, however, could not be erected into an axiom, as the Second World War made clear. From that conflict the United States and the Soviet Union emerged much stronger than before, both absolutely and relatively, in spite of vast expenditures by the former and great devastation of the latter. In the past the conclusion that war did not pay was pragmatic rather than axiomatic. Today, however, nuclear weapons could destroy more in a few days than years of large-scale war had destroyed in the past. The belief that war did not pay would now act as a deterrent to a potential warmaker whether or not he expected to win an ultimate military victory.

Such a belief was much less likely to be held in Stalin's time, when official doctrine held that the air battle, with the use of nuclear weapons, would be more important than ever before, but still not decisive. That doctrine put a ceiling, as it were, on the potential destructiveness of nuclear weapons. As long as the enormous destructive possibilities of nuclear weapons were less than fully admitted, it was difficult to advance the hypothesis that other nations, or even one's own, would be deterred from initiating nuclear war because the costs—win or lose—would be too high.

In estimating Western intentions from the Stalinist point of view, the Soviet analyst had to assume that the capitalist powers would make a last desperate effort when they saw political dominance passing to communism. Nuclear weapons, however, introduced a fresh consideration into this old dogma. Unless the capitalists could reconcile themselves to suffer the destruction produced by nuclear weapons, they would prefer gradual decline to nuclear war. Under the Stalinist formula, the Soviet analyst might conclude that the capitalists would be deterred from making war if they felt that victory was in doubt. After the reappraisal of nuclear weapons, however, it was legitimate to argue that capitalism might be deterred from making war, irrespective of its chances of victory.

The belief that the capitalist powers would probably not attack the Soviet Union brought with it a profound modification of the traditional fear that national catastrophe was possible sooner or later. The country must continue, of course, to ensure itself against catastrophe by building up its military strength, but the constant preoccupation with impending disaster was no longer justifiable.

The Soviet analyst, however, could scarcely admit that he lived in a relatively secure new world until he was assured that the Soviet Union really had the nuclear power to deter the United States and that the United States recognized the existence of that power. Evidence on these points is presented in later chapters.

The new Soviet position rested on the possession of nuclear weapons and the ability to deliver them. It was simple enough to count the nuclear weapons in the Soviet stockpile, but it was difficult to be sure that the Soviet Union had the capacity to deliver against the United States a punishing retaliatory blow, if the latter attacked first. Nothing less than this capacity constituted an adequate deterrent. The ability to strike a first blow could constitute only a threat, not a deterrent.

In estimating the probable effects of a Soviet retaliatory blow the Soviet analyst had to consider a great many variables. He had to establish the probable weight of the American first strike, for which he depended on a knowledge of the numbers, efficiency, and strategic uses of American aircraft and weapons. He had to decide how far the weight of the American blow would be reduced by effective warning and defense measures. Having made due allowance for these factors, he had to calculate the effectiveness of a Soviet counterstrike.

The ability of the Soviet striking force to employ what power it still retained depended on many imponderables. If one assumed that the American attack aimed to reduce the size of the Soviet striking force, then the destructiveness of individual weapons became an important factor. Would the American force bring a large or a small number of hydrogen bombs? How effective would the Soviet chain of command be after an American blow?

This list of factors required for an estimate of the retaliatory capability of the Soviet Union could be extended, but it is probably clear already that it was extremely difficult for Soviet planners to determine the precise moment when the Soviet Union acquired a retaliatory capability adequate to her requirements for deterring an American attack. There seems to be little question that the Soviet Union did not have such a capability in 1950, or that she does have it in 1958. Even if one had all the facts available to both Soviet and American military planners, one could not fix with certainty a point in time when the Soviets acquired a deterrent nuclear capability. For deterrent capability is, so to speak, in the mind of the deterrer. One can, as it happens, learn within reasonable limits the period when the Soviet planners decided that their military power met the requirements of deterrence.

In March, 1954, some persons in the Soviet Union stated quite unmistakably that the Soviet Union possessed a deterrent capability. The best known of these were Malenkov and Mikoian. That they were sincere in their opinions is made probable by the fact that other persons publicly disagreed with them. Once again one has the feeling that a genuine debate was in progress. Those who opposed Malenkov's views repeated the old shibboleth about capitalist encirclement of the Soviet Union and indicated quite clearly that they did not accept the fact of Soviet deterrent capability, at least as of that moment. The most notable in this group were Khrushchev, Bulganin, Kaganovich, and Molotov. Only a directed verdict could have produced uniformity in statements of opinion on the subject, but at this early date such a verdict was not forthcoming. At this time, as we shall see, differences of opinion about military and other matters extended into the highest ranks of the Soviet leadership.

It is interesting, but by no means surprising, that the Soviet military leaders were not among the first to shout that the age of Soviet nuclear deterrence had arrived. While some civilian leaders believed that the mere possession of nuclear weapons and aircraft constituted a deterrent capability, military leaders by virtue of their experience did not make this mistake of oversimplification. Moreover, the caution and conservatism characteristic of military leaders in powerful countries must have delayed the recognition that so important a change had really taken place.

If the United States did not know that the Soviet Union could answer an air-nuclear attack in kind, she could not be deterred from making such an attack merely by fear of retaliation. It only takes one party to commit an act of aggression; it requires an unspoken agreement between two to deter such an act. For the doubters, including the military, it was extremely important to determine whether the United States was framing her policy on the assumption that an American attack on the Soviet Union would result in a level of damage to the United

States that her leaders would find unacceptable. The answer to this question was bound to make a tremendous difference in the Soviet sense of security. True, the Marxist might reason that the United States would refrain from making war on the Soviet Union because one group of capitalists wanted peace, because the population had not yet been properly prepared for war, because of contradictions in the relationships among capitalist countries, or because the capitalist military establishment was not yet ready. Under any of these hypotheses, however, the Soviet Union was secure against attack only as long as the restraining factors existed. By their very nature, these factors were transitory. Only the capitalist fear of unacceptable retaliation could be counted on to provide the desirable degree of security.

Had the United States been deterred, either transitorily or permanently, from launching war against the Soviet Union? The indicators were contradictory and confusing.

The United States had not minimized the importance of nuclear weapons while she possessed a monopoly of them and had frequently stated that these weapons constituted a deterrent to aggression. Yet during the Korean War, the only major act of Soviet-sponsored aggression in the period when the United States had a clear superiority in nuclear weapons and delivery capability, the United States exercised restraint. Far from being willing to engage the Soviet Union directly with nuclear weapons, America was clearly anxious to avoid any expansion of the war. This was true of both the Democratic and Republican administrations.

Thus far the omens were favorable to the Soviet Union, but the situation was not clear cut. While those in power in the United States were relatively cautious about committing American resources to the Far Eastern conflict, several military and political leaders urged the expansion of the war in Asia and the use of nuclear weapons against China, even at the risk of precipitating a war with the Soviet Union. The Korean War may well have forced on the Soviet military leaders a heightened awareness of how exposed they were to a nuclear attack if the Americans decided to make one.

The Korean War ended early in President Eisenhower's first term of office. The new President expressed his abhorrence of nuclear war. In a major speech of December, 1953, he began to advance his conviction that current weapons development made general war unthinkable. The leaders of the Soviet Union might well have regarded the President's remarks as evidence that their own possession of nuclear weapons was already effectively deterring the United States from making war against them.

In January, 1954, however, Secretary of State Dulles announced the latest policy of the National Security Council. The United States would meet aggression with "massive retaliation at places and times of our own choosing." Since the issue of massive retaliation in response to a massive Soviet attack was not in question, the Secretary's announcement seemed to mean that the United States might initiate a nuclear exchange with the Soviet Union if provoked by less than an all-out attack on her own positions. This interpretation implied that the United States would not be deterred by the Soviet nuclear capability from greeting local aggression with an all-out nuclear attack. But the almost instantaneous reaction of America's British ally to the Dulles statement made it obvious that the United States could not use British bases without British permission. For this and other reasons, as later chapters will show, the Soviet Union concluded that probably the United States either could not or would not use nuclear weapons against her under the provocation of limited Soviet aggression.

Since no major act of Soviet provocation comparable to the attack on South Korea has occurred since Dulles's speech of January, 1954, no real test of the readiness of the United States to execute the policy of massive retaliation has been possible.

The very idea that it was possible to count on nuclear weapons to provide immunity from attack by the United States (capitalist hostility being axiomatic in the Soviet mind) opened up many seemingly attractive vistas for the Soviet Union. First, the Soviet leaders could hope to gain parity with the United States in the newest weapons much more rapidly than in conventional armaments, where the industrial mobilization base was of prime importance. Even by optimistic estimates the Soviet Union would require decades to approach American industrial potential capacity. To achieve parity in nuclear weapons, however, might take only a matter of years.

In the months after Stalin's death, Malenkov and some others contended that possession of nuclear weapons could assure the Soviet Union of immunity from American attack, if the country concentrated on the deterrent aspects of military posture. Under such a program military expenditures could be kept at a level that would permit the Soviet Union to use its resources to raise the standard of living at home. Other Soviet leaders, notably Khrushchev, were hostile to these ideas and branded reliance on a deterrent posture as a policy of complacency which could lead to disaster. After a little time the second group prevailed.

A theoretical distinction, never precise, has long been made between a military posture that will deter the enemy from undertaking war and one designed to bring war to the enemy, destroy his forces, and occupy his territory. One might say that the second is an extension of the first. With the advent of nuclear weapons, the distinction has survived but its character has changed. Soviet military and political thinkers have addressed themselves to present-day problems with this distinction in mind. Their conclusions may be more readily understood if, at this point, a few general observations about military deterrence are introduced.

Traditional deterrents against a war of the opponent's choosing can be divided into three categories. First, an overwhelming military superiority residing in one power group will deter other powers from a calculated decision to attack that group. In 1907, France increased her ability to deter a hostile Germany by entering into the Triple Entente of Great Britain, France, and Russia, for the combined might of the three countries seemed to exceed Germany's. The existence of this alliance, however, failed to deter a German attack on France. But neither side, as it turned out, had an overwhelming superiority over the other.

In the First World War victory was believed to depend on

the rapid destruction of the enemy's military forces, an obvious maxim of war. When the front lines bogged down, the wearing effects of blockade and attrition began to play a role. Had German statesmen been faced in mid-1914 with Allied military forces unequivocally superior, and therefore clearly able to defeat an invader, one can scarcely doubt that they would have been deterred from making war. In such a case the deterrent force and the warmaking force are one and the same. The theoretical distinction between them does not apply. A marked superiority in over-all fighting capacity has been the most common deterrent to aggression on the part of the weaker powers, as it has been a frequent cause of aggression on the part of the stronger.

The second type of deterrent may be called the "sturdy rampart." For centuries England's island position, combined with an effective naval force, deterred invasion and facilitated successful military campaigns on the Continent. Similarly, the mountains of Switzerland have protected her independence for seven centuries. In each of these examples we find an excellent natural barrier supplemented by appropriate military measures. A favorable combination of geographical position and military art is required to make such a deterrent effective. Unfavorable changes in the military art may deprive a natural rampart of impenetrability, and hence of deterrent value. To be effective as a deterrent, the rampart need not discourage all attempts to breach it; it need merely prevent their succeeding. But the failure of such an attempt is likely to deter future attacks.

Where a strong natural rampart exists, the military forces required to deter a presumptive aggressor are far from identical with those required to destroy the opponent's military forces. The former are usually organized for purely defensive purposes and hence are incapable of inflicting strategic defeat on a powerful enemy. Great Britain, for example, could seldom bring war to a European enemy and defeat his land forces without the assistance of continental powers that possessed large armies.

Besides water and mountain barriers, sheer physical distance may act as a deterrent to war. Ancient Rome and China, for example, could not come to grips with each other. In this connection the transportation facilities possessed by the potential aggressor are bound to affect his decision to make war over great distances, as well as the drain on his other resources that such a war would entail.

The sturdy-rampart type of deterrent seems to be obsolete in the nuclear age. Only extraordinary developments in the art of defense seem likely to make its revival possible. At present such developments are not in sight.

The third type of deterrent is that of "disproportionate cost" and is of great antiquity. Here the presumptive aggressor is deterred because he decides that the game is not worth the candle. A potential aggressor is persuaded not to initiate a war because the cost of victory seems likely to exceed its value. As one might expect, this type of deterrent has often been used by the weak against the strong. It is, indeed, a variant of the first type. While overwhelming military superiority (the first type) will deter relatively weak powers from aggression, the latter may in turn protect themselves from strong powers by possessing and publicizing their ability to inflict an unacceptable level of damage on the attacker.

There is a certain similarity between this type of deterrent and those factors that may induce a strong power to abandon a war against a weaker one. Among such factors one may include difficulty of access to the weaker power's territory and military forces, unfavorable or strange fighting conditions, and guerrilla activity. All these factors played a part in Great Britain's abandonment of the American Revolutionary War, in spite of her obvious ability to continue it. In 1783, and again in 1814, the United States gained surprisingly favorable terms from the British. Indeed the granting of such terms by the British would be inexplicable if one were to take into account only the military forces that each contestant could muster. In view of the limited military forces that the British could transport to, or raise in, the North American Continent, however, and of the difficult fighting conditions imposed by wooded terrain on soldiers trained in the formal maneuvers of the parade ground, the Americans could exact from the British a price for continuing to fight that the latter found disproportionate to what they hoped to gain from the war.

Today the principle of disproportionate cost has become one of paramount importance. Considerations related to this principle have become the major deterrent to large-scale war involving the use of nuclear weapons. In the First and Second World Wars, though the destruction of the enemy's economic base began to play a larger role than before, the major strategy of the contestants was to destroy the enemy's military forces. Today and in the future, however, a war in which nuclear weapons are extensively employed will result in wholesale destruction of life and economic assets. Under modern conditions, damage to the economic base of each contestant is bound to be a major consequence of all-out war. Whether or not such destruction will be a major strategic aim of the contestants, it may well be the consequence of an effort to destroy numerous and widely dispersed targets in the opponent's country by the employment of megaton weapons. Such destruction is even more likely if the delivery vehicle is a ballistic missile, for the inaccuracy of fire of such missiles must be compensated by a large radius of destruction if the target is to be destroyed. Hence arises the thought that no potential aggressor can reasonably hope for victory in general war at a cost acceptable to himself. Thus the principle of disproportionate cost has become the major deterrent to nuclear war. To a greater extent, perhaps, than ever before the great powers are deterred from a head-on clash more by the threat of destruction to their economic resources and population than by the threat to their military forces. This historic change in the relative weight assigned to the various deterrent factors has blurred whatever practical significance once resided in the distinction between forces designated primarily to deter the enemy and forces designed primarily to destroy his military forces.

Before 1945 certain military arrangements were often valuable both as deterrents to aggression and in active defense should war break out. The numerous coastal guns placed on American shores in the nineteenth century were clearly meant to deter a possible invader; they were certainly not meant to carry the war to the enemy. The Dutch preparations for flooding before World War II were not intended primarily to destroy the enemy's forces, but to deter him from attempting an invasion of the Netherlands. The French fortress system built before World War I was meant to deter an invasion across the Franco-German border.

Each of these deterrent devices could be used in a defensive role in the event that deterrence failed. Although the American coastal artillery never fired a shot in anger, the flooding of Dutch lands briefly delayed the advance of the German invaders. For nearly a century before 1914 the British navy not only maintained the Pax Britannica but deterred others, at least until 1898, from attempting to compete for mastery of the world's oceans. In the First World War the navy was an essential element in Britain's fighting forces. Thus it is clear that the deterrent role of a given military arrangement is seldom, if ever, its only role. Nevertheless, the distinction between a deterrent force and a warmaking force is worth maintaining, if only as a tool for analyzing the motives behind a country's development of this or that kind of military power. Consider, for example, the case of the huge German naval program of 1900. Since Germany, from a military point of view, was essentially a land-locked power, observers supposed that the intended role of the new German navy was offensive rather than deterrent or defensive. It was not possible to detect such a distinction in the case of the British navy.

Considerations such as the above suggest that there has more frequently been an identity between the requirements of defense and deterrence than between those of offense and deterrence. Since the development of nuclear weapons, however, the relationship between offensive capabilities and deterrence has become much closer. Conversely, a large investment in defensive arrangements may very well indicate not *primarily* a desire to deter nuclear attack, but rather a form of insurance against retaliation. Where this is true, the heavy investor in defense may well be hoping to reduce the risks of initiating offensive action. As we shall see in a later chapter, the Soviet Union has invested a great deal more in measures of active and civil defense than the United States.

Why have nuclear weapons brought about this change in the mutual relationships of offensive, defensive, and deterrent capabilities? An answer has already been suggested above. The major consequence of nuclear war (and therefore the major deterrent to its initiation) is the destruction of population and economic resources; hence the tendency to devote ever more attention to minimizing this destruction, should war break out, by the development of defensive systems.

In the chapters that follow we shall present evidence indicating that the Soviet position is based on reasoning similar to the above. The group around Malenkov, which tended to rely on mutual deterrence as a guarantee of prolonged peace, was stigmatized as complacent and defeatist: complacent because they thought that Soviet nuclear weapons precluded a war not of Soviet choosing; defeatist because they did not believe in the possibility of surviving a nuclear war. The Soviet Union would suffer fearful destruction, answered Khrushchev, but it would win the war.

Khrushchev's theoretical and political victory over Malenkov had immediate practical consequences for Soviet military planning. No Soviet leader had opposed the building of long-range aircraft and missiles, weapons that were at once of offensive and deterrent value. Khrushchev's insistence on the possibility of victory in a nuclear war, however, demanded still more expensive additions to the Soviet military posture. Should deterrence fail, the country must have a defensive system capable of minimizing destruction. There is a more or less definite limit to what a country can usefully spend on offensive nuclear weapons; there seems to be no limit to the returns from added increments of expenditure on defense against such weapons. This discrepancy is a direct consequence of the unprecedented destructive potential of modern weapon systems. The great destructiveness of individual weapons requires active defense to destroy a very high percentage of the delivery vehicles. The marriage of nuclear weapons to high-speed aircraft and missiles makes a low rate of interception futile. Even an inadequate defense, however, is extremely expensive to build and maintain.

The Soviet decision to prepare to fight a war if need be, rather than to rely on the effectiveness of deterrence, involves enormous expenditures and sets severe limits on the non-military sector of the country's economy. The condition of the Soviet peoples, therefore, is directly and powerfully affected by the present military policies of the Kremlin.

*   *   *

Once it had been decided that the major mission of the Soviet armed forces was to fight a full-scale war if the need arose, the choice of strategies open to the planners was automatically narrowed. If war came the Soviet aim was victory, and the well-understood characteristics of nuclear weapons made it necessary to conceive of victory primarily in terms of the survival of a substantial proportion of the population and the economy. Now that nuclear weapons make wholesale devastation of the homeland an almost inescapable concomitant of war, the destruction of the enemy's military forces can no longer be *in itself* the main object of military operations. That mission has now become the means to a more fundamental end, namely the preservation of that proportion of one's own population and economic resources that one believes to be compatible with "victory." The Soviet strategy, therefore, is to destroy the enemy's military forces before those forces can destroy Soviet population and cities. This strategy has the greatest promise of success if the Soviet Union is able to initiate the use of nuclear weapons. If the Soviet leaders believe that the United States is about to attack, they must try to effect a pre-emptive nuclear assault. A retaliatory attack on their part might come too late to achieve the main object of any major war, the salvation of the Soviet population and economic wealth.

Such a pre-emptive strategy requires that the Soviet Union get timely and unequivocal warning of the enemy's intention to attack. It may be said that the cold-blooded planning of a preventive war would obviate the necessity for warning.

Soviet strategic plans, then, demand the ability to destroy

a large part of the presumptive enemy's warmaking force at its bases, to knock out such elements of this force as may reach the Soviet Union, and to minimize by civil-defense measures the effects of the weapons that get through the active defenses. Such requirements necessitate a striking force able to hit with considerable precision. The more the targets to be destroyed have been "hardened," the greater the required precision of delivery. Underground installations protected by thick concrete must receive near-direct hits.

An important role in this over-all strategy has been assigned to ground forces, at least for the next decade. If the main object of the war is to protect the Soviet population, enemy missiles moved to new bases in Western Europe after the initiation of hostilities will constitute a major menace. The surest way of eliminating them is to occupy the ground. A rapid Soviet advance across Europe is therefore essential for the successful execution of the whole Soviet strategy.

The present Soviet strategy, as outlined above, is designed for a period when the Soviet Union has no retaliation-proof capability. But if that country should continue to develop its warmaking capability to the point where its high-yield weapons have great accuracy and reliability, and if its presumptive opponents should fall behind, the strategy of the initial blow may become much more attractive to the Soviet leaders than it is now. As soon as such a blow seems to promise immunity from retaliation, the Soviet planners will have greater freedom in making major military decisions.

At present, however, the planners must rely on the least of several evils, namely their ability to get in a first blow upon receipt of warning, though not necessarily with the hope of eliminating retaliation. At best this means, for the Soviet Union, that the enemy chooses the time for initiating hostilities; at worst it means that the Soviet homeland may be devastated if warning comes too late. Nevertheless, the Soviet Union has to aim for the expected advantages of getting in the first strike, should war threaten. Without the power to obliterate the enemy's striking force by a single, all-out blow, the Soviet Union would court destruction by launching a nuclear strike "out of the blue." Such a strike would be insane, and we have no reason to think that the present Soviet leaders are anything but shrewd and calculating. For this very practical reason, their professed abhorrence of "preventive war," that is, of the cold-blooded planning of all-out war, is no doubt sincere.

Should the Soviet Union ever acquire what her leaders consider a retaliation-proof capability, the world situation will alter radically. One need exercise little imagination to visualize the dangers inherent in such a development. No one can say that the acquisition of such a vastly improved capability would induce the present Soviet leaders to plan a cold-blooded "preventive" war. In such circumstances, however, the United States would have to fear constantly that the Soviet Union might be tempted to initiate war in the conviction that the first blow would decide it.

For a few years the United States possessed a monopoly of both nuclear weapons and delivery vehicles. Yet there was no general war. This seemingly hopeful analogy departs from the hypothetical situation just described in two important respects. First, for much of the earlier period the Soviet leaders did not really believe that the employment of nuclear weapons could decide the outcome of war. Second, in this period the Soviet Union did not possess the capability of making *any* kind of nuclear strike against the United States. This fact emphasizes the principal danger in one power's gaining a retaliation-proof strategy. That power's presumptive enemy will possess the capability of making a first nuclear strike. The weaker power is bound to consider that making a first strike, in its own time and without specific provocation, may well be the best insurance against national extinction. Hence an imbalance of this unprecedented kind is likely to lead to an unprecedented danger of all-out war.

Should the Soviet Union ever acquire a retaliation-proof capability, she would have to consider the possibility that any small international crisis might be the occasion for the execution of an American nuclear strike. For the Russians would surely argue that a desperate American attempt to reap the benefits of surprise and priority was more likely now that the United States lacked the power to recover from an initial Soviet blow. Hence, the Soviet leaders would feel tempted, on grounds of reason and prudence, to plan an obliterating strike in their own time and without any specific provocation.

CHAPTER TWO

BREAKING THE OLD MOLD

In this chapter we shall examine in detail the revolution in Soviet military doctrine that occurred between the latter part of 1953 and the spring of 1955. The influence of this revolution on Soviet strategic posture will be considered in a subsequent chapter.

First, let us consider Soviet military history in the fifteen years before Stalin's death. One can detect a pattern in the wars initiated by the Soviet Union in this period: the attack on Poland in 1939; the Finnish war of 1939-1940; the war against Japan in 1945; and the war against South Korea through the agency of the North Koreans in 1950-1953. In all these cases the Soviet Union hoped that the employment of limited means would achieve ends proportionate to the effort expended. The Soviet Union expected to, and did, obtain important objectives by occupying Eastern Poland in 1939 and Manchuria in 1945, with a negligible expenditure of resources and with little risk of an expansion of the conflict beyond what was justified by the expected gains. In the wars against South Korea and Finland the Soviet Union was unable to obtain her planned objectives in the time allotted and therefore abandoned the original objectives rather than risk an expansion of the war and an expenditure of resources incommensurate with the ends desired.

The defensive campaigns against Japan in 1938 and 1939 also demonstrated the Soviet willingness to fight a limited war for limited ends. Numerous border incidents had occurred along the Manchurian-Russian and Manchurian–Outer Mongolian borders. In 1939 these culminated in a series of full-scale military engagements. In all cases the Japanese took the initiative, successfully advanced across the Manchurian border, and were then beaten back by the Russians. The Russians' primary object in fighting these engagements was obviously to defend their territory, but in doing this successfully they demonstrated their strength and determination to the Japanese. The latter were thereby put on notice that they could hope neither to expand piecemeal, after Hitler's example, nor to win a cheap victory over the Soviet Union. The Russians, however, did not push their advantage beyond the limited requirements of defense. By limiting the geographical scope of their operations, when they had won the power to extend it at Japan's expense, and by their care to avoid even the suggestion in their propaganda that their actions presaged a large war, the Russians made it clear that they sought only the limited objectives of throwing the Japanese back into Manchuria and deterring them from further aggression.[1] In all the wars so far initiated by the Soviet Union the objective has been limited, both in the planning stage and in the aftermath. The temptation to expand the conflict when the resources needed to attain the original objective turned out to be excessive has always been resisted.

In the only war imposed on the Soviet Union since 1921, the Russo-German war of 1941-1945, the German aim was to conquer the Soviet Union. The latter was obliged to seek the complete defeat of the enemy and whatever further advantages might accrue from victory. Since this war has been the major military event in the life of the Soviet Union, its course is worth considering briefly.

As in most wars, the period of preparation was crucial in determining the course of the conflict. It was for such a war with a great power that the Red Army had been prepared and trained in the thirties. The resources of personnel and materiel available to this army were limited by the political and economic facts of Soviet life. The Soviet Union's industrial establishment, on the whole, could not produce goods of quality comparable to that of its likely enemies, although some items of military equipment compared favorably with their German and British counterparts. To compensate for these deficiencies the Soviet Union gradually built up vast quantities of military equipment. By the time the desired quantity of certain items was reached many of them were obsolete. Hence a relative superiority in the numbers of such items was not necessarily of any military significance. As events proved, however, the very great numbers of tanks possessed by the Soviet Union compensated in some degree for their obsolescence.

Besides great masses of military equipment the Russians had great masses of men in their armed forces. No other sovereign state except China could equal the reserves of population possessed by the Soviet Union. The efficiency of the huge Russian military machine was relatively low. Though they might not admit it, many Russians probably knew that their officers were not to be compared with German officers, as the course of the war was to demonstrate. While some individual generals and officers proved competent, the Army command as a whole was lumbering and clumsy.

The military weaknesses of the Soviet Union in the nineteen-thirties put rather stringent limits on the foreign aims that it was prudent to pursue. It was obviously risky to become embroiled in war with one of the great powers, especially with the most likely antagonist, resurgent Germany. Soviet diplomacy, therefore, was mainly directed toward avoiding war with Germany. There can be no doubt that in 1939 it was the Soviet Union that made overtures to Germany for a *rapprochement*. There is evidence that since 1935 she had made repeated but vain efforts of this kind.

With the advantage of hindsight it is now easy to see what few Westerners realized in the late thirties: that Soviet policy was to further the "natural" tendency of capitalist nations to make war on one another, leaving the Soviet Union as *tertius gaudens*. Once we accept the fact that Stalin had no preference for "democratic capitalism" over "fascist capitalism," we can understand why the Soviet Union used its not inconsiderable influence in German domestic politics to help bring Hitler to power in 1933. Having no ideological preference for Western democracy, Stalin hoped and believed that the rise of German fascism would mean war among the capitalists rather than a capitalist war against the Soviet Union. When the Nazi-Soviet pact was signed in 1939, it seemed as if Stalin's policy had been crowned with success. As we know, however, the triumph was short lived.

The same inadequacy which made it advisable for the Soviet Union to avoid war with a great power affected whatever preparations the country might make for a war imposed on her. It did not matter what kind of defenses the Soviet Union wanted; she could have only what her resources permitted.

In the twenties and thirties some Soviet theoreticians had made radical proposals for the reorganization of the armed forces. They emphasized the value of airborne troops, the high mobility of tanks, and the usefulness of other "team-operated" weapons. But by 1937 the Soviet leaders had decided that infantry ruled the battle and that the army must consist primarily of great masses of individual fighting men. They may have reached this conclusion partly as a result of misinterpreting the "purely localized experience of the Spanish Civil War."[2] In the nineteen-thirties, however, it would have been pointless to impress on the Soviet leaders the theoretical superiority of a small, mobile, concentrated force over a mass army, for the Russians had no choice but to rely on the latter. The state of technical expertness in the society as a whole and the unwillingness to permit commanders to exercise initiative determined the dependence on a mass army. It would have been preferable, of course, to have an army as efficient as the German and as large as their own, but this was not a practicable alternative.

Within limits the Russians were free to vary their military posture. They could disperse their tanks through the infantry units, as they did at the beginning of the war, or concentrate them in special armored units, as they did later in the war. No matter how they arranged the elements of their massive army, however, the only basic strategy open to them was to use superiority in numbers of men and amounts of equipment to smother the Germans. Such a strategy, though the only practicable one, was far from a guarantee of victory. The Russians could not wear down the Germans unless they could first deny them a quick victory. Here Hitler's rashness played into Russian hands. Hitler failed to mobilize the German economy as thoroughly as the Russians did their own. He expected to gain victory over the Russians with less than the utmost effort. The success of German mobilization measures in 1943 and 1944 when the situation had deteriorated demonstrated that fuller mobilization would have been possible in 1941, when it might have saved the day for the Germans. In 1943 it was too late, for the Red Army continued to outnumber the German forces, and Soviet command, weapons, and morale improved, while German strength declined. German units had to be taken away from the Russian front in increasing numbers as the Western allies advanced across North Africa and into continental Europe. By 1943 it was possible for the Soviet Union to win by employing the strategy of massive attack and attrition.

Because the German blitzkrieg strategy failed in 1941, the Russians were confirmed in their belief that surprise could not determine the outcome of wars and that no single arm in warfare could be decisive. If the Russians had been more cautious they might have concluded merely that the inferior manpower of the Germans, coupled with the onset of a Russian winter, had outweighed the advantages obtained from surprise. This more modest interpretation would have left the Russians free to recognize that surprise might have been successful in somewhat different circumstances. If the Russians had been followers of Clausewitz, they would have tried to analyze surprise in relation to other factors bearing on the issue of victory or defeat, balancing one against another. Instead, they laid it down virtually a priori that surprise could never succeed without superiority in every major aspect of military strength. The Soviet tendency was to elaborate rigid rules of warfare, rather than to develop a pragmatic approach to particular military problems. They asserted that the strategy they had successfully employed against the Germans in 1941 would always be a winning strategy. That the only strategy open to the Russians turned out to be a winning one served to bolster their conservative prejudices.

The lessons the Russians drew from World War II may readily be traced in Soviet published materials. In the second edition of *Bol'shaia Sovetskaia Entsiklopediia* (*Great Soviet Encyclopedia*) an unsigned article on the military art postulated that "bourgeois military science [has] sought the secret of victory in the use of surprise and other transitory factors which could only have given temporary successes."[3] This statement was consistent with the view that in World War II the Germans depended on deciding the issue at the outset of the war and lost the war because they were not strong enough to do so. It did not necessarily imply a universal rule that initial successes deriving from surprise can only have temporary effects.

Another article on military science in the same encyclopedia makes it clear that about 1950 the merely temporary importance of surprise was viewed as a universal principle. In commenting on the significance of Stalin's formula concerning the permanently operating factors (the stability of the rear, the morale of the armed forces, the quantity and quality of divisions, the equipment of the fighting services, and the organizational abilities of the military commanders), the encyclopedia article characterized factors such as surprise as "transitory" and the permanently operating factors as "decisive."[4] This contrast made it quite clear that transitory factors, in the Soviet view, could not be decisive. The same article insisted that the Soviet Union would always be superior in the permanently operating factors: "The military science of the Soviet socialist government assumes the invincible superiority in economic and morale potential of the Soviet Union over any coalition of possible opponents from the imperialist camp."[5]

One military writer, in a book published shortly after Stalin's death in 1953, showed that little had changed in the Soviet view of war since 1951, the date of the article cited above:

> Soviet military science rejects the bankrupt position of bourgeois military theory which exaggerates the importance of temporary factors for the outcome of war and thereby relies on the triumph of the transitory elements. Recognizing the limited role of transitory factors in the

course of military events, Soviet military science considers that the main elements determining the course of war according to the rules are the permanently operating factors. The adventuristic and anti-scientific theories of "atomic blitzkrieg," "lightning," "aerial" wars, etc., are alien to the military science of a socialist government. It [military science] realistically takes into account and utilizes all factors assuring victory in warfare. It is this that constitutes the invincible strength of Soviet military science and its indubitable superiority over bourgeois military science.[6]

This theory, in characteristically Soviet style, insists that the course of events in a given historical period follows definite laws and rules. The author, in a manner typical of those years, asserts that bourgeois theory is bankrupt because it says that a blitzkrieg or an atomic strike can win wars.

The old Soviet formula was not content to say that in the conditions of 1941 a blitzkrieg could not win the war, or that in 1953 a nuclear strike would not be decisive. Soviet theory, before the modifications to be discussed, held that in the machine period (as opposed to the period before World War I) blitzkriegs and atomic strikes did not win wars in any circumstances. Such an attitude is consistent with the Soviet application of Marxian determinism. Soviet Marxians have believed that human events can be predicted because laws govern their unfolding. Marx predicted the coming of socialism on the basis of his scientific analysis of the laws of historical development. Most present-day Russian thinkers probably believe in the validity of the Marxian analysis of historical change. We in the West would say that Marx based his analysis of history on a minute examination of mid-nineteenth-century British capitalism, whose tendencies as he discerned them, he projected into the future and into other countries. According to Marx, capitalism was bound to become more oppressive and, by creating an ever larger proletariat, to generate the conditions for its own destruction. One may wonder if a knowledge of the next hundred years of capitalist history might not have caused Marx to modify his predictions, as many Marxians have since done and as the Bolsheviks have conspicuously avoided doing. The Bolsheviks believe Marx's prediction of the doom of capitalism to be as reliable as Newton's Law of Gravitation. In the materialist view of the world, it is sacrilege to suggest that large-scale human events cannot be predicted by using the "laws of history."

The Bolsheviks have clung desperately to their belief in the predictability of the future. When we recall how much the Bolsheviks wrote about the danger of their own destruction, the importance of being able to predict the future becomes understandable.[7] Those who feel secure are confident of their ability to cope with whatever the future brings; those who are uncertain of their strength need to reassure themselves about the future. For example, Churchill's optimism about the outcome of the First and Second World Wars sprang from the self-confidence of the man himself and of the society in which he grew up, not from any conviction that the future was predictable and therefore manageable.

While all statesmen are concerned in varying degrees with the probable course of future events, the Bolsheviks fear that a failure to predict accurately the broader trends of history means catastrophe. This attitude has pervaded Soviet military thinking. The following is typical of hundreds of quotations from Soviet military writers:

> The demonstration that the laws of economic development are objective laws expressing the process of economic development and that people can discover these laws, comprehend them and employ them in society's interests, but that they cannot destroy old or create new economic laws—has great significance for the comprehension of the rules of war and military affairs and furnishes an opportunity for the scientific understanding of the superiority of Soviet military science (which rests on the unshakable foundation of materialistic theory) over bourgeois military science, which is permeated with the spirit of idealism. . . .
>
> Soviet military science, built on the theoretical foundation of Marxism-Leninism, assumes that the phenomena of war, as of other spheres of the life of society, are completely

knowable, and that our knowledge of the rules of war, based on experience, is trustworthy knowledge which has the importance of objective truths. A knowledge of the rules of war is a necessary condition for the scientific prediction of the events of war and the successful leadership of troops on the field of battle.[8]

Here is an instance of anxiety to control the future by following the laws governing it, which are "completely knowable." No wonder Stalin felt it necessary to attack Clausewitz, who was essentially the proponent of a pragmatic approach to military science.

After Stalin died, many long-established formulas were reexamined. The most dramatic episode in the revision of Stalinism was Khrushchev's speech at the Twentieth Party Congress in 1956, but by then certain less obvious modifications of Stalinist principles had already occurred. One of these was the revision of military doctrine.

Before the principles of war enunciated by Stalin in 1942 could be applied to the conditions of the early fifties it was necessary, at the very least, to subject them to a critical review. Stalin's formula concerning the permanently operating factors, which were said to determine the outcome of wars, had been put forward when a qualitatively inferior but quantitatively superior Soviet force had been forced to fight a German army with the converse attributes. Stalin's concept of war, with its emphasis on morale and war production, prescribed a strategy of attrition. By 1953, when there was no great rival land power on the Continent, when the most powerful putative enemy, the United States, was superior in airborne nuclear weapons, it was no longer certain that a Soviet strategy of attrition could be put into practice, or that if practicable it would lead to victory.

The Soviet military, realizing the need for a revision of doctrine, employed old terminology to ease the transition to a complete revolution in military thought. The seeds of this revolution were sown in a discussion ostensibly initiated by Major General Talenskii, who had been editor of the daily organ of the Ministry of Defense, *Red Star,* and who was then editor of *Voennaia mysl'* (*Military Thought*), the monthly organ of the Ministry of War. These high positions guaranteed that he was not speaking lightly and suggested that he had powerful official backing.

In the September, 1953, issue of *Military Thought,* a periodical written for Soviet officers, Major General Talenskii took the first step toward a revision of the Soviet view of warfare. The discussion that ensued extended to other military journals, which were intended for all ranks. Talenskii's article bore the title "On the Question of the Laws of Military Science."[9] It began with the statement that objective laws govern wars as they do all human activity. In order to win wars one must understand these laws. Military science has as its purpose the establishment of the rules which govern the armed conflict, the conduct of the war in accordance with these rules, and the organization of a military establishment capable of meeting the demands imposed by the laws of war.

The laws of war will reflect two distinct but related tenets. On the one hand, both capitalist and socialist societies have similar military equipment, and the character of the equipment is an important factor in determining the methods used in the armed conflict. On the other hand, the difference between the two great social systems is such that there exist two incompatible sets of laws governing human society. The socialist laws of society alone are objective and realistic. Upon this foundation Marxism-Leninism has built certain laws of war that only socialists can understand and only socialist states exploit. Military science, in the technical sense, reveals that over time wars have been expanding in scope and intensity; but only Marxism, with its understanding of the nature of capitalism in its imperialist stage, can explain why this has happened.

Soviet military science assumes the "objective" character of the laws of war. As a rule, however, capitalist military science fails to do this, built as it is on an "idealistic" basis. (Idealism, in Soviet terms, is that theory of history which explains major events in terms of individual leaders who embody a world idea; whereas materialism explains history in terms of broad social classes.) Clausewitz, according to Talenskii, is idealistic because he puts so much stress on accidents in war and on the personality of the military leader.

As an example of what he means by an objective law of war, Talenskii offers: victory is gained by advance and not by retreat. Another such law is that modern war cannot be won by one arm such as the air force, since the means by which war is waged have become steadily more complex. There has been no case, for example, where a new weapon, such as the airplane, the tank, poison gas, or the recoilless gun, has won a war. This applies to atomic weapons too. The objective rule is that only the employment of a whole complex of weapons can secure victory. Armed with such objective laws, Soviet military science can foresee future military developments.

To posit a Marxist law does not mean to lay down an eternal and absolute rule. These laws apply to concrete but changing historical situations. For example, when muskets and guns had smooth bores and a range, accuracy, and rate of fire far below present standards, it was cold steel rather than firepower that was decisive. This law has lost its force in a later historical era.

Military science has not completed its task when it has discovered the rules of war. These rules have to be applied to specific situations, in some of which they have to be modified. For example, the rule that it is impossible to win a war with only one type of force has to be qualified for countries having common land borders or great expanses of ocean in between. (The probable implication is that in the first case the armies will be preponderant and in the second, the navies.)

It is possible, says Talenskii, to arrive at a basic law of war, but he ventures his own opinion that the statement about the permanently operating factors determining the outcome of wars is not such a law, because it does not allow sufficient importance to the armed conflict or say how a war should be waged. Though the permanently-operating-factors formula is important, argues Talenskii, it is not basic. There can only be one basic law of war and it must be concerned primarily with the armed conflict. Stalin's permanently-operating-factors formula had not usually been described as a law, so that technically Talenskii was not rejecting Stalin's theory when he denied that it constituted a law of war. Since the political goal of war is achieved through victory in the armed conflict, the basic law should provide the key to victory. /

Talenskii offers the following as his statement of the basic law of war:

> Victory in modern war is attained by the decisive defeat of the enemy in the course of the armed conflict through the employment of successive blows accumulating in force, on the basis of superiority in the permanently acting factors which determine the fate of war, and on the basis of a comprehensive exploitation of economic, moral-political, and military potentialities in their unity and interaction.

This formulation, argues Talenskii, meets the criteria he has established for a satisfactory law of war. In concluding his own evaluation of it, he adds a capital qualification that, with the tentativeness characteristic of the whole article, is not made part of the definition:

> While taking as a point of departure the concept of contemporary world wars as extended wars, the basic law in the above-cited formulation does not exclude the possibility of a decisive defeat in a limited time of one or another opponent, given the existence of certain conditions.

We shall return to this key idea later.

According to the unqualified basic law, not a single blow, but a series of blows of cumulative force, is required for victory. Under some conditions, however, it will be possible to win strategic victory without recourse to such extended operations. These conditions will be exceptional and the special case in which they arise will not affect the essence of the military art.

The armed conflict is a two-sided process, and the activity of both sides is governed by the same set of rules, but both sides do not have the same opportunities under these rules. The leaders of capitalist states, who by definition do not have just war aims, cannot exploit the moral force of their people, and this limits the extent to which they can exploit the basic law of war on which victory hinges. As Talenskii's qualification of the basic law indicates, Soviet military science does not deny the importance of chance in military affairs. Chance is thought to be more prominent in warfare than in other social phenomena. A commander who knows the laws of war can fail in an operation because of an accident, and a skillful one can turn an accident to his advantage, "but not a single commander has attained victory in war despite the laws of the armed conflict using accidents only."

Denying the objective laws leads to adventurism, that is, taking unjustified risks; but denying the subjective factors leads to passivity and to collapse in the face of an active enemy. The objective law of the armed conflict declares that, other things being equal, the side superior in strength wins. The operation of this law, however, does not reduce the weaker side to helplessness. It can

> . . . find means for neutralizing "the negative" aspect of this law. . . . History shows examples, when as a result of skillful action by military leaders and troops, this general law was neutralized and an opposite result was achieved—the side with inferior forces won. . . . In the light of this proposition the aphorism "not numbers, but skill wins" has as good a claim as the other aphorism, "the biggest battalions win."

Another example of the modification of the rules governing warfare is presented by Talenskii. A surprise enemy attack, which theoretically should yield gains to the attacker, can be more or less paralyzed by a system of measures developed by Soviet military science.

As Stalin pointed out, attacking nations are usually better prepared to fight, as well as having the advantages of the initiative. Once more Talenskii could discern a loophole in the law of war:

> The action of this law can also be neutralized or weakened by a system of international political measures as well as by appropriate organization in governments threatened by an aggressor's attack, by a system of organization and military service, by the preparation of the country for war, by the

organization of the anti-air defense of the country and the troops, by a skillful and vigilant intelligence, etc.

Knowing the objective laws, it is possible to foresee events, to prepare for them as much as possible, and to direct them. Therefore the great military leaders are those who have understood these laws.

Talenskii concludes by saying that he does not pretend to have given a comprehensive elucidation of the laws of war, and he calls for discussion.

Various deductions can be made from Talenskii's article, which opened the Soviet discussion on the character and content of the laws of war. Obviously Talenskii was dissatisfied with the state of Soviet thinking on the nature of war, and just as obviously he failed to make a clear, logically consistent statement of what the laws of war should be. In his thrashing about for a solution, however, he laid the foundation for a new Soviet conception of war.

In the same breath Talenskii talked of the permanently operating factors and of the possibility of the "decisive defeat in a limited time of one or another opponent." The permanently-operating-factors formula had been so long associated with Soviet strategy in World War II that it almost automatically implied an extended war of all-out mobilization, in which morale on the home front and the ability to command vast resources would tell in the end. Yet Talenskii also asserted the possibility of defeat in a limited time. In other words, he implied that in certain circumstances the Soviet Union might be unable to utilize her power to mobilize vast resources. This, in turn, implied that the permanently operating factors had lost a good deal of their former importance. Talenskii, however, approached the weaknesses of the Stalin formula obliquely rather than directly. First he stuck to a quasi-religious faith in "the laws of history" and the existence of a basic law of war; then he advanced the idea that the action of these "objective" laws could be paralyzed by an intelligent regard for "subjective" factors. Clearly Talenskii was attempting to pour new wine into old bottles.

It appears that Talenskii appreciated that the pragmatic approach to military problems was genuinely objective. At the same time, he seems to have questioned the objectivity of Stalinist dogma. Traditionally, however, dogmatism had been officially characterized as "objective" and pragmatism as "subjective." Talenskii's first article seems to have been an awkward attempt to dignify the pragmatic approach, at the expense of the dogmatic, by reversing the definitions of the terms "objective" and "subjective." Moreover, he had to perform this *volte face* without appearing to move. Hence he found himself postulating the existence of basic laws, the knowledge of which was essential to victory, and simultaneously suggesting that a little human ingenuity could readily evade these laws.

In any case individual thinkers rarely come up with a set of ideas entirely new in content and terminology. The guiding ideas in human societies tend to change very gradually, and by the efforts of many. Perhaps these generalizations alone are enough to explain the peculiar mixture of tradition and innovation in Talenskii's article.

The most obviously traditional feature in Talenskii's treatment was his insistence that war is governed by the action of "objective" (that is, dogmatic) laws. Here he used as his authority Stalin, who a year before in his *Ekonomicheskie problemy sotsializma v SSSR* (*Economic Problems of Socialism in the U.S.S.R.*) had issued a dictum on the subject and admonished those who were then deviating from it:

> Some comrades deny the objective nature of scientific laws, in particular the laws of political economy under socialism. They deny that the laws of political economy cover processes governed by objective law which occur independently of the will of man. In view of the special role allotted by history to the Soviet state, they hold that the Soviet state and its leaders can negate laws of the existing political economy, can "establish" new laws, "make" new laws.
>
> These comrades are profoundly mistaken. . . . Men may discover these laws, may learn them and, relying on them and applying them in the interests of society, may impart a

different direction to the destructive operation and allow fuller scope to other laws which are forcing their way to the forefront; but men cannot negate nor make new economic laws. . . .

The laws of political economy under socialism are objective laws which reflect the fact that the processes of economic life have their own rules and proceed regardless of our will. Those who deny this thesis are really rejecting science, and in rejecting science are denying the possibility of prognosis and therefore any possibility of guiding economic life.[10]

Stalin is here dealing with one of the recurrent problems of Western civilization. Determinism, whether it be Calvinist, Marxian, or Freudian, automatically raises a question as to the existence of free will. If God, history, or parents have predetermined the fate of an individual, class, or nation, can there be any such thing as free will? In each case the danger of fatalism and passivity has been overcome by a feat of intellectual legerdemain.

The Marxians worked out this dilemma as it applied to historical changes in class relationships. No one could accuse Stalin or the Bolsheviks of being fatalistic or quietistic. Stalin's passage, quoted above, embodied the standard Bolshevik rationale of activism. History is a juggernaut that will roll forward in its prescribed course no matter what men do to oppose it. It is man's role to discover and accept the laws of history, and to push the juggernaut in the direction that these laws have given it. Thus it is possible at once to be certain of the ultimate future and to enjoy a sense of power and importance in speeding the juggernaut on its predestined path.

If you deny that the course of history obeys objective laws, you are, in Stalin's words, "really rejecting science, and in rejecting science are denying the possibility of prognosis and therefore any possibility of guiding economic life."

The Bolshevik emphasis on the necessity for accurate prediction reflects the belief that mistakes by the human agents of history can cause a very long, or even indefinite, postponement of the earthly heaven of worldwide communism. Talenskii adopted this point of view in his treatment of the laws of war. His insistence that the laws of war are knowable and that the Marxists know them better than the capitalists, who follow a false idealistic philosophy of history, is standard Bolshevik theory that has been reiterated a thousand times, both before and since Talenskii's article.

This article, however, also contains viewpoints that are completely incompatible with the traditional view of the world, and states them matter-of-factly as if they followed naturally from the old premises. When Talenskii says that the action of fundamental laws can be paralyzed, he is breaking with Marxism as it has been interpreted in the Soviet Union. Stalin allowed that human activity could limit the scope of the action of a law and that when one historical era was giving way to another, human activity could "allow fuller scope to the other laws which are forcing their way to the forefront," but he was completely opposed to the idea that human beings can paralyze the action of a law and regarded it as a contradiction of Marxism.

It is not clear that Talenskii consciously set out to revise Marxism, but the numerous important exceptions that he cites to the operation of basic laws suggest some such motive. Although he assumes that modern wars will be extended wars, Talenskii "does not exclude the possibility of a decisive defeat in a limited time of one or another opponent, given the existence of certain conditions." It is a law that the stronger side wins, but the weaker side does not have to lose. Surprise is known to yield important advantages to the attacker, yet "the effect of an enemy surprise attack can be more or less paralyzed by a system of measures worked out by Soviet military science. . . ." An aggressor attacks first and thereby gains the advantage of surprise, but "the action of this law can also be neutralized" by good preparations, particularly in air defense and intelligence. It is a law that strategic victory is won not by a single blow but by the development of a series of blows, but "perhaps in certain conditions and situations it will even be possible to win a strategic operation without recourse to consecutive operations."

All these statements are in the pragmatic spirit of Clause-witz, who is condemned by Talenskii as "idealistic." Gone is the old refrain that the Soviet Union is bound to win wars because their outcome depends on permanently operating fac-tors such as morale and industrial potential. This sober evalua-tion of the risks and hazards of an uncertain future testifies to a growing Soviet self-confidence far more than the loud boast-ing of an earlier period. Now that the Russians feel strong, they are ready to face the future without wishful thinking. Talenskii's arguments imply a spirit of self-confidence without ever explicitly appealing to it.

It seems that Talenskii's confidence in Soviet strength and his realism about the effects of the new weapons helped him to break the mold of the "laws-of-war" framework without his being fully aware of how much he had weakened the older arguments. As we shall see shortly, some of his critics pounced on the fact that he had broken the older framework, but his viewpoint, with all its contradictions, was nevertheless gen-erally accepted.

Talenskii was, as far as can be ascertained, the first Soviet official to say that the permanently-operating-factors formula is not adequate as a law of war. Even without taking into con-sideration the complaints against his bold statement (as we shall do shortly), it is obvious that Talenskii seriously ques-tioned whether the strategy demanded by this formula was the only possible one for the Soviet Union.

In 1953 Russia did not have to expect that she would once again fight a numerically inferior but better-equipped and more skillful opponent with contiguous land borders. It seemed more likely that the opponent of the future would be separated from her by an expanse of ocean. This Talenskii specifically pointed out, suggesting that the strength of the rival "forces in being" at the outset of the war might not be significantly disparate. This would apply more to the air forces, of course, than to the ground forces. Therefore it was neither necessary nor sensible to concentrate only on the strategy of wearing down the enemy over a long period by superior weight of numbers. Hence the concentration of attention on the armed conflict.

Talenskii also specifically raised the possibility (not the probability) that the armed conflict might not be extended, and that under certain conditions the decision could be reached in a short time. Later writings made it clear that this was a reference to nuclear weapons. Talenskii implied a relationship between surprise and the possibility of a war being decided in a short time, when he wrote that the effects of surprise, great as they potentially were, could be more or less paralyzed by suitable active air defense and intelligence. When the connections that he fails to make are made, his position would be this: given the use of nuclear weapons, a surprise strike against an opponent who has not adopted the proper measures in advance may be decisive. Such a strike against the Soviet Union is possible but not likely, since Russian leaders know what the proper measures are.

Talenskii struck out against the statement often made that the Soviet Union, as a socialist country, was subject to laws of war different from those applying to capitalist countries. This statement had some significance in the context of the kind of war that the Russians had fought with the Germans. The argument derived from it fell into two parts, of which the first part was better grounded than the second. The first part of the argument was that the superior economic organization of the Soviet system (a euphemism for the ruthless pressure on civilians) made it possible for Soviet industry to convert to a war footing more quickly and completely than the industry of capitalist countries. In the Russian view, this generalization held in a comparison of German and Russian mobilization, and presumably would hold in any future comparison of American and Russian war mobilization. The second part of the argument was that civilian morale was much better in socialist countries than in capitalist. The Russo-German conflict hardly furnished unequivocal proof of this assertion. In fact a good case can be made for the belief that German morale on the whole was better than Soviet, while it is very difficult to make a case for the contrary. Every government, of course, is constrained to assert publicly that its country's morale is superior to the enemy's.

By insisting that the same laws of warfare applied to both capitalist and socialist states, Talenskii questioned the inevitability of Soviet superiority in mobilization and in morale. To minimize these "permanently operating factors" is to imply that the outcome of wars may be determined by the forces in being at the outset. Talenskii, however, granted only that the outcome might be so decided in an exceptional case. By making the victorious surprise attack an exception to the rule, Talenskii returned by implication to the position that he had just abandoned, namely, that the permanently operating factors are of fundamental importance in deciding the outcome of wars. In effect what he has done is to challenge the determining role of the permanently operating factors while leaving open the question as to how much weight should be added to the factors of surprise and "forces in being." In challenging the old formula he clearly abandoned the tenet that the strategy of attrition is the only strategy open to the Soviet Union.

The last point on which Talenskii overtly diverged from the standard formula was his emphasis on the skillfulness of commanders. While recognizing the paramount importance of basic, "objective" factors, he cautioned against neglecting the "subjective" factors, in particular the skill of the commanders. He assigned much more importance to the qualities of the individual general than had been customary. From one point of view this may have been a foretaste of the later campaign to deny Stalin the exclusive credit for winning the war and to give the generals their proper due. At the same time, however, Talenskii was justifying his own emphasis on the armed conflict. If the battle is the thing, the general must be more than a pawn of his superiors.

The critical discussion aroused by Talenskii's article shows that his professional readers realized whither his ideas were tending. There can be no doubt that many felt Talenskii's formulations to be both radical and pernicious. The feeling that Talenskii threatened to subvert the whole framework of accepted thinking was expressed in several different ways. One line of rebuttal was the flat assertion that military science did not require the kind of basic law that Talenskii sought to frame for the first time in the Soviet Union. A Colonel M. Shvarev characterized the attempt to find a law of war as contrived and artificial. Every science did not need to have its basic law: "For military practitioners and theoreticians what is important above all are those factors determining final success in war. The thesis on the permanently operating factors gives an exhaustive answer to this question."[11]

A Major Balashov sought to demonstrate the futility of the search for a basic law of military science. There could be no special law for the "armed conflict"; the only basic law was the general one governing the development of society.[12]

Not only majors and colonels contended that the proposition on the permanently acting factors was the be-all and end-all of Soviet military doctrine; no less a personage than Marshal Vasilevskii, in an article written for the widely circulated *Red Star* in February, 1954, asserted that Soviet military science "is based on the permanently acting factors determining the fate of a war. . . ."[13] In May of the same year, Vasilevskii reiterated his stand that the old formula was adequate by quoting Stalin approvingly to the effect that "the outcome of a war is determined not by transitory factors but by the permanently operating factors."[14]

Other statements in the open press made it clear that Talenskii did not represent official opinion when he described the permanently-operating-factors formula as insufficient. Colonel V. Petrov, in an article that appeared in a collection on Soviet military science, argued that the formula was adequate for both wartime and preparation for war. The following excerpts from his article convey its tone:

> The proposition on the permanently operating factors gives an exhaustive, scientific answer to one of the most important questions of military science, to the question of which of the numerous and varied factors influencing the course and outcome of a war are the chief and decisive and which are transitory and temporary. . . .

These transitory factors could have a positive influence on the course of the whole war only if they rested on a secured superiority over the opponent in the permanently operating factors. . . .

An investigation of the role of the permanently operating factors in the Great Fatherland War reveals the wisdom and genius-like prophetic power of our Communist Party, which long before the war with its profound comprehension of the rules governing contemporary war had shown ceaseless concern for the comprehensive strengthening of the Soviet rear and for the broad expansion of our economic, politico-moral, and military potentialities. . . .

This proposition [on the permanently operating factors] shows the people of the U.S.S.R. and the toilers of the countries of the people's democracies the only correct and reliable way to the further strengthening of their defensive capability.[15]

The collection of articles in which these words appeared was published by the Ministry of Defense. Talenskii's views, then, did not at this time represent ordinary official opinion, but at some later point they were adopted as the official view.

The first publicly expressed modification of the permanently-operating-factors formula occurred in an article written by General Rotmistrov in March, 1955. Rotmistrov did not reject the formula out of hand. It would have been unreasonable to insist that the country with the larger, better-equipped, better-led forces, with better morale, and a better industrial base did not enjoy great advantages. Rotmistrov repeated, as many had done before him, that superiority in the permanently operating factors was a condition of victory. His assault was on the narrow and unimaginative use of this formula that precluded further thought about the conditions of victory. The victims of his scorn were M. Taranchuk and V. Petrov, whose words were quoted above.

Rotmistrov complained about Petrov's conclusion, on the basis of some "verbose talk about the permanently operating factors," that surprise attack "had no significance."[16] Rotmistrov felt that a surprise attack might even have decisive significance.

He quarreled with complacent reliance on the permanently operating factors and with the futile argument that the Soviet Union would win wars because she would win wars.

Rotmistrov objected to the writers who said, in effect, that

> . . . only Soviet military science understands the permanently operating factors of war, and that this is not the case for bourgeois military science. And, if this is so, we can be untroubled: we, they [Taranchuk and Petrov] say, understand the permanently operating factors, the socialist system permits us to secure a lasting superiority in them, and this will have its results in any war.

> It is impossible to agree with this of course. . . .

> In the past many strategists in the pursuit of victory also took into account the permanently operating factors as determining the outcome of war to a greater or lesser extent. . . .

> M. Taranchuk takes the well known and incontrovertible position that he who seeks to attain victory using temporary factors and not taking into account permanently acting factors suffers defeat. But who is that "he"? There are no military leaders, as there were none in the past, who do not take into account the stability of the rear, the quantity and quality of divisions, the weapons of the armies, and the organizational abilities of the leaders on the staff level.[17]

Rotmistrov, however, agreed that there was a difference between bourgeois military science and Soviet military science. First, Soviet military science understood the laws of warfare and military affairs better; second, only bourgeois military science furthered the goals of the capitalist system:

> In all this, indubitably, one has to see the basic difference between Soviet military science and bourgeois military science. But what is not understandable is that M. Taranchuk when he comes to the examination of the question of the permanently operating factors suddenly asserts that it is precisely on the question of these factors that "the radical difference between Soviet military science and bourgeois

military science is expressed." Such an assertion cannot but leave the reader at a loss.[18]

Rotmistrov apparently believed that the permanently-operating-factors formula, while sound enough in general, had proved to be more of a hindrance than a help in dealing with the vital question of surprise attack with the employment of nuclear weapons.

The inadequacy of the formula was proclaimed even more unequivocally by the editors of *Military Thought* in the article that concluded the discussion of Talenskii's article:

> Can one really accept the adequacy of an argument such as the following? "For military theoreticians and practitioners it is most important to know what factors determine the final outcome of the war; inasmuch as the thesis on the permanently operating factors determining the fate of a war gives an exhaustive answer to this question, it is not necessary 'to discover' a basic law of military science."

> It is easy to see that in the best case this avoids a solution of the problem and is not a solution, and in the worst case it is a voluntary or involuntary withdrawal from the position of Marxist materialism. Indeed, this style of analysis can lead one unwittingly to conclude that there is neither "necessity" for a basic law of military science nor for other laws, general and special, since in every general and particular case it will be permissible to substitute some factors or other for a law, saying each time that the law is not important. . . .

> The assertion was also made that, since the thesis on the permanently operating factors determining the fate of a war "helps the leading organs of our society to mobilize the forces of the people for the solution of the basic problems on which the course and outcome of the war depends, military science does not need a basic law and there is no such thing in nature." What! The understanding of the objective laws of the armed conflict makes more difficult rather than helps the leading organs of our society to mobilize the forces of the people for the solution of the basic problems on which the course and outcome of war depends?[19]

In writing these lines the editors of *Military Thought* gave official approval to the position that Stalin's permanently-operating-factors formula did not meet present-day requirements. In reducing the importance of Stalin's formula the editors referred to it merely as "some factors or other" that tended to obscure the true laws of military science. The underlying tendency of Talenskii's argument was in the direction of considering each case on its merits, and the editors saw in that approach the royal road to an "objective" law of war. In this context the term "objective" has shifted its meaning and come closer to Western usage.

The editors of *Military Thought* did not admit specifically that the permanently-operating-factors formula had hitherto been treated as the basic law of Soviet military science. They simply said that the formula was no substitute for such a law. In other words, the true law was to be found outside the Stalinist frame of reference.

After April, 1955, the Soviet press carried but a few scattered references to the permanently operating factors and in 1956 none at all. In 1957 the old formula concerning these factors was specifically proscribed as leading to rigidity and complacency. Reviewers writing in *Red Star* objected to a book by P. A. Chuvikov that repeated "the old propositions."* The tone of condemnation was that customarily reserved for effete doctrine:

> In a number of cases, he [the author] almost literally repeats old propositions which at the present time are treated differently in the Soviet military-theoretical literature. . . . Thus, questions concerning the conditions for the attainment of success in modern war are presented in the book in the old way, as the question of the five permanently operating factors. It would have been more correct to talk about the moral-political, economic, and military factors and seek a comprehensive elucidation of their place in securing victory in war. . . .

* By the time a book is published, of course, it may reflect viewpoints that are already outdated.

The question of the role of such a factor as surprise is treated in a one-sided fashion in the book. The book talks about the growing role and potentialities of surprise in modern war but does not indicate that it obligates the Soviet military cadres to [accomplish] much in their practical work of perfecting the military readiness of our troops.

The critics also took the hapless writer to task for following Stalin in translating the rules of political struggle to military affairs. In political life, they said, it may be necessary to stick to a course of action once adopted, but the execution of a military plan "cannot but change in dependence on the actual situation."[20]

A month later another writer in *Red Star*, addressing students and teachers of Marxian theory, was for improving on Lenin's dicta as well as Stalin's:

We have had attempts to reduce all military theory to I. V. Stalin's propositions on the permanently operating factors determining the course and outcome of war. This proposition essentially reproduces Lenin's ideas on the conditions of victory over aggressors. However, it does not completely exhaust the question of the factors determining the course and outcome of modern war. It would be possible for example, to show that it does not include such important factors as the preparation of troops, their organization, the military art, the state of the military theory of the warring armies, and others. It is impossible also not to note that in present conditions the significance of the surprise factor has grown.

Basing itself on the unshakable foundation of Marxism-Leninism, Soviet military science makes a searching generalization of the experience of past wars and the latest developments for the preparedness of the Soviet Armed Forces.[21]

In 1953 Talenskii had stated that the permanently-operating-factors formula was correct but not exhaustive; three years later it was officially rejected as old fashioned. Dismissing the Stalin formula was a prerequisite for the re-examination of the problems of war in the nuclear age. The next important step, taken by Talenskii, was the argument that the laws of war were the same for both contending sides. Here, of course, he was striking directly at the comforting theory that a socialist society at war with a capitalist society must win because, being socialist, its cause alone is just and imparts high morale to its citizens; because it mobilizes more efficiently; and because it better understands the laws of war.

It is natural to insist that victory in war will somehow be a consequence of the very character of one's society. Naturally one does not go about voicing fears of defeat. But when a litany of inevitable victory prevents one from taking the necessary steps to avoid defeat, it is time to call a halt.

By insisting that the laws of war were essentially the same for both sides, Talenskii focused attention on the battle, "the armed conflict," and made it more difficult for the Soviet Sir Galahad to say:

> My strength is as the strength of ten,
> Because my heart is pure.

Talenskii's argument that the armed conflict was subject to its own laws, and not to social laws that differed in different societies, aroused the most violent objections. Talenskii was clearly felt to be striking at the *mystique* that insisted that the Soviet Union would win any war she fought because she was bound to do so. As one Soviet officer wrote:

> The conditions of socialist and capitalist society are qualitatively different and the objective laws of military science, which are the expression of these conditions, must also be different. . . .[22]

Colonel V. Vronin objected to the concept of a general law for war applicable to both socialist and capitalist states. Only a socialist government, he argued, could really transform a national economy to a war basis. Talenskii spoke of victory achieved by consecutive blows, growing in strength. Germany's blows had diminished in strength, partially because of the anarchy of production in capitalist countries, and because the popular masses could not be made to wage an extended war that was not in their interests. Germany, therefore, was unable to employ Talenskii's formula for victory because she was a capitalist state. It followed that there were special rules for each side in an armed conflict between socialist and capitalist governments.[23]

Colonel R. Gusakov also gave reasons for the unacceptability of a universal law of armed conflict.[24] Leninism taught that the goals of the warmakers influence the course of the war: "One of the immutable objective laws of the conduct of war is that a just war furthers in the highest degree the development of the military art and an unjust war hampers it."[25] That is why the Germans followed stereotyped tactics.

Others adopted the same line of criticism. Their arguments boiled down to the assertion that in the nature of things the same laws of warfare could not be applied to different social systems. Colonel A. Kapralov carried the argument against Talenskii to its ultimate: "The law of victory formulated by Talenskii differs very little in principle from the well-known theories of bourgeois military theoreticians such as Douhet, who asserted in his time that victory in modern war could be attained by crushing aerial blows, and Fuller and many others who sought to find the means of victory beforehand [that is, in the forces in being at the outset]."[26] It is a measure of the emotions that Talenskii aroused in his opponents that they likened him to a Douhet or a Fuller. This was fully equivalent to calling an American general officer a communist.

Some of his critics, mostly younger men nurtured in the Soviet system, were quite willing to accept that there could be a basic law of war valid for all social systems, but they insisted that there must also be special laws applicable in different degrees and ways to the capitalist and socialist systems. Colonel Chalik argued that there were universal laws governing war as a social phenomenon, its outbreak, development, and outcome; but that the attitude of the popular masses in a capitalist society toward war belonged to a special law of war applicable only to capitalist society.[27] Although Chalik was willing to accept the existence of a universal law of war, he still wanted the Soviet Union to be in a special category with better prospects than any potential capitalist enemy.

The editors of *Military Thought*, in the article that summed up the doctrinal discussion and laid down the new line, took Talenskii's side: "One cannot consider as well founded the assertion of some participants in the discussion that the recognition of the 'generality' of objective laws is incorrect and unacceptable since it supposedly would lead to the denial of the difference in principle between Soviet and bourgeois military science. . . ."[28] The editors of the magazine agreed, however, that capitalist military scientists could not understand and interpret the laws of science as well as Marxists and that a country waging a just war was superior in morale to a country waging an unjust war; they even claimed invincibility for a people conducting a "war in the interests of their socialist Motherland."[29] Unquestionably, two military sciences exist, they said, but this "does not demonstrate the existence of two different kinds of objective laws."[30]

Upon first examination the controversy about a general objective law of war seems futile. The purpose of all this theorizing was to arrive at some satisfactory picture of the war of the future and, as a consequence, to make the proper military dispositions to wage the war to the best possible effect, if they did not actually deter its outbreak altogether. However similar the military doctrine and the outlook of two warring states, the differences between their social systems would be reflected in diverging reactions to attack and recovery. Did it really make any difference whether the socialist protagonist believed that there was a universal law of war governing the armed conflict or a separate body of law for each society participating in the armed conflict?

The Soviet problem was not simply one of developing a more rigorous mathematical and scientific analysis. In the past the grand strategy of wars has not been worked out with slide rules. Although rigorous scientific methods had become increasingly necessary for planning particular segments of war activity, the greater complexity of warfare demanded sound subjective judgment as much as ever. Rigid procedures could not deal with imponderables such as the adaptation of habits and practices suited to a tried weapon system to systems yet untested in combat. Sound judgment depended on more than comprehensive information and close reasoning; an essential component was detachment, a state of mind difficult to attain when one's firmest prejudices were called in question. Before 1953 one of the most deeply rooted Soviet prejudices was that socialist and capitalist states operated under different sets of social laws. War was a social phenomenon. Therefore a universal law of warfare could not exist. These views were incompatible with the detachment that must enter into reliable militar calculations. After 1953 a spirit of genuine objectivity began to invade Soviet military writings and made possible a rapid advance toward the recognition that all societies are affected by the same laws of warfare.

How did the changing Soviet outlook affect views on the significance of nuclear weapons in surprise attack? It was quite clear, especially after the American hydrogen bomb tests of March, 1952, that the physical effects of nuclear weapons were vastly greater than those of the weapons available to, say, the Germans in 1941. The Russians naturally wanted to know what these effects meant for the future of warfare.

The believers in two separate laws governing the military behavior of two contending societies inevitably stressed the difference in the responses of the societies to the effects of these weapons. The Soviet analyst, intent on the imperative of victory, pointed to the high level of Soviet morale, which derived from the superiority of Soviet society and from the feeling of fighting for the right; to the superior endurance and performance of the Soviet people in adversity; to the more rational organization of Soviet society and its ability to mobilize faster and more thoroughly than the capitalists. For these and many similar reasons the Soviet Union could sustain a surprise nuclear attack better than the capitalists and would win any war that began with such an attack. It was the old Soviet theme: we will win because it is in the nature of things.

The exponents of a universal law of the armed conflict argued quite differently. They accepted that the Soviet Union was a superior society and that its prospects in war were therefore brighter, but they refused to concede that the outcome of the armed conflict would be determined by such considerations. If other things were equal, the side with the larger forces would win the war; if other things were equal, the side with the superior morale might well have a determining advantage; under favorable conditions a surprise attack employing nuclear weapons might be decisive. These views were clearly incompatible with the proposition that separate social laws determine the fate of contrasting societies, for these statements applied equally to all societies.

A group of Talenskii's critics perceived that his concept of the content of military science differed greatly from the prevalent one and took issue with him in very sharp language. Colonel A. Pshenichkin thought it impermissible to ignore the social and political aspects of war as Talenskii did. He therefore categorically opposed limiting military science to the problems of the armed conflict. Such circumscription of the subject would contradict "the Marxist-Leninist teachings on war and the army."[31] Colonel S. Pekarskii viewed this limitation as "the intrusion of idealism into military science," which "should concern itself simultaneously with all the laws of war, both the social-political and those of a special character, since they are all indivisible from each other."[32] Colonel M. Marienko held a similar opinion:

> Military science should investigate the rules of war not only as the armed conflict but also the rules of war as a social phenomenon (the rules of the social-political aspects of war) and not be limited to a passive recital of these rules in the form given by Marxist-Leninist science. But this means that General N. Talenskii's proposition on what the subject matter of military science should be and his definition of the military science evoke doubts.[33]

Colonel R. Zverev was less restrained in his criticism. Talenskii, he wrote, views

. . . the armed conflict apart from its dialectical inter-
dependence with the social and political aspect of wars,
and this leads to a non-Marxist, non-scientific point of view
on the nature and character of war, and on the nature and
character of the rules of military science, and reduces military science to a mere military art. . . .

He [Talenskii] thinks that the armed conflict exists in general without a human being as the representative of a definite social structure, of definite classes, that a bare military
science exists, a naked strategy, a naked operational art, a
naked tactics, naked, eternal military rules which are the
same for all. Such things do not exist in nature. This attempt to "work out" "a pure military science, one and the
same for all times and peoples" is idealistic in essence and
should be decisively rejected.[34]

Colonel R. Gusakov criticized Talenskii along much the
same lines:

Following Marx and Engels, Lenin always viewed the
armed conflict in its interconnections with social and political questions. He placed the revolution in the military art
in direct dependence on revolution. The most striking
demonstration of the influence of revolution on the military art was the great October Revolution . . . which created
immeasurably more profound and greater transformations
in military affairs than did the bourgeois revolution. Therefore in investigating the laws of military science the question of the connection of science with economics and
politics should occupy a most prominent place. In the
article under review it obviously occupies a most modest
role.[35]

Talenskii also had defenders for his attempt to focus military thinking on the battle. Colonel G. Sapozhkov wrote that
military science should certainly take into account the difference in economic potential and morale between the contending
sides, but this was the proper concern of the Communist Party
and the Soviet Government: "It is impossible to convert military science into a science without boundaries and to set inappropriate tasks for it."[36]

Colonel E. Chalik, who it will be remembered differed with Talenskii on some points, agreed with him as to the appropriate content of military science. While recognizing completely the influence of economic, social, and moral factors on Soviet military prospects, Chalik found it impossible to agree with "some comrades who seek to reduce Soviet military science to a popularization of these factors. This leads to a diminution of the role of the military art." Military science properly took into account questions of morale and the economies of warring countries, but "subordinated all this to the chief and basic thing—the elaboration and perfection of the military art on the basis of Marxist-Leninist teachings." The tasks of strengthening the government economically and politically and of building up the armed forces were "the function of the government and its apparatus as a whole."[37]

On the subject of the content of military science the editors of *Military Thought*, in their resolution of the discussion, took Talenskii's side of the argument without any equivocation. They criticized those participants in the discussion who included too much within the bounds of military science. They could not agree to the inclusion of "the whole complex of questions of war as a social and historical phenomenon." "Some partisans of this [inclusive] view even assert that military science includes the Marxist-Leninist teachings on war and the army, which go into the question of the origin and nature of wars as a continuation of politics. Such an expanded conception of the subject matter of military science cannot be recognized as correct." Lenin, wrote the editors of the journal, described the armed uprising as a special kind of struggle with special laws of its own. Special laws are all the more applicable to a war between governments:

> The subject of military science is above all the investigation of these very special laws of . . . the armed conflict. But the expanded interpretation of the subject matter of military science leads away from the resolution of its specific tasks. . . . Therefore to include in military science questions going beyond the limits of its competence means to doom military science as a special branch of knowledge.

Military science, however, properly has to take into account matters other than the strictly military:

> Military science in investigating the cause of the armed conflict and the methods of its conduct does not disengage itself from the economic, moral, and political factors, but examines them and studies them in the interests of the attainment of victory in the armed conflict and in the interests of the military art.

Naturally an advanced military science can only be created on the basis of Marxist-Leninist theory.

The absence of proper attention to the problem of basic doctrine, the editors continued, has been a serious deficiency of Soviet military science. The true basic law should express that aspect of the armed struggle which relates directly to military operations, as well as to morale and politics. Talenskii's formula is to be recommended in that it comes close to a correct understanding of the subject matter of military science, since it includes the particular and specific matters peculiar to the armed conflict. Some topics examined by Talenskii, however, require explanation or support; for example, "the essence of consecutive blows growing in force, the place in war of other combinations of blows or other means of pursuing the armed conflict, the relationship of the various factors determining the fate of war. . . ."

Perhaps as revolutionary as any statement in the summing up was the following:

> The editors [of *Military Thought*] suggest that it is not yet possible to propound any final and definite formulation of the basic law.[38]

This matter-of-fact recognition that there was no guiding dictum, no last word, contrasted sharply with the older atmosphere in which it was assumed that everything fundamental was known.

In April, 1955, when the editors analyzed the results of the discussion opened by Talenskii and gave their own views, official Soviet ideas about the nature of war and the functions of military science had already changed radically. The editorial comment, as the above quotations show, was in sharp contrast to the official line of 1951, when the *Great Soviet Encyclopedia* started its article on military science with the following four paragraphs:

> MILITARY SCIENCE is the system of knowledge about the rules governing warfare, the methods of preparing for it, and its conduct in a given historical situation. Military science encompasses the *military art* [q.v.], the questions of the organization and preparation of the armed forces, and the questions of the economic and morale potentialities of one's own country and that of the opponent.
>
> The rules governing war arise from the rules governing the development of class society; therefore military science is a social science. Military science assumed those views, ideas, and concepts which comprise the military ideology of a given class. The contemporary military science of the imperialist governments is identified in the best case with the military art and being basically reactionary serves the interest of the bourgeoisie and their aggressive aspirations. Soviet military science serves the interests of the Soviet people and is a powerful weapon of the socialist government and its Armed Forces.
>
> Bourgeois military science, which expresses the idealistic and metaphysical views of the bourgeois military ideologists and which believes in the existence of eternal and unchanging principles of war, is incapable of discovering the rules governing it and correctly determining the content of true military science. . . .
>
> The only real military science is Soviet military science, since it is built on the firm foundation of Marxism-Leninism and relies on the Leninist-Stalinist teachings on war.[39]

By 1955, the whole atmosphere had changed. No longer were the permanently operating factors the sacred limits of Soviet military thinking. No longer did a statement on the laws of war have to include the conclusion that the Soviet Union would win wars because it possessed a more advanced political system. No longer did every statement about capitalist military science have to say it was bankrupt because it was only interested in the battle itself. For the first time Soviet military thinkers could openly discuss the possibility of the defeat of the Soviet Union. That country was now strong enough militarily, and conscious enough of her strength, to consider the chances of defeat in an objective way. Her leaders had lost the need to comfort themselves by repeating the formula: we will win because we are we.

NOTES

1. Clark W. Tinch, "Quasi-war between Japan and the U.S.S.R., 1937-1939," *World Politics,* January, 1951, pp. 174-199.
2. N. Galay, "The Problem of Quantity and Quality in the Soviet Armed Forces," *Bulletin,* Institute for the Study of the U.S.S.R., Vol. 3, No. 10, October, 1956, pp. 3-14. An excellent treatment of this point.
3. "Voennoe iskusstvo" ("The Military Art"), *Bol'shaia Sovetskaia Entsiklopediia (Great Soviet Encyclopedia),* 2d ed., Vol. 8, Leningrad, 1951, p. 439.
4. "Voennaia nauka" ("Military Science"), *Bol'shaia Sovetskaia Entsiklopediia,* 2d ed., Vol. 8, Leningrad, 1951, p. 409.
5. *Ibid.,* p. 410.
6. Colonel I. V. Maryganov, *Peredovoi kharakter sovetskoi voennoi nauki (The Advanced Character of Soviet Military Science),* Moscow, 1953, p. 37.
7. See Nathan Leites, *A Study of Bolshevism,* The Free Press, Glencoe, Illinois, 1953, pp. 399-404.
8. Maryganov, *op. cit.,* pp. 19, 20.
9. N. Galay, "New Trends in Soviet Military Doctrine," *Bulletin,* Institute for the Study of the U.S.S.R., Vol. 3, No. 6, June, 1956, pp. 2-12, contains an account of the article and of one critique of the article.
10. I. Stalin, *Ekonomicheskie problemy sotsializma v SSSR (Economic Problems of Socialism in the U.S.S.R.),* Moscow, 1952, pp. 10, 11, 15, and 24; Leo Gruliow (ed.), *Current Soviet Policies,* New York, 1953, pp. 2, 3. This is a convenient translation, from which the present one differs only in minor details.
11. "On the Question of the Character of the Laws of Military Science," *Voennaia mysl' (Military Thought),* No. 11, November, 1954, p. 30. Review of comments on Major General N. Talenskii's article "On the Question of the Character of the Laws of Military Science," *Voennaia mysl',* No. 9, 1953.
12. *Ibid.*
13. Marshal of the Soviet Union A. Vasilevskii, "On Guard over the Security of Our Soviet Motherland," *Red Star,* February 23, 1954. (An exception to the general practice of citing Soviet publications in the Russian will be made for the well-known *Red Star.*)

14. Marshal of the Soviet Union A. Vasilevskii, "The Great Lesson of History," *Red Star*, May 7, 1954.

15. Colonel V. Petrov, "On the Permanently Operating Factors, Determining the Fate of a War," in *O sovetskoi voennoi nauke (On Soviet Military Science)*, Moscow, 1954, pp. 96-97. Delivered to the printer on April 25, 1954; galleys approved by the censor on June 30, 1954.

16. Tank Marshal P. Rotmistrov, "For Creative Examination of the Questions of Soviet Military Science," *Red Star*, March 24, 1955.

17. *Ibid.*

18. *Ibid.*

19. "On the Results of the Discussion on the Character of the Laws of Military Science," *Voennaia mysl'*, No. 4, April, 1955, p. 20.

20. Colonel V. Gorynin, Candidate in the Philosophical Sciences, Colonel P. Derevianko, Candidate in the Historical Sciences, Colonel V. Seregin, Candidate in the Historical Sciences, "Inadequacies of a Book on an Important Subject," *Red Star*, February 19, 1957.

21. Colonel N. Baz', "V. I. Lenin on the Basic Factors Determining the Course and Outcome of War," *Red Star*, March 6, 1957.

22. "On the Question of the Character of the Laws of Military Science," *Voennaia mysl'*, No. 11, November, 1954, p. 38.

23. *Ibid.*, p. 40.

24. Colonel R. Gusakov, "A One-sided Approach to the Study of the Laws of the Armed Conflict," *Voennaia mysl'*, No. 9, September, 1954, pp. 33-36.

25. *Ibid.*, p. 35.

26. "On the Question of the Character of the Laws of Military Science," *Voennaia mysl'*, No. 11, November, 1954, p. 39.

27. Colonel E. Chalik, "On the Question of the General and Special Laws of War," *Voennaia mysl'*, No. 9, September, 1954, pp. 26-32.

28. "On the Results of the Discussion of the Character of the Laws of Military Science," *Voennaia mysl'*, No. 4, April, 1955, p. 18.

29. *Ibid.*

30. *Ibid.*, p. 19.

31. "On the Question of the Character of the Laws of Military Science," *Voennaia mysl'*, November, 1954, p. 33.

32. *Ibid.*, p. 34.

33. *Ibid.*

34. *Ibid.*, pp. 33, 34.

35. Colonel R. Gusakov, "A One-sided Approach to the Study of the Laws of the Armed Conflict," *Voennaia mysl'*, September, 1954, p. 34.

36. "On the Question of the Character of the Laws of Military Science," *Voennaia mysl'*, November, 1954, p. 36.

37. Colonel E. Chalik, "On the Question of the General and Special Laws of War," *Voennaia mysl'*, September, 1954, p. 26.

38. The passages quoted and paraphrased are from "On the Results of the Discussion of the Character of the Laws of Military Science," *Voennaia mysl'*, April, 1955, pp. 16, 17, 20, and 21.

39. "Voennaia nauka" ("Military Science"), *Bol'shaia Sovetskaia Entsiklopediia*, 2d ed., Vol. 8, Leningrad, 1951, p. 406.

CHAPTER THREE

IS DETERRENCE RELIABLE?:
THE SOVIET VIEW

After the first employment of atomic weapons many Western commentators wrote that war had abolished itself because it had become too horrible. They knew full well that their predecessors had greeted other new weapons, such as high-explosive projectiles, with similar hopes, only to see those hopes dashed by wars of unprecedented severity. The destructiveness of nuclear weapons, however, seemed to promise that at last, war had become so fruitless that all must avoid it. This kind of comment was still, as in the past, a product of wishful thinking rather than of careful analysis.

Would the same writers have made statements about war having abolished itself if only the Soviet Union had possessed nuclear weapons? What they meant was that the United States would not use nuclear weapons to initiate war, and that no other country would risk starting a major war while the United States had a monopoly of atomic weapons. Western writers were saying in effect that the West was peacefully inclined, so that terrible weapons in its hands virtually assured the continuance of peace. To the Soviet leaders, however, capitalist states were aggressive by definition, and the more powerful their weapons, the more probable their aggression. This position was not immediately affected by the Soviet acquisition of nuclear capabilities. It is therefore all the more striking that soon after Stalin's death, when the Soviet Union possessed fission bombs but a poor delivery system, a few Soviet leaders cautiously expressed the hope that mutual possession of nuclear weapons made it reasonable to count on peace.

In his last published work Stalin had said that war was inevitable as long as imperialism existed, but he limited his whole discussion to the question of war among "imperialists." The popular peace movements might prevent a specific war, but sooner or later war among the capitalists was inevitable. Stalin clearly meant, and was read in the Soviet Union to mean, that as long as capitalism existed, war involving the Soviet Union was inevitable.[1]

This viewpoint did not long survive the death of the old dictator. At the end of 1953 and the beginning of 1954, the Chairman of the Council of Ministers, Malenkov, and other by no means unimportant persons advanced the idea that perhaps there would be peace in their time. Obviously the elevation of such a hope to the status of a prediction would have had far-reaching consequences for Soviet military posture, foreign policy, and domestic conditions. Shortly Malenkov's power declined and his optimistic views were proscribed. The official Soviet analysis became that of Khrushchev and others, who asserted that war initiated by the capitalists was always possible, and that the military posture, foreign policy, and domestic arrangements of the Soviet Union should be shaped accordingly. The dismissal of Malenkov from the premiership did not in itself guarantee the ascendancy of the less optimistic policy. As recently as June, 1957, it was necessary to demote Malenkov still further and charge him with having jeopardized Soviet security. The persistence of the rejected ideas makes it all the more important to understand their history.

For years before 1953 all Soviet writers had repeated the familiar theme that the natural aggressiveness of capitalism made war inevitable. This theme furnished the permanent background to all Soviet discussions on international politics. The premises of what we may call the Malenkov argument were initially stated by little-known persons. The first to make a change in the monotonous litany of Stalinism was an obscure writer, M. Gus.

Following the style required of Soviet writers who consciously depart from official doctrine, Gus started with a low bow to orthodoxy: Lenin made the great discovery that capitalism suffers from uneven development; as one capitalist nation outstrips others, the economic balance of all is upset; capitalism knows no way to right the balance without economic crises and war. Thus far Gus's doctrine was unexceptionable to the orthodox, since it had been propounded in almost the identical phrases thousands of times in the Soviet press. But only a taste cloyed by the endless repetition of this formula could have found Gus's next paragraph palatable:

> Experience has shown and proved that we are in a position to prevent war, and to paralyze the action of this law [of the inevitability of war]. As one bourgeois radio commentator expressed it, in previous years people looked at their calendars anxiously as the pages came nearer and nearer to August, the classic month for the beginning of world wars, but in 1953 for the first time people drew an easy breath in the certainty that such an obvious threat of war had been significantly reduced this year, and had considerably receded.[2]

Although Gus began by appealing to Lenin's authority, he went on to deny one of the latter's most important theoretical formulations, namely that capitalism inevitably breeds war. If the law of the inevitability of war could be paralyzed, in Gus's unprecedented phrase, one or both of two heterodox propositions had to be true: first, capitalism had changed its nature; second, now that war had become so destructive to all participants, the fear of its consequences outweighed the capitalists' aggressive propensities. The acceptance of either of these propositions meant a radical revision of the prevalent doctrine.

Other Soviet writers immediately apprehended the implications of Gus's remarks and refuted them in no uncertain terms. No less a personage than V. Kruzhkov, then chief of the Agitation and Propaganda Section of the Central Committee of the Communist Party, attacked Gus's theory but without mentioning him by name. Kruzhkov recalled Stalin's criticism of those Soviet philosophers, economists, and historians who wanted to formulate or create new laws. The incidence of such mistakes had declined, but it was still necessary to direct attention to them when they appeared. Talk about the possibility of paralyzing the laws of the development of capitalism was not Marxism-Leninism.[3]

Other writers differed with Gus's view but did not always mention his name.

Colonel G. Fedorov, writing in *Red Star* for January 6, after echoing Stalin's dictum that the popular masses could prevent a particular war or delay its outbreak, specifically reaffirmed the standard formulation that Gus had challenged. Fedorov said:

> In this connection it must never be forgotten that as long as capitalism exists wars are absolutely inevitable. Only with the destruction of the last system of exploitation— capitalism—will wars become impossible.[4]

Stalin had been satisfied with the epithet "inevitable," but Fedorov insisted that wars are "absolutely inevitable." Any informed Soviet reader who had seen Gus's original deviation from the old formula would realize that the redundant term "absolutely" pointedly contradicted the idea of the paralysis of this law.

Gus's thesis was refuted, in the journal that published it, by a V. Tereshkin, who accused Gus of taking a capricious attitude toward the laws governing the historical development of society. Tereshkin argued that even under the conditions prevailing since 1945 the law of the inevitability of war held true and would do so as long as capitalism existed. Only the destruction of capitalism could remove the inevitability of war. It was impossible to speak of the paralysis of a social law, although once a specific historical period had passed, the laws applicable to that period gave way to new ones:

> But, according to Gus, if a law cannot be destroyed then it can be, it seems, paralyzed and thus voided. But a paralyzed law is no longer a law; it is in the situation of a paralytic and cannot move. Either it is a law or not a law.[5]

Colonel Piatkin, writing for officers in *Military Thought,* without referring specifically to Gus, also declared that in contemporary conditions capitalism was still giving birth to wars and that the Leninist proposition on the inevitability of war had not lost its force. "Imperialism cannot live without force and bloody wars."[6]

In the traditional Bolshevik view, since a capitalist-made war was inevitable, the Soviet Union must be fully prepared for war. The problem was how best to prepare.

Gus, who probably had supporters in Soviet higher circles, also received some support from the other side of the Atlantic. The President of the United States himself, in an address to the United Nations on December 8, 1953, indicated that war might not be inevitable. President Eisenhower had insisted that the United States then had a great superiority in nuclear weapons, but even that was no guarantee against "fearful material damage." As consequences of a nuclear war he foresaw "the probability of civilization destroyed . . . and the condemnation of mankind to begin all over again the age-old struggle upward from savagery." Here indeed was an argument supporting the thesis that the United States would not initiate a war because it abhorred the consequences. Little more than a month after the President's speech his arguments were employed by an anonymous retired general writing in *Izvestiia,* the Malenkov organ. The general "agreed completely with the appraisal of the danger contained in present-day atomic weapons which was expressed by Eisenhower." This strongly suggested that Malenkov and his group stood behind Gus.

The article drew attention to the fact that American military theoreticians, commentators, journalists, and occasionally people in high positions had been in the habit of describing an easy atomic war against the Soviet Union, since they believed they had a monopoly of atomic weapons. Looking into the past for the source of this American attitude, the author first observed that there had been a time when great powers could participate in wars without subjecting their own territories to destruction and devastation. Great Britain was able to do this in the eighteenth and nineteenth centuries because the English

Channel was then an insuperable barrier. Even in the First World War Great Britain suffered air raids, and the Second World War demonstrated England's high vulnerability to air attack. The United States had hitherto benefited from a more favorable geographical position, but times were changing:

> The postwar development of the technical facilities of warfare has advanced so far that now the ocean is no longer a reliable protection against blows in war. The contemporary development of aviation, missiles, and the submarine fleet makes it possible to deal crushing blows across a distance of many thousands of kilometers. . . . Why, there are already appearing even in the American press sufficient admissions of the fact that the age of invulnerability of overseas states is a thing of the past.

The author of this article did not say specifically that new Soviet weapons made the United States home territory vulnerable or that this fact would deter the United States from making war; but for the first time the Soviet general reader was given such optimistic hints about new Soviet technical capabilities that he might make them the foundation for a theory of deterrence.[7]

On January 21, 1954, two days after the general in retirement published his article in *Izvestiia,* a fairly high-level person, P. N. Pospelov, a secretary of the Central Committee of the Communist Party, made a major speech on the thirtieth anniversary of Lenin's death, in which he said that the Soviet Union was seeking ways and means of employing atomic energy for the good of mankind and not for the "destruction of the peoples or the annihilation of world civilization." Rather indirectly Pospelov was echoing Eisenhower's warning of December 8 that a nuclear war would destroy both sides. He touched upon the possibility of deterring the United States from war, taking comfort from the technical and economic might of the Soviet Union, which had sobered some of the more vigorous capitalist proponents of a crusade against the Soviet Union.

On the whole, the speech was one of the mildest major Soviet speeches in years, without a single reference to the possibility of war. Furthermore, after the standard analysis of the contradictions of capitalism in its imperialist stage, the standard conclusion that war was inevitable was missing. Pospelov said merely that imperialism was vulnerable and the general crisis of capitalism was intensified by the widespread opposition to imperialist policies.[8]

In a speech on March 12 Premier Malenkov pointed out that it was not necessary for mankind to choose between a new world war and the so-called cold war. The Soviet government, he said, resolutely opposed the cold war, "for this policy is a policy of the preparation of a new world holocaust which, with the present means of warfare, means the destruction of world civilization."[9]

What Malenkov hinted in a few phrases was elaborately spelled out by Mikoian on the same day in a speech at Erevan, Armenia. The following paragraphs from the Erevan speech were not published in the Moscow press and appeared only in the Erevan party newspaper:

> The danger of war has receded to a large extent in connection with the fact that we now have not only the atomic but also the hydrogen bomb. These successes of the Soviet Union are striking evidences of the fact that our physics and chemistry have attained the heights of modern human knowledge and that the U.S.S.R. has reached tremendous industrial might.
>
> In the course of the last four or five years the ruling circles of the U.S.A. have declined negotiation with the Soviet Union, while trying to convince public opinion that these negotiations were useless and that it was not even worthwhile to initiate them. It is quite instructive therefore that after the Soviet Union made the hydrogen bomb, and it is not yet known whether the United States of America has such a bomb, the government of the United States of America proposed to the Soviet Union the initiation of negotiations on questions of atomic energy. We agree to this because our principle is to resolve all international questions by the method of negotiation. Such negotiations are in progress and the fact of these negotiations speaks for itself.

. . . Atomic and hydrogen weapons in the hands of the Soviet Union are a means for checking the aggressors and for waging peace.

If former wars in which the United States participated did not spread to the territory of the United States of America and not one of their factories, not one of their homes was destroyed, now the situation would seem to be different.

Hence a new tone in the American press:

If, not so long ago, the American bourgeois press printed insolent articles illustrated with maps showing Soviet cities as targets of atomic bombings, so now the very same newspapers and magazines describe the destruction of American cities in the future atomic war.[10]

The group of leaders who had less confidence in Soviet deterrent power was able to prevent the dissemination of Mikoian's arguments. Manifest differences of opinion on what would deter the United States from war indicated a major political dispute in the Soviet Union. The opponents of the policy of relying on deterrence were soon heard from. In conformity with the custom of minimizing public differences on policy they exercised restraint, but not at the cost of obscuring their position.

Small verbal clues were the first signals of what soon revealed itself as an important political debate. On New Year's Day, 1954, in a written reply to questions put by an American correspondent, Malenkov said that he knew of "no objective impediments to the improvement in the relations between the Soviet Union and the United States of America." On the same day, Voroshilov, the occupant of the honorary post of Chairman of the Presidium of the Supreme Soviet, said that the power of the Soviet Union had grown, "despite the designs of the external and internal enemies of socialism." Thus one major Soviet political figure denied that there were barriers to continuing peace with the United States, while another stressed the hostility of the capitalist enemies.

In March, 1954, a number of important Soviet figures in

unison contested the view that the Soviet acquisition of nuclear weapons had made the United States more pacific. On March 6, Khrushchev accused the reactionary capitalist forces of seeking a way out of their difficulties "by the preparation of a new war."[11] Voroshilov, speaking on March 10, said that despite Soviet economic and diplomatic successes "we live in encirclement all the same."[12] The phrase "capitalist encirclement," so often used by Stalin to justify domestic sacrifices, had become rare in the Soviet Union since Stalin's death. Kaganovich argued that the collapse of the colonial system made the imperialists seek a solution in war.[13] Bulganin also rejected the notion that Soviet strength forced peaceful ways on the United States when he dismissed as reckless the assumption that the imperialists "spend enormous material and financial resources on armaments only to frighten us. We cannot depend on the humanitarianism of the imperialists who, as life has shown, are capable of using any weapon of mass destruction."[14] Molotov and Khrushchev, in speeches on March 11, again stressed the aggressive intentions of the imperialist camp.[15]

These statements might have passed unnoticed but for the fact that only a few weeks later Malenkov retracted his optimistic views about the prospects for peace. The opposition to Malenkov was implicit rather than explicit. The latter possessed enough political power in the early part of 1954 to confine his opponents to oblique criticism. None took the obvious course of quoting Malenkov against himself by recalling that at the Nineteenth Party Congress in 1952 Malenkov had said that a new war would mean the collapse of capitalism. More recently he had spoken of the collapse of civilization, indicating a mutual compelling interest in the preservation of peace.

Malenkov's opponents apparently were able to prevent the public repetition of the phrase "destruction of world civilization." A careful search has uncovered only one instance to the contrary: on March 27, 1954, a Soviet domestic radio commentator said that a war in which atomic and hydrogen bombs were used meant colossal destruction: "More than that it threatens the very existence of human civilization."[16]

There were no more references to the destruction of world

civilization. Indeed the major party organ, *Kommunist,* pointedly rejected the Malenkov view without mentioning his name. The journal said that if the imperialists unleashed a third world war it would lead to "the complete destruction of that whole [capitalist] system."[17] A week later, on April 26, Malenkov reversed his March position by saying that a third world war "would inevitably lead to the collapse of the capitalist social system." This went beyond his statement of October, 1952, at the Nineteenth Party Congress, where he did not use the word "inevitably." Nevertheless the retraction of his recently adopted views seemed to contain a certain reservation. Malenkov did not specifically repudiate his words of a month before, and used the term "collapse," rather than "destruction of," to describe what would happen to capitalism. In doing so he avoided the exact words of the *Kommunist* editorial of the week before. Malenkov's description of how such a war could come about was also so phrased as to suggest reservations:

> If, however, the aggressive circles, relying on atomic weapons, should decide on madness and seek to test the strength and might of the Soviet Union, then it cannot be doubted that the aggressor would be crushed by that very weapon and that such an adventure would inevitably lead to the collapse of the capitalist social system.[18]

This was something less than a total abandonment of his earlier position. True, he no longer said that an American war against the Soviet Union would be deterred. Should Soviet deterrence fail, however, war would come because the enemy had decided on madness. This is a strange phrase; people rarely decide to be mad.

Malenkov had implied very strongly that peace was assured because all would lose by the destruction of civilization. Defeatism is the only epithet a good Bolshevik could apply to such an analysis. To suggest that the Bolsheviks could do nothing to win a war initiated by the capitalists was defeatist. To suggest that such a war was ruled out because the capitalists did not want it was complacency. In the years that followed, Soviet statements expressed increasing confidence that Soviet military strength would deter the United States from making war, but never again did any Soviet statement even imply that increasing military strength guaranteed peace to the Soviet Union. Rather, the tone adopted was that aggression had been restrained. Mikoian, speaking on the day of Malenkov's retraction, typified the dominant Soviet position when he argued that

> . . . the newest weapons—the atomic and hydrogen bombs —which are the means for unleashing wars in the hands of the aggressors, in our hands are the best means for safeguarding the peace because they tie the hands of those who would like to fight. . . . The aggressive forces are preparing a new world holocaust for the sake of profit, for the sake of the unlimited increase of their profits.[19]

Malenkov's revised formulation, to the effect that capitalism would collapse in a new war, was widely repeated. On May 3, for instance, a Soviet marshal in command of troops in the Ukraine used the formula.[20] Marshal Vasilevskii repeated the same phrases.[21] On June 12, Khrushchev in a speech in Prague used the very words of Malenkov.[22] Three days later Khrushchev apparently spoke extemporaneously when he slipped the following sentences into a speech at Prague:

> Comrades, I think that Hitler's last war should teach some people sense. Hitler also thought that the Soviet Union stood on feet of clay. But you and I, comrades, are alive while Hitler has already rotted. [Applause] If we remain strong, all those enemies who raise their hand against us will follow Hitler's example and that of Mussolini. Only the latter was hanged by his feet, and the former just killed himself.[23]

Although in the latter half of 1954 most important public figures continued to insist that a future war would mean the collapse of capitalism, the opposition had not been finally demolished. No one said as yet that Malenkov had been mistaken in declaring that the whole of civilization would be destroyed by a future war. The rejection of Malenkov's views continued to be indirect: it took the form of a flat statement

that only capitalism would collapse, and did not refer to Malenkov. Furthermore, Gus's radical statement on the possibility of
paralyzing laws continued to be attacked. For example, in a
book on military theory that went to press in October, 1954,
Colonel Piatkin attacked certain comrades who still talked
about destroying objective laws and paralyzing the action of
these laws. As an example he gave the attempt to show that the
law of the irregular economic development of capitalist countries could be paralyzed.[24] It will be recalled that this theory of
the irregular economic development of capitalist countries is
the basis of Lenin's proposition on the inevitability of war in
the imperialist stage of history.

It was not until the beginning of 1955, when it became
clear that Malenkov was about to be demoted, that the theory
of the possible permanent deterrence of the United States
was subjected to direct attack and officially designated as incorrect. The likelihood of war and the amount of Soviet defense
expenditures was an important issue in Malenkov's political
defeat, as the next chapter will demonstrate. It was not until
his dismissal from the premiership that the party magazine
Kommunist made a direct attack on his thesis concerning "the
destruction of world civilization." The magazine described the
thesis as essentially a capitalist trick to induce a false sense
of security. By saying that the existence of atomic weapons had
liquidated the danger of a new war, the capitalists were trying
to pose as saviors of peace while actually pursuing aggressive
purposes. In propagating this thesis of the destruction of world
civilization the capitalists were exploiting the sincere desire of
the peoples to maintain peace and prevent an atomic war:

> This circumstance explains to a considerable extent the
> fact that the thesis of "the destruction of world civiliza-
> tion" has been accepted on faith and disseminated to some
> extent even among those who are opposed to war and its
> imperialist instigators. A few, it turns out, have been in-
> clined to believe in the "absolute power" of contemporary
> weapons of mass destruction and have exaggerated the
> strength of the instigators of a new war. . . . These people
> were unable to discern promptly the real sense and purpose

of the fable about the "destruction of world civilization"
. . . and began to repeat it uncritically in their oral and
written statements.

> However grievous the consequences of atomic war might
> be, it must not be identified with "the destruction of world
> civilization." Such an identification willynilly brings grist
> to the American imperialist mill; it can create the incor-
> rect concept among the partisans of peace that, as they say,
> the atomic threat is such that the instigators of war will not
> dare to use their own bombs, since they will not decide to
> commit suicide. Such a concept blunts the vigilance of the
> people toward those who in the preparation of atomic war
> would like to take the peoples by surprise.

The article went on to explain that capitalism, not world
civilization, would be destroyed in a future atomic war. The
capitalists disseminated the slogan of the destruction of world
civilization, according to *Kommunist,* in order to spread fatalistic and pessimistic ideas among the masses so that they would
feel: "Why struggle? Nothing will change anyhow! The end
of the world is coming."[25]

As soon as Malenkov was deposed, then, his thesis of a
peace based on mutual deterrence was characterized as a capitalist slogan whose purpose was to lull vigilance and spread defeatism.

After Khrushchev and Bulganin installed themselves as
the leaders of the new government, they never altered their
basic position that war was always possible, although they
estimated the likelihood of war as circumstances required. From
February, 1955, when Malenkov fell, to the summit meeting
in July, the new leaders avoided stressing the likelihood of war;
they seemed compelled to represent themselves to their own
people as peacemakers. Yet immediately after Khrushchev's
acquisition of control in the Presidium of the Central Committee of the CPSU, it became official policy to acquire and
maintain the ability to deliver a pre-emptive attack against
the United States. The fantastically expensive preparations to
get in a first blow should an American attack appear probable
were only justifiable on the theory that war was possible. The

decision to be ready to make a pre-emptive attack if necessary was mentioned discreetly in several public statements by generals in April, 1955, but these were drowned out by the strident optimism that heralded the Geneva Summit Conference of July, 1955. Although before this conference the Soviet leaders expressed hopes for the further improvement of international relations and an abatement of the cold war, they never said that a complete mutual understanding was possible or that there was no more danger of war. Nor have they done so since that time.

At the end of 1955, during their trip to India and Burma, Khrushchev and Bulganin went further than ever before in describing the horrors of a nuclear war. They continued to eschew the theme of mutual destruction, although they came closer to it than they had done in the past. The Soviet version of the joint statement issued by the Russians and Indians at the end of the tour referred to "conditions leading to a devastating and ruinous world war." The Indian rendering of the same phrase referred to "conditions leading to the inconceivable disaster of another world war."[26] The Russian version of the text seems deliberately to stop short of Malenkov's phrase, "the destruction of world civilization." "Devastating" is the term ordinarily employed in Russian to describe the destruction of World War II; "inconceivable," the word employed by the Indians, suggests an unprecedented disaster such as the destruction of world civilization.

Bulganin seems to have made a slip and overstepped the agreed limit when he endorsed one of Nehru's statements:

> The Prime Minister of India . . . was absolutely right to demonstrate that coexistence was the only sensible possibility for all governments because in the opposite case there would be only one alternative—mutual destruction.[27]

The phrase "mutual destruction" is even closer to the idea of mutual deterrence than "the destruction of world civilization," and it is significant that the Soviet press made little mention of Bulganin's words.

Perhaps to correct any misapprehension, Bulganin stated

flatly on New Year's Day, 1956, that it was incorrect to say: "As long as East and West possess hydrogen bombs the possibility of thermonuclear war is automatically excluded." Such assertions, he said, only lull the vigilance of the fighters for peace, but "naturally the fact that in present conditions atomic and hydrogen weapons cannot be employed with impunity exerts a certain deterrent influence on those circles who want to unleash war employing the means of mass destruction."[28]

Since 1956 official Soviet spokesmen have continued to increase their estimates of how grievous the consequences of a nuclear war would be for the whole world. In a speech made on March 14, 1958, Khrushchev came very close to approving the hitherto proscribed formula that a nuclear war would mean the end of world civilization:

> A future war, if it breaks out despite the will of the peoples, threatens to be the most destructive of wars—a nuclear war. In addition to immediate destruction, the employment of nuclear weapons will poison the atmosphere with radioactive fall-out and this could lead to the annihilation of almost all life, especially in countries of small territory and high population density. There all will be literally wiped off the face of the earth.[29]

The difference between the phrases, "annihilation of almost all life" and "destruction of world civilization," seems trivial at first glance. The latter phrase, however, implies that a nuclear war is not worth fighting because victory would be meaningless; the former phrase, Khrushchev's, implies that enough could be saved to assure the ultimate victory of communism. One Soviet leader's failure to maintain this distinction was immediately corrected by the press. On April 26, 1958, Voroshilov referred, in a talk over the Moscow radio, to two wars of bloodshed unleashed by German militarism. "Today it would not be [merely a matter of] bloodshed," he continued, "but simple annihilation of all life on earth. We know what nuclear weapons are." These two sentences did not appear in the account published by *Pravda* on the following day.

A corollary of the growing admission that a new war would

be terribly destructive to all was the growing conviction that such a war would not occur. At the Party congress of February, 1956, Khrushchev significantly modified the Party doctrine concerning war in a world where "imperialism" still existed.

Khrushchev's report to the Twentieth Party Congress devoted several paragraphs to the possibility of preventing war. He recalled the Marxist-Leninist proposition that war was inevitable as long as imperialism existed, but unlike standard Soviet textual exegesis he put the formula into the perspective of time. The theory of the inevitability of war had been developed when imperialism controlled the whole world and when the political and social forces opposed to war were weak and poorly organized and could not make imperialism refrain from wars. These conditions had changed: imperialism had become weaker and socialism stronger. Although this proposition had been absolutely right in its time, the present position was radically different. Nevertheless, while the camp of socialism had become stronger, the basis for the outbreak of war continued to exist because imperialism still existed. The greatest vigilance was necessary, for as long as capitalism existed the reactionary forces would seek the course of military adventures and aggression and might try to unleash war. "But," he added in very non-Leninist fashion, "there is no fatal inevitability of wars."

There were many well-armed forces in the world, continued Khrushchev, which would not permit the imperialists to start a war, or would spoil their plans if they managed to start one. All these antiwar forces ought to be strong and ready. They should not weaken their efforts for the preservation of peace.[30]

The phrase "no fatal inevitability of wars" seems awkward. Khrushchev could simply have said that, while war always remained possible, the prospects for peace were better, but he and the Party had to tread warily. On the one hand the new regime needed peace and wanted the credit for making a virtue of necessity. If they continued to insist that war was inevitable as long as imperialistic capitalism existed, no one would believe that they meant what they said about "peaceful coexistence." On the other hand, since they actually believed that war was possible and became more likely as the Soviet Union relaxed its guard, they could not afford to imply that imperialism had changed its nature and no longer threatened war. Hence Khrushchev's somewhat equivocal optimism, as it appeared in the phrase "no fatal inevitability of wars."

Other major speakers at the Twentieth Party Congress more or less elaborated Khrushchev's ideas. Only Molotov and Kaganovich departed noticeably from them. Molotov, in expanding Khrushchev's new formula, avoided implying that Lenin's theory of the inevitability of war in the imperialist stage of history was outdated and needed qualification. He described the Leninist theory in terms of a conflict between the forces that wanted war and those that wanted peace. Now that the forces for peace had grown greatly, a real possibility of preventing war existed. Molotov stressed, however, that there could be no reliance on the ability of these forces to deter capitalism from initiating war:

> We should not minimize the danger of war nor surrender to the illusion that peace and a quiet life are assured in all circumstances. We must always be vigilant and watchfully follow the aggressive plans of the imperialists. We should not surrender to complacency as if it were possible to convince the imperialists with nice speeches and pacific plans.[31]

Like Molotov, Kaganovich avoided saying that Lenin's formula about the inevitability of war had become dated. In the increased strength of the forces opposing the imperialist pressure toward war he found the reason for "the contemporary balance of forces," which led to the conclusion "that there is no fatal inevitability of war. . . ." The prevention of war was possible, but only if several conditions were met. These were the exposure of imperialism's aggressive schemes, a fruitful struggle for disarmament, the strengthening of the defensive might of the Soviet Union, and the perfecting of her armed forces.[32]

During 1956 Soviet publicists pushed two themes: one, that nuclear weapons were equally dangerous to all, and two, that the West might still employ nuclear weapons in an aggressive surprise attack against the Soviet Union. For example, in a letter to Eisenhower in January, 1956, Bulganin wrote: "Everyone knows that the newest means for the conduct of war . . . place the people of all countries in an equally dangerous position. . . ."[33] The theme was repeated a week later. An article in *Pravda* talked of the reliance of the Americans, especially Generals White and Twining, on nuclear weapons whose destructive force was "equally dangerous for all." Generals should know this better than anybody else.[34]

In a reply to a letter by Bertrand Russell that had been published in *Pravda,* the Soviet academician Skobel'tsyn took issue with Russell's statement that the mutual possession of nuclear weapons created a balance of forces and therefore promised peace. Even Russell, wrote Skobel'tsyn, recognized that such a balance was precarious and therefore could readily be disturbed.[35]

General Pokrovskii, who was already prominent in his own country and who was soon to become well known abroad through some of his statements on the ballistic missile, made clear why Soviet official opinion regarded the nuclear balance as precarious. His explanation was so vivid and so unusual in its specificity that it merits quotation in full:

> No one can guarantee that there will not emerge in some country a reactionary military dictatorship similar to that of Nazi Germany which would recklessly disregard all considerations of the peoples' peace and security. In that event sudden atomic attack would become a by no means unlikely prospect. Of course it would not be left without retaliation. But there can be no doubt that technically nuclear weapons make it easier to unleash war than conventional weapons.

> Thus, if the development of conventional armaments in no way prevents the outbreak of war, there is still less reason to believe that nuclear weapons can play the role of peace preservers. Experts know only too well that the stockpiling of atomic weapons does not diminish but greatly aggravates the danger of another war.[36]

Throughout the first half of 1957 the general tone of the Soviet press conveyed the opinion that, although Soviet strength had greatly increased, the danger of war was still very real. A Soviet officer writing in *Red Star* pointed with obvious pleasure to the difference between General LeMay's present opinions and those of five years earlier. Five years ago General LeMay had said "that the United States could win a war against the Soviet Union without suffering serious losses." Now, however, LeMay was afraid to make such predictions because he understood that "Soviet atomic bombers could deal serious destruction" to America itself. Despite the greater realism of LeMay's present attitude, many important political and military figures in America still did not share this view and continued to seek means to destroy others while themselves remaining unharmed.[37]

In February, 1957, Foreign Minister Shepilov made a major foreign-policy speech in which he painted a more optimistic picture of the likelihood of peace, a picture which, as we shall seek to demonstrate later, was connected with his dismissal a few days afterwards. This speech was an aberration: the press in general and the military press in particular re-emphasized that there was no assurance of peace through deterrence. A writer in a philosophical journal, for example, explained that nuclear weapons had the double-edged effect of sobering the capitalists and simultaneously arousing in them baseless hopes for a new blitzkrieg. Therefore the danger of war would continue to exist.[38]

A military writer in *Red Star* pointed out forcefully that the absence of "absolute inevitability" did not imply the improbability of war. He seems to have been the first to draw public attention to the fact that recent Soviet propaganda had drawn too optimistic conclusions from Khrushchev's somewhat vague words at the Twentieth Party Congress:

> It is necessary, if even briefly, to note that some of our propagandists give a one-sided interpretation of the question of wars in the contemporary epoch. In explaining this proposition of the XXth Congress of the Communist Party of the Soviet Union they often concentrate chief attention on the question of the possibility of *preventing* wars in

contemporary historical conditions. And insofar as the possibility of the *outbreak* of new wars prepared by the imperialists is concerned—of this they speak in passing as if it were something secondary and insignificant. Such an approach to the question of wars in the contemporary epoch contradicts the very spirit of Soviet military ideology. What is basic for Soviet military ideology is the proposition of the XXth Congress of the Communist Party of the Soviet Union . . . that even now the economic basis for war exists and that the imperialists will seek to unleash war. Our chief attention should be devoted to that aspect of the question.[39]

The theme of the increasing likelihood of war was very prominent in the first few months of 1957. (The reasons for this will be explored in a subsequent chapter.) Khrushchev himself, in two interviews with foreigners, raised the specter of a war started by accident, a new theme. In an interview with Turner Catledge of *The New York Times* on May 10, 1957, Khrushchev implied that the chances for war were increasing with the continued accumulation of nuclear weapons:

In this connection it should be realized that, given the existence of atomic and hydrogen arms and given the existence of rocket technology and intercontinental missiles it is not to be excluded that a war can be unleashed as a result of some kind of fatal error, which will lead to untold tragedy for the peoples not only of our two countries but for the peoples of the whole world.

Expanding on this theme, Khrushchev asserted that some irresponsible American statesmen were pursuing an adventuristic policy:

It is one thing when a skilled acrobat balances on a tightrope. If he loses his balance and falls off only one person perishes. Even that is a pity. But if a statesman who is conducting a policy of "the brink of war" falls, then his mistake can lead to the death of millions of people. This must not be forgotten. It cannot be forgotten also that certain American officials themselves talk of how they conduct a policy from "a position of strength" and conduct it "to the brink of war."

Later in the interview, when Khrushchev was asked whether he thought the chances for peace or the chances for the outbreak of war were greater, he replied that it was very difficult to say which way the scales would tip:

> The questions of war and peace depend on many circumstances and depend not only upon the Soviet Union but upon other governments. I shall speak concretely, most of all on the United States of America and the Soviet Union. There are many generals in the United States who make very stupid statements that they can wipe the Soviet Union "from the face of the earth." But these braggarts should remember that the other country too can reply in kind. In general a hubbub on this question is a stupid hubbub. It is hard, I repeat, to say in which direction the scales will tip.[40]

Khrushchev's imagery is interesting. The role of a statesman walking a tightrope, falling, and then plunging the world into war was clearly not one for which the speaker was casting himself. The reference to "brinkmanship" made it obvious enough to whom Khrushchev was referring. He pictured a United States that was playing a dangerous game with alarms of war, though not necessarily making a deliberate plan to attack the Soviet Union. Earlier Soviet statements had implied unequivocally that the United States was plotting war on the Soviet Union at an opportune moment. On May 28, 1957, in his interview with a Japanese newspaperman, Khrushchev again pointed to the danger of war being unleashed because of some accident.[41]

Khrushchev's new emphasis on accident suggests that he considered the United States to be deterred from making war by Soviet strength. By stressing war by accident instead of a war planned by the United States, Khrushchev implied that Soviet military strength was already exerting a deterrent influence. One might also argue that Khrushchev in an effort to be tactful said war by accident when he meant war by design. But Khrushchev's repeated mention of the war-by-accident theme and the increasing detail in which he described the outbreak of an unwanted war suggests that he really believed in the possibility of war by accident. Whatever relative weight Khrushchev privately assigned to the possibilities of war by accident or by design, he has insisted that war continues to be possible, and that as long as this is true the Soviet Union has to prepare for war. On one occasion, when he was very anxious to make a good impression on Americans, he nevertheless stuck to this point of view. During a television interview, later widely disseminated in the United States, Khrushchev was asked how he could talk of coexistence with the United States if he really believed that the United States was planning a war against the Soviet Union. Khrushchev answered:

> But what should we do? We would like it if you are not planning war, but you are planning it. And we take this into account.[42]

In his interview with the Japanese newspaperman, Khrushchev spelled out the theme at even greater length. The Japanese suggested that if the Soviet Union unilaterally ceased testing nuclear weapons this could lead to a general cessation of tests. Khrushchev rejected the suggestion and gave as his reason the dangers of reducing Soviet strength when its deterrent effect was an essential support of peace:

> If we stop our tests then we weaken our defensive might to some extent. And it is our own power that deters the forces of war and strengthens the forces of peace. Would not some weakening of our power impel the imperialist forces to an adventuristic step? They might be heartened by such a circumstance.

Khrushchev then cited some "bellicose" statements made by General Norstad to prove that one must not forget the hotheads who talked about destroying the Soviet Union in a few hours. Khrushchev, drawing his imagery from the animal world, then drew an imaginary picture of a weak Soviet Union:

> We do not want to be like the lamb defenseless before the
> wolf. Both the lamb and the wolf live on the same earth.
> But by the right of might the wolf eats the lamb. We do
> not want to be in the lamb's spot. We want to have fangs
> so that the wolf knows that an attack on the peace-loving
> cannot be carried out with impunity. The wolves may lose
> their skins and, perhaps even worse, their heads.

When Khrushchev's Japanese interviewer asked if he agreed
with the American position that the mutual possession of
nuclear weapons could be made to serve the interests of peace,
Khrushchev replied that the Russians did not share such views.
These were the views of men of war, not men of peace. Khrushchev feared that as these weapons accumulated some would be
tempted to use them: "Hotheads begin to think: 'Isn't it time
to begin real war?' "[43]

Since 1953, when the possibility of mutual deterrence was
cautiously broached in the Soviet Union, the dominant Soviet
attitude has been consistent. It was only for the brief period
of a month between the middle of March and the middle of
April, 1954, that Malenkov's statement about "the destruction
of world civilization" was permitted to stand. That phrase implied only the possibility, not the guarantee, of a continued
peace. Since even this mildly optimistic implication was not
permitted to remain unmodified, one may be sure that strong
feelings were aroused among Malenkov's opponents at the very
hint of a trend toward complacency. They have uniformly
maintained the position that, no matter how strong the Soviet
Union, the possibility of war always exists. Various reasons
were given for this stand. According to Bulganin, the capitalists
were not accumulating all these weapons just to frighten the
Soviet Union. Even if they were not planning a war at the
moment, argued Khrushchev, they might be propelled into
some kind of madness and unleash a world war. The forces of
peace and the forces of war were in constant struggle within
each capitalist country and there was always the chance that the
more bellicose elements would win out. Even if it were accepted
that Soviet strength sobered the feverish warmongers in capitalist countries, there was always a chance that through some

accident war would break out. Thus, in the mind of the Soviet leaders, there existed the constant possibility of an outbreak of war.

NOTES

1. I. Stalin, *Ekonomicheskie problemy sotsializma v SSSR* (*Economic Problems of Socialism in the U.S.S.R.*), Moscow, 1952, pp. 85, 86.
2. M. Gus, "The General Line of Soviet Foreign Policy," *Zvezda* (*The Star*), Leningrad, November, 1953, p. 109.
3. V. Kruzhkov, "V. I. Lenin, the Coryphaeus of Revolutionary Science," *Kommunist*, No. 1, 1954, pp. 21, 22.
4. Colonel G. Fedorov, "Marxism-Leninism on War and the Army: 1. The Origin and Essence of Wars," *Red Star,* January 6, 1954.
5. V. Tereshkin, "The Great Mass Movement of the Present Day," *Zvezda*, Leningrad, February, 1954, pp. 139-140.
6. Colonel A. Piatkin, "Some Questions of the Marxist-Leninist Science of War," *Voennaia mysl'* (*Military Thought*), No. 3, March, 1954, p. 16.
7. A General—Retired, "Where the 'Policy of Strength' Leads," *Izvestiia,* January 19, 1954.
8. "On the Thirtieth Anniversary of the Day of V. I. Lenin's Death. Comrade P. N. Pospelov's Report at the Ceremonial Memorial Meeting in Moscow," *Pravda,* January 22, 1954.
9. "The Speech of Comrade G. M. Malenkov at a Meeting of the Electors of the Leningrad District of the City of Moscow, March 12, 1954," *Pravda,* March 13, 1954.
10. "Speech of A. I. Mikoian," *Kommunist* (Erevan), March 12, 1954, full text. *Pravda,* March 12, 1954, contains the abbreviated text.
11. "Speech of Comrade N. S. Khrushchev at the Meeting of the Electors of the Kalinin Electoral District of the City of Moscow, March 6, 1954," *Pravda,* March 7, 1954.
12. "Speech of Comrade K. E. Voroshilov at the Meeting of the Electors of the Kirov Electoral District of the City of Leningrad, March 10, 1954," *Izvestiia,* March 11, 1954.
13. "Speech of Comrade L. M. Kaganovich at a Meeting of the Electors of the Tashkent-Lenin Electoral District, March 11, 1954," *Pravda,* March 13, 1954.
14. "Speech of Comrade N. A. Bulganin at a Meeting of the Electors of the Moscow City Electoral District, March 10, 1954," *Izvestiia,* March 11, 1954.
15. "Speech of Comrade V. M. Molotov at a Meeting of the Electors of the Molotov Electoral District in Moscow, March 11, 1954," *Pravda,* March 12, 1954; "Speech of Comrade N. S. Khrushchev at the Second Congress of the Polish United Workers' Party, March 11, 1954," *ibid.*
16. Viktor Shragin, Soviet Home Service, Moscow, March 27, 1954.
17. Editorial, "The Invincible Movement of Mankind toward Socialism," *Kommunist,* No. 6, April, 1954, p. 8. This issue went to press on April 20, 1954.

18. "The Speech of the Chairman of the Council of Ministers of the U.S.S.R., the Deputy G. M. Malenkov," *Izvestiia*, April 27, 1954.
19. "The Speech of the Deputy A. I. Mikoian," *Pravda*, April 27, 1954.
20. "Speech of the Commander of Troops of the Kiev Military District, Marshal of the Soviet Union V. I. Chuikov," *Pravda Ukrainy*, May 4, 1954.
21. Marshal of the Soviet Union A. Vasilevskii, "The Great Lesson of History," *Red Star*, May 7, 1954.
22. "The Speech of Comrade N. S. Khrushchev at the Xth Congress of the Communist Party of Czechoslovakia, June 12, 1954," *Izvestiia*, June 13, 1954.
23. N. S. Khrushchev, speech at a workers' rally in Prague, June 15, 1954, as broadcast by Radio Prague, June 15, 1954. This text differs quite extensively from the official text published in the Soviet newspapers.
24. Colonel A. Piatkin, "Some Questions of the Marxist-Leninist Theory of War" in *Marksizm-Leninizm o voine armii i voennoi nauke (Marxism-Leninism on War, the Army, and Military Science)*, Moscow, 1955, pp. 70, 71.
25. "The Peoples Decide the Fate of the World and Civilization," *Kommunist*, No. 4, March, 1955, pp. 12-23, particularly p. 16.
26. The official Soviet version of the text in English appears in *Documents Supplementary to "New Times,"* No. 51, December 15, 1955; for the Indian version I have used the text of the Joint Soviet-Indian Statement, *The New York Times*, December 14, 1955.
27. *Pravda*, November 24, 1955. *Missiia druzhby (Mission of Friendship)*, Vol. 1, Moscow, 1956, p. 62, has the same text.
28. "The Answer of the Chairman of the Council of Ministers of the U.S.S.R., N. A. Bulganin, to Questions of the Chief of the Washington Bureau of the Telenews Television and Chronicle Company, C. Schott," *Pravda*, January 1, 1956.
29. "The Speech of Comrade N. S. Khrushchev," *Pravda*, March 15, 1958.
30. *XX S"ezd Kommunisticheskoi partii Sovetskogo Soiuza 14-25 Fevralia, 1956 goda Stenograficheskii otchet (XXth Congress of the Communist Party of the Soviet Union, February 14-25, 1956, Stenographic Report)*, Vol. 1, Moscow, 1956, pp. 37, 38 (hereinafter cited as *XXth Congress Report*).
31. *Ibid.*, pp. 457, 459.
32. *Ibid.*, p. 512.
33. "Message of the Chairman of the Council of Ministers of the U.S.S.R., N. A. Bulganin, to the President of the United States of America, Dwight D. Eisenhower, January 23, 1956," *Pravda*, January 26, 1956.
34. V. Borovskii, "Atomic Weapons Should Be Prohibited," *Pravda*, February 3, 1956.
35. Active member of the Academy of Sciences of the U.S.S.R., D. Skobel'tsyn, "The Problem of Disarmament Should be Solved," *Pravda*, March 29, 1956.
36. Professor Georgi Pokrovskii, "Atomic Deadlock?" *News*, Moscow, No. 6, 1956, pp. 13-14.
37. A. Turov, "The U.S.A. Brandishes Atomic Weapons," *Red Star*, January 25, 1957.

38. E. G. Panfilov, "Has War Ceased To Be the Continuation of Politics?" *Voprosy filosofii (Questions of Philosophy)*, No. 1, 1957, p. 246.

39. Colonel G. Fedorov, Candidate in the Philosophical Sciences, "On the Content of Soviet Military Ideology," *Red Star*, March 22, 1957.

40. "N. S. Khrushchev's Interview with the Chief Editor of the American Newspaper, *The New York Times*, Turner Catledge, May 10, 1957," *Izvestiia*, May 14, 1957.

41. "Interview of N. S. Khrushchev with the Chief Editor of the Japanese Newspaper, *Asahi Shimbun*, Mr. Tomo Hirooka, Transcript of Proceedings," *Pravda*, June 30, 1957. The interview took place on June 18.

42. "Interview of N. S. Khrushchev with Correspondents of the American Radio Television Company, Columbia Broadcasting System, May 28, 1957," *Pravda*, June 4, 1957.

43. Khrushchev interview with Hirooka, *Pravda*, June 30, 1957.

CHAPTER FOUR

THE LIKELIHOOD OF WAR AND SOVIET DOMESTIC POLITICS: 1953-1954

The last chapter sought to demonstrate that the Soviet leadership, despite some tentative detours, has adhered to the policy of preparing for the worst contingency. However likely that contingency, the same thorough preparations were required. Thus one would suppose that budgetary discussions were unaffected by the question of the likelihood of war. Indeed this question was irrelevant to the true Bolshevik, who prided himself in furthering the trend of history no matter what the cost.

The ascetic bent of Bolshevism sees peril in self-indulgence; the Bolshevik is psychologically conditioned to regard self-sacrifice as the necessary concomitant of a sound policy. He has no difficulty in accepting the axiom that the Soviet Union must always be ready for war as long as war is possible. In the period after Stalin's death, however, the desire to relax tugged hard. If peace were indeed 95 per cent assured, as the Malenkov school of thought seemed to believe, could not military expenditures be somewhat reduced and life become easier? This mood was familiar enough in democratic countries; its appearance in the Soviet Union demonstrated the strength of the reaction against conditions of life under Stalin.

The Soviet debates over the likelihood of war are not easy to analyze, because public discussion in the Soviet Union does not necessarily reflect the basic problems confronting the leaders. The debate on the likelihood of war was the public manifestation of different points of view among the leaders on several varied issues. First and foremost was the question of the distribution of military strength in the world. If some political leaders feared that Soviet military strength was inadequate, or growing too slowly in comparison with Western military strength, they did not think of referring publicly to this weakness. Instead of arguing openly for what they really wanted, namely that military expenditures be expanded to make good an existing deficiency, they called attention to some such external danger as "increasing international tension." The principle embodied in this style of debate applies, with modifications, to other countries. A democratic government that has held office long enough to be responsible for the current state of the military establishment is not likely to be able to increase it except on the ground that the international situation has changed for the worse. To ask for more funds because the military forces are too weak to perform what may be required of them is to admit a past error in judgment. The opposition to the government in power is usually willing to make political capital out of poor military preparedness. It is at this point that Soviet practice diverges from democratic experience. There is no organized opposition, and if there were, the Bolsheviks would see something close to treachery in a public airing of the weakness of the Soviet Union. Thus any public debate on the adequacy of the military establishment must necessarily be carried on in terms of changes in the international situation.

A public Soviet discussion on the likelihood of war may be a front for fears, not only of current weakness, but also of future dangers. Statesmen of any country rarely describe a situation in terms of a threat that will materialize in the future. It is more usual to say "The wall is cracking and the building is about to collapse," than "If the crack in the wall is not repaired now, the building will become unsound in five years." The Soviet leaders conform to this pattern. A Soviet appraisal of the ratification of EDC, which promised the eventual rearming of Germany, presented it as an immediate threat to the Soviet Union.

Public Soviet discussions of the likelihood of war serve to conceal issues of basic domestic importance. The question "What is to be done?" is still as urgent as when Chernyshevskii posed it in 1863 and Lenin posed it again in 1901. Now that Stalin's death has proved to mark an epoch in Soviet history, the new political leaders cannot agree among themselves how far to modify existing institutions and practices. Differences over the allocation of resources to investment and to military strength have become public. If the satisfaction of consumer demands is still to be postponed, the Party, whose task it is to exhort and drive, still has a major function; if on the other hand consumer needs are to be met, the Party will be over-shadowed by the executive. In the past, priority for heavy industry and Party pre-eminence were always associated with the slogans "We live in capitalist encirclement" and "The backward are beaten." The people must make sacrifices in a time of national danger. Thus the likelihood of war is closely linked to the fundamentals of Soviet domestic policy. The answers to such questions as "What is to be done?" and "Whither Russia?" depend on the official estimate of the safety of the state.

Alarms of war may offer political advantage to the alarmist in a factional fight. To the factionary, of course, his attaining office, or continuing in it, is a matter of major ideological import. The opponent's faction, he believes, will take the country to the dogs by perverting true Bolshevism or by failing to adjust it to the changing situation. When, in the early months of 1957, Khrushchev raised a wholly contrived danger of war, he himself and those who supported him probably believed that his displacement would be accompanied by dangerous political changes. The alarm of war was raised to keep one faction in office, and this suggests that a lower probability was assigned in fact to the likelihood of war. It is difficult to resist the conclusion that in the Soviet Union the employment of such alarms for minor purposes betokens a low estimate of the likelihood of war. The one element seemingly never present in a public Soviet debate on the likelihood of war is a real danger of war. If such a danger were believed to exist it would be considered much too important for public discussion.

A particular controversy may encompass several or all of the strands described above. It is the variety of latent motives behind any public Soviet discussion of the likelihood of war that makes it at once instructive and difficult to untangle.

In the Soviet Union when a man publicly makes a far-reaching prediction, it can only mean that he has reached a high level of political importance. In short, he speaks for the Party. If such a man retracts his prediction under duress, he thereby demonstrates that he has lost some of his political importance. The power to make or unmake important predictions is an attribute of political predominance within the Soviet leadership. From the Soviet leader's point of view, to make predictions is to enjoy the feel of power. If he is a leader, others expect him to make predictions. But prediction is much more than a mere symbol of authority. Today's prevalent prediction is the basis of today's policies.

As we have seen, the difference of opinion about the likelihood of war that arose within the top Soviet leadership provided one of the criteria for identifying the winners in the factional struggle between Malenkov and Khrushchev. The outcome of that debate became the basis for determining the internal policies of the Soviet Union. Evidence will now be presented to demonstrate the contention that it was Khrushchev and his group who always inclined in moments of crisis to stress the likelihood of war, while Malenkov and his group tended to belittle it.

There were two periods in which this sharp difference of emphasis became important: the early part of 1954 and the first few months of 1957. In 1954, just before and just after Mr. Dulles announced his policy of massive retaliation, the likelihood of war was the subject of a public debate, which concealed differences among the leaders on other basic issues, of which the most apparent concerned the allocation of resources to heavy industry and light industry and, to a lesser extent, to Soviet satellites and allies. In April Khrushchev's faction succeeded in imposing on its opponents a public recognition of the need to increase the armed forces, but the victory was not complete until the beginning of 1955 when Malenkov was forced out of the premiership.

In the conflict between Khrushchev and Malenkov it became abundantly clear from public statements that the Soviet military leaders, possibly excepting those in the air force, were ranged on Khrushchev's side.

With the accession of Khrushchev and Bulganin to power in February, 1955, a paradoxical development took place: military preparations were accelerated but the alarms of war dropped off. In *Military Thought* the military stated the official requirement for a pre-emptive capability, arguing that surprise attack had assumed major importance in modern warfare. Since it was now thought possible for a successful surprise attack to shape the outcome of a war, the Soviet Union had to be prepared to slip in a paralyzing blow before the enemy could do so. The military posture required for such a state of readiness was much more expensive than one designed primarily to deter enemy attack. It necessitated great expenditures not only on weapons of offense but also on measures for active and civil defense.

Nevertheless the public statements of the top leaders about the dangers of war became much calmer and more reassuring. Almost from the moment that Khrushchev and Bulganin acquired full power the prospects for peace seemed to improve. Starting with the reconciliation with Yugoslavia and the signing of the Austrian Peace Treaty, Khrushchev and Bulganin seemed intent on proving to the Soviet Union and to the world that they could preserve peace more effectively than their predecessors. The summit meetings at Geneva climaxed their program for easing world tensions. The "spirit of Geneva" brightened the international scene for a short time, only to be dimmed, though not extinguished, by later events. In 1956 predictions of war with the West were avoided. Only after the Hungarian and Egyptian crises were safely resolved did the Soviet leaders again talk of the imminence of war. In the first months of 1957 the top leadership was divided once again over the likelihood of war. Shepilov publicly took a more optimistic view than Khrushchev, thus breaking with him. Shepilov's subsequent dismissal from the post of Foreign Minister was the penalty for changing sides.

Conflict continued among the Soviet leaders. Apparently the persons dismissed from their high posts in June, 1957, were opposed to Khrushchev's formula for governmental reorganization. Their failure to speak for Khrushchev's plan signalled their opposition. In his struggle with this group, Khrushchev again employed the argument that war was much more likely than his opponents thought. As soon as he had secured the approval of his reorganization plan, he dropped the alarms of war and reverted to a more temperate appraisal of the future. In the crisis of June, 1957, Khrushchev enjoyed the support of the military leaders who, in the aftermath of the crisis, seemed eager in their published writings to hold Khrushchev to promises of continued emphasis on heavy industry.

This interpretation of Soviet views on the likelihood of war is based on rather imperfect evidence. Soviet information policy leaves one very much in the dark as to what is going on in Soviet governing circles. From the materials presented in the rest of this chapter, and in the following one, the reader can judge for himself the validity of the conclusions reached.

* * *

One of the first hints of a high-level Soviet debate on how to adjust Soviet policies to the realities of the nuclear age was contained in the Soviet reaction to President Eisenhower's speech of December 8, 1953, which sharply presented the opportunities and dangers arising from the mutual possession of nuclear weapons.

Eisenhower stated that at least one Soviet test up to that time had involved thermonuclear reactions and frankly recognized that the American monopoly of atomic weapons had "ceased to exist some years ago." He expressed horror at the prospect of the two great powers remaining permanently armed to the teeth and threatening "the probability of civilization destroyed."* He made a direct appeal to the Soviet leaders to begin to negotiate in a modest way on the problems of nuclear disarmament.

The President's speech must have meant a great deal to the Soviet leaders. Even today we cannot be sure of the exact nuclear strength possessed by the Soviet Union at the end of 1953, but it does seem clear that the numbers of her weapons and her delivery capability were then far behind those of the United States. The tone and content of Eisenhower's speech, therefore, left ample leeway for future developments and applied to the present only in a limited sense. The Soviet leaders, however, could readily interpret the President's words to mean that the United States recognized the existence of something like nuclear parity at that time or in the near future. Those Soviet leaders who were not irrevocably set against any form of *détente* with the United States could argue that here was their chance to negotiate from strength. Those who felt that Eisenhower's offer was only a trick to induce the Soviet Union to relax its guard were likely to see only danger in negotiation. Arguing a priori, then, we may say that Eisenhower's speech was likely to be a divisive influence among the Soviet leaders. The available evidence confirms this speculation.

On December 9, the day immediately following Eisenhower's speech, the Soviet press made no reference to it. This was to be expected, for the Soviet press rarely reacts immediately to major foreign events. On December 10, *Pravda* was the only newspaper that appeared on the Moscow streets; *Izvestiia, Trud (Labor)*, and *Komsomolskaia Pravda* failed to appear. In this unique occurrence the Yugoslavs detected evidence of a dispute between two factions in the Presidium, one favoring some kind of accommodation with the West on an international basis and the other opposing it. The Yugoslav press speculated that the suppressed editions of *Izvestiia, Trud,* and *Komsomolskaia Pravda* had carried a blast against Eisenhower's speech.[1] With the advantage of hindsight, however, one may wonder whether *Izvestiia* did not plan to report Eisenhower's speech

* The TASS rendering of "destroyed" was *unichtozhen,* which means literally "annihilated."

too extensively or too favorably. This interpretation is consistent with the paper's attitude a year after these events. Whatever the details of the case, the suspending of three newspapers strongly suggests a divergence of opinion at the top.

The official Soviet reply to the President's address was dated December 22, 1953, and it is consistent with the hypothesis of a high-level debate. The Soviet declaration carried water on both shoulders. It was pessimistic about any large results from token transfers of nuclear material from warlike to peaceful uses; it insisted that the abolition of nuclear weapons was the only solution. At the same time it agreed to accept Eisenhower's invitation to negotiate. Interestingly, the reply did not comment on Eisenhower's statement that both societies would suffer mutual destruction in a nuclear war.

Public statements of the Soviet leaders gave hints of disagreement. In his New Year's statement Voroshilov spoke of the enemies of the Soviet Union, while Malenkov, on the same day, insisted that there were no objective impediments to the improvement of relations between the Soviet Union and the United States. At a lower level, Gus's views on the possibility of lasting peace evoked, among other things, Colonel Fedorov's extreme statement that wars were *absolutely* inevitable as long as capitalism existed. From the side of the optimists, apparently, came an extremely mild Lenin anniversary speech delivered by Pospelov on January 21, 1954.[2]

The clearest signs of a dispute concerning the likelihood of war and the Soviet military posture appeared during the elections to the Supreme Soviet .We sometimes forget that there are elections in the Soviet Union and that the custom of delivering election speeches has been retained there. The election addresses of 1954 are useful to the analyst because the two factions within the leadership favored different policies that a single party formula failed to conceal. The party line was in effect bifurcated.

Before the elections for deputies to the Supreme Soviet, the Communist Party normally publishes an appeal to all the electors. It is essentially a collection of generalizations about the domestic and international situation and embodies the

Party's official line. In the 1954 election the appeal had a few paragraphs on the international situation and its implications for military posture. These attempted to smooth over certain inconsistencies, but did not quite manage to conceal them. Two paragraphs in particular seem to reflect divergent outlooks about military preparedness. The first of these reminds one strongly of Malenkov's point of view:

> In the postwar years our county has become still more strong and powerful. *It possesses everything necessary* to guard the peaceful toil of our people and to bring to his senses any one who dares encroach upon our freedom and independence. We do not fear threats on the part of any aggressors and we stand firmly and consistently for peace and the interests of our people and the people of the whole globe. We are certain that there are no disputed questions in the present international situation which cannot be resolved in a peaceful way [author's italics].[3]

"It possesses everything necessary. . . ." This was to be the refrain of the Malenkov forces until almost the end of the year 1954.

Another paragraph addressed itself to the dangers to peace and the possible need to fight a war:

> Vigilantly standing guard over the interests of the people and their peaceful toil, the Communist Party cannot help but consider that there are reactionary imperialistic forces abroad who strive to sharpen and strengthen international tension and to unleash a new war. Therefore, while conducting a firm and consistent policy of peace and defending and guarding with all its might the cause of peace, which is great and holy for all the people of the world, *the party considers it necessary steadily to perfect and strengthen the armed forces of the Soviet government in order to assure the security of our motherland* [author's italics].[4]

These two paragraphs were different in emphasis but not incompatible in logic. The Soviet Union might well be satisfied with her current military posture while planning to increase her strength to meet future developments. This interpretation would be acceptable were it not for the way each faction pressed its own policy by emphasizing one or the other paragraph. *Pravda, Izvestiia, Sel'skoe khoziaistvo (Agriculture)*, the organ of the Ministry of Agriculture, and *Red Star* in the first issues following the election appeal, set the pattern for the majority of the Soviet press by paraphrasing both paragraphs. In contrast, *Trud,* the newspaper of industry, and *Red Star* in its later issues, quoted editorially only the second paragraph, which referred to the need to strengthen the armed forces, and omitted any reference to the paragraph saying that the Soviet Union possessed everything necessary to guard the country.[5]

The military, taking advantage of the anniversary of the Red Army when generals traditionally publish articles in the Soviet newspapers, made it abundantly clear on which side of the argument they stood. Lieutenant General Kozlov wrote for *Red Star* and omitted any reference to the first of the two paragraphs quoted above.[6] General Zheltov did not raise the question of the adequacy of current Soviet defenses, but called for strengthening the defensive capacity of the whole motherland, together with the armed forces, as the best means to curb aggression.[7] Marshals Sokolovskii and Vasilevskii cited only the paragraph from the appeal that stressed the need to increase the strength of the armed forces.[8]

The faction advocating expansion of the military forces was to prevail. The relatively complacent views of Malenkov, Pospelov, Pervukhin, and Saburov were heard through March, but Khrushchev, Bulganin, Molotov, Kaganovich, and Voroshilov expressed the views of what was to become the dominant faction. The trade-marks of the Malenkov group were, first, their concentration on the message contained in the phrase, "It possesses everything necessary . . .," and second, their failure to call for a strengthening of the armed forces. The Khrushchev trade-marks were the citation of the second paragraph quoted above and a summons to increase military power.

Pospelov restricted himself to repeating almost verbatim the Malenkov paragraph from the appeal to the voters and he failed to call for an increase in military strength.[9] Pervukhin, who spoke in Tbilisi, Georgia, repeated almost without change the Malenkov paragraph, and this part of his speech was omitted in the Moscow reports. Pervukhin also failed to call for an increase in the armed forces.[10] Saburov's speech was clearly on Malenkov's side, since it failed to call for expansion of the armed forces.[11]

Mikoian seemed to take a somewhat special position in the debate over military policy. He had been more unequivocal than anyone else about his belief that Soviet nuclear strength was sufficient to deter the United States from making war. At Erevan in Armenia, he argued that great destruction would be visited on both sides in the event of a nuclear war and gave this as the main reason for the recession of the danger of war. This part of the speech was not printed anywhere in the Soviet Union except at Erevan. Unlike other members of the Malenkov group, however, he called for strengthening the armed forces, just as did those who were minimizing the prospects of peace. This part of Mikoian's speech was picked out for emphasis in all the generally available newspaper versions. These versions included everything but the paragraphs about the receding danger of war.

It is a measure of the strength of the Khrushchev group that it was able to keep out of the central press Mikoian's trenchant arguments against its position. The speeches of lesser figures in the provincial cities were reprinted in condensed versions in the Moscow press without any indication that they had been abbreviated so as to favor the arguments of the Khrushchev-Bulganin group.

It was Malenkov himself who made the most radical statements concerning the imperative need for peace in the nuclear age. He even seemed to imply that it might be possible to eliminate the cold war:

> Every thinking person cannot but reflect on the question of how to take a further step forward, how to find a real basis for the firm foundation of peace and the security of the peoples. It is not true that mankind faces a choice between just two possibilities: either a new world holocaust or the so-called cold war. The peoples [of the world] are

vitally interested in a firm consolidation of peace. The Soviet government stands for further relaxation of international tension, for a firm and lasting peace and resolutely opposes the policy of cold war for this policy is a policy of preparation for a new world holocaust, which, with the present means of warfare, means the destruction of world civilization.[12]

This declaration ran counter to the orthodox Bolshevik analysis of international politics, which allowed of only two alternatives: war brought about by the imperialist powers or a period of uneasy peace during which the communist forces of peace would restrain the capitalist aggressors. Malenkov did not give a very elaborate description of his third alternative, but the rejection of "the policy of cold war" seemed to look toward a permanent accommodation between capitalism and communism, some lasting agreement to live and let live. Here is what he said:

> It is thus understood that as long as aggressive circles which still hopelessly dream of devastating our socialist country exist in the world, the Soviet Union is obligated to maintain its armed forces in such a situation that they can make short shrift of any adventures of the aggressors.[13]

A careful reading of this paragraph reveals that the barrier to the third alternative was the existence of "aggressive circles," not simply the existence of capitalism and imperialism. Aggressive circles might become less aggressive, especially as it was clearly in their interest to do so. The issue of the inevitability of war in a world divided between capitalists and socialists had been sidestepped. Malenkov's most belligerent phrases were not incompatible with an ultimate reduction of the Soviet armed forces, for "aggressive circles" might fade into the background. The opposition emphasized that capitalism might always fight.

The plausibility of this analysis is heightened by the fact that Malenkov never again mentioned the possibility of a third alternative, just as he never again repeated his statement about the destruction of world civilization. It can be deduced that the majority faction among the leaders linked these views with complacency about military preparedness.

Malenkov's opponents presented a very different picture in their election speeches. On March 6 Khrushchev said that "the Communist Party and the Soviet government cannot but realize that there are reactionary forces in the capitalist countries which seek to find a solution to their economic difficulties and the exacerbated contradictions of the imperialist camp by the preparation of a new war."[14] Five days later in Poland, Khrushchev said that "the reactionary forces of the capitalist countries impede in every way the weakening of tension in international relations."[15] Sharper even than the party chief, Molotov found it "impossible not to take into account that before everyone's eyes the policy of the preparation of a new war is being carried out by the reactionary forces. . . . It is impossible, of course, to ignore the circumstance that the aggressive forces continue to proceed in the same direction as always. The arms race continues."[16] Kaganovich referred to Lenin's 1921 thesis that the collapse of the colonial system meant the ultimate collapse of capitalism and concluded: "Thence their nervousness, their desire—however they can—to change the developing international situation by force and to find an 'escape' through war. That is why they create tension in the international situation and develop the arms race."[17] Voroshilov talked of an imminent economic crisis in the United States that would be accompanied by a reduction in the standard of living and a consequent increase in unemployment: "This explains the attempt of the reactionary circles to avoid economic crises by inspiring a war psychosis and creating an international atmosphere of even more tension and by continuing the arms race."[18]

All the election speeches of the Khrushchev group argued that the war plans of the capitalist countries were a natural feature of capitalism. Sweet reasonableness, even a full understanding of the great evils to be suffered by all from a nuclear war, could have no effect on their warlike course, which was predetermined by the laws of history. Bulganin had this to say:

We would commit an irreparable error if we did not strengthen our armed forces. Very many facts indicate that the imperialist forces headed by the U.S. are openly conducting a policy of the preparation of a new war against us. . . . The intensified arms race, which has developed in the countries of the Anglo-American bloc, and the construction of military bases in Europe and on other territories, and the policy of the revival of German militarism all show quite clearly the direction in which the imperialist circles are trying to go.

In these conditions we do not have the right to waste time, and even less right to sink into complacency and to reassure ourselves because we emerged victorious in the war and because our army is the strongest in the world. It is well known that he who does not go forward falls behind; and the backward are beaten. . . .

The most important thing in military affairs is the uninterrupted perfection of the armed forces. This is especially true of aviation, where technological progress is very rapid. All these years we have sought to develop our air technology and not to fall behind the demands of the present; and we have succeeded. . . .

We cannot assume that the imperialists expend enormous material and financial resources on armaments only to frighten us.

We cannot depend either on the humanitarianism of the imperialists who, as life has shown, are capable of using any weapon of mass destruction.

We must always be ready to give a crushing rebuff to any enemy no matter what weapons he possesses.[19]

Bulganin's statement was the most direct rebuttal of Malenkov's views. Over the years, indeed, Bulganin had always been sharpest in condemnation of the Malenkov line. After Malenkov was dismissed from the chairmanship of the Council of Ministers in February, 1955, Bulganin delivered slashing attacks on the former Premier's policies.

In his election speech Bulganin did not content himself

with a routine statement that the Soviet armed forces must be increased; he declared that it would be an irreparable error not to strengthen them. Furthermore, instead of making trite remarks about eternal vigilance, Bulganin called attention to the specific dangers of wasting time, of sinking into complacency, and of trying to live on past successes. The implication was quite clear that some people were guilty of these mistakes. Bulganin heightened the effect of his admonitions by repeating the phrase that Stalin had employed to justify his heavy industry program, namely, "the backward are beaten." He suggested very strongly that the imperialists were planning to attack the Soviet Union and would not be satisfied with maintaining a balance of power and mutual deterrence. This seems to be the only possible interpretation of Bulganin's statement that it could not be assumed that the imperialists were expending enormous resources only to frighten the Soviet Union and of his statement that it was impossible to depend on the humanitarianism of the imperialists, who were known to be capable of anything.

An important element in Soviet appraisals of the danger of war was the current estimate of American intentions. In 1954, first Mr. Dulles's speech on massive retaliation, and then the culmination of the Indochina crisis in the spring furnished the data for a Soviet assessment of American intentions. Early Soviet fears, soon to be modified, apparently forced Malenkov to retract his more optimistic opinions.

On January 12, 1954, Secretary of State Dulles analyzed Soviet policy as one aimed to divide and weaken the free nations by forcing them to overextend their strength and bring themselves to "practical bankruptcy."[20] That would be the "moment for the decisive blow," said Dulles, quoting Stalin. The Soviet Union with its extensive land borders could impose a series of Koreas upon the free world. Although the free world intended always to challenge local aggressions as they arose, it would be better advised to seek a policy more suited to the long run. Dulles argued for local defenses all over the world, "but there is no local defense which alone will contain the mighty land power of the Communist world." Local defenses must be reinforced by the further deterrent of massive retaliatory power. A potential aggressor must know that he cannot always prescribe battle conditions that suit him: "Otherwise, for example, a potential aggressor who is glutted with manpower might be tempted to attack in confidence that resistance would be confined to manpower. He might be tempted to attack in places where his superiority was decisive."

"The way to deter aggression is for the free community to be willing and able to respond vigorously at places and with means of its own choosing." Dulles made it quite clear that this departure from the old policy of meeting each emergency as it arose had been decided by "the President and his advisors, as represented by the National Security Council." The Secretary's announcement was no mere trial balloon: "The basic decision was to depend primarily upon a great capacity to retaliate, instantly, by means and at places of our own choosing. Now the Department of Defense and the Joint Chiefs of Staff can shape our military establishment to fit what is *our* policy instead of having to try to be ready to meet the enemy's many choices. That permits of a selection of military means instead of a multiplication of means. As a result, it is now possible to get, and share more basic security at less cost."[21]

A reasonably careful reading of Dulles's statement made it clear to Western observers that it was not the American intention to retaliate with a nuclear strike to every and any local emergency. But in the American as well as in the European press it was interpreted to mean simply that henceforward the United States would be more likely than before to retaliate to local aggression with a massive nuclear attack. The world press, and especially the Western European press, was agitated about the implications of Dulles's speech, fearing that the new policy might miscarry.

From the first the Russians obviously took Dulles's speech on massive retaliation very seriously. The speech was delivered on January 12, 1954, and reported in the Soviet press on January 14, after the standard time lag. The press reports were brief and the most noteworthy feature of Dulles's speech, his reference to massive retaliation, was not even mentioned. Evidently more time was required to develop an agreed official interpretation of this important policy statement. When Soviet propagandists do not react immediately and in a routine way to a major foreign statement, the matter is probably undergoing review at the highest level. Not until March 17 was the Dulles speech again mentioned in the Soviet press and then only in passing. The first evaluation of it came as late as March 26.

On March 17, an editorialized news account of foreign events pointed out that the Americans intended to expand the war in Indochina. Eisenhower had stated at a press conference that, if American technicians and instructors sent to Indochina were killed, the United States could not be drawn into the war without a declaration by Congress. The Soviet writer interpreted Eisenhower's reply to a journalist's question about the technicians to mean that the United States was considering how to enter the war. According to this writer the American press could not make out whether or not the President's answer contradicted "Dulles's recent statement about the so-called 'instantaneous retaliatory (?) actions'."* According to the Soviet analysis, as published in *Pravda*:

> *The essence of the matter is that such a statement by the Chief of State of the United States of America can be explained only by the desire not to be limited in the future to the provision of materiel, arms, and equipment for the war in Indochina but to pass to even further intervention directed toward the expansion of the war in this area of Asia. . . .*
>
> *Furthermore, the President did not find it necessary to deny the view expressed by the American Senator Stennis and by the correspondents at the press conference that the fact of the loss of American soldiers on the field of battle in Indochina might be the occasion for the official entrance of the USA into a war against the people of Indochina.[22]*

On the day these words appeared in *Pravda*, *The New York Times* printed an article written by Dulles for the April Issue

* The question mark is in the original.

of *Foreign Affairs* making it clear that the policy of massive retaliation depended on the co-operation, and implicitly on the agreement, of America's allies. In some cases an attack by a communist power would mean a general war, but the United States meant to have the means for response on a selective basis. In some areas, however, the main reliance would have to be on retaliation with great force in places of America's own choice, but this did not mean that every local war would become a world war. Naturally the United States would not announce in advance what it would do in a specific situation. Here Mr. Dulles recalled his earlier warnings that if there were open Chinese aggression in Indochina there "would be grave consequences which might not be confined to Indochina."[23]

The first full Soviet treatment of Dulles's "massive retaliation" speech appeared in a *Pravda* editorial on March 26, 1954. Quite unusually, it was on the right-hand side of the page, while in the normal editors' space on the left was a routine piece on the necessity of improving navigational techniques. Perhaps for this reason, the editorial was not picked up and reported by American correspondents in Moscow. According to *Pravda*, Dulles had delivered his speech of January 12 in "a bellicose fever, losing all sense of reality." The editorial interpreted him to have said that "the United States intended in case of any local conflict, wherever it happened, to begin military operations where they pleased and against whom they pleased using all kinds of weapons including atomic bombs." To Dulles was attributed the implication that America's allies in the NATO and the Rio Pact would automatically participate in this warfare and that their consent did not even have to be requested. The result, said the Soviet editorial, was widespread domestic and foreign criticism. More balanced Americans, like Adlai Stevenson, pointed out that the execution of such a policy "could lead to the destruction of our cities."

The foreign allies of the United States were alarmed at the thought that their countries could be drawn into a new world war by "a handful of American politicians who were capriciously trying to seize the right of deciding the fate of other governments as they thought fit." *Pravda* provided facts to support the argument. The Canadian Minister of Foreign Affairs, Lester B. Pearson, when in Washington on March 15, had expressed dissatisfaction that the fate of Canada "could be decided not by us ourselves but on the other side of the border." The English press had pointed out that the United States could draw England into a world war not of her own choosing.

In his appearance before the Senate Foreign Relations Committee (March 20) Dulles had tried to smooth over the bad impression made by his January 12 statement on massive retaliation, but in essence American policy remained unchanged.[24] *Pravda* did not trust Dulles's second thoughts.

It seems quite obvious from the long delay between Dulles's speech and the Soviet commentary on it that the analysts were both puzzled and shaken. The tone of the editorial just quoted seems to be one of relief that things were not quite as bad as they had thought. It also seems very likely that the editorial was written with the purpose of smoking out some further American reaction which would give the Russians some clues as to what was meant. Writing a few days later, one of the important foreign editors of *Pravda*, Yuri Zhukov, complained that no American correspondents accredited to Moscow had written a line on the March 26 editorial. Zhukov attributed this silence to the embarrassment of the warmongers after they became "convinced that their maneuvers had suffered defeat." He summarized an Acheson statement in *The New York Times* arguing that the massive blow advocated by Dulles would only bring destruction to the United States in the form of a counterblow. According to Zhukov, Acheson had emphasized that the administration's policy would destroy the American alliance system, because the allies would consider that their very existence had been thoughtlessly subjected to a needless risk. Acheson had pointed out that the United States could not count on the allies' permission to use bases on their territory. American newspapers, said Zhukov, had ignored the Soviet exposure of the emptiness of Dulles's threat because they did not want to make matters worse for themselves.[25]

The Russians interpreted the Dulles speech to mean that

the United States would refuse to settle local conflicts, in order to use them as a springboard to larger conflicts. They implied very strongly in their press treatment that America intended to extend the Indochina fighting to China and possibly beyond but did not suggest the possibility of an American surprise attack on the Soviet Union. The Soviet appraisal of events in Indochina is important as a clue to the Soviet estimate of the world political situation at the time when Malenkov was forced to revise his optimistic estimates of the future.

The Russian analysts had a knotty problem in judging American intentions in Indochina. In 1950 Secretary of State Acheson had clearly indicated that the United States did not consider South Korea a vital area; the Russians could not have received stronger assurance that the Americans were unwilling to defend South Korea. The almost instantaneous reaction of the Americans to the North Korean attack in 1950 came as a surprise to the Russians. The Russians must surely have concluded either that the United States had laid a trap for them, which would have been explaining American behavior in Soviet terms, or that Americans were quite unpredictable. Since the Americans had intervened in Korea after they had indicated that they probably would not, how could one be sure that they would not intervene in Indochina when they had already threatened to do so? Even a shrewd American analyst could not have been confident in March or April, 1954, that there would be no American intervention in Indochina. Indochina was more important strategically to the United States than Korea and communist domination of it would have been a setback to the whole policy of containment. Numerous American statements, one by the Vice-President, urged intervention in Indochina. In March and April, 1954, the Russian analysts could not reasonably have excluded the possibility of American intervention in Indochina.

The Soviet press reports seemed to demonstrate the American intention to participate in the Indochina war and to expand its scope. On March 22, 1954, they announced that a communications and transport squadron of American planes had been sent to Indochina from Japan. This squadron included B-26's. The dispatch quoted Stassen as saying that the United States would continue to supply Indochina up to and during the Geneva talks on peace in Indochina.[26] On March 24, *Pravda* quoted an American article "Will American Soldiers Fight in Indochina?" as saying that the Americans had to intervene in the war because the French were not prepared to fight.[27]

On the following day *Pravda* quoted James Reston in *The New York Times* to the effect that the Pentagon had discussed the possibility of recruiting an international corps of aviators to aid either the French or the Bao Dai Government. *Pravda* stressed the importance of the second alternative, because it implied American readiness to carry on the war in disregard of, or counter to, French interests.[28]

The Soviet press' reporting of events fitted into the arguments of Malenkov's opponents. Malenkov suggested that the United States was seeking an amelioration of international tension because it feared the future nuclear strength of the Soviet Union, and that the latter could seize this opportunity to arrive at an accommodation with the United States and to make an end of the cold war. Malenkov, if challenged to explain Dulles's talk of "massive retaliation" and the American plans for intervention in Indochina, could have said only that Dulles's views were those of a minority and that the dominant group in the United States administration had effectively repudiated the policy of massive retaliation. The dominant group of Soviet leaders rejected such a reassuring explanation. To them the apparent dangers seemed real enough to be taken at face value. America, they recognized, was far ahead of the Soviet Union in nuclear strength and in delivery capability. Why should Eisenhower want to drag the Soviet Union into some sort of international agreement whereby each power would deliver stocks of nuclear material to those countries which wanted to operate reactors for peaceful purposes? It could only be because he hoped to gain something at the expense of the Soviet Union. The more cautious Russians would enter no agreement that might involve an open confirmation of American superiority in nuclear weapons. For this reason alone they could not allow disarmament talks to progress. The impediments placed by the United States in the way of the liquidation of the Indochina war obviously meant that the American strategy was to expand the war in Asia and then, perhaps, to make war against the Soviet Union.

For Malenkov's opponents to overcome him and make his policy appear reckless it was not necessary to prove the imminence of war. So serious were the implications of their analysis that it was enough to demonstrate the mere possibility that it was correct. The Soviet Union had to be prepared to meet the worst eventualities, even if no more than a possibility of their occurrence could be demonstrated.

Under the pressure of events at home and abroad, therefore, Malenkov was forced on April 26, to retract his optimistic prognosis of March 2 and to adopt the more pessimistic view of the future of peace. Malenkov's retraction has already been described in part. It will be recalled that he withdrew his prediction of the destruction of world civilization in the event of nuclear war. He was also forced to modify his low estimate of the likelihood of war, but was able to maintain the position that international tension had been recently relaxed in an important way, an index of his residual power. Even here, however, he had to qualify his opinion with a warning against the dangers of overestimating the significance and extent of the relaxation. Malenkov himself ascribed this counsel of caution to others:

> A sober approach to the evaluation of the international situation has always characterized the Soviet people and today they warn against overestimating the significance of the relaxation of international tension already achieved, because the opponents of peace have not abandoned their aggressive aspirations. . . .

Malenkov's April speech differed from his March speech in another important particular. Whereas in March he conspicuously failed to call for an increase in military strength, while his opponents were calling for one, in April he not only made good that failure but also promised that "in the future" the armed forces would have everything they needed.[29] The phrase, "in the future" was almost unprecedented in Soviet statements about increasing military appropriations. Soviet statements usually called for increases in the armed forces without committing themselves to continued expansion in the future. In April Malenkov did so commit himself.

The policy of not increasing, or of decreasing, military appropriations was finished. The reduction of emphasis in Malenkov's April speech on the consumer goods program, long associated with Malenkov's name, was the corollary of his retreat on the military issue. Speaking on the same day, Pervukhin, then a supporter of Malenkov, also called for the further strengthening of the defensive capability of the country, something he had signally failed to do in March.[30]

Malenkov's opponents revealed in their subsequent speeches that although he had made major concessions he had not abandoned his basic position. Differences on the assessment of the international situation and the likelihood of war continued. In April, as we have seen, Malenkov was still insisting that international tension had decreased. Meanwhile Kaganovich repeated his March statement that the Soviet Union was encircled—the old Stalinist formula that had fallen into disuse—and Khrushchev insisted that the imperialists "were increasing tension . . . and were not sparing in threats to the Soviet Union."[31] Where Malenkov had only mentioned American irrationality as a bare possibility, Khrushchev, in a long tirade against Dulles, went so far as to cast doubts on the latter's mental balance:

> Mr. Dulles acts as if he had become sick with some sort of rage. We know that a person in a rage is mad. But is it fitting for a statesman to announce the foreign policy of his country when he is drunk with fury and malice toward other people?[32]

From that point onward Malenkov's opponents continued to stress publicly that war might come at almost any time, and that surprise had become important in determining the outcome of wars. The statement about military surprise had appeared hitherto only in the military press.

Malenkov's opponents did not attack him on his own ground. Instead of denying his contention that the terrible consequences of nuclear war would effectively deter one power from attacking another and so open the way for a decline of international tension, they contented themselves with reiterating that anything could happen and that the Soviet Union must be prepared for all eventualities. In the spring, summer, and fall of 1954 the possibility of a surprise attack against the Soviet Union was not a major theme of Soviet propaganda. But since prominent figures such as Bulganin warned against surprise, the new theme apparently had political importance.

Bulganin, as we noted above, warned against complacency and stressed the impossibility of counting on American humanitarianism when the United States was investing billions in weapons. The next statement along these lines was made by Marshal Vasilevskii in an article in *Red Star* for May 7, 1954. Particular interest attaches to Vasilevskii's arguing the danger from surprise, for he had been one of the most conservative champions of the validity of the permanently-operating-factors formula. This formula minimized surprise so that it was noteworthy that Vasilevskii now insisted that the Soviet Union must constantly be on guard "so that nothing unexpected can catch us unawares. Whoever forgets vigilance and is slack about it commits the greatest crime against the government and against the people." The possibility of surprise attack was a new and still uncommon theme in Soviet public speeches. Perhaps Vasilevskii was willing to shift a bit on the subject of surprise in order to attack Malenkov. In a rare reference to "the head of the Soviet Government, Malenkov," Vasilevskii quoted, against Malenkov's early position, his retraction that talked about capitalists deciding on madness, making war, and suffering the destruction of their system.[33]

Following this line, the Soviet press started to pay more attention to items stressing American unpredictability and the possibility of anything's happening. For example, in June, 1954,

General Gruenther had made a speech in which he said that atomic weapons would be required for infantry support in Europe in the event of war. The Soviet commentator explained this attempt to make nuclear weapons compensate for small armies as a realization of the difficulty of getting cannon fodder. Furthermore, said the Soviet writer, "General Gruenther and those who stand behind him are apparently possessed by the mania of world conquest which possessed Hitler too."[34]

When Malenkov suggested that the capitalists would have to be mad to unleash war, his opponents countered by trying to show that they were indeed mad. In April Khrushchev hinted that Dulles was of unsound mind. In May Vasilevskii drew special attention to Malenkov's phrase about capitalist insanity. In June a Soviet writer said that General Gruenther and the people behind him were just as crazy as Hitler.

Some Soviet leaders may have had sincere doubts about American rationality and may have been genuinely concerned about the international situation, but it seems more likely that the cry, "the Americans are mad," was only a dramatic justification of the warning, "anything can happen." That talk of American insanity was deliberately fostered to justify a program of the expansion of the military forces is further suggested by Khrushchev's speech at a workers' rally in Prague on June 15, 1954. The speech was broadcast by Prague radio and was printed next day in the Soviet press in a severely edited version, with the poor sequences eliminated, the incorrect grammar improved, and much of the content changed. Unusually blunt, Khrushchev spoke not just of "aggressive circles," but of "enemies." He came very close to saying that the much excoriated policy of "the position of strength" was sensible. In describing the reluctance of the West to negotiate when they had a monopoly of the atomic bomb, he asked:

> And what does it indicate? It indicates that which Churchill has said so well from, one might say, the point of view of his class. He said: "with the Bolsheviks one should talk from a position of strength because they are our class enemy."

Khrushchev implied that the stronger side would not negotiate because it aimed to dictate. After an awkward, halting detour around the politically impossible statement that the Soviet Union must operate from a "position of strength," Khrushchev quoted Krylov's couplet: "To live with the enemy one must be strong." Then he described how the Soviet Union had made herself strong by creating the atom bomb and outstripping the capitalists in the construction of the H-bomb.

Although Khrushchev spoke unrestrainedly of capitalist stupidity and lack of judgment, he did not suggest that capitalist leaders were insane. This suggests that the theme of "American insanity" was polemical and did not represent a true Soviet concern. He warned that the capitalists might share Hitler's fate if they, too, underestimated the strength of the Soviet Union. Soviet strength was required first as a military safeguard and second to improve the Soviet bargaining position in international negotiations. Failure to increase her military strength might deprive the Soviet Union of security in the event of war and of political advantage in time of peace.

Malenkov moved more and more into the shade partly because he failed to get a summit meeting which might have given substance to his assertion that there was a way out of the grim choice between hot war and cold war. Only two months after Malenkov had become Chairman of the Council of Ministers, Churchill had publicly revealed his hopes for success in dealing with the post-Stalin government:

> It would, I think, be a mistake to assume that nothing can be settled with the Soviet Union until all has been settled. . . . I think that a conference of the highest level should take place between the leading powers without long delay.[35]

Churchill's speech offered the Soviet leaders some grounds for believing that it was possible for the Soviet Union to deal with the West on equal terms. As the months passed, however, it became clear that Churchill's willingness to negotiate at the highest level was not matched in the United States. All the facts have not yet been made public, but it seems that Churchill was eager and Eisenhower cool. The President never ruled out the possibility of a top-level, four-power conference, but he repeatedly stated that such a conference would have to wait upon a Soviet demonstration of good intentions.

On July 4, 1954, Churchill wrote privately to Molotov that the United States would not participate in a high-level conference at that time, though Eisenhower had become more favorable to the idea. Instead of a four-power meeting Churchill suggested an Anglo-Russian meeting. Molotov approved, but Churchill then asked for a postponement and, after a Russian counterproposal for a general European conference with the participation of the United States, the negotiations died.[36] The Churchill-Molotov correspondence appeared in the London *Soviet News* in March, 1955. The British government has never denied its authenticity. It affords only a glimpse into the matter, and we do not know whether the United States was asking only for a small down payment of Soviet reasonableness in return for her willingness to negotiate, or whether Malenkov's opponents sabotaged the negotiations to undermine his prestige. What is important to our argument is that Malenkov's failure weakened his political position within the Soviet Union. Had Malenkov succeeded in a summit conference he might have imposed on his colleagues the view that nuclear weapons made war unlikely and he might have fared better. Public approval of his success in reducing international tension would have been a political asset. The genuine popular desire for peace, of little weight in affairs under Stalin, is now a factor in the power struggle at the top in the Soviet Union.

Through the summer and early fall of 1954 Malenkov's opponents emphasized the possibility of war and the need for Soviet vigilance. Bulganin said it was self-evident that, until the United States agreed to renounce nuclear weapons, "the Soviet Union will need to have these weapons so that, in the event of the unexpected happening, we shall not be disarmed."[37] At the end of July a *Pravda* article discussed the danger of war. After charging American diplomacy with opposition to collective security, the author contended:

However, having said "a," one must says "b," i.e., that United States diplomacy is not out to ease international tension and consolidate peace but to prepare a new war. . . . It is also impossible to ignore the openly provocative speeches made by the military leaders of the Atlantic bloc. The Supreme Commander of the North Atlantic armed forces, United States General Gruenther, in an interview in *Newsweek* stubbornly pursued the idea that the alleged present superiority at the disposal of the bloc will decline noticeably in the next few years. Is this not an instigation for a so-called preventive war?[38]

A *Red Star* article was able to list a goodly number of American statements to support the thesis of American aggressiveness:

On March 29, Secretary of State Dulles spoke of the possibility of armed intervention in Indochina. Then the Chairman of the Joint Chiefs of Staff, Admiral Radford, demanded the extension of the war from the territory of Indochina to the territory of the Chinese National Republic. Following him on May 27, Admiral Carney proposed beginning "a preventive war" against the socialist camp. On June 8, at a dinner given by the Union of English Speaking Peoples, the Commander-in-Chief of the North Atlantic bloc in Europe, General Gruenther, threatened the Soviet Union with the employment of atomic weapons. A list of similar speeches by the warmongers could be extended.[39]

William Bullitt, the Soviet writer continued, was proposing an aerial and naval war against China.

At the end of September, in China, Khrushchev said that the Soviet Union did not want war, "but if the imperialists, losing control of themselves, dare to initiate war against us, then imperialism will suffer total defeat." Khrushchev also charged that the imperialists, who had not yet abandoned hopes of reimposing the yoke of imperialism on the liberated peoples, sought to ignite the flame of war in Asia.[40]

Before suffering dismissal, Malenkov made one last sally. Since the spring the Soviet press had devoted less and less attention to him, yet he was not completely beaten. His man, Saburov, was chosen to deliver the major speech on the anniversary of the Russian Revolution. (The speech was actually given on November 6.) Saburov effectively reneged on the concessions made by Malenkov and Pervukhin during the previous April and reiterated Malenkov's optimistic views about the prospects for peace. Saburov was breaking the pattern set by Beria, Pervukhin, and Voroshilov in the three previous major speeches of November 7, when he failed to call for an increase in military might. Moreover, his speech was imbued with a sober optimism about the prospect of an international settlement, although he did mention the difficulties in the way.[41] Malenkov's opponents seem to have had prior knowledge of Saburov's address. Immediately before and immediately after it, the press directly challenged Saburov's failure to call for an increase in the armed forces and questioned his optimism about the prospects for a relaxation of tension. This concerted attack indicates that Saburov's omission of a call for an increase in armaments was due to the survival, as late as November, of policy differences at the highest level.

On November 5, the day before the Saburov speech, *Red Star,* the newspaper of the Ministry of Defense then under Bulganin, called for an increase in the fighting power of the Soviet armed forces.[42] This had been the usual way of countering the past statements of the Malenkov group. On the same day, General Kolesnichenko also called for a further strengthening of the defensive capacity of the Soviet Union. Although he gave the Soviet Union credit for having successfully prevented war so far, he called attention to the continued imperialist policy of initiating war.[43]

In his Order of the Day to soldiers participating in the Red Square parade, an order that was published simultaneously with Saburov's speech, Bulganin said that it would be necessary to continue strengthening the might of the armed forces because the capitalists were continuing the policy of the preparation of a new war.[44] In his speech on Red Square Bulganin took issue with Saburov's optimism when he pointed out that "so far no changes have taken place in the international situation which would give us grounds for reducing our attention in any degree to the question of strengthening our defensive capability."[45] In Minsk, Marshal Timoshenko also called for strengthening the armed forces, on the grounds that "the easing of tension should not be overestimated."[46]

On November 12 *Red Star* went even further in opposing Saburov's position than before the speech. Repeating Bulganin's call for strengthening the armed forces, the editorial added: "The Communist Party considers that there is no sphere, including military affairs, where it is possible to stop at what has been attained."[47]

Foreign policy and military posture, although of great importance, did not exhaust the areas of disagreement among the Soviet leaders. The proportionate effort to be devoted to heavy industry and to light industry, an issue in its own right, was directly affected by the debate on military preparedness. The relative roles assigned to the Party and to the governmental organs were a subject of dispute and of shifting emphasis. The breaking in of new lands was being advanced as an alternative to a more intensive agriculture, with greater incentives to the peasantry. The great variety of issues and the imperfection of our information make it impossible to say whether foreign policy and military posture were the only major areas of policy on which differences of opinion existed, or whether Saburov's failure to call for an increase in armaments had a wider significance.

Saburov's speech makes one wonder whether world events between April and November worked in Malenkov's favor. Had they emboldened him to one more attempt to promote his views? The Soviet press had been making a great fuss about Western plans for a European Defense Community (EDC), which would have facilitated the rearming of Germany. For all we know, Malenkov may have used the French rejection of EDC at the end of August to argue among his colleagues that America was impotent to impose her will on Europe. The French rejection of EDC induced a tone of optimism in the Soviet press that reached a climax in November. This is a puzzling circumstance because on October 3 events had taken a turn that strengthened the position of the Western allies. That day Great Britain made a solemn pledge to keep four divisions on the continent. Anyone reasonably familiar with Western European politics must have known that such a pledge was unprecedented in British history and also that the chief French objection to some kind of Western defense community was the previous British reluctance to bear burdens that France was expected to assume. Therefore some explanation is required for Saburov's optimistic assessment of the international situation after the British commitment. The British move practically guaranteed German rearmament.

Either the Russians misunderstood the Western European political situation (which is not at all impossible) or Malenkov had improved his position in the factional struggle to the point where he could once more press his optimistic views about the international situation. The second explanation is particularly attractive because the issue of *Kommunist* for November, 1954, presented a sanguine view of events. Since *Kommunist* was the most authoritative Party organ, Malenkov's views were for the moment being put forward as the official line. The editorial in this issue connected the failure to ratify EDC with a reduction of the war danger:

> Favorable conditions for the regulation of other unresolved international problems [other than Korea and Indochina] have been created. . . . The Soviet people are convinced that at the present time there are no questions which cannot be justly resolved in the interests of all people given good will on both sides. . . . The characteristic feature of the present political and strategic situation is that the forces which strengthen the cause of peace are growing but at the very same time the subversive activities of those who are trying to push mankind into a new world war are being intensified. . . . However, the present relationship of forces on the international scene proves the hopelessness of any such attempt by the imperialists. . . . The USA only in the most recent years has spent about fifty billion dollars in creating aggressive blocs. . . . And yet right now American imperialism is just as far from accomplishing its plans of world mastery as at the mo-

ment that it entered upon this hopeless task. The brandishing of atomic weapons, military hysteria, and the adventurous policy of provocations lead to the isolation of the USA on the international scene. Subversive activities in Asia raise up the Asiatic peoples against the USA. *Despite the USA and as a result of opposition to it, a certain diminution of international tension has been attained* [author's italics].

The foreign policy of American monopoly capital has suffered failure after failure but it has not yet suffered final defeat and dreams madly, is ready to rush into any adventure and to take up any provocation.[48]

This editorial passage in the most authoritative of journals, *Kommunist,* breathes a confidence not to be found in the analyses of the preceding months. Conditions for an improvement in the diplomatic situation are said to be favorable. In the present state of international forces imperialism cannot hope to accomplish its aims. The billions that the United States has spent on its alliance system and on its bases have been wasted. American militarism has served only to isolate the United States: it has not prevented a weakening of international tension. The Soviet editor expressly related his optimistic tone to the French failure to ratify EDC: "Not a single modern war has begun without the prior hammering together of aggressive blocs," nor has a single modern war begun without being started by militaristic Germany. The French failure to ratify EDC means no consolidation of the Western alliance system and no German rearmament.

The optimism of the editorial extended to the internal politics of the Western nations. Not a single aggressive war has started without the imperialists' first stupefying a significant part of their own population and stifling all opposition to their aggressive plans. But the American progressives (the Communists and fellow travelers are meant) and even the liberals are infused with the peace spirit and have spoken out for it. Even the "right-wing leaders of the social democratic parties" (much hated by Soviet officialdom) dare not oppose the wishes of the masses for peace and, in Germany and France, they have opposed German rearmament.

Had this editorial appeared a month previously, its hopes for Western disunity would have been more understandable. The Soviet press reported these events in a way that suggested lack of understanding of European politics. Its argument was about as follows: the French Parliament rejected EDC at the end of August because the forces of peace triumphed within France. The fear of revived German militarism effected the rejection of this plan. At the end of October the London and Paris meetings worked out a substitute for EDC, which would permit German rearmament, and dropped some of the supranational features of EDC. The Soviet press described the great opposition to these arrangements in terms that made it seem unlikely that the agreements would be ratified. The Soviet press hardly noticed the unprecedented British commitment, and concentrated on the hubbub raised by the plan's opponents.

Such a misreading of the situation accords with the doctrinaire Soviet outlook on foreign policy. The conviction that England runs the Continent and that the United States runs England caused the Russians to interpret the British concession as a staged gesture, for the Bolsheviks assume that all is prearranged in the capitalist world. Moreover, Soviet hopes were bolstered by Mendès-France, who then seemed to be the most influential statesman in France, and who made his misgivings about German rearmament quite clear.

Some such reconstruction of the Russian analysis helps to explain Soviet optimism one month after the British commitment, and eight or nine days after the Paris Agreements on West European Union had been signed by the French, British, German, and other governments. Ten days later, on November 13, a Soviet official protest described the Paris Agreements as a threat to stability and made a counterproposal for an all-European security pact.[49] The tone was more hostile than alarmed.

Another *Kommunist* editorial, written about this time, took a sober and calm view of the situation. The ratification of the Paris Agreements, said the Soviet commentator, would make it very difficult to solve urgent European problems, especially the German problem, yet the partisans of peace were still a force to be reckoned with.[50]

An article in the December issue of *Kommunist,* although retaining the line that the defeat of EDC had decreased international tension, was perhaps as alarmist about the danger of war as anything since Stalin's death. The defeat of EDC, it was argued, impels the enemies of peace to so frantic an activity that it has "created a real danger to peace." The situation is serious, the editorial said, because "the aggressive forces of imperialism who suffered such a failure with EDC are trying, but now under a different banner, to carry out their criminal schemes and to put into the hands of the German militarists—yesterday the hangmen of Europe—the weapons which were dashed from the hands of their soldiers by the anti-Hitlerite coalition." The Paris Agreements of October 23, 1954, envisaged a military alliance "whose purpose it is to speed up preparation for a new war." The West German revenge seekers do not hide the fact that twelve divisions are only a beginning and that they hope soon to have thirty and then sixty divisions.

In typical communist style the previous month's estimate was not merely modified but reversed. Now readers were told that Churchill, in October, 1942, had prepared a plan for making Germany a member of an anti-Soviet alliance. Whereas the month before even the American liberals were said to be "infused with the peace spirit" and to be speaking up against war, now *Kommunist* insisted on the connection between "the preparation of a new war and the accelerated process of making the United States of America fascist." There was no support for the idea, so recently expressed, that international tension had decreased. "The most recent events," said *Kommunist,* "especially the program of the Western powers for the ratification of the Paris Agreements . . . increase the danger of war. There must be no illusions on that score."

Having stated the awful prospects facing Europe and the Soviet Union, the writer concluded, not surprisingly: "The nations of the camp of peace, democracy, and socialism, in the full realization that the war is designed primarily against them, will not permit themselves to be taken by surprise. They are doing everything necessary to guard their peaceful toil, to guarantee the inviolability of the frontiers and territory of their governments and to assure defense against any possible aggression."[51]

Less than a month after *Kommunist's* reversal of judgment about the danger of war, *Pravda* launched a campaign against Malenkov. The approaching remilitarization of Germany made it possible for Malenkov's opponents to repudiate him, since his policies assumed the possibility of agreement with the West.

Malenkov had hoped for a summit meeting to dramatize Western willingness to make such an agreement. He had seemed to argue, as we shall see shortly, that Western European nations retained enough sovereignty and independence not to be classed as American puppets. Although a four-power summit conference had failed to materialize, the French Government had demonstrated its independence by refusing to ratify EDC. Up to this point events had supported Malenkov's cause. The Western European nations, however, had been able to overcome the strong opposition to the rearming of Germany and were now on the point of making legal arrangements to that end. According to the Russian concept of war as described in Chapters 2 and 7, German militarization was a necessary preliminary to a Western war plot.

In a future war, the Russians expected the United States to rely greatly on the effect of a surprise aerial attack, but also to assign a large role to tactical atomic weapons. In the Russian view the United States could not deploy the tactical weapons and advance overland without German troops. The Russians had scant regard for the French, but respected the Germans who had beaten them badly and had withdrawn from Russia only when greatly inferior in strength.

The Russians at that time had to reckon with the fact that West European political-military power was potentially equal to Russia's. From the viewpoint of each single Western European nation the Soviet Union seemed overwhelmingly stronger, but from the Soviet viewpoint the West European industrial complex and population resources were comparable to those of the Soviet Union. Germany had recently dealt a nearly fatal blow to the Soviet Union with little help from others. A union of Germany, France, Britain, and Italy—not to speak of the United States—could represent a serious threat.

Since the communists assumed that capitalism would make a desperate effort to prolong its existence before its inevitable demise, German rearmament seemed to them the harbinger of the final conflict between the two world systems. The growing danger to the Soviet Union happened also to furnish ammunition against the Malenkov faction. With a sense of righteous self-assurance Malenkov's opponents went over to the attack in December, 1954.

It would certainly be an error of oversimplification to assert, in the absence of detailed knowledge, that Malenkov's foreign policy was diametrically opposed to that of Khrushchev. One would have to suppose that Malenkov had been a secret noncommunist all his life. Such a notion is absurd. The truth seems to be that Malenkov believed Western unity to be a mere façade. A combination of war weariness, fear of the great destructiveness of nuclear weapons, and the Soviet possession of those weapons, seemed to create a situation favorable for dividing the Western alliance.

As soon as he took office in March, 1953, and again on August 8, Malenkov held out the hope of the disintegration of NATO if international tension were reduced. Malenkov was suggesting that the Western alliance system was so fragile that a change in the international atmosphere could cause its collapse.[52]

We do not know what tactics, if any, Malenkov had in mind to bring about the collapse of the NATO system. But an article written by Gus in November, 1953, suggests that Malenkov did have a plan and offers some clues as to what it was. The previous chapter described Gus's suggestion that the law of the inevitability of war could be paralyzed. The condemnation of his idea by military writers and especially by Khruzhkov, the chief ideological opponent of Malenkov, suggests that Gus was putting up a trial balloon for Malenkov. Gus's article contains the only known argument in Marxian terms for Malenkov's ideas. Whether or not Malenkov approved every item in Gus's article, the fact is that its arguments went much further in support of the Premier's thesis than he himself had done in his public statements.

Gus contended that all Western schemes for a united Europe were reactionary. The Americans talked of "the obsolete principle of the sovereignty of nations" and of the necessity for "world government." They were dreaming of the American Twentieth Century. But Soviet policy was for the independent existence of sovereign nations.[53]

Developing the theme of dissension within the Western camp, Gus pointed out that American insistence that their allies curtail normal economic relations with communist nations was inspired by economic competition between the United States and Western Europe. Pressure for the restoration of the China trade had grown sharply, especially in Britain, since the conclusion of the Korean armistice.[54] Here Gus was demonstrating the validity of Malenkov's prophecy of August that the relaxation of international tension would open more widely the fissures in the Western alliance system.

A limited accommodation with capitalism was made possible by the divisions within the capitalist camp. The limit was "Collaboration cannot lead to the transformation of one system into the other."[55] Within this limit Gus argued for major Soviet policy changes:

> Every agreement between the two systems should be the fruit of a reasoned, mutually advantageous, voluntary deal [sdelka] and not the result of the imposition of one country's dictate upon the other. . . . This was the case even in the first years of the existence of the Soviet government. And now when the international position of the U.S.S.R. is firm as never before there is not the slightest chance for the success of a diplomacy of threats and blackmail or the imposition of any conditions whatsoever upon the Soviet people.
>
> Therefore our agreements with the capitalist world always have been and always will be the fruit of mutual agreement and the result of mutual concessions [ustupki]. . . .

> In other words, we always remember that our bourgeois opposite number, whether it be a trading, economic, or political bargain, will not enter upon it if he does not receive "a just profit," and in certain cases we are ready even to go as far as giving him an "increased gain" but in order that we too receive a proper benefit.[56]

Later in the article Gus warned, as did Malenkov in his speech of August, 1953, that the capitalists misinterpreted "expedient and necessary concessions" as a sign of the weakness of the Soviet government.[57]

If we supplement Malenkov's speeches with this article of Gus's we get a clearer view of the former's intentions. The advantages the Soviet Union might derive from the disintegration of the NATO alliance were so great that a few concessions from the Soviet side would be amply rewarded if they led to dissension among the Western allies. Against this argument we can set a speech by Khrushchev in June, 1954, in which he declared that Soviet concessions would only provoke further demands. Since this was the opposition's line, we can more readily understand the Malenkov group's almost pathetic insistence that the capitalists must not misinterpret the Soviet desire for peace as a sign of weakness.

Since his retraction in April, 1954, Malenkov seems to have been on the defensive, with only intermittent bursts of offensive activity. During December, 1954, and January, 1955, the political forces gathered that were to bring about his resignation from the premiership in February.

NOTES

1. Novosad, Vojvodina Regional Service in Hungarian, December 12, 1953. I am indebted to Melville J. Ruggles for calling this Yugoslav reaction to my attention.
2. See Chapter 3.
3. "Appeal of the Central Committee of the Communist Party of the Soviet Union to All Electors, to the Workers, Peasants and Soviet Intelligentsia and to the Fighting Men of the Soviet Army and Navy," *Red Star*, February 11, 1954.
4. *Ibid.*

5. "The Inspiring Appeal of the Communist Party," *Pravda*, February 13, 1954; "Toward New Victories in the Struggle for Communism," *Izvestiia*, February 13, 1954; "For the Victory of the Bloc of Communists and Non-Party Members," *Sel'skoe khoziaistvo (Agriculture)*, February 13, 1954; "The Great Unity of the Party Government and People," *Trud (Labor)*, February 13, 1954; "The Communist Party, the Organizer of the Victory of the Soviet Armed Forces," *Red Star*, February 21, 1954.

6. Lieutenant General Kozlov, "The Communist Party—The Organizer and Leader of the Soviet Armed Forces," *Red Star*, February 16, 1954.

7. A. Zheltov, "The Armed Forces of the Soviet Government," *Pravda*, February 23, 1954.

8. Marshal of the Soviet Union V. Sokolovskii, "Guard the Peace and Security of the Motherland," *Izvestiia*, February 23, 1954; Marshal of the Soviet Union A. Vasilevskii, "On Guard over the Security of Our Soviet Motherland," *Red Star*, February 23, 1954.

9. "The Speech of Comrade P. N. Pospelov at the Meeting of Electors of the Kursk Election District, March 10, 1954," *Red Star*, March 11, 1954.

10. "Speech of Comrade M. G. Pervukhin at the Meeting of Electors of the Tbilisi Kalinin Electoral District, March 11, 1954," *Zaria Vostoka (Dawn of the East)*, March 12, 1954. The reduced text is in *Pravda*, March 12, 1954.

11. "The Speech of N. Z. Saburov," *Sovetskaia Belorussiia (Soviet Belorussia)*, March 13, 1954.

12. "The Speech of Comrade G. M. Malenkov at a Meeting of the Electors of the Leningrad District of the City of Moscow, March 12, 1954," *Pravda*, March 13, 1954.

13. *Ibid.*

14. "Speech of Comrade N. S. Khrushchev at the Meeting of Electors of the Kalinin Electoral District of the City of Moscow, March 6, 1954," *Pravda*, March 7, 1954.

15. "Speech of N. S. Khrushchev at the Second Congress of the Polish United Workers' Party, March 11, 1954," *Pravda*, March 12, 1954.

16. "Speech of V. M. Molotov at the Meeting of the Electors of the Molotov Electoral District in Moscow, March 11, 1954," *Pravda*, March 12, 1954.

17. "Speech of Comrade L. M. Kaganovich at a Meeting of the Electors of the Tashkent-Lenin Electoral District, March 11, 1954," *Pravda*, March 13, 1954.

18. "Speech of Comrade K. E. Voroshilov at the Meeting of the Electors of Kirov Electoral District of the City of Leningrad, March 10, 1954," *Izvestiia*, March 11, 1954.

19. "Speech of Comrade N. A. Bulganin at the Meeting of the Electors of the Moscow City Electoral District, March 10, 1954," *Izvestiia*, March 11, 1954.

20. "Outlines of Strategy: Address by the Secretary of State before the Council of Foreign Relations, January 12, 1954," *Documents on American Foreign Relations, 1954*, New York, 1955, pp. 9-10.

21. *Ibid.*

22. Observer, "Peaceful Regulation or the Expansion of the War," *Pravda*, March 17, 1954. Italics, which are in the original, mark specially important passages.

23. "Text of Magazine Article by Dulles on Present Defense Policy," *The New York Times*, March 17, 1954; "Text of Statement by Dulles before Senate Foreign Relations Committee," *The New York Times*, March 20, 1954.

24. Editorial, "The Sowers of Fear and the Instigators of War Hysteria," *Pravda*, March 26, 1954.

25. Iu. Zhukov, "International Review," *Pravda*, March 31, 1954.

26. A. Kozhin, "The Schemes of the Enemies of Peace in Asia. The Chinese Press Reveals the Intrigues of the Imperialist Aggressors," *Pravda*, March 22, 1954.

27. Anonymous, "Plans Directed Toward the Expansion of the War in Indochina," *Pravda*, March 24, 1954.

28. M. Afonin, "How the Pentagon 'Prepares' for the Geneva Meeting," *Pravda*, March 25, 1954.

29. "The Speech of the Chairman of the Council of Ministers of the U.S.S.R., the Deputy G. M. Malenkov," *Izvestiia*, April 27, 1954.

30. "Speech of the Deputy M. G. Pervukhin," *Pravda*, April 27, 1954.

31. "Speech of the Deputy L. M. Kaganovich," *Pravda*, April 27, 1954; "Speech of the Deputy N. S. Khrushchev," *Izvestiia*, April 27, 1954.

32. "Speech of the Deputy N. S. Khrushchev," *Izvestiia*, April 27, 1954.

33. Marshal of the Soviet Union A. Vasilevskii, "The Great Lesson of History," *Red Star*, May 7, 1954.

34. A. Belskaia, "General Gruenther Makes It Clear . . .," *Literaturnaia gazeta (Literary Gazette)*, June 12, 1954.

35. "Churchill's Statement on Foreign Policy," *The New York Times*, May 12, 1953.

36. "Correspondence between Sir Winston Churchill and V. M. Molotov on a Meeting between the Heads of the Governments of Britain and the U.S.S.R.," *Soviet News* (London), March 22, 1955.

37. "Speech of Comrade N. A. Bulganin at the Celebration of the Tenth Anniversary of the Polish Peoples' Republic in Warsaw, July 21, 1954," *Izvestiia*, July 22, 1954.

38. Iu. Pavlov, "The Policy of Setting Up Aggressive Blocs Endangers the Security of the Peoples," *Pravda*, July 31, 1954.

39. Colonel P. Vasil'ev, "On Bullitt's Provocative Article," *Red Star*, August 10, 1954.

40. "Speech by Comrade N. S. Khrushchev at the Great Meeting in Peking Honoring the Fifth Anniversary of the Founding of The Chinese Peoples' Republic, September 30, 1954," *Pravda*, October 1, 1954.

41. "The Thirty-seventh Anniversary of the Great October Revolution. A Report by M. Z. Saburov . . . on November 6, 1954," *Pravda*, November 7, 1954.

42. "The Soviet Army—A Real Peoples' Army," *Red Star*, November 5, 1954.

43. Major General I. Kolesnichenko, "The Socialist System Is the Basis

of the Power of the Soviet Government and Its Armed Forces," *Red Star,* November 5, 1954.

44. "Order of the Minister of Defense of the U.S.S.R.," *Pravda,* November 7, 1954.

45. "The Speech of Marshal of the Soviet Union N. A. Bulganin," *Pravda,* November 8, 1954.

46. Speech by Marshal Timoshenko at Minsk as broadcast on November 8, 1954.

47. "Persistently Strengthen the Might of the Soviet Armed Forces," *Red Star,* November 12, 1954.

48. Editorial, "Socialism and Peace," *Kommunist,* No. 16, November, 1954, pp. 3-12. This issue went to the printer on November 4, 1954.

49. "The Note of the Soviet Government to the Governments of the European Countries and the USA," *Pravda,* November 14, 1954.

50. V. Zagladin, "The Paris Agreements Are Incompatible with the Interests of Assuring Security in Europe," *Kommunist,* No. 17, November, 1954, pp. 112-122.

51. Editorial, "The Peoples Will Not Reconcile Themselves to the Policy of the Preparation of a New War," *Kommunist,* No. 18, December, 1954, pp. 3-13.

52. "Speech by Comrade G. M. Malenkov, Chairman of the U.S.S.R. Council of Ministers," *Pravda,* August 9, 1953.

53. M. Gus, "The General Line of Soviet Foreign Policy," *Zvezda (The Star),* Leningrad, November, 1953, p. 110.

54. *Ibid.,* pp. 113-114.

55. *Ibid.,* p. 113.

56. *Ibid.,* p. 114.

57. *Ibid.,* p. 115.

CHAPTER FIVE

THE LIKELIHOOD OF WAR AND SOVIET DOMESTIC POLITICS: 1955-1957

On February 8, 1955, Malenkov resigned his post as Chairman of the Council of Ministers of the U.S.S.R. Malenkov's career and downfall were, as the previous chapter pointed out, closely connected with the development of Soviet military policies. In tracing this connection to February, 1955, we have made certain general assumptions about the manner in which Soviet policy differences are resolved. It is now time to examine these assumptions more closely, so that the reader may himself judge the validity of the reasoning based on them. The first step will be to review briefly the history of the Malenkov era.

Immediately after Stalin died in March, 1953, Malenkov became both Chairman of the Council of Ministers and Secretary of the Communist Party. He held the second post for only a few days before he resigned it to Khrushchev. Beria held high posts and received considerable press prominence until he was arrested as a traitor in July, 1953. Malenkov's eminence was progressively reduced until, in February, 1955, he was demoted to the office of Minister of Electric Power Stations. Two years later he was removed from this post and assigned to an obscure managerial position in Soviet Asia.

This brief recapitulation of well-known events serves to illustrate the absence of constitutional provisions for the transmission of the powers of state in the Soviet Union. Despite intermittent efforts to assert that ultimate power lies with the Central Committee of the Communist Party, it remains a fact that each shift of power has come about through an alteration in the balance of forces at the highest political level. Exactly how these forces are brought into balance we do not know. The reasons for the shifts in power, however, are less obscure.

Stalin had ruled by virtue of the awe and fear he inspired in the whole Soviet Union. Continual arbitrary arrests and imprisonments maintained his hold of terror. When Stalin died his successors feared an explosion of forces they could not control. In what was practically their first announcement the leaders warned of the dangers of panic and disorder. Later they asserted that some capitalists had wanted to take advantage of Stalin's death to attack the Soviet Union.

The very fact of Stalin's death worked an organic change in Soviet society. His successors, in adjusting to that fact, made changes that in turn created the necessity for further changes. No constitutional framework existed to circumscribe the form and extent of these changes. For example, when the top members of the ruling clique found it necessary to expel Beria from their number and to reduce the activity and the influence of the secret police, the only method considered effective was drastic: the arrest of Beria, his secret trial, and his execution as a traitor. The course of the political crisis of June, 1957, showed that policy changes are made as a result of *ad hoc* shifts in the balance of political power and not through established channels. While these shifts of power do not occur according to law and are not susceptible to any kind of judicial review, it would be a mistake to imagine that custom does not govern them to some extent. There are in the Soviet Union, as in any other settled society, certain permanent social groups with relatively unchanging interests and outlooks. Through these an element of uniformity is imposed on top-level political changes.

Two types of groups influence national policy. Among the first type are the police, the army, and the Party—groups that can make their weight felt directly since they are official institutions. Among the second type are the peasantry, the youth, and the intellectuals—social groups whose influence is indirect.

The importance of the secret police is obvious. With their intimate knowledge of the personal history of important persons, and with their unlimited powers, they occupied a unique position as an instrument of Stalin's dictatorship. Almost immediately upon his death the chief symbol of that instrument, Beria, was liquidated. Such a step was probably considered an urgent necessity by representatives of several interest groups. A police of tremendous powers held firmly in the hands of a single dictator made sense, but in a collective dictatorship, in which Beria occupied what seemed to be the second position, who could guarantee that the instrument of power would not seek to become the wielder of power? The elimination of the police as a major power in the state was bound to be popular since almost all had suffered at their hands in the past, and all feared them in the future.

Among the interest groups that acquiesced in, or actively supported, the elimination of the police, the armed forces occupied a special place as the only armed group besides the police. The professional army cadres had suffered humiliation and decimation at the hands of the secret police in 1937 and 1938. The ubiquity within the armed forces of secret police officers who reported up through an independent chain of command was a constant reminder that another purge could be instituted.

Stalin's death breathed political life into the inert Army. Once active support had been solicited from the Army by the new civilian leaders, the Army could not be debarred permanently from participation in internal politics. The demotion of Zhukov in 1957 demonstrated that the Army already had a political role and that the Party had been successful in reducing it. There is a general tendency in the Soviet Union for the once-dependent instrument of power to seek an independent political role. It is this that makes the political importance of particular institutions at any given time so difficult to assess.

The Communist Party of the Soviet Union has also changed

its role considerably since the death of Stalin. Stalin had converted the Party, which had originally been the holy vessel of communist doctrine, into a mere instrument for the execution of his personal will. Its more than six million members, whether acting of their own volition or at Stalin's instance, provided the mechanism that moved the countless levers of Soviet society. In the months following Stalin's death the Party's area of competence seemed to shrink, while governmental institutions expanded their authority. This shift of weight favored Malenkov's policy of greater emphasis on consumer goods. Sacrifice of present comforts for the sake of the future has always been the Party's credo. The improvement of the standard of living demanded the talents of the industrial manager rather than those of the party boss.

Khrushchev's displacement of Malenkov in February, 1955, marked a revival of the Party's influence. Yet Khrushchev himself, by his scathing denunciation of Stalin in the ''secret speech'' at the Twentieth Party Congress in February, 1956, by implication rejected much of the Party's past. He brusquely told the party leaders to learn the business that they presumed to direct in the name of the Party. Since then Stalin's reputation has been partly restored, the Party's prestige has been somewhat elevated, and its members have been assigned by Khrushchev to new and important positions in the decentralization of industry. Furthermore the constant repetition since 1953 of the fiction that the Central Committee of the Party is the ultimate authority in the Soviet Union may have enhanced the committee's position.

The industrial managers have always played a vital economic role. Under Stalin the industrial manager lived well when most fared badly, but at any moment he might be capriciously imprisoned. He had to concentrate on fulfilling the state plans, without resistance to what was absurd or impracticable and without the possibility of independent action. The industrial managers of today do not seem to have become an independent political force. But the state prefers to elicit their initiative and enthusiasm rather than the automatic obedience that characterized the Stalin era.

The army, the police, the Party, and to a lesser extent the industrial managers, are clearly marked groups. Less highly organized groups must be taken into account, though their disaffection would not present an immediate political crisis. Of these, the Soviet peasants are the largest, if not the most important. In their public speeches the Soviet leaders, especially Khrushchev, have emphasized the past mismanagement of agriculture and have admitted that past governmental policies forced the peasants to act against their own and the common interest. The post-Stalin regime, by fits and starts has sought active co-operation and improved efficiency from the peasants by large-scale investment in agriculture. Unless food and labor shortages are mastered, the consumer goods program cannot progress. In a sense, therefore, the government must woo the peasantry, but the latter, scattered over the country, have no means of bringing direct pressure on the leadership in order to promote their own interests.

Another potentially powerful but presently impotent group comprises the students. The political inconsequence of students in the Stalin period represented a break in the Russian tradition. Today numerous travelers to the Soviet Union report the agitation of the student body, which finds expression in pointed questions about the internal and external policies of the regime. Some believe that the student body is merely letting off surplus steam and that the regime is wise to permit this. Others assert that student pressures can lead to consequences even more serious than the riots of 1956 in Poland and Soviet Georgia. No one, not even the Soviet leaders, can foresee the future role of the students.

These considerations apply, of course, to other social groups. If each group formulated its demands and secured their acceptance, the present regime could not survive. On the other hand, the regime must go some distance in meeting these demands if only to prevent them from growing too insistent. Meeting one demand reduces the resources available for meeting others. The present regime's freedom of action is severely limited by the need to satisfy the economic, political, and psychological demands of so many groups without any firm knowledge of what groups can be slighted without danger of an explosion. The inevitable tendency is to play safe and give each group something. The list of fixed requirements is long.

The general standard of living must continue to rise; it cannot safely turn downward for any length of time. The wages of the industrial class, including the managers and the shock workers, must be increased to improve morale. The curtailment of the sources of new urban labor, the increased mechanization of industry, and the greater demands for industrial output make the improvement of labor efficiency a requisite. At this stage forced labor is less economical than in the past and apathetic workmen are as undesirable as ever. Agricultural production must increase through greater investments in equipment and labor. Common prudence would recommend a steady expansion of basic industry; the Bolshevik faith demands great efforts to that end. Nuclear war can be avoided, or survived, only if a most expensive military establishment is maintained.

These vast requirements, formidable as they are, do not exhaust the constraints on the freedom of action of the present Soviet regime. Ideological taboos flourish in all their vigor. It is an article of faith that Soviet socialism is the best system of political economy and government. The one party system, the dead-end *kolkhoz* system, cannot be changed without tempting the wrath of the god of history. In the Bolshevik view only extreme emergencies justify temporary retreats in the advance toward their historical goals.

To adjudicate the claims of conflicting interests in society is the function of any government. This task is especially difficult in the Soviet Union where there are no commonly accepted procedures for making such decisions. Each crisis has been worked out somehow, although we do not know exactly how. Take the protracted crisis we have been discussing. Until January, 1955, Malenkov headed the preponderant faction in the Soviet leadership. His military and economic policies had been under fire from an opposing faction that was free to offer discreet public criticism and to achieve preponderance by detaching some of Malenkov's support. This procedure is at once similar to, and profoundly different from, that by which majorities are achieved in parliamentary governments. Realignments, pooling of interests, and sacrifice of principles are common to both systems, but in the parliamentary system the fate of the loser is known beforehand. Since Stalin, it is true, only Beria has paid with his head for losing, but who can guarantee that the next loser will not suffer the same fate? It testifies to the essential unity of aim and solidarity of Stalin's successors that they have managed to frame and execute policy with some success in this most uncertain atmosphere without physically liquidating more than one major figure.

Khrushchev owes his retention of office and his extension of power to his knack for choosing the winning side—and for helping it to win. A master of equivocation, he seems to promise all things to all men, to pursue incompatible courses, to juggle many balls in the air. His policy seems inconsistent and improvised. If some of his associates, unknown to us, have accused him of sacrificing principles to expediency, others must have observed that by his very flexibility he is carrying the entire communist system through a period of most delicate readjustment.

The above analysis of top-level Soviet politics puts into perspective the events of December, 1954, and January, 1955. The available press evidence shows that the anti-Malenkov forces first threw down the gauntlet. In a *Pravda* article written on the seventy-fifth anniversary of Stalin's birth, December 19, 1954, heavy industry was described as the cornerstone of the socialist economy and the source of the wealth, might, and defensive capability of the Soviet government. Malenkov had indicated that heavy industry and military strength had already achieved a satisfactory level and that now consumer goods could be sharply increased. The *Pravda* article contradicted this point of view, arguing that "in the conditions of the present international situation, the further strengthening of the defensive might of the Soviet government, the elevation of vigilance, and the strengthening of the Soviet armed forces acquire special significance. . . ." The Communist Party always had devoted, and was now devoting, primary attention to the comprehensive development of heavy industry, the cornerstone of the might of the Soviet Union: "And now while carrying out the program of the further improvement of all branches of the socialist economy and the program of the systematic improvement of the material welfare of the people, the party will push heavy industry forward above everything else and unswervingly."[1] Here was a clear indication that Malenkov's program for giving priority to light industry was considered dangerous to the security of the Soviet state. Two days later both sides of the argument were stated in unequivocal terms, one in *Pravda* and the other in *Izvestiia*.

V. Kruzhkov, the same who had dismissed as contrary to Marxism the possibility of paralyzing the laws of the development of capitalism, wrote an article on Stalin for the *Pravda* issue of December 21. Kruzhkov quoted Lenin on the need to build up heavy industry in order to maintain the independence of the Soviet Union, as if nothing had changed since Lenin's day. (Malenkov had described Lenin's dictum as the correct basis for policy in Lenin's time.) Over and over again Kruzhkov described heavy industry as the cornerstone of Soviet power. He quoted Stalin as having said the backward were beaten. Heavy industry had been decisive for the victory in the last war. Kruzhkov pointed out that, in conditions where the aggressive imperialist forces were aggravating the international situation, the armed forces should be strengthened: "The Party calls upon the Soviet people to direct its primary attention . . . to the growth of heavy industry."[2] Here gathered in one place are all the familiar themes of the anti-Malenkov group.

In an editorial in the same issue of *Pravda*, the same points were made, if anything more sharply: "The growth of heavy industry is the basis for the further development of the whole economy and the guarantee of the inviolability of the borders of our motherland. . . ." The need to strengthen the defensive might of the Soviet Union was directly linked with imperialist plans for a new war and the revival of the German army, which was to serve as the shock force against the Soviet state.[3]

Izvestiia took the opposite side in the debate. Konstantinov, in an article on the date of Stalin's birth, devoted paragraph after paragraph to the importance of the masses and to the great role the Party had played in victory in the Great Fatherland War, but he failed to make the familiar connection between heavy industry and Soviet victory. In the following statement he differed flatly with *Pravda:*

> The chief concern of the Communist Party in the sphere of internal policy is for the further rise in the productive forces of the country so that the material welfare and cultural level of the popular masses should grow without interruption and that the life of millions of toilers should become even better from year to year.[4]

The editorial in the same day's *Izvestiia* was not quite as uncompromising as Konstantinov's article, but its divergence from *Pravda* was clear enough:

> The chief concern of the Party and the government is the maximum satisfaction of the constantly growing material and cultural demands of all members of the society.[5]

Never before had the two conceptions of state policy been contrasted more clearly: "The Party calls [for] primary attention . . . to heavy industry," and "The chief concern of the Party . . . is the maximum satisfaction of the constantly growing material . . . demands of all. . . ." During the month of December Khrushchev twice put himself on the heavy industry side of the argument. In a speech on improving building methods, he said that heavy industry was the basis of the whole economy and the source of the country's defensive capability. The further development of heavy industry was necessary to assure the inviolability of the Soviet borders and to achieve success in raising the standard of living.[6] The only possible counterargument was that the Soviet borders were quite secure. As early as September, 1954, Khrushchev had told a visiting English scientist, John Bernal, that the development of all branches of Soviet industry would proceed according to an existing plan that devoted the main attention to heavy industry.[7] The interview was printed late in December. It seems unlikely that the publication of an interview three months after it took place was a mere coincidence. The decision to do so must therefore be placed in the context of the Khrushchev group's struggle against Malenkov and his policies. The publication of this interview only three days after *Pravda* and *Izvestiia* had taken directly contrary views served two purposes. First, it reminded people of Khrushchev's great importance, for his tone in addressing Professor Bernal was that of a confident spokesman for the whole regime. Second, it made clear that Khrushchev was then, as he had earlier been, a proponent of continued emphasis on heavy industry.

The Khrushchev faction, having re-emphasized the long-established connection between heavy industry and the security of the Soviet Union, proceeded to drum up support for its policies by pointing to the danger of war. Major General Talenskii, in an article written for wide circulation, said that "at any moment . . . mankind might be faced with the accomplished fact of the beginning of a destructive atomic war."[8] This was the sharpest public statement about the likelihood of war made by a Soviet official in the entire period under review. A few days later General Gritchin recalled that American aircraft had penetrated Soviet air space and sarcastically referred to the Forty-ninth Air Division's "tactical" capability, implying that its true mission was a strategic attack against the Soviet Union.[9]

On January 8, 1955, Khrushchev told an audience of young people, about to go out to the new virgin lands, that the industrialization of the country was the Party's general line. That policy had brought victory in the last war. Now the Soviet Union was in capitalist encirclement and Soviet industrial triumphs made the enemies of the Soviet Union fearful.[10]

Khrushchev's opponents gave the impression of fighting a rear-guard action against superior forces, but they had not yet surrendered. In a lecture passed for the press on January 10, an economist, discussing the proportion of resources to be allocated to capital formation and to the production of consumer goods, admitted that heavy industry had to continue to expand, but stated flatly that "a certain backwardness in the production of goods in popular demand had not yet been mastered." At the present time it was possible to develop heavy industry and light industry simultaneously. Here was an echo of the basic theme of Malenkov's speech in August, 1953, namely, that the period of forcing forward heavy industry was past and that a new stage had been reached.[11]

The basic tone of Khrushchev's remarks on January 8 had been that the requirements for heavy industry were exactly the same as they had always been in the past. The editor of *Pravda*, Dmitri Shepilov, elaborated Khrushchev's terse statement in a signed article. Shepilov took direct issue with the dangerous counsels of the Malenkovites to whom he ascribed the belief that the primacy of heavy industry had only been necessary when the country was backward. Now that a mighty industry had been created the situation had altered radically and therefore, said the "pseudo-economists," *since 1953* the Soviet land had entered a new stage of economic development. (The phrase here put in italics clearly intimated that Malenkov was the leading "pseudo-economist.") These pseudo-economists, continued Shepilov, wanted equal rates of development for heavy industry and light industry and even advocated preferential treatment for light industry. Such a program could only injure the country: "Stalin showed more than once that in the face of capitalist encirclement we cannot halt the tempo of the forward movement of heavy industry. . . . To hold it back means to fall back. And the backward are beaten." Shepilov went on to quote some highly technical language from the writings of the economists whom he was attacking, and concluded:

> In generally understandable language this means: we surrender the advantage of forcing forward the development of heavy industry, machine construction, energy, chemical industry, electronics, jet technology, guidance systems, and so forth, to the imperialist world. . . . It is hard to imagine a more anti-scientific, rotten theory, which could disarm our people more.[12]

Shepilov's catalogue proceeded from the general to the particular, from "heavy industry" to "guidance systems." He implied that the Malenkov faction was not only guilty of a general negligence to push heavy industry but also of a specific failure to develop guidance systems, an essential component of both long-range missile systems and active air-defense systems.

It is not surprising to find that three days later an editorial in the official organ of the Ministry of Defense repeated Shepilov's remarks about the dangerous errors of the pseudo-economists, which would lead to the weakening of the defensive capacities of the Soviet Union "in conditions where the imperialist countries are openly conducting a policy for the preparation of a new war."[13] It does come as something of a surprise, however, to read in the same editorial that certain economists on the teaching staffs of higher military institutes shared these "anti-Marxist" views. Colonel Kuznetsov was singled out for his zealous defense of these terrible views at the Zhukovskii Air Academy. This revelation that the whole military establishment did not speak with one voice is indeed rare in Soviet official publications. The hapless Colonel Kuznetsov was almost certainly expressing more than his personal views when, at the most important institute of air force research and higher education, he advocated more emphasis on light industry. Perhaps the air force, heretofore the least politically important of the Soviet armed services, had decided that its interests lay in the support of Malenkov and his views. One may surmise that Malenkov, who relied so heavily on deterrence, was willing to maintain the rate of growth of the air force or even to increase it, while making his economies at the expense of the ground forces. No other explanation offers itself for *Red Star*'s deliberate linking of the air force with Malenkov's ideas. There is nothing intrinsically unreasonable, of course, in the three services competing for position and funds during a period of major revision of strategic concepts, or in their appealing to different factions within a divided top leadership Unfortunately, almost nothing more is afforded us than this single glimpse into the effects of the political conflict on the military. The successful elimination of the Malenkov heresy from the air force school was referred to twice later, and that is all we know.[14]

The speeches and printed interviews of early February carried forward the theme of the optimists' unforgivable recklessness in the shadow of war clouds. Most critical of all was Bulganin, who succeeded to Malenkov's vacated post. He had been among the first to call attention to the danger of surprise attack and was the sharpest in attacking Malenkov. He echoed many others in his remarks about the importance of heavy industry for defense, but was the only one to suggest that Malenkov had depleted the state reserves in his efforts to economize: "It would be an unforgivable mistake to slacken our attention to this very important matter [of the state reserves] or to yield to the temptation to solve individual current problems at the expense of state reserves. . . . To increase the state reserves . . . is our most important task."[15]

Marshal Zhukov, who gained greatly by Malenkov's dismissal, warned that the very existence of atomic weapons made it necessary to reckon with the possibility of their employment because "certain madmen might go to the length of using them in spite of everything."[16]

At the very meetings of the Supreme Soviet where Malenkov's resignation was formally accepted, however, it became apparent that war alarms had been raised mainly as a pretext for deposing Malenkov. The cries of "imperialist aggression" and "capitalist encirclement" were hyperboles meant to convey that Malenkov's satisfaction with the current military posture was unsound. In Soviet political disputation it is insufficient to charge that the opponent has a policy that may ultimately bring great dangers. The policy under attack is always described as having already created a critical situation.

On the very day of Malenkov's resignation Molotov made a speech analyzing the international situation that indicated the trumped up nature of the war warnings. As a matter of routine he condemned American aggressiveness, but he went on to offer evidence of the weakness of the American cause. In an unusually realistic analysis of the American political scene, Molotov argued that the Democratic Party's involvement in the Korean war caused it to lose the 1952 election. The Republicans won the Presidency, said Molotov, not because they had announced an aggressive foreign policy, but because they then seemed to favor the conclusion of the war in Korea. All this goes to show, argued Molotov, that the situation is characterized by numerous contradictions within the capitalist camp and that the public opinion of wide circles of voters plays a role in the formulation of policy in the imperialist camp. These differences within the imperialist camp afford an opportunity for the execution of the Soviet foreign policy which is, of course, in the interests of the strengthening of peace.[17] The attribution of political power to "voters," instead of to "capitalists" and "the forces of peace," was quite unusual. The implication that the danger of war could not be so great if the Republicans had won on a peace platform had been avoided by spokesmen of the Khrushchev school while Malenkov was under attack. Now that Malenkov was out, his successor promised peace through military preparedness. A continuation of the cries of capitalist encirclement and the danger of war would have detracted from the promises of peace. From this time until the summit conference the incidence of statements on the likelihood of war fell sharply.

A long *Kommunist* article, already referred to, had interpreted the theory of the destruction of world civilization in a nuclear war as a propaganda tool of capitalist aggressors, who hoped thereby to spread defeatism among their enemies. Konstantinov, who had argued the Malenkov case in *Izvestiia* on December 21, 1954, now recanted and lumped the theory of the destruction of world civilization with the discredited policy of emphasizing light industry. Now the argument was complete. The capitalists promoted the theory of the destruction of world civilization in order to foster complacency. Emphasis on light industry was a consequence of that theory.[18]

In the months that followed Malenkov's downfall Khrushchev trumpeted the relaxation of international tension. After Soviet overtures to Austria and what really amounted to a bilateral arrangement with her, a four-power agreement to withdraw from Austria was promulgated on May 15, 1955. Simultaneously a rapprochement with Yugoslavia was achieved, and by the end of May the Big Four Summit Conference was settled. Against all these visible signs of the relaxation of tension, it would have been inappropriate to insist on the likelihood of war. In the early part of 1955, therefore, the Soviet press took the line that tension had been reduced, though it was pointed out on several occasions by military people that peace could not be counted on. Marshal Rotmistrov pointed out in an article that had appeared somewhat earlier in *Voennaia mysl'* (*Military Thought*), and now appeared in slightly different form in *Red Star,* that surprise was more likely than before because of the developments in weapons and the preference of Americans for this tactic. Essentially, Rotmistrov was arguing that nuclear weapons made surprise attack a possible winning strategy and therefore that to count on deterrence was ridiculous.[19]

Shepilov, in a speech on the eighty-fifth anniversary of Lenin's birth, pointed to the continuing intrigues of the enemies of peace and said that the Soviet Union was taking the necessary steps to increase the strength of the armed forces. The Soviet Union, he promised, would not be caught unawares by the imperialists if they unleashed a new world war.[20] This indirect reference to military surprise was far more moderate than Talenskii's statement a few months before that destructive atomic war might break out at any moment. Shepilov's tone implied that the imperialists had not given up their war plans, but that the Soviet Union was strong and the imperialists would rue the day if they made war.

Marshal Zhukov, speaking on the tenth anniversary of Germany's surrender, struck a balance between the deterrent strength of the Soviet Union and the continuing danger of war. While he emphasized the destructiveness of hydrogen weapons in densely populated countries—a theme to become increasingly prominent in Soviet propaganda—he insisted that the ratification of the Paris Agreements and the arrangements for rearming Germany had increased international tension.[21]

In May the Soviet military press made numerous statements about the nature of surprise.* These emphasized the changes wrought in warfare by the new weapons. They did not suggest, as Talenskii had done, that war might be imminent. Public

---

* Examined in Chap. 6.

statements about imminent war would not have contributed to the success of the forthcoming Geneva meetings. Success at Geneva would yield domestic political advantages to the leadership. Malenkov had offered the prospect of peace through amicable negotiations; Khrushchev now offered peace through military strength. Moreover, he stole Malenkov's thunder by negotiating as well.

Today we know that Khrushchev's position was not as secure in 1955, or even in 1956, as it became subsequently. Had the victory of his policies brought an increase of international tension his opponents might well have tried to unseat him. Khrushchev's policy of carrying the big stick had prevailed; to maintain his position he had to speak softly, at least for a while. Domestic and international policy were both served by an almost total absence of statements on the war danger during the rest of 1955 and 1956. The official Soviet line, as reported by Bulganin to the Supreme Soviet when he and Khrushchev returned from a much-publicized trip to India and Burma, was that the prospects of peace had greatly improved:

> The past year will go down in history as the year of a definite turning point in the tense international situation which has existed in recent times.[22]

An editorial in *Kommunist,* the main party organ, quoted Bulganin's report and described the events of 1955 as representing a gradual improvement in the international situation. The Geneva Conference had been forced on the West by public opinion. The Bandung Conference of Asiatic countries also had been a great contribution to peace. Events that earlier would have been treated as evidence of the imperialists' appetite for armed aggression were now interpreted merely as part of an effort to spread the cold war. Thus the formation of SEATO was said to evince a desire to spread the cold war to the Asian continent. *Kommunist* referred to Dulles's article in *Life,* which used the much-discussed phrase "brink of war," as "playing with fire" and emphasized that even the Western proponents of the policy of strength had criticized Dulles for his tactlessness. That the forces of peace were growing daily was borne out by the events in French Indochina and by communist electoral victories in France.[23]

The relatively moderate tone of this editorial is not difficult to explain. When Khrushchev at the Twentieth Party Congress introduced the formula that wars were not "fatalistically inevitable," he suggested that the prospects for peace had improved. A simultaneous press campaign to the opposite effect would have hurt Khrushchev politically by calling in question his powers as a prophet. It would have been inappropriate, at the very least, for the Soviet press to say after Khrushchev returned from his visit to England that the prospects for peace had diminished. A *Kommunist* editorial, dealing with the possibility of preventing war, declared that Bulganin and Khrushchev's London conversations had taken place in an atmosphere of frankness and realism and had "made an important contribution to the improvement of relations between the U.S.S.R. and Great Britain and to the extension of the general peace and the security of the peoples."[24]

In mid-1956 political developments in the satellites took a turn that threatened the Soviet position in Eastern Europe and Soviet prestige throughout the whole world. A crisis arose for which the blame could be placed at Khrushchev's door. By choosing the party leaders in the satellite countries he had assumed responsibility for what happened there. His "secret" speech to the Twentieth Party Congress, made public in June, 1956, brought matters to a head. By the fall of 1956 revolutions in Hungary and Poland were brewing and the possibility of Western intervention could not be excluded. If Khrushchev's opponents could make the point that the international situation had deteriorated so far that war with the West was possible, the Party chief's position would be as weak as it possibly could be. On the other hand, if Khrushchev could maintain that international tensions were abating, the crisis in Eastern Europe could be represented as a serious but surmountable problem. This explains why he chose the second alternative, to belittle the danger of war.

The situation in the satellite countries was extraordinarily complex. During the war some of them had been allied with the Germans. Others had been occupied and brutally mistreated. Some of these countries had been transferred from German rule to Russian rule by action of the Russian armies alone. Others, most notably Yugoslavia, had played a role in their own liberation from the Germans. Immediately after the war the Russians installed in each of these countries (except Yugoslavia) a regime that permitted an amount of opposition that was harmless from the Russian point of view.

By comparison with the situation only a few years later Russian rule in the satellites was then moderate and restrained. The American government interpreted Russian wartime promises to mean that the Russians would introduce parliamentary democracy to these areas after the war. To the Americans the political regimes in Eastern Europe even in the early postwar years were far from satisfactory. Moreover, the West understandably viewed Chinese communist territorial gains, Ho Chih Min's successes in Indochina, and the Greek communists' threat to the Greek government, as part of a Soviet grand design for expansion. If these troubles were instigated by local communists against Soviet wishes, as some evidence suggests, it remains a fact that the Soviet Union never denounced their actions. In 1947, therefore, the United States set forth the Truman Doctrine and declared her intention to stem the tide of communism by force if necessary.

A radical change followed in the satellite countries. Soviet control became direct in one country after another, culminating with Czechoslovakia, and noncommunist parties were either suppressed or denied any real power in the satellite governments. Even in Yugoslavia, the one country where a native communist party had established a measure of control before the arrival of Russian troops, the Russians sought to tighten their controls, with the result that the most forceful of the satellite leaders, Tito, rebelled and was branded a heretic. Tito's defection was the signal for redoubled witch-hunting in the satellite countries, the imposition on them of programs of forced industrialization and compulsory collectivization of agriculture, and the creation of large armies presumably intended for disciplining Yugoslavia.

This program caused profound dislocation in the satellites. Stalin, with a lack of historical sense that accorded ill with his professsed historical materialism, precipitately sought to force countries with the most varied histories and social composition through a process of development that had taken a quarter of a century in the Soviet Union. In the Soviet Union the civil war had been followed by a period of consolidation that lasted from 1921 until 1928 or 1929. During this period much of the communist economic program was held in abeyance. The old classes with specialized skills were partially liquidated by emigration, intimidation, or execution and supplanted by new cadres. Not until all this had happened was the assault on the peasants undertaken and collectivization carried out. Only in 1934, when the industrialization program was under way, did Stalin make his assault on the older party cadres and inaugurate the reign of terror that did not subside until 1938.

In the satellites everything was done at once: collectivization, industrialization, elimination of the former governing classes, the purge of the older generation of party members, and establishment of the terror. When Stalin died none of these processes was yet complete, although it seemed as if this cruel and rapid surgery might have been completed had Stalin lived. Suddenly the pressure relaxed. The changes introduced into the Soviet Union after 1953 were automatically applied to the satellites. The reduction in the role of the police and in the tempo of industrialization were imitated in the satellites. Renewed hope in the satellite countries brought open signs of discontent of which the East German uprising was the most serious, but order was reimposed.

Into this situation Khrushchev injected himself. If Stalin had increased international tension without benefit to the Soviet Union, Khrushchev would decrease it with corresponding benefit to the Soviet Union. If Stalin had lost the most stalwart of the satellite leaders, Tito, to the capitalists who supplied him with weapons and money, Khrushchev would win him back to communism. But Tito's position in 1955 differed greatly from his position in 1948. A mere promise from the Russians to refrain from pressing the kind of claims that Stalin had insisted on in 1948 was no longer sufficient to restore good relations. In 1955 Tito required that the verdict of heresy against him be reversed, without any formal commitment on his part to be bound in ideological matters by the Communist Party of the Soviet Union or by any international communist organization. Khrushchev had to accept these demands as a start, whatever his hopes for the future may have been. The initial concessions to Tito opened up a Pandora's box. Polish and Hungarian jails had to disgorge communists who had been subjected to painful and humiliating treatment on the grounds that they had been infected by the Titoist heresy. These communists were restored to membership in the Party with their former persecutors. Amidst the resulting uncertainty and confusion came Khrushchev's "secret speech" against Stalin. The chief crimes that he ascribed to Stalin were crimes against the personnel of the Party. The restored members of the Polish and Hungarian parties had good cause to look at their former jailors and wonder who were really the criminals. The police, who were now being purged for what they had been ordered to do, naturally became inactive.[25]

These were the basic causes of unrest that culminated in an armed uprising in Hungary and in the accretion of a certain independence to the Polish Communist Party. During the fall and early winter of 1956, no one in the Soviet Union could predict the end of all these troubles that had mushroomed so suddenly. Would the map of Eastern Europe be rolled to the Soviet border of 1939? Would the Soviet student body go beyond sympathetically watching the events abroad and reading the Polish and Yugoslav newspapers? Would the Western powers enjoy greater success in their subversive activities in Eastern Europe? Might they go over to overt military support of the dissident communists? These questions must have been put many times in Moscow in those anxious months. Many must have laid these calamities at Khrushchev's door, for it was he who had pushed the rapprochement with Tito and had excoriated Stalin for his crimes against Party personnel. This was not the time to talk of the danger of war. There was trouble enough without inventing more. Alarms of war might serve to unite the Soviet people and to divert their minds from domestic problems, but they had no power to unite peoples who aspired to national independence.

From the summer of 1956 to the end of the year the Soviet press soft-pedaled the likelihood of war. In July, for example, *Kommunist* charged that the enemies of socialism were taking advantage of temporary difficulties within socialist countries and of some socialist mistakes to deceive the people. The recent Poznan riots provided an example of how international reactionaries seized their opportunities. In all this there was not a single war alarm of the kind so common in 1954.[26]

In September a *Kommunist* editor discussed a doctrinal innovation of the Twentieth Party Congress, namely, that a parliamentary transition to socialism was possible. He emphasized that the whole world situation had changed markedly in favor of the communists. The communists parties were larger, the Soviet Union was stronger, the colonial system was disintegrating. All this had combined to change the relationship of world political forces and to create new opportunities for a peaceful transition from capitalism to socialism. In former days the conclusion of such an argument was often that the imperialists, maddened by the prospect of destruction, would strike out like a wounded beast. NATO and SEATO, once described as alliances for the preparation of war against the Soviet Union, were now said to have as their primary object the suppression of revolutionary activity within the member countries. By this interpretation NATO was directed against the French communists rather than the Soviet Union.[27]

A month later the strongest accusation that *Kommunist* could make against the imperialists was that the cold war, their creation, was not in the interests of the people. The bourgeoisie were accused, not of preparing a war, but of seeking to drive a wedge between the communist parties of the peoples' democracies and those of the capitalist countries.[28] In the same issue, an article on American military preparations in the Pacific accused the United States of seeking to create a war psychosis in an international situation otherwise characterized by the reduction of tension. The American naval program, said the article, aimed at ejecting the smaller British navy from the Pacific. Popular opposition in Asia had seriously hampered American military plans. The writer made no mention of the danger of war.[29]

In January, 1957, *Kommunist,* reviewing the events of 1956, said a great deal about the bankruptcy of imperialism but not a word about the desire of the imperialists to make war.[30]

For almost two years there had been no warnings in the press about the danger of war. At this moment Khrushchev chose to launch a new campaign stressing the likehood of general war. The international situation did not justify such alarms. American disapproval of the British, French, and Israeli invasion of Egypt had displayed for all to see a difference within the Western alliance, rather than a consolidation of that alliance for war. The Egyptian adventure had been liquidated and the Hungarian uprising suppressed without even a hint of Western intervention, so that if anything the prospects for peace were better. Why, then, did Khrushchev start to beat the war drums again? As before, we must look for an explanation within the Soviet Union, rather than outside it.

Lacking direct evidence, we can nevertheless be fairly certain that Khrushchev's position was badly shaken by the Hungarian events. It was easy to explain all the disturbances in Eastern Europe as the result of the Party chief's rapprochement with Tito and denunciation of Stalin. When the Plenum of the Party's Central Committee met on December 20-24, 1956, for the first time since February when they had convened for a day, Khrushchev's name was not even mentioned. The newspapers said that Bulganin reported on the improvement of leadership in the Soviet economy, and Saburov and Baibakov on the economic plans for 1957. After these reports the Central Committee resolved to present to the Supreme Soviet (which was to meet at the beginning of 1957) several economic proposals described as putting a greater emphasis on meeting the requirements for raising the standard of living, and as designed to secure "a reduction in the scale of capital investments."[31] This sounded more than a little like the old Malenkov line.

The Plenum, in which Khrushchev apparently played either

a small role or none at all, viewed the international situation calmly. There was no word about any increased danger of general war. The conferees emphasized the competition within the capitalist camp and thought that the standard of living was falling in capitalist countries. The imperialist attempts to expand aroused popular opposition and strengthened the movements for national liberation. This led to the further militarization of the capitalist economy, which in turn aggravated its internal contradictions.[32] In other words, the capitalist camp was in rather a mess and, by implication, not unduly dangerous to the Soviet Union.

Khrushchev was obviously slighted by the December Plenum. Major party decisions were taken, according to the press, without the participation of the man whose name had overshadowed all others for almost two years. Perhaps this circumstance explains the reconvocation of the Plenum in February, remarkably soon after its last meeting. At the second meeting Khrushchev dominated the proceedings. He proposed a reorganization of the economy that differed in many essentials from the plan of December. The most prominent party members did not speak up in favor of Khrushchev's plan and only after several months of politicking did Khrushchev obtain its acceptance.

Khrushchev's recovery of the spotlight and the initiative in February lends interest to the statements on the likelihood of war that he began to make almost immediately after the conclusion of the December Plenum. In written answers to question presented by the editor of a Czech newspaper, Khrushchev took the line that peace would be strengthened in 1957, although the events in Egypt and the fascist plot against Hungary had "sharply increased the threat of a new world war."[33] At a New Year's party in the Kremlin, Khrushchev said that the Soviet people were thirsting for peace, but added: "We should not forget that a feverish arms race is being conducted in a number of capitalist countries, and therefore we must not for a second forget about our Army. We should provide it with first class equipment and supplies. We have done this, are doing it, and will do it in order to secure and extend peace, because we should defend the conquests of the Great October [Revolution], the Soviet Power."[34]

During January others, probably following Khrushchev's cue, began to take a stronger tone on military preparedness. Bulganin, in the middle of the month, spoke of the necessity of being able to protect socialism "from enemy blows from wherever they may be dealt."[35] A joint Chinese-Soviet declaration, summarizing the results of conversations held during January, observed that "the development of international events took a tortuous course. All the peace loving nations of the globe should be constantly vigilant and prepared for a persistent and prolonged struggle with the camp headed by the United States." America was pursuing a "policy of aggression and preparation for war."[36] Here, for the first time since 1955, the Soviet press accused the United States of preparing for war.

Molotov made a speech at this time in which he said that the Soviet Union, while seeking a reduction in international tension, "could not but reckon with the fact that the imperialists would not be imperialists if they were not making plans for new aggressive wars and were not continuing the arms race." A lesser figure, speaking in Siberia, stated that the threat of war and of new military adventures was far from removed. Now the task was to give a stunning rebuff to the enemy's schemes and to strengthen the Soviet armed forces.[37] Kaganovich, instead of drawing attention, like *Kommunist* early in January, to the slackening of international tension, declared that "the aggravation of relationships and the strengthening of tension is characteristic of the contemporary international situation." The reason was that the reactionaries were seeking military adventures.[38]

Red Star, in a signed article reviving a long-discarded theme, charged the American imperialists with seeking to initiate a new war in order to establish world domination. Despite the fact, recognized by General LeMay himself, that the Soviet Union had grown so much stronger, the Americans still sought ways to destroy others and to remain unharmed themselves.

The general American idea was to deflect retaliatory blows on their allies.[39]

A joint Soviet-Czechoslovak declaration of January 29 said that the imperialists were increasing international tension by undertaking new and dangerous adventures that seriously threatened the peace of the world.[40]

The old Stalinist bogey of espionage by foreigners was revived. On February 7 more than a page of *Pravda* was devoted to a press conference called by the Soviet Ministry of Foreign Affairs to demonstrate continued American subversive activities. The report alleged that some spies had entered the Soviet Union in December and January, but most of its espionage stories were more dated. The intention was obvious: to instill a sense of danger.[41]

The most authoritative statement on the war danger was made by the Minister of Foreign Affairs, Shepilov, in his speech to the Supreme Soviet on February 12. Since less than three days later Shepilov was no longer Foreign Minister, his speech merits particular attention. Amidst a mounting crescendo of warnings that war was imminent, Shepilov struck a quieter note. He seemed to be carrying water on both shoulders. The main argument of his very long speech was that there were two political tendencies in the West: the more sober one leaned toward a relaxation of tension; the other, more dangerous one had come to the fore in the latter half of 1956. The second policy had inspired the counterrevolutionary uprising in Hungary and the aggression in Egypt, but the defeat of both showed that the capitalist system was growing weaker. These events demonstrated, said Shepilov, that under modern conditions war is not fatalistically inevitable and can be prevented. The imperialists had learned that the forces opposing war were stronger, but nevertheless went on intensifying their preparations for war.

It cannot be said that Shepilov ignored the theme of growing international tension. In the first two minutes of his speech he indicated that tension had both risen and fallen in recent months. This, of course, was a more equivocal view than those recently expressed by Khrushchev, Kaganovich, Molotov, and others, who had flatly postulated an increase of international tension. Moreover, Shepilov's remarks about the possibility of an accommodation with the United States had a tone of optimism that departed even further from the Khrushchev position than the noncommittal statement that tension had had its ups and downs:

To return again to the question whose importance is obvious to all, namely the question of the future development of relations between the U.S.S.R. and the United States of America: a myth exists, disseminated abroad by certain circles, that the normalization of Soviet-American relations is impossible because both sides are divided by insoluble problems. As a matter of fact, it is well known that our governments have lived in peace and friendship for decades. With the exception of the period of foreign intervention against the young Soviet Republic, the U.S.A. and the U.S.S.R. have never made war against each other. The deceased President of the U.S.A., Franklin Roosevelt, emphasized that between our peoples "for more than a century there has existed the happy tradition of friendship, beneficial to both sides." This tradition began to be destroyed when American ruling circles began to expand the tendency toward world dominion and to exclude international co-operation on an equal basis.

The Soviet government believes, as it did before, that no matter how different the American and Soviet social systems there are not a few important problems in which the interests of our people go together. Both the American and the Soviet people are equally interested in the preservation of peace and in the development of peaceful co-operation. On this basis we propose to the U.S.A. the conclusion of a treaty of friendship with the Soviet Union. More than a year has passed since this proposal was made by us, however, we have not yet received an answer and this naturally is no accident. In the United States there are influential circles interested in inflaming hatred between countries. However, we do not confuse these circles and the American people and we are certain that sooner or later the good common sense characteristic of the American nation and sober understanding will conquer over the egotistical conceptions of those who seek to intensify tension in American-Soviet relations.[42]

The evidence seems fairly strong that this speech, with its overtones of optimism about the future, was not well received by those who found it useful to insist on the likelihood of war. The Central Committee of the Communist Party met suddenly on February 13-14 and immediately thereafter Shepilov retired from his ministerial position.

On February 14 the Central Committee adopted a resolution on a report by Khrushchev on the reorganization of the management of the Soviet economy. Everybody who read the resolution must have been struck by the contrast between it and the resolutions of the December Plenum, where Khrushchev had been so inconspicuous. Although it is difficult to point to any particular phrase, the whole tone of the resolution tended to emphasize heavy industry. There was no hint of the December resolution to reduce the scope of investment.[43] Clearly the February Plenum of the Central Committee had eaten out of Khrushchev's hand.

A few days later Major General Kozhedub of the air force, writing in the organ of the Soviet air arm, presented a picture of the prospects of foreign policy that lacked the optimism of the retired Shepilov. The aggressive circles in the capitalist countries, above all, in the United States, were said to oppose peaceful coexistence and to be spinning plans for the initiation of a new war. The United States was spending as many billions as during the Second World War and was behind the Hungarian counterrevolution. The Twentieth Party Congress, wrote the General, had emphasized the need for the greatest vigilance, because as long as capitalism existed the reactionary forces representing the interests of capitalism and monopoly would continue to seek military adventures and aggression. Major General Kozhedub, perhaps significantly, failed to add the formula, devised by Khrushchev, to the effect that wars are no longer fatalistically inevitable.[44]

At a reception in the Bulgarian Embassy on February 18,

Khrushchev made a speech marked by two novelties. First, he talked about his capitalist opponents as "enemies," something that he had not done in any published speech heretofore; second, he hinted for the first time at the danger of surprise attack. (Others, of course, had mentioned it before him.) The most significant passage was as follows:

> The capitalists . . . are assigning hundreds of millions of dollars to subversive espionage and diversionary activity against the Soviet Union and other socialist countries. They spend many billions of dollars on arms, on the building of military bases on foreign territory. Should we smile and make believe that we do not notice it? No. We see what all the enemy schemes are and adopt the necessary measures in order that the enemy should not take· us unawares. . . . We do not want to fight and we are not preparing to attack anyone. But if we are attacked then we will defend ourselves and when we defend ourselves it will be difficult for the attacker to defend himself.[45]

On March 18 a *Pravda* writer once more raised the whole question of the inevitability of war. The dictum of the Twentieth Party Congress that there was no fatal inevitability of war, he wrote, certainly did not mean that a new peaceful phase in the development of capitalism had arrived: "Capitalism has been, remains, and in the future will be the source of threats of aggression and war." The very fact that the sphere of capitalist rule was being restricted intensified the capitalist desire to start a new war, through which they hoped to recover their lost positions. These formerly standard Marxian arguments had been almost absent from the Soviet press during 1956. In the early part of 1957, when it suited Khrushchev's purpose, the analysis once more went beyond the conclusion that capitalism was declining. It now went on to say that the continuing losses of capitalism would drive the imperialists to desperate measures, including war.[46]

In an interview given to a small American newspaper, Khrushchev continued to support the theme that the international situation had become worse. He dodged a question as to when in the preceding eleven years the war danger had been greatest, but made it clear that he believed the present danger to be great. All danger of war came from the American policy of working from "a position of strength." The dangers of war spreading from Korea and Indochina had been liquidated by negotiation. The Geneva meeting of 1955 did cause a certain dispersion of international tension. "Unfortunately this period didn't last long. The attack on Egypt and the subsequent attempts of some powers to fill in the 'vacuum' invented by themselves in the Arab east has again significantly aggravated the international situation and created a serious threat to peace in this region." Thus Khrushchev contended that the present danger of general war was more serious than at any time since the settlement of the Indochina question in the spring of 1954.[47]

As might be expected, *Red Star,* the newspaper of the Ministry of Defense, reinforced this line, emphasizing the need to recognize the possibility of an outbreak of a war. The writer accused Soviet propagandists of perverting the true balance, established at the Twentieth Party Congress, between the possibility of preventing wars and the possibility of the outbreak of wars. The propagandists, said *Red Star* with a good deal of truth, had been concentrating their chief attention on the possibility of preventing war and had slighted the possibility of its outbreak.[48]

The diplomatic correspondence of the Soviet Union, obviously intended for publication, reflected the Soviet estimate that the danger of war was closer. Bulganin, for example, in a message to the Norwegian Prime Minister published on March 27, noted: "The international situation has recently seriously deteriorated. Dangerous attempts have been undertaken to undermine the relaxation of international tension already achieved and to place the peoples at the brink of war. Indeed it is a secret to no one that in November of last year there were days when we stood before a serious danger of war." Bulganin went on to say that the rebuff received by the aggressors in Egypt and the liquidation of the fascist uprising in Hungary had prevented this terrible danger from materializing, but that the situation remained tense. The arms race continued and the United States did not conceal her intention to employ her armed forces in the Near East. The anounced plans of the United States to locate special atomic units in new places spoke neither for the policy of peaceful coexistence nor for the desire to reduce international tension.[49] In a similar message to the Danish Prime Minister, Bulganin spoke of American international policy as "leading to the increased threat of a new war."[50]

At practically the same moment the Central Committee of the Communist Party was assembling to hear Khrushchev report on his scheme for reorganizing the economy of the country. In concluding his long speech, Khrushchev made it clear that his plans would further the policy of priority for heavy industry. The Party, he warned, had always condemned "surrendering to the false concept of directing basic resources to the development of light industry," which might yield the temporary appearance of success, but would undercut the basis for future economic development. Eight months later Khrushchev told a foreign newspaper man that the reorganization plan, by decentralizing management, had "improved our strategic position."[51]

As might be expected, Khrushchev also emphasized that armaments were necessary for the maintenance of the defensive capability of the U.S.S.R.: "That is why the enemies of the Soviet Union always have directed and are directing their efforts to the discrediting of this great Leninist idea [of priority for heavy industry] which is the general line of the Communist Party of the Soviet Union."[52]

In conformity with his political style of promising everybody everything, Khrushchev went on to pledge a sharp increase in the production of meat and dairy products in the near future. He did not explain how priority for investment in heavy industry could be reconciled with such a startling increase in the production of consumer goods.[53]

It is not quite clear just how far Khrushchev's reorganization plan differed from the one proposed without his participation. Both plans were extremely complicated, and a detailed comparison of them would be inappropriate here. It is sufficient for present purposes to establish that it was a political necessity for Khrushchev to ensure that the plan adopted was his.

It is suggested that Khrushchev revived talk of the imminence of war in order to overcome, at the least, reluctance to support him and his plan, and more probably, active opposition. The speed with which he reversed his position on the danger of war once he had had his way with his opponents cannot be explained by any notable change in the international situation, for there was none. It can be understood only against the background of Soviet domestic politics. Only two weeks later Khrushchev was saying that life had again become normal:

> International events became even more strained in connection with the imperialist aggression in Egypt. As is known, here too, the imperialists miscalculated and met with a deserved rebuff. Now the passions, if they have not subsided altogether, have quieted down noticeably and life flows in its normal course. We should direct all efforts to reduce international tension and attain an improvement in the relations between all countries. . . .[54]

In a joint Soviet-Albanian communiqué, published the following day, it was laid down as a general statement that, "as a result of the joint efforts of the socialist governments and the peace loving forces of the whole world, a relaxation of tension in international relations had been attained."

On April 23 Madame Furtseva, whose rapid advance in the Soviet hierarchy had coincided with Khrushchev's, continued the theme of the relaxation of tension. She argued that the healthy nationalist groups in Western Europe and in the United States, who realized the disastrous nature of their governments' policies, were indubitably capable of changing them to conform with the true national interests of their countries. Most optimistically, considering the alarms of war in January and February, Madame Furtseva said:

> It is possible to count both on common sense prevailing and on the triumph in international affairs of the policy of peaceful co-existence between different governments.

> We believed and continue to believe that a stable peace
> can be assured in and for our time. . . . We are convinced
> that the present somewhat sharpened international situa-
> tion is a temporary phenomenon. . . . If the peoples will
> be vigilant and not permit themselves to be involved in a
> struggle against each other and if in the future they con-
> tinue to be guided by the defense of peace which is of com-
> mon interest to them, no plots and sallies of the imperi-
> alists will menace the solid camp of the progressive forces.[55]

All the evidence presented in this and the preceding chapters seems to point to the conclusion that public Soviet statements about the imminence of war are often employed for
domestic political purposes, whether or not they happen, at
the same time, to represent a genuine fear of war. In some
cases, as in 1957, alarms of war clearly have no relation to the
international situation and are employed only as a weapon in
domestic arguments. As we have seen, Khrushchev was dis-
inclined to use such a weapon when there seemed to be a
real danger of general conflict—in the Suez affair, for example.
It may be, therefore, that the private and the public Soviet
estimates of the likelihood of war seldom if ever coincide.
When the danger is great, there is little disposition to cry wolf.
When the danger recedes, there is a temptation to make domestic political capital out of the fear of war. Soviet leaders who
succumb to this temptation do not worry that their war alarms
will precipitate the very disaster they warn against. One of
their basic beliefs is that American policy is determined, not
by Soviet statements, but by the necessities of the capitalist
system. Moreover, they have been convinced for some time that
Soviet power effectively deters the United States from making
war.

The seemingly mercurial Russian views about the likelihood of war, then, have little to do with Soviet long-term plans
to be fully prepared for any military emergency. They have still
less to do with Soviet analyses of the nature of a future war,
should one break out. The next chapter is devoted to Russian
ideas on the possible nature of a future war.

NOTES

1. Academician M. Mitin, "I. V. Stalin—The Foremost Theoretician of Marxism," *Pravda*, December 19, 1954.
2. V. Kruzhkov, "I. V. Stalin—The Great Continuator of V. I. Lenin's Work," *Pravda*, December 21, 1954.
3. Editorial, "The Great Triumph of the Idea of Marxism-Leninism," *Pravda*, December 21, 1954.
4. F. Konstantinov, "The Great Continuator of Lenin's Immortal Work," *Izvestiia*, December 21, 1954.
5. Editorial, "Under the Great Banner of Marx, Engels, Lenin, Stalin," *Izvestiia*, December 21, 1954.
6. "Speech of Comrade N. S. Khrushchev to the All-Union Conference of Builders . . .," *Trud (Labor)*, December 28, 1954. This speech had been delivered on December 7, 1954.
7. "Interview of Comrade N. S. Khrushchev with the English Scientist and Public Figure, John Bernal," *Trud*, December 24, 1954. This interview was published in the whole Soviet press.
8. Major General N. Talenskii, "On Atomic and Conventional Weapons," *Mezhdunarodnaia zhizn' (International Life)*, No. 16, 1955, p. 22.
9. Lieutenant General I. Gritchin, "What the American Atom Brandishers Should Not Forget," *Pravda*, January 7, 1955.
10. "Speech of Comrade N. S. Khrushchev," *Komsomolskaia pravda*, January 8, 1955.
11. I. D. Shirinskii, "The Law of Plans (Proportional Development of the Economy)," Moscow, 1955. A public lecture passed for the press on January 10, 1955. Date of delivery of lecture was not given.
12. D. Shepilov, "The General Line of the Party and the Vulgarizers of Marxism," *Pravda*, January 24, 1955.
13. "The Bases of the Might of the Soviet Fatherland," *Red Star*, January 27, 1955.
14. Editorial, "Ideological Work among the Troops Should Be on the Level of the New Demands," *Red Star*, June 10, 1955; editorial, "The New Academic Year in the Higher Military Schools," *Red Star*, September 1, 1955.
15. "The Speech of N. A. Bulganin," *Izvestiia*, February 10, 1955.
16. Interview with G. K. Zhukov by the American Journalist, William Randolph Hearst, Jr., . . .," *Pravda*, February 13, 1955.
17. "Report of the First Vice Chairman of the Council of Ministers and the Minister of Foreign Affairs of the U.S.S.R., Deputy V. M. Molotov," *Pravda*, February 8, 1955.
18. F. Konstantinov, "I. V. Stalin and the Question of Communist Construction," *Pravda*, March 5, 1955.
19. Tank Marshal P. Rotmistrov, "For Creative Examination of the Questions of Soviet Military Science," *Red Star*, March 24, 1955.
20. D. T. Shepilov, "The Ideas of Lenin Illuminate the Road to Communism," *Pravda*, April 23, 1955.
21. Marshal of the Soviet Union G. Zhukov, "The Tenth Anniversary of a Great Victory," *Pravda*, May 8, 1955.

22. Bulganin's Report to the Supreme Soviet as quoted in the editorial, "The Inspiring Example of Socialist Labor and the Struggle for Peace and the Friendship of the People," *Kommunist*, No. 1, 1956, p. 5.

23. *Ibid.*

24. A. Nikonov, "In the Contemporary Era War Can Be Prevented," *Kommunist*, No. 6, April, 1956, p. 44.

25. See Paul Kecskemeti, "Limits and Problems of Decompression: The Case of Hungary," *The Annals of the American Academy of Political and Social Science*, May, 1958, pp. 97-106 for a lucid and persuasive treatment.

26. Editorial, "The Unity of the International Communist Movement Is Unshakable," *Kommunist*, No. 11, July, 1956, pp. 6, 7.

27. A. Sobolev, "On the Parliamentary Form of the Transition to Socialism," *Kommunist*, No. 14, September, 1956, pp. 14-32.

28. Editorial, "October's Cause Lives and Conquers," *Kommunist*, No. 15, October, 1956, pp. 3-12.

29. M. Petrov, "American Military Preparations in the Pacific," *Kommunist*, No. 15, October, 1956, p. 90 *et passim*.

30. Editorial, "Raise High the Banner of Marxist-Leninist Ideology," *Kommunist*, No. 1, January, 1957, pp. 3-14.

31. "Resolution of the Plenum of the Central Committee of the Communist Party of the Soviet Union (Adopted on the Basis of the Reports of Comrades Baibakov, N. K., and Saburov, M. Z.)," *Pravda*, December 25, 1956.

32. *Ibid.* On the following day a *Pravda* editorial on the Plenum also failed to mention Khrushchev's name.

33. "The Answers of N. S. Khrushchev to Questions by the Editors of the Newspaper *Rude Pravo*," *Pravda*, January 1, 1957.

34. "Bringing in the New Year in the Kremlin," *Pravda*, January 2, 1957.

35. "Speech of Comrade N. A. Bulganin at the Chinese-Russian Friendship Meeting," *Pravda*, January 18, 1957.

36. "Joint Soviet-Chinese Declaration," *Pravda*, January 19, 1957.

37. "Speech by N. I. Beliaev in Barnaul," *Pravda*, January 20, 1957.

38. "Speech of Comrade L. M. Kaganovich in Krasnoiarsk," *Pravda*, January 23, 1957.

39. A. Turov, "The U.S.A. Brandishes Atomic Weapons," *Red Star*, January 25, 1957.

40. "Joint Soviet-Czechoslovak Declaration Dated January 29, 1957, Signed by the Chairman of the Council of Ministers, of the U.S.S.R., N. A. Bulganin, and by the President of the Czech Republic, William Shiroky," *Pravda*, January 30, 1957.

41. "L. F. Il'ichev's Statement," *Pravda*, February 7, 1957.

42. "Speech of D. T. Shepilov," *Pravda*, February 13, 1957.

43. "Resolution of the Plenum of the Central Committee of the Communist Party of the Soviet Union on the Report of Comrade Khrushchev, N. S., Adopted February 14, 1957," *Pravda*, February 16, 1957.

44. Deputy of the Supreme Soviet of the U.S.S.R., Thrice Hero of the Soviet Union, Major General of Aviation I. Kozhedub, "Always on Guard," *Sovetskaia aviatsiia* (*Soviet Aviation*), February 17, 1957.

45. "The Speech of Comrade N. S. Khrushchev at a Reception in the Embassy of the People's Republic of Bulgaria, February 18, 1957," *Red Star*, February 20, 1957.
46. M. Marinin, "Peaceful Coexistence—The High Road of International Relations," *Pravda*, March 18, 1957.
47. "Comrade N. S. Khrushchev's Answers to the Questions of the Editors of the American Newspaper, *Grand Rapids Herald*," *Pravda*, March 19, 1957.
48. Colonel G. Fedorov, Candidate in the Philosophical Sciences, "On the Content of Soviet Military Ideology," *Red Star*, March 22, 1957.
49. "Message of the Chairman of the Council of Ministers of the U.S.S.R., N. A. Bulganin, to the Prime Minister of Norway, Einar Gerhardsen," *Pravda*, March 27, 1957.
50. "Message of the Chairman of the Council of Ministers of the U.S.S.R., N. A. Bulganin, to the Prime Minister of Denmark, H. K. Hansen," *Red Star*, March 31, 1957.
51. "N. S. Khrushchev's Interview with Henry Shapiro . . .," *Pravda*, November 17, 1957.
52. "On the Further Perfection of the Organization of the Direction of Industry and Construction, Theses of Comrade N. S. Khrushchev's Report," *Pravda*, March 30, 1957.
53. "Speech of Comrade N. S. Khrushchev at a Meeting of the Agricultural Workers of the Central Black Soil Zone Regions on March 30, 1957," *Pravda*, April 1, 1957.
54. "Comrade N. S. Khrushchev's Speech at a Reception in the Embassy of the Albanian People's Republic, April 15, 1957," *Red Star*, April 17, 1957.
55. "Report of E. A. Furtseva at the Celebration of the 87th Lenin Birth Anniversary," *Pravda*, April 23, 1957.

CHAPTER SIX

SURPRISE AND THE INITIATION OF WAR

To find a precedent for the employment of war alarms to advance particular factions within the Party it is necessary to go back as far as the late twenties. In the thirties Stalin had suppressed all the Party factions that did not render him unquestioning obedience. Public emphasis on foreign dangers, contrived or genuine, was no longer needed as a weapon in intra-Party disputes. Furthermore, in the late thirties the danger of Soviet involvement in a major war was only too real, and common prudence argued against the dangerous game of playing with war scarces. The death of Stalin and the reappearance of factions within the Party leadership have obviously provided the conditions for a revival of the war scarce as an instrument of domestic politics. This revival would scarcely have been possible, however, without a genuine change in Soviet views about the likelihood of war.

A great many factors affect Soviet estimates of the likelihood of war. Since the advent of nuclear weapons an important factor has been the growing realization in the Soviet Union that the seizure of initiative and the consequent achievement of surprise give much greater advantages in modern war than ever before. Another consideration is the Russian conviction that as the Soviet Union becomes stronger in comparison with her strongest opponent the danger of a war not of Soviet making recedes. Since 1953 these beliefs have jointly affected Soviet views on national security, but for analytical purposes it is convenient to treat them separately. Both factors, however, arise from a common source, namely the changes brought about in Soviet strategic thought by a growing appreciation of the role of nuclear weapons. These changes are the subject of the present chapter.

Since the publication of Talenskii's article in November, 1953, Soviet ideas on strategy have undergone continual modification. Before 1953 there is no evidence that Soviet leaders had done any serious thinking about strategy in the nuclear age. Even after that time, many years passed before the new ideas became operative.

Every discovery must pass through several stages before it achieves its maximum effect on society. Elaborate institutional arrangements are required to put military theories into effect. Thousands, if not millions, of people must participate. Often years of research, development, training, and indoctrination must precede the desired state of readiness. Especially under modern conditions, generals cannot execute a strategy, no matter how brilliantly conceived, until great numbers of officers and noncommissioned officers have been trained to execute their various parts in the whole plan. Even when the generals have fully realized the implications of a new weapon, much planning and training are required to exploit its potentialities in practice. To take an example in the field of logistics, the American Civil War demonstrated how important railroads were for the deployment and supply of troops; but not until the Franco-Prussian War were mobilization and the initial campaign planned in terms of rail transport. When World War I broke out, all the major powers were organized to use their railroads to maximum strategic effect.

Let us suppose that a major European power, before World War I, had regarded its railroads as primarily of commercial importance in wartime, and only ancillary in mobilization and supply. Such a power would have been at a military disadvantage, not through ignorance of the principles or lack of skill in the operation of railroads, but through a failure of doctrine: the absence of an official military policy for the employment of railroads in wartime. This hypothetical case points to the importance of doctrine in military affairs. Without a suitable policy and proper training and indoctrination throughout all ranks, the possession of the latest weapons and other materiel may be of little strategic importance.

When the muzzle-loading musket was the main weapon of armies, indoctrination and discipline were suited to its qualities. The musket, although its accuracy was poor and its range short, could stop an advancing enemy when fired en masse by a compact line of musketeers. Since reloading was slow, a second line of men was ready to fire while the first was reloading and, by the time a third line had fired, the first line of musketeers was ready to fire again. If any of the musketeers fell the ranks were closed by men from behind, for the line formation had to hold. When the infantry weapon had such a low fire power, perfection in parade-ground drill and an almost mechanical obedience to command were the primary objects of indoctrination and training. With the advent of rifles, and later machine guns, the doctrine of infantry tactics had to change, for increasing fire power made the old compact line more of a liability than an asset. In the realm of infantry tactics, as in other military spheres, the introduction of new weapons has tended to precede the evolution of doctrine that they necessitate.

The problems of developing doctrine and standard procedures for the employment of nuclear weapons have been difficult for all the nuclear powers because of the enormity of the weapon and the paucity of experience in its use. A satisfactory doctrine for the employment of a new weapon usually has to wait on the tests of war. Strategic bombing is a good example. Before the Second World War British and American officers had grasped the broad strategic possibilities of air bombing, but they were far from understanding how it could be made strategically decisive. Only actual experience in war demonstrated how great a weight of bombs was required to effect a given object and the nature of the priorities in target systems that could contribute most to victory. It was not until almost the end of World War II that the principles of aerial bombardment were properly adjusted to the capabilities of the weapons involved.

The terrible destructiveness of nuclear weapons makes it undesirable, to say the least, that the birth of a sound doctrine for their employment should depend on the test of battle. It has become imperative to develop doctrines in peacetime for using them and for defending oneself against them.

Russian military writing has always stressed the importance of doctrine and of the indoctrination of officers and men. In line with this policy, Russia has probably permitted less independence and initiative to junior officers in practice than most other great powers. The absence for several years (1945-1953) of any Soviet press discussions of the strategic and tactical implications of nuclear weapons can be interpreted to mean that the Soviet Union was backward in nuclear doctrine and indoctrination and that in the event of a war, she would not have been able to use whatever nuclear weapons she possessed to the best advantage. It will be argued below that this interpretation is correct.

Until the latter part of 1953 the Soviet press, including the military press, had almost no information about the effects of nuclear weapons. The propaganda line, repeated year after year, that the Western powers were mistaken in their exclusive reliance on nuclear weapons was a poor substitute for a Soviet doctrine governing the employment of the country's brand-new, if limited, nuclear arsenal. Not only the newspapers but the military publishing houses and academies were afraid to discuss the new military problems that had arisen since 1945. The editors of *Voennaia mysl'* (*Military Thought*), writing in March, 1955, after Malenkov had been deposed and after the publication of Rotmistrov's article on the importance of surprise, looked disapprovingly at the past:

> At a meeting of the leading staff of the armed forces, Marshals of the Soviet Union N. A. Bulganin and G. K. Zhukov gave a high evaluation to our military cadres and . . . [advocated] a thorough study of modern military technology and advanced military theory. . . . But in this regard, as speeches at the meetings noted, everything is not

in good order. Military scientific work in the armed forces still lags. For too long our military scientific cadres have confined themselves to repeating truths long and well known—to the detriment of the situation and to the detriment of the investigation of a number of urgent new problems. . . .

We have no new interesting books . . . which pose the problems of military science with adequate sharpness and which propose original methods for their resolution.

Our periodical military press still does not do everything to develop Soviet military science. The articles published in the military journals are often far removed in their theme and content from urgent military problems; they are general and unspecific, one-sided and poorly conceived. In a number of cases discussions, which are one of the effective instruments for the development of military theory, are on secondary problems, proceed sluggishly, drag out; some are still not completed. These faults characterize all our journals, including . . . *Military Thought*.

The editors of our journal in particular held back without good grounds the publication of the article by Tank Marshal P. A. Rotmistrov, "On the Role of Surprise in Modern War," thereby revealing an absence of the boldness required to pose a new, urgent question of great significance for the correct understanding of the character of modern war.

If we are talking about the reasons which cause the backwardness in the development of our military science in general, then the chief of these is the *fear* to say something new, or to say something different from what has already been said by one or another authority. It is enough to familiarize oneself with the military scientific literature issued in the postwar period to become convinced of this.

Instead of taking the statements of authorities as starting propositions for the expansion and creative elaboration of military theory, and instead of boldly presenting new questions, many research people have limited themselves to mere logic chopping, to commentary on well-known statements and to the endless production of quotations. As a result of this, views once expressed by great theoreticians or important men of affairs are converted into dogma and these research works acquire a Talmudic character and actually delay further progress in military science.

Such a pernicious style in military scientific work leads to marking time and hinders correct understanding. As historical conditions change many propositions once completely justified no longer meet the requirements of a new situation. . . .

It cannot be recognized as normal, however, that books and articles issued during and after the war, instead of being objective scientific research in military theory and in the historical facts, are in the majority of cases merely a repetition of what Stalin said at various times. This business [military theory] was bound to harbor toadies eager to employ what was already prepared and quite convenient, which they often presented as their own. It was easiest of all to copy existing statements, especially from such an authority as I. V. Stalin. Such copying, which freed one from the necessity of thinking about serious questions, held back creative thought and obviously damaged our military science. . . .

One must also point to the serious neglect of theory in some important aspects of the military art, particularly strategy. Our military scientific institutes actually do not concern themselves with the theory of strategy, considering it to be a sphere for the creative activity only of the supreme high command. Therefore they do not prepare qualified scientific cadres for that purpose.

The necessity to elaborate strategic theory thoroughly in modern conditions is perfectly obvious, since the circle of persons concerned with strategic questions and participating in wartime strategic leadership is becoming ever larger. These persons, certainly, should have a comprehensive knowledge of theory for the preparation and conduct of war. . . .

Our military academies have not yet really become the creative and organizational centers of military and scientific theory. The academies have not yet acquired the rights of full citizenship in military scientific work.

Scholasticism and Talmudism are still cultivated in the scholarly practice of the academies. There are still not a few teachers who accustom the students to answering questions with memorized quotations and formulas. . . .

One of the most serious causes retarding the development of military science is the incorrect attitude toward the selection of military scientific cadres and the absence of a well thought out training system. We have not yet put an end to the bad practice of assigning to scientific and pedagogic work people who cannot cope with their work with the troops and people who have no fighting experience. . . .

The situation in the publication of military scientific literature is poor. In the postwar years hardly a single significant work in the sphere of military theory was published. Books are lacking on the history of the Soviet Armed Forces, on the theory of military science, on military ideology; there are no books on the Soviet military art and no memoirs of the prominent Soviet and foreign military leaders. . . .

The Military Publishing House publishes military literature only if articles on the subjects have appeared in the military journals more than once or if the manuscript has already traversed a long road of editing, approval, agreements and consultation. Why such a system to pass military scientific works? Is it really necessary to have so many consultations, reviews, and opinions in order to print a book on a particular military scientific theme? Unquestionably, it is not necessary. The explanation is the fear of the Military Publishing House that something might happen. The majority of reviews, assessments, and opinions are not employed to help the author in his work on the book but as an umbrella for protection against the issuance of an unsuccessful book.

This leads to a situation where every original view and thought is levelled and adjusted to the officially promulgated position. The main . . . departments of the Ministry of Defense are thereby overburdened with the superfluous work of reviewing and approving all sorts of books and works, with obvious detriment to their main tasks. . . .[1]

The underlying import of these strictures seems to be as follows. Early in 1955 the military academies were still conducting their instruction in terms of World War II; and war planning, in the absence of an up-to-date official doctrine, could not take proper account of such novelties as nuclear weapons. It may be argued that the long quotation from *Military Thought,* authoritative as it undoubtedly is, condemns dogmatic conservatism in very general terms and says nothing specific about a lack of doctrinal provision for nuclear warfare. One may argue that the Soviet Union has developed nuclear weapons speedily and has achieved still more remarkable advances in ballistic missiles. How, then, can presumably intelligent Soviet planners have lacked an adequate doctrine for nuclear warfare as late as 1955? We have tried to demonstrate above that the mere possession of the latest weapons does not automatically produce a military doctrine to maximize their effectiveness. Progress in the development of nuclear weapons and delivery vehicles does not necessarily bring the concomitant development of an up-to-date doctrine for their employment. That doctrine has not kept pace with weapons development in the Soviet Union is strongly suggested by the Soviet conception of war over the years.

In the spring of 1947 the famous Soviet historian, Eugène Tarlé, described in a public lecture the nature of a hypothetical war between the United States and the U.S.S.R. As soon as the war started the Soviet Union would occupy Western Europe. The Red army would meet little resistance, for one Frenchmen in three was a communist. The bombing of Moscow and Leningrad, or of Russian-occupied Europe, would accomplish nothing. The two sides would never be able to come to grips and would fall back on a war of nerves. The war would begin with the atomic bomb but would not end with it, because American bombs would be unable to solve the problem posed by the Russian army, the largest and best in the world.[2]

Tarlé's picture of the war of the future is quite consistent with what we know of Soviet weapons development in 1947. In the Russian view of that time the war would be *with* the United States but *for* Europe. If the Soviet Union could eject the United States from the continent of Europe and take or neutralize Great Britain, then neither side could really get at the other. The destructiveness of nuclear weapons has so permeated our thinking that we now tend to dismiss such a view as some kind of a propaganda smokescreen. Yet, as matters were in 1947, it was not an unreasonable blueprint for a major war. An American nuclear assault on the Soviet Union would then have had two weak points: the number of bombs and the delivery vehicles.

The number of bombs in the American stockpile was very low. In 1949 the Congressional Joint Committee on Atomic Energy published reliable testimony that the American weapons position in 1947 had "verged upon the tragic" and that disclosure of the small number of American bombs would have threatened the deterrent position of the United States.[3] Without the information provided by espionage, which apparently was considerable, the Russians could have deduced from their own progress and their knowledge of physics that the United States then possessed only a limited number of nuclear bombs.

Whether each of the few American nuclear bombs would reach a target in the Soviet Union depended on the American delivery system and the Soviet defenses. In the early years after World War II the mainstay of the American bombing force was the B-29, which had been designed during the war to bomb cities from forward bases. In the event of another war it was intended to employ these bombers in the same way, so that an American bombing campaign against the Soviet Union would depend on the continued operation of overseas bases. Soon after the World War the Soviet Union manufactured many Tu-4's, essentially copies of the B-29, which if skillfully employed could harry the air bases from which the B-29's had to fly, thus reducing the damage that the American Air Force could inflict. Furthermore, the Soviet Union early began to make heavy investments in warning systems and interceptors. The warning and interception plan was essentially that of

World War II and was designed to destroy a certain percentage of the attacking force. Since single atomic weapons were so destructive, an air-defense system that would probably let some bombers through was far from satisfactory. Nevertheless, in view of all the other factors then prevailing, the situation would be far from desperate for the Soviet Union. Once she had overrun the continent and knocked out Great Britain by a submarine campaign more destructive than either of the German ones, she could reasonably hope that after some bomb damage to her territory, neither the Soviet Union nor the United States could get at each other, so that eventually the United States would have to accept the Soviet possession of Europe.

It would be a mistake, however, to suppose that the Soviet leaders actively sought a war because they could envision a favorable outcome. The hazards of war are notoriously uncertain and the Soviet leaders had to reckon with the possibility of internal disaffection in the event of war. Soviet diplomacy at that time strongly suggests the desire to avoid a large war. Nevertheless, if war should come, the Soviet Union could reasonably expect a favorable outcome. Why establish a doctrine for the employment of nuclear weapons when you have none and you can foresee attaining your ends without them?

By 1949 the Soviet Union had mastered the technique of producing nuclear weapons. One would expect the Soviet leaders to have begun to think about war in terms of nuclear weapons. The evidence suggests that they believed in the importance of the new weapons but did not consider that the nature of warfare had changed. They needed no doctrine of nuclear warfare to justify heavy investments in atomic bombs and delivery systems. It was enough that the fission reaction was the most powerful explosion yet created by man, and that the United States had harnessed this reaction to military purposes. Moreover, prestige was enormously important to the Soviet leaders. The attractiveness of keeping up with, perhaps outstripping, the West in weapons development and thereby demonstrating Soviet technical mastery should not be underestimated.

That a new military doctrine was not an ingredient in the Soviet scheme of things is suggested by the history of the development of missiles in the Soviet Union. In the Second World War the Germans had developed and employed the V-2 to good effect. This missile had caused damage to London and later had interfered with the operation of the port of Antwerp. Its effects would have been far more serious had it been used in greater numbers over a longer period. Its effective range was over 100 miles and the warhead of about one ton was adequate for its purpose, area bombing. From the Soviet point of view it seemed an excellent idea to develop the V-2 further. A 1000-mile range, a two-ton warhead, and greater accuracy would make it a very promising weapon in a war of the kind foreseen by Tarlé. It could seriously hamper the operation of ports and airfields in Great Britain and make an American landing on the continent very difficult. Thus the use of ballistic missiles could be fitted into a picture of war not essentially modified by the existence of nuclear weapons.

A program of rocket-motor development could be justified for a "defense-of-Europe" role, but the recent launching of earth satellites demonstrates that the Soviet scientists must long ago have been permitted or instructed to develop rocket motors of far greater thrust than would be required to interdict ports and airfields in Great Britain and North Africa. It is unlikely that the Soviet leaders thought as early as 1947 of using missiles to carry intercontinental nuclear weapons, for the latter were then too heavy. Although it is possible that the Russians thought of improving the atomic-weapons design for missile warheads, it seems safer to follow an account furnished by the defector Tokaev in 1950. The passage of time has confirmed both the essentials and the details of Tokaev's statement. Here we read that the Soviet leaders determined in 1947 to develop very-long-range missiles and very-long-range aircraft in order to be able to hit the United States. In the long and circumstantial account furnished by Tokaev, nuclear weapons are not even mentioned.[4] Apparently the Russians decided that if rocket motors were improved they could deliver either very heavy loads of explosives at short and medium ranges or modest loads at intercontinental range. In Peenemünde, the German scientists, some of whom the Russians had captured, had already planned a ballistic missile with a 3000-mile range. The Russians probably also expected improvements in chemical explosives and perhaps even the use of nuclear warheads, but in 1947 long-range rockets meant first and foremost the ability to hit the United States with *something*. Even if the most expensive missile could do no more than deliver a thousand pounds of TNT to New York, the political and psychological value of possessing this capability must have seemed priceless to the Russians.

The Soviet leaders, as we have seen, had many reasons for adapting new weapons to an older military philosophy. When these reasons are properly understood, the complaint in *Military Thought* in March, 1955, that doctrinal stagnation had prevailed since 1945 does not seem inconsistent with the successful weapons developments of the same period.

In 1947 Tarlé's description of a war over a helpless Western Europe, in which the Soviet Union would suffer no more than an acceptable amount of damage from American nuclear weapons, was not implausible. As time passed, however, it became much less convincing. As nuclear weapons and delivery vehicles developed, what had been a sober judgment of Soviet prospects in a war with the United States became reckless complacency. A combination of factors gradually transformed the situation. The major ones were an increase in the number of American nuclear weapons, the greater effectiveness of these weapons and their delivery systems, and changes in the Soviet ability to reduce this effectiveness.

Although the number of nuclear weapons in the American stockpile has always been a closely guarded secret, official spokesmen and Congressional and other hearings have revealed that the Russian nuclear explosion of 1949 and the outbreak of the Korean War accelerated American production of these weapons. One can surmise that each year saw an increase and that by the time Stalin died the United States probably had a formidable number of bombs. The H-bomb tests of 1952 and

1954 demonstrated how greatly the destructive effect of nuclear weapons had grown.

The improvement in American delivery systems constituted a growing threat in the eyes of the Soviet leaders. The B-36's, which became operational in the late forties, were a great improvement over the B-29's largely because of their greater range, but they obsolesced as Soviet fighter aircraft outclassed them in speed. The B-47's, introduced during 1953 and 1954, again represented a great improvement because when refueled they had adequate range and their speed made them less vulnerable than the B-36's.

Soviet defenses were far from capable of meeting the growing American threat. The Soviet warning system suffered from serious gaps in altitude coverage. In 1953 Soviet interceptors were so designed that maximum attrition of an attacking bomber force could be expected only in good daylight weather.

These statements are very general, but the point that they are intended to support is probably valid: since some indefinite time about 1953 an American strike against the Soviet Union might well have meant damage so serious that the latter could never have recovered sufficiently to redress the balance and win the war. The destruction would be maximized if the United States achieved surprise. After 1953 the picture of a future war drawn by Tarlé in 1947 was hopelessly out of date. Such views could only be supported by wishful thinking.

The changes in weapons were so far-reaching that Soviet theories and practices would probably have adapted to them even if Stalin, whose name and prestige had been closely associated with the older military theories, had lived another ten years. The death of the dictator, however, probably made the task of the innovators easier. Part of the intellectual preparation for doctrinal progress was the controversy about the nature of war, described above in Chapter 2, in which the preponderant role of Stalin's "permanently operating factors" was questioned. Between the end of 1953 and the beginning of 1958 the elements of a new grand strategy emerged. It is helpful to divide this development into two stages. In the first stage, from 1953 to the spring of 1955, the older strategic views were attacked and somewhat modified, but no official position was taken in favor of a revision of Soviet military doctrine. In the second stage, from 1955 onward, the initial nuclear strike, with all its implications, was officially recognized as being critically important; and thereafter the aim of Soviet policy was to create and maintain the ability to deliver the first blow.

Appropriately, all the early evidence of ferment in Soviet thinking about military strategy was concerned in one way or another with surprise attack. As long as the old formula about the permanently operating factors remained official dogma, surprise by definition remained a subordinate factor and could not possibly decide the outcome of a war. Until 1955 surprise could only be presented as the most important of the secondary factors contributing to victory.

An article by a Soviet colonel in the issue of *Military Thought* for October, 1953, contained what appears to be the earliest public statement on the increased importance of surprise. The new weapons were now described, for the first time, as highly dangerous instruments of attack, capable of causing untold suffering. Hitherto their destructiveness had been minimized. In conformity with the still-reigning emphasis on the permanently operating factors, the author continued:

> Surprise attack, it is understood, has been and remains a collateral factor which does not decide the fate of a war. It is known from the experience of war, however, that surprise can bring great advantages to the aggressor and great harm to the one suffering attack. It would be unforgivable, therefore, not to reckon with this factor, or to underestimate it.[5]

This statement magnified the role of surprise without contradicting the existing doctrine of the primacy of the permanently operating factors.

In the journal *Voennyi vestnik* (*Military Herald*), Major General Pukhovskii singled out surprise as the temporary factor most capable of playing a significant role, especially in the initial period of a war. Development of new military weapons, he went on, meant that the factor of surprise could be even more important in a future war than in the past.[6]

A few weeks later a much more important soldier, Marshal Vasilevskii, published an article in *Red Star* that seemed to brush away these attempts to ascribe greater significance to surprise. He repeated the old statement that Soviet military science, unlike the bourgeois variety, "did not exaggerate the significance of such transitory factors as . . . surprise."[7] Only five days later two colonels stated in the same newspaper that Soviet military science, while recognizing the decisive influence of the permanently operating factors on the course and outcome of a war, was "far from denying the influence of temporary factors, particularly surprise attack, upon the course of the war."[8]

In an article written at almost the same time for *Military Thought,* Colonel Piatkin, too, gave surprise attack more than the traditional emphasis. He said it was the most important of the temporarily acting factors, and assumed still greater importance when atomic weapons were used: "However, the temporary factors cannot give permanent successes nor decide the fate of the war as a whole."[9]

In May, speaking on the anniversary of the victory over Germany, Marshal Vasilevskii said that surprise attack had a limited significance, without adding as he had done in February that it was improper to "overestimate" the importance of surprise. He continued to insist that the outcome of the war would be determined by the permanently operating factors.[10]

These verbal evidences of an unresolved conflict over the importance of surprise attack with nuclear weapons become more impressive when viewed in conjunction with the controversy then raging over Talenskii's article on the nature of war. Moreover, in February, 1955, *Military Thought* published an article on surprise by Rotmistrov that went far beyond the compromise formulations of early 1954, and the editors confessed their error in refusing publication until that time. Thus hindsight helps us to see the verbal peculiarities of the 1954 articles as harbingers of a new doctrine that was soon to put the permanently operating factors in the shade.

The switch from tentative suggestions to outright revision-ism was made almost in passing by a naval captain, Avramenko, who emphasized the decisive role of the permanently operating factors, and then fairly contradicted this orthodox view by calling it incorrect to underestimate "such a factor as surprise [which], especially if new and mighty weapons were employed, might in certain conditions even determine the outcome of the war. . . ."[11]

Colonel Kargalov, in a contribution to an anthology on mili-tary science said that the newest military technology had very greatly increased the role of the surprise factor, although in an earlier version of the same article, written for *Red Star*, he had been less definite.[12] In the same collection Major General Pukhovskii made a strong statement on the growing importance of surprise:

> Of the temporary, transitory factors Soviet military science singles out the element of surprise as the most effective and capable of playing a significant role, especially in the initial, first, period of a war. It should be said that, with the development of military technology and the employ-ment of new means of destruction, the surprise element acquires even more significance than it had in past wars. The employment by the opponent of the element of sur-prise cannot impose any serious damage upon the country suffering the attack if that country and its armed forces are always ready to repulse the foe. If, however, the enemy catches that country unawares [i.e., with unready defenses] and acquires the initiative even if only for a few hours, then by employing modern powerful weapons he inflicts tremendous disaster and destruction.[13]

Later in the same article Pukhovskii explicitly assumes Soviet superiority in all the permanently operating factors, as well as in atomic fission and fusion weapons: "Soviet military science assumes that at the present time the role of surprise has in-creased and has become one of the factors decisive for victory. But the Soviet armed forces will not permit the enemy to employ that factor and will reply with crushing counterblows to any aggressor's attempt at attack."[14] In other words, the enemy may strike the first blow, but he will fail to reap the advantages of surprise.

In the same anthology Colonel Vasilenko stated that some Americans, notably Senators McCarthy and Knowland and Admirals Radford and Carney, had proposed a preventive war against the Soviet Union. Given Soviet vigilance, such an attack

> . . . could not bring the imperialists success because the fate of war is decided in the last analysis by the permanently acting factors. . . . However, it is impossible to underestimate the very great damage of which an aggressor who attacks unexpectedly is capable. The role of the factor of surprise attack in connection with the appearance of the atomic and hydrogen bomb has grown seriously. This relates not only to the moment of the outbreak of the war, to its beginning, but to the whole course of the war. It should be recalled that the best means against the crafty schemes of the aggressors is the constant readiness of our army, air force, and fleet to foil the surprise attack and to deal crushing counterblows immediately against the opponent.[15]

In 1954, then, we find Soviet military writings that insist on the primacy of the permanently operating factors and at the same time suggest that a surprise attack with nuclear weapons may determine the course, and perhaps the outcome, of the whole war. This combination of ideas is at best obscure, at worst inconsistent. The insistence that general strength will determine the outcome of the war in the long run does not at first seem consistent with the suggestion that the outcome can be determined in the initial phase by nuclear surprise attack. The difficulty disappears, however, when we notice the further insistence on the role of defense. Adequate defenses, say Pukhovskii and others, coupled with vigilance, can and will deny the enemy the advantages of surprise. He will be repulsed and counterattacked. At this stage in Soviet thinking there seems to have been a certain acceptance of the idea that the enemy would get in a first blow. But not for long, as we shall see.

The debate over military surprise was not settled until early in 1955. Meanwhile the man who initiated the debate on basic military policy, Talenskii, was relieved of his post as editor of *Military Thought* some time in 1954. As soon as Malenkov was replaced, the editors of *Military Thought* published a statement on the role of surprise in modern war going far beyond anything said in 1954. Further, the editors said, as we have seen, that they had been in error in refusing to print this article when first submitted. It is not in the least surprising that the political implications of the contending strategic concepts played such an important role. The existence of a debate about the best military strategy, involving massive allocations of money and readjustments in foreign policy, necessarily aroused strong feelings in the highest decisionmaking bodies of the state. Until these bodies resolved all differences of opinion, the formulas advanced by lesser persons had to straddle two or more views. Meanwhile further development took place in the ideas of Soviet officers about the importance of the initial nuclear strike and its place in Soviet strategy.

The most important single article arguing that surprise attack with nuclear weapons differed in essentials from surprise attack in any earlier period was the one whose publication had been held up by the editors of *Military Thought*. The author, Tank Marshal Rotmistrov, carefully demonstrated how much had changed in the last few years. In the first paragraph, Rotmistrov stated the basic thesis of the revisionists, that surprise could decide the fate of the whole war:

> The experience of history has shown that the skillful employment of surprise brings true success, not only in battles and operations, but also in war. If a war starts with a surprise attack, then as a rule it [the surprise attack] essentially determines the strategic victory in the first stage of the war and secures the conditions for the advantageous development of subsequent military activities, which [development] is obtained if the initial strategic result is correctly assessed and forces and means for the purposeful exploitation of the success are prepared while the opponent has not yet been able to localize it.[16]

Rotmistrov showed how surprise had always been important in military operations and how the Russian military heroes

Suvorov and Kutuzov had employed surprise to good effect. He analyzed some surprise attacks that had been strategically important. The Japanese assault on the Russian Far East naval squadron during the night of February 8-9, 1904, eliminated Russian sea power in the Pacific and removed any danger to the supply line between Japan and her ground forces in Manchuria. In planning for the First World War, the German General Staff expected that a surprise thrust through Belgium would assure victory. The Germans counted on superior military ability and superior artillery to bring quick success. Underestimation of their opponents' military capacities and of the length of the war, however, brought defeat. The failure of the Germans to gain victory by strategic surprise did not stop them from seeking success a second time by the same method. In the Second World War the Germans did succeed in defeating Poland, France, Holland, and Belgium by employing surprise and superiority. In the forty-five-day campaign of 1940 Hitlerite Germany completely destroyed the Anglo-French army. Not only surprise, Rotmistrov explained, but political factors, made this victory possible. As a result of surprise attack Germany not only gained "intermediate strategic goals but in a very short time obtained the capitulation of a number of European governments."

In its surprise attack against the Soviet Union, continued the Russian marshal, the German army had the advantages of two years' wartime experience and a certain superiority in the quantity of military equipment. The Germans used these advantages to gain strategic results in the first phase of the war and put the Soviet army in a very difficult position.

The surprise Japanese aerial blow against Pearl Harbor in December, 1941, caused important damage to the American navy and "predetermined its two-year passivity in the subsequent phase of the war." From these historical facts Rotmistrov concluded:

> Thus on the basis of the experience of past wars it is possible to assert that surprise, successfully accomplished, not only influences the course of battles and operations but in

certain circumstances can influence to a significant extent the course and even the outcome of the whole war.[17]

This does not mean, cautioned Rotmistrov, that surprise is the only condition for victory, as some imperialists say, but it does mean that one cannot afford to underestimate the significance of a surprise blow in the first phase of the war: "To the extent that equipment has developed and new, powerful, and effective weapons have appeared and have been incorporated, the significance of surprise in war grows more and more." In other words, surprise is even more important today than it was in the historical cases cited to demonstrate its importance.

Rotmistrov took up the theme that the past was not a reliable guide. Even if one recognized the importance of surprise attack in earlier wars, one could "not now be limited by this experience alone."[18] Rotmistrov went on to give what has since remained the official Soviet appraisal of the importance of surprise attack:

> Surprise attack, employing atomic and hydrogen weapons and other modern means of conflict, now takes on new forms and is capable of leading to significantly greater results than in the past war. It must be plainly said that when atomic and hydrogen weapons are employed, surprise is one of the decisive conditions for the attainment of success not only in battles and operations, but also in war as a whole. . . . Surprise attack with the massive employment of new weapons can cause the rapid collapse of a government whose capacity to resist is low as a consequence of radical faults in its social and economic structure and also as a consequence of an unfavorable geographic position.[19]

Rotmistrov felt that surprise attack played an important part in the strategy of the United States and Great Britain, and that the American and British leaders would expect, by bombing the deep rear of the Soviet Union, to put her war facilities and industrial centers out of commission, to paralyze transportation, and to demoralize the population. Although the Americans expected so much from surprise attack, they realized that aerial blows alone could not decide the outcome of a future war and therefore they were also assembling mighty land forces. Rotmistrov had no better answer to this imagined threat than that German surprise did not succeed, an argument that was outdated by his own admission. Imperialist strategy, he continued, was forced to rely on the surprise attack because the capitalists could not expect to sustain the strains of a long war. Moreover the imperialist aggressors had often in the past attacked by surprise. The Soviet Union "should always be ready for pre-emptive action against the aggressor's schemes." The imperialist desire to achieve surprise and take the Soviet Union unawares made it necessary for the Soviet government to be constantly ready.

Rotmistrov brought to its logical conclusion the discussion and controversy of 1953-1954. If a surprise attack could indeed determine, or even seriously affect, the outcome of a war it was even more necessary to surprise, and avoid being surprised, than in the past. A surprise attack could be frustrated if the enemy were himself surprised as he prepared to strike:

> The duty of the Soviet armed forces is not to permit an enemy surprise attack on our country and, in the event of an attempt to accomplish one, not only to repel the attack successfully but also to deal the enemy counterblows, or even pre-emptive [*uprezhdaiushchie*] surprise blows, of terrible destructive force. For this the Soviet army and navy possess everything necessary.[20]

The pre-emptive blow, then, was one designed to forestall an enemy strike. This was a new element in Soviet thinking. The success of a pre-emptive strategy, Rotmistrov continued, required prompt detection of a concrete war danger. The Soviet armed forces must not only discover the best means to repel enemy blows but also to deal advance counterblows, completely unexpected by the enemy about to attack the Soviet Union.

After advocating a Soviet strategy of "pre-emptive" attack to forestall the known aggressive plans of an enemy, Marshal

Rotmistrov carefully distinguished it from a strategy of "preventive" war:

> The growth of the role of surprise, in combination with the changed character of contemporary war, indicates that if we are forced to take up arms we should be able to gain the strategic initiative by using the surprise element to the full. . . . The aspiration to seize and hold the strategic initiative should not be understood as an intention to begin a preventive war against the enemies of the U.S.S.R. who are preparing to attack us. The Soviet Union threatens no one nor is it preparing to attack first, even though some governments are conducting a provocative military policy, surrounding the territory of our country with a network of bases, and feverishly pushing their satellites to war against us. But in this connection it is necessary always to remember that historically aggressors have frequently used the excuse of preventive war to justify pure aggression. Any such attempt, however it may be masked, demands that the Soviet army give the aggressor who ventures to this extreme a fitting rebuff, according to all the rules of the Soviet military art.[21]

The subtle distinctions that can be made between the terms "pre-emptive" and "preventive" will be discussed later. At present it is more important to note that readiness to strike a pre-emptive blow became, early in 1955, a principal aim of official Soviet policy. This bald assertion will shortly be supported by more evidence. But first it should be emphasized that it is *not* Soviet policy to admit the adoption of a pre-emptive strategy.

In January, 1958, an article in *Foreign Affairs** stated the case for the proposition that the U.S.S.R. had adopted a policy of readiness for pre-emptive war. Soviet General Kurasov stoutly denied the truth of this proposition. His argument was this:

> As history shows, the Soviet Union has more than once suffered aggressive attacks and has been forced to conduct hard and bloody wars in order to defend her independence

---

* Written by the author of this book.

as a state. A study of the initial period of the Great Fatherland War could not but direct the attention of military thinking to the significance of the factor of surprise in modern wars. It became patently obvious that the surprise attack of the German fascist troops permitted them temporarily to seize the strategic initiative at the beginning of the war. The appearance of nuclear weapons and the possibility for their mass employment against troops and targets in the rear produced different opinions on the significance of surprise attack in a future war and on the measures for opposing such an attack. This prompted some military authors to engage in an investigation of the significance of the factor of surprise in modern war. Theoretical statements in the press by individual authors on measures to frustrate an aggressor's surprise attack were interpreted in the Western press as a summons to preemptive war.[22]

This somewhat equivocal denial of the existence of an official requirement that the Soviet Union be able to strike preemptively is open to question on two grounds. In the Soviet Union high officials writing in an organ of the Ministry of War, as Rotmistrov did, do not make "theoretical statements," nor can they be considered to write as "individual authors," unless (and this is rare) the article is characterized as being part of a discussion. The debate opened by Talenskii in 1953 was so characterized and all the articles pro and con were clearly designated as parts of that discussion. Second, the editorial in *Military Thought* for March, 1955, which was certainly an official statement, criticized the magazine's former policy in holding up Rotmistrov's article, and then made the following unambiguous statement:

> We cannot ignore the lessons of history and we must always be ready for pre-emptive actions against the perfidy of the aggressors.[23]

Is it not conceivable, one may ask, that Rotmistrov's article in February, 1955, and its editorial endorsement in March represented merely a temporary aberration of official policy? The subsequent wide circulation of Rotmistrov's ideas makes this explanation extremely improbable, to say the least.

Rotmistrov soon repeated a number of the conclusions of his *Military Thought* article in *Red Star,* a far more widely read organ. The new version omitted a great deal of the historical argument that appeared in the earlier one and avoided the explicit statement that the Soviet Union should be ready to strike a pre-emptive blow under the appropriate circumstances. The *Red Star* article took the form of a polemic against two writers who had written about the permanently operating factors in a tone that had been standard, if not obligatory, only a year earlier. The essential points of Rotmistrov's two formulations, however, were the same. In each he used identical phrases to say that surprise attack with nuclear weapons could be one of the decisive conditions for success not only in the initial phase but in the whole war. Instead of directly advocating a pre-emptive attack, however, he used circumlocutions about frustrating the "aggressors' schemes" and "not permitting a surprise attack." The latter soon became standard in mass-media references to the subject.

At this stage Rotmistrov did not deny the validity of the formula about the permanently operating factors, but he felt that Soviet military writers erred when they said that the capitalist nations did not take the permanently operating factors into account.[24]

An editorial in the May issue of *Military Thought* left no doubt as to the official character of the pre-emptive strike doctrine:

> The matter goes beyond the exhaustive clarification of the significance of the surprise factor and the study of cases and examples of the employment of surprise in recent wars. The task is the purposeful elaboration of all aspects of this question, especially the elaboration of ways and means to prevent an enemy surprise attack and to deal the opponent pre-emptive blows on every scale—strategic, operational, and tactical.[25]

General Kurochkin, writing in the same issue of *Military Thought,* said: "In order further to guarantee the security of our Motherland against an aggressor's surprise attack, it is necessary to be in a state of full fighting readiness and to be able to deal pre-emptive blows against an enemy who is preparing to attack."[26]

Several public statements in the same month reaffirmed the need for a pre-emptive strategy. Of these, Vasilevskii's was particularly striking because he had earlier insisted on the primacy of the permanently operating factors, probably in resistance to the growing emphasis on the importance of surprise. Vasilevskii now said that the Soviet Union had everything necessary "to deprive the aggressor, should he unleash a new war, of the advantages which long preparation and the suddenness and treachery of the attack could give him."[27] Lieutenant General Braiko of the air force, writing for an air force magazine, said that this service had the duty "to deprive the aggressor of the factor of surprise and not let ourselves be taken unawares. It is necessary for us to nip in the very bud the scheming plans of the warmongers if they dare begin to execute them."[28] The editorial in the same issue of the magazine said that it was not "enough to be prepared and capable of returning blow for blow at the instigator of war." It was also "necessary to deprive the aggressor of the factor of surprise and not let ourselves be taken unawares."[29] General Shatilov, writing a month later, was even more explicit:

> Knowing the savage character of the aggressors, we cannot ignore the plans they are hatching. The Soviet Union threatens no one and is not preparing to attack anyone. But those who think they will find us passive or unprepared to repel aggression will be bitterly disappointed. It would pay the immoderately warlike generals and admirals of the imperialist camp to remember that atomic weapons as well as surprise action are double-edged weapons and that it is hardly sensible to jest with them.[30]

The point of calling surprise a "double-edged weapon" seems unmistakable: the enemy who seeks to surprise us may himself be surprised.

A few months later Marshal Rotmistrov reviewed a book

on surprise attack, written by General Popov before the new policy had been officially adopted. He was merciless in exposing the inconsistencies and absurdities of trying to say at once that surprise was terribly important and that the permanently operating factors were still all-determining. Following the usual Soviet style, Rotmistrov ignored the circumstance that the book he was criticizing had been delivered to the printer at the end of 1954. Thus he used a recently outdated book to drive home a doctrine established since the book was written.[31]

General Popov, who made a hopeless attempt to reconcile the old view of the permanently operating factors with the new view of surprise, was an easy mark. He made the point that surprise could be successful only with superiority in the permanently operating factors. Rotmistrov argued that the side inferior in a number of the permanently operating factors could employ surprise to compensate for its relative weakness. Popov, wrote his critic, had been forced to conclude from his faulty premise that Soviet surprise attack succeeded in the last war because of superiority in the permanently operating factors and that imperialist surprise attack was only adventurism. This, Rotmistrov argued, was unscientific. If success in surprise attack depended on, and was guaranteed by, superiority in the permanently operating factors—a superiority preordained for the Soviet forces—then there was no point in discussing the matter at all. Popov's thesis demonstrated his "incorrect interpretation of the significance of the permanently operating factors as a panacea for all ills." Here Rotmistrov was taking a real step forward from his position of February and March, and from the ideas expressed by the editors of *Military Thought*. No one had said in so many words that the permanently operating factors were being employed as a panacea for all ills. Rotmistrov was approaching a point where the old permanently-operating-factors formula would have to be explicitly abandoned because it interfered with the proper appraisal of surprise.

Rotmistrov attributed more to Popov than the latter meant, in order to prove that the new pre-emptive strategy was best. Popov had said that "aggressive countries, as a rule, attack the peace loving countries when they are not mobilized."[32] Rotmistrov presented this as meaning that there was a "fatalistic inevitability that the peace loving peoples must suffer the aggressor's [opening] blows, and moreover, suddenly." Using this as a point of departure, he outlined his own idea of a strategy to prevent it:

> What is all this for? What is the use of such "theoretical" calculations? What can they offer military practice? Indeed, the problem really is: *by studying the lessons of the past to avoid in the future any kind of possibility of surprise attack on our country by a putative opponent,* which demands constant vigilance by the Soviet armed forces. And in this case the author [Popov], by his assertion expressed on page 9 of the impossibility of foreseeing "the moment of surprise" and of the inevitability of its appearance, unwittingly does a disservice to the cause of inculcating vigilance and battle readiness in our troops.

> Naturally it is impossible to foresee every trifle in all cases, but when such events as surprise attack by an aggressor are involved it is possible and, frankly, necessary under any conditions not to permit the moment of surprise whose consequences might at the present time be difficult to overcome. It is absolutely clear and beyond argument that Marxist-Leninist science is fully capable of foreseeing such a significant phenomenon in the life of society as the transition from a condition of peace to a condition of war.[33]

In this statement Rotmistrov added two new facets to the doctrine of the pre-emptive strike. First he made the point that the consequences of a successful surprise attack might be difficult to overcome. This was a corollary of his proposition, made earlier in the year, that surprise might be one of the decisive factors affecting not only the course but also the outcome of the war. More novel, and more important for the formulation of a pre-emptive strategy, was his second point, that the Soviet Union could reasonably expect timely warning of the enemy's preparations for a surprise attack, so that it would not be surprised. In the absence of a belief that timely warning was possible, the whole pre-emptive strategy would be meaningless.

By definition and by logic "pre-emption" required the receipt of warning.

These points were reiterated in 1956 in a long, ambitious book entitled *Militarism*, also published by the Ministry of Defense. The author, Skopin, re-emphasized what had become the standard Soviet line, that strategic surprise could be of tremendous importance and that the Soviet Union, if threatened with attack, would find some way of getting in the first blow. Skopin argued: "Thanks to nuclear weapons strategic surprise has become unusually and unprecedentedly dangerous. Any other evaluation would be blind and naïve. But from this follows not the victory of militarism [that is, the initiator of aggression], but only the very great price of victory over militarism." The capitalists, he continued, thought a surprise nuclear attack the only promising way to win the duel between Capital and Labor. But monopoly capital underestimated both the military strength of the Soviet bloc and its constant readiness to deal with surprise. Furthermore, "the massive popular genius always finds new infallible ways and means for rebuffing treacherous surprise attacks of any size." Then Skopin rhetorically affirmed what had now become an article of faith, that the Soviet Union would always have timely warning of attack: "Just as the chain reaction within the atom produces the sudden splitting of the nucleus, so the surprise attack by militarism produces a 'chain reaction' of retaliatory activity."[34] Virtually the same statements were made as late as October, 1957, when a second edition of Skopin's book was in galleys.[35]

Once it became official doctrine that a successful surprise attack could determine the ultimate outcome of the whole war, the Soviet version of the events of 1941 had to be revised. The very editorial in *Military Thought* that praised Rotmistrov's article and repeated his advocacy of "pre-emptive actions" started a campaign against the then-current doctrine that a planned "active defense" had held off defeat in 1941 and 1942. The relevant passages read:

> The authors of many works [on the war] do not give a correct objective evaluation of events, but give a one-

sided account of the course of the war, seek to embellish and idealize many of the phenomena of the war, do not treat the difficulties adequately, and either maintain silence on our mistakes and shortcomings or minimize them. In research on the war the chief attention has been erroneously devoted to the military events of the second half of the war and to the offensive operations of the Soviet Army . . . in 1944 and 1945 . . . when the enemy had lost the initiative and the ability to conduct offensive operations on a more or less large scale.

As a result of its treacherous invasion the German Fascist Army, as is well known, succeeded in the initial period of the war in gaining important successes. . . . However, people are to be found to this day in our scientific institutes, academies, and the editorial boards of our military journals who represent the failure of 1941 as a victory, characterizing this as the period of the classic form of the so-called "active defense. . . ."

The paeons to active defense and its misinterpretation as something planned in advance lead not only to the distortion of what really happened in 1941 but also to the idealization of this form of war, and incorrectly orient our cadres to the possibility of its repetition in a future war.

The very designation of the initial period of the war as the "period of active defense," which has wide currency in military literature and has entered the programs of instruction of our military-pedagogical institutes, incorrectly represents the actual character of that period, since the military activities of our troops for the most part had the character of withdrawal operations.[36]

Here the editors of *Military Thought* drew attention to a particularly striking example of the danger of falling victim to one's own propaganda, that is, of accepting as guiding principles statements made only for political purposes. Marshal Rotmistrov, obviously a leader in the fight for more realism, took issue with a writer who had written in the traditional way that the German surprise attack had turned into an unexpected catastrophe for the Germans and that the planned retreat of the

Soviet army had surprised the enemy by turning into a victorious advance. Rotmistrov commented sarcastically:

> Thus the [German] surprise attack is converted into an advance into catastrophe, and the unexpected [Soviet] withdrawal becomes a victorious advance for that side. Such conversions and transitions do not occur in life. A surprise blow is a surprise blow and a withdrawal is a withdrawal. One cannot be converted into the other. If it is admitted, as apparently the author of this book wants to say, that similar conversions might recur and should be expected, then nothing remains but to present the opponent with freedom to deal surprise blows and turn them into a sure path to his downfall. These enemy blows would represent no danger for us since they would not be supported by superiority in the permanently operating factors. (According to the author, surprise not backed up by the permanently operating factors is not effective.)[37]

After March, 1955, many writers echoed the editorial position of *Military Thought,* sometimes using the same phrases. On May 6 an editorial in *Red Star* chided Soviet writers and thinkers for having concentrated only on the successful battles and operations of the last war and for not having reviewed Soviet mistakes and failures.[38] In an article on the tenth anniversary of the victory in Europe Marshal Sokolovskii also referred to the necessity of studying the experience of the first difficult months of the war.[39] General Shatilov was explicit on this point. He insisted that the German advantage of surprise, although temporary, made the war develop very differently from the way it would have done otherwise. He complained that Soviet literature

> . . . often idealizes the first period of military operations and presents it as the so-called classic form of "active defense" in operation. Furthermore the authors, contrary to the true facts, try to present "active defense" as if it had been planned in advance and had been included in the calculations of our command. In fact the initial period of the war, in view of the suddenness of the enemy attack and

his numerical superiority in tanks and airplanes, was very unfavorable for our country and for our army which suffered the bitterness of retreat despite the stubbornness and bravery of her fighters, who defended every inch of native soil.

Such a view, Shatilov pointed out, "distorts the historical truth and incorrectly orients our people by creating the impression of the possibility and even of the desirability of treating these events as precedents for the future."[40] Shatilov was clearly castigating those who minimized surprise on the ground that the Soviet Union had undergone a surprise attack and yet had emerged victorious from the war. Since the spring of 1955 this view has been out of favor and military journals and books have continued to describe "active defense" as complacency.

Only once has there been a significant variation in this theme, and the occasion was a difference on political rather than strategic matters. In April, 1956, the editors of *Military Herald,* the journal of the ground forces, wrote that the defeats in the initial period of the war were largely Stalin's fault. Furthermore, "one of the most important reasons for our military shortcomings in the initial period of the Great Fatherland War was that Soviet industry had not been promptly and properly mobilized for the production of the necessary weapons and munitions. As a result, despite the fact that industry had attained a level of development adequate to guarantee completely everything the troops required and even before the war had produced excellent pieces of military equipment, the Soviet Army until the end of 1942 suffered shortages in artillery, tanks, and aircraft."[41] The implication of the whole editorial was that Stalin and the political leaders, not the armed forces, bore responsibility for the early defeats. The editors of *Red Star,* no doubt in response to pressure from party leaders, protested the opinions of *Military Herald:*

One cannot but be shocked and pained at the completely incorrect and harmful judgments appearing in the editorial article of the fourth issue for 1956 of *Military Herald.* The article asserts that our army had to retreat

and wage difficult defensive battles allegedly because the
troops had not been put into fighting readiness. . . . The
article crudely distorts the mobilized readiness and the
potentialities of our industry.

Whether or not they wanted to, the authors of the article
just cited from *Military Herald* have minimized the significance of our victory in the past war and have minimized
the decisive role of the Soviet people and their Armed
Forces in the winning of that victory.[42]

These incorrect judgments, the *Red Star* writers added, were
advanced in the guise of criticism of the cult of personality,
which had been one of the main features of the Twentieth
Party Congress: "But it is impossible, under the guise of un-
masking that cult, to minimize the role of our Party and its
Central Committee, the role of our people and of the Soviet
Government, both in strengthening the defensive capability of
our country and in the organization and accomplishment of the
defeat of Fascist Germany."[43] The Party leaders apparently felt
that the military were carrying things too far in implying that
the Party and its Central Committee had let the country down.
The army seemed to be challenging the good judgment of
several of the present Party leaders as well as of Stalin, in
economic matters as well as military, and to be claiming more
of a voice in the sphere of state policy. Nevertheless, *Red Star*
soon modified its shocked reaction to the editorial in *Military
Herald*. On July 19 the editors wrote a new article[44] about
Party leadership of the armed forces that made no reference to
their May editorial, but that was clearly a revision of it. In
defense of the Party, they stated that it had always been aware
of the danger fascism represented, had preached vigilance, and
had ultimately led the army to victory. Only Stalin had failed
to take the necessary measures. So far the article seemed to
make no retreat in its championship of the Party. But when it
admitted that "industry was not promptly and properly mobilized so as to insure to our army an adequate quantity of
military equipment and munitions," it was paraphrasing the
very sentence that *Red Star* had characterized as a distortion

two months earlier. Moreover the article went on to flatter the generals: "Certain important factors, particularly the role of the Soviet army generals in determining the outcome of the war, had been underestimated."

The reason for *Red Star*'s change of attitude is not hard to find. Marshal Zhukov, who had recently become Minister of Defense, had raised the whole question of the honor of the armed forces and the responsibility for early Soviet defeats in World War II in a manner that could not but reduce the prestige of the Communist Party. This was probably a major reason for his ultimate dismissal in 1957, when he was taken to task for vainglory and for trying to deprive the Party of its due. In 1957 there was not a word about the army's criticism of "active defense." Any revision of the now-official policy of attacking active defense could easily have been interpreted as a revival of the idea that surprise was of secondary, not crucial, significance. The party leaders had no intention of taking such a backward step in military doctrine. Zhukov's dismissal was inspired by political differences, not by any disagreement between Party and army on basic military thought.

In the first half of 1955, as we have seen, the Soviet leadership adopted a basic innovation in military strategy. The requirement that the Soviet Union be prepared to strike a pre-emptive blow in order to forestall an enemy attack was bound to affect military planning, procurement, and training. In addition, suitable ways had to be worked out for presenting the new policy to domestic and foreign audiences.

What did the Soviet Union have to do in order to bring her military posture into line with the new requirement? In crude terms, she had to be able to beat the enemy to the draw. But when nuclear weapons are to be delivered by aircraft, by intercontinental ballistic missiles, by cruise missiles from submarines, or by a combination of these vehicles, "the draw" is an enormously complicated act. When the aim is pre-emption, the act of drawing is further complicated by the need to interpret the enemy's moves and to learn his intentions.

A modern strategic air force always has some fraction of its aircraft ready to start instantly on a bombing mission. The fraction grows larger during alerts and practice maneuvers. An increase in the number of aircraft at maximum readiness is not necessarily an indication of intention to start hostilities. Even detailed information on the activities of an opponent's air force does not yield unequivocal conclusions about the orders being executed by that air force. These considerations apply even more strongly to ballistic missiles than to manned bombers. How is one to know the exact time to pre-empt, and can one be ready by then?

Let us assume that a decision to strike pre-emptively has been taken on the basis of what is considered adequate warning. How much time is then required to make the strike pre-emptive rather than merely retaliatory? When aircraft are the chief means of delivery, one must count as a minimum the time of flight. It is more realistic to add the time required to make ready more crews and planes than those available at the moment of warning. Even if the main delivery system is intercontinental ballistic missiles, time is required for a count-down on those at maximum readiness and more time to get other missiles into firing position. These necessary time lags mean that even unequivocal warning may not permit an effective pre-emptive blow, that is, one that knocks the opponent's weapon from his hand.

If the chances of getting in a telling pre-emptive strike are so poor, why, one is bound to ask, did the Soviet leaders lay down the requirement for one as their guiding principle? A nation will surely adopt the strategy that seems to offer the best chance of victory. It does not follow, however, that even a very powerful nation is at all times in a position to devise and employ a promising strategy. There may be periods in a country's history, especially transitional ones, when her official strategy must be merely the best of several poor alternatives.

What were the Soviet alternatives at the beginning of 1955, when the policy of pre-emptive capability was announced? The traditional aim had been to avoid war with any great power. This policy assumed the military weakness of the Soviet Union and the probable loss of such a war. To ward off calamity no concession was too great; no insult too humiliating. In the months before June, 1941, Stalin appeased Hitler on almost every issue. Hoping that German mobilization was a bluff, Stalin feared that preparations against a German attack might provoke it and felt that passivity might prevent it. This seems to be the explanation of his otherwise inexplicable failure to heed the most unequivocal of warnings. To Soviet leaders in 1955 a policy of appeasement seemed indefensible. First, it had failed miserably in 1941; second, Eisenhower presented no such threat as Hitler; and third, the Soviet leaders felt immeasurably stronger in 1955 than in 1941. Moreover, to leave the initiative to a possible enemy, as Stalin had done, would be far more dangerous under present conditions. If nuclear weapons were used, the victor in the first campaign might well be the victor in the whole war. If the Soviet Union were to suffer the first strike she could not count on a repetition of her successful recovery and counterattack in World War II. Traditional passivity was no longer a workable basis for military planning.

Another alternative was to ensure Soviet priority by initiating a strike against the United States. The object of a war thus begun had to be at least an improvement of the prewar position. The weapons balance could not hold out such a promise to the Soviet leaders. Although it is impossible to say exactly what the weapons balance was in 1955, or what the Soviet leaders thought it was, it is clear enough that American retaliation to an initial Soviet strike would have been devastating. No matter how many nuclear weapons the Soviet Union then possessed, she had a delivery system much inferior to the American one. Even if the Soviet leaders counted on all accidents and unforeseen circumstances favoring them, they could not confidently expect to obviate American retaliation by making a surprise nuclear attack on Western bases. We have no reason to think that the Soviet leaders ever seriously contemplated any such reckless solution to their problems. A preventive war, at a time of their own choosing, was not an acceptable policy in 1955.

The third and last alternative strategy, and the least unsatisfactory, was that of the pre-emptive blow. The requirements for a successful pre-emptive blow were unequivocal and

timely warning of an impending enemy attack, and the ability
to destroy the enemy striking force before it could get in its
strike. As far as unequivocal warning was concerned, Soviet
leaders took a very sanguine view. Talenskii, in his opening
article, pointed out that the advantages accruing to an aggressor
could be minimized "by a skillful and vigilant intelligence."[45]

In May, 1955, the editors of *Military Thought,* in the same
editorial in which they advocated preparatory measures for a
pre-emptive blow to prevent an enemy surprise attack, dealt
with the problem of warning. Marxism-Leninism, they wrote,
taught that wars are always preceded by the formation of aggressive military coalitions, and history has demonstrated quite
clearly that "not a single modern war began without a series of
provocations preceding it."[46]

In his "secret" speech on Stalin, delivered at a closed session of the Twentieth Party Congress, Khrushchev reviewed
the warnings of a German attack in 1941. On April 3 Churchill
warned Stalin through Cripps, but "Stalin ordered that no
credence be given to information of this sort, in order not to
provoke the initiation of military operations." Khrushchev
cited two separate warnings from Soviet military attachés in
Berlin on May 6 and May 22, and a new warning from the
British on June 18. On the eve of the invasion a German citizen
crossed the border and told of the coming invasion.[47] Khrushchev might also have mentioned even sharper warnings from
Soviet intelligence sources in Japan and Switzerland.[48] From
these warnings the editors of *Military Herald* argued that the
German attack should have been expected:

> The very ideology of fascism and also the whole prewar
> policy of the Hitlerite clique was irrefutable evidence of
> the preparation for an attack upon the U.S.S.R. and,
> moreover, the fascists did not even conceal their plans.
> Thus, despite the conclusion in 1939 of a non-aggression
> pact, there was no doubt of the possibility of a treacherous
> blow against the Soviet Union by Hitler. In the spring of
> 1941 this possibility was converted into a real threat.
> Numerous facts revealed in good time by Soviet military

intelligence* testified to this threat. In particular it was learned in good time that a tremendous number of German fascist troops, including strong tank units, had been concentrated along the Western U.S.S.R. border.

But the German fascist attack was a surprise to the Soviet Armed Forces all the same, although it cannot possibly have been a surprise to the highest leadership of the country—which at that time was concentrated entirely in the hands of J. V. Stalin. The main point is that, despite every obvious sign of the preparation of aggression, the measures of readiness necessary to exclude surprise were not taken.[49]

Statements of this kind often did more than throw the blame for the defeats of 1941 on Stalin: they also expressed the confidence that similar failures to heed warnings need not recur.

Nevertheless the analogy between the events preceding the German attack on the Soviet Union and those likely to precede a third world war was obviously far from perfect. The deployment of more than a hundred German divisions along a two-thousand-mile frontier was hardly comparable to the preparation of a nuclear air strike. On the other hand the Soviet leaders might expect that no Western parliamentary democracy would go to war without giving some kind of notice or warning. It will be recalled that in November, 1954, when the magazine *Kommunist* pointed to the growing danger of war, one of the arguments adduced was the curtailment of liberties in the United States and the strengthening of fascist tendencies. As long as the present system of government prevails in the United States, the Soviet leaders will probably not worry very much about a "bolt from the blue." For all these reasons, the Soviet policymakers are optimistic about the feasibility of receiving timely warning of any nuclear attack.

As for the likelihood of a Soviet pre-emptive blow to destroy the American striking force before it can get to its targets, one can do little more than isolate the elements that would enter into a Soviet decision to attempt a pre-emptive nuclear blow against the United States. If this capability be poor, the need

* Such Soviet references to their own espionage are extremely rare.

for reliable warning signals will rise. In other words, the greater the risk of retaliation, the greater the desire not to risk a nuclear exchange. If minimal retaliation is expected, the attacker may think it worth while to strike pre-emptively, even though he is far from certain of the putative enemy's intentions. If we assume (as we have suggested the Soviet leaders assumed) that in 1955 a nuclear war could have been a disaster for the Soviet Union no matter who enjoyed the advantage of the first strike, then we must also assume that it was Soviet policy to wait until the very last moment before initiating such a war.

In the unlikely event that the Soviet Union should ever acquire a striking capability so strong and sure as to preclude retaliation, a Soviet pre-emptive blow would assure a Soviet victory, at little or no cost in terms of damage to the homeland. In that case it is difficult to imagine Soviet leaders risking a seizure of the initiative by the enemy. At best, a policy of waiting would raise the cost of an ultimate Soviet victory; at worst, it would result in final defeat. Let it be emphasized, however, that the circumstances of this hypothetical case are unlikely to occur.

Since a "retaliation-proof" attack is out of the question in the foreseeable future, the Soviet leaders are likely to be influenced by various subtle political factors in defining the conditions under which a pre-emptive blow would be justified. They will certainly take into account the character of the American presidential incumbent and the domestic situation in the Soviet Union. The possibility cannot be excluded that in certain circumstances a Soviet political leader or faction, convinced of Soviet ability to win a nuclear war, will overestimate the indicators of a possible American attack and underestimate the danger from American retaliation. As we have seen, Khrushchev has not hesitated to provoke war scares for partisan political advantage.

The difficulties of coming to a decision to make a pre-emptive strike are so obvious that the Soviet leaders must have realized them in 1955, at or about the time they adopted a policy of readiness to strike pre-emptively. These reflections pointed to something more than a generalized military expansion; they pointed to the kind of military program that would aim at a retaliation-proof capability. This capability could be used to strike "preventively" and thus circumvent the weakness of the pre-emptive strategy, with its dependence on unequivocal warning. Ideally this capability would preclude damage to the country possessing it. Obviously this was a goal worth shooting for.

Without assurance that warning of an enemy attack will come in good time and that pre-emptive action will be speedy, dependence on pre-emption becomes effectively only dependence on retaliation. The only real guarantee that a nuclear strike will be early enough to damage the opponent's striking force before he can employ it is to hit the opponent before he has begun to prepare a strike of his own. This is the long-established and widely excoriated principle of preventive war.

Whatever the possible advantages of preventive war, American public opinion and the American political system do not permit an unprovoked, or even pre-emptive, attack. Therefore the United States has to rely mainly on her capacity to retaliate if she or her allies are attacked. In the Soviet Union, however, the Party controls military policy and is a law unto itself. The leaders have only to be convinced of the correctness of aggressive policy; it requires no popular mandate. This basic characteristic of Soviet politics makes it legitimate to inquire whether the Soviet leaders are employing the phrase "pre-emptive blows" as a euphemism for preventive war.

Preventive nuclear war makes sense for the Soviet Union only if that country can be reasonably sure to emerge unscathed. Even if the Soviet leaders were convinced that they possessed the required military preponderance, they would not necessarily decide to start a preventive war. That decision would depend on many other circumstances that cannot now be foreseen. It is possible, however, to list some factors that would tend to produce such a decision and some that would work against it.

The Soviet leaders, whether or not in command of a retaliation-proof capability, might conclude from available evidence that the United States would soon have such a capability. Preventive war might then seem a worth-while gamble.

It would be oversimplification to suggest baldly that the Soviet political leaders may seek to extricate themselves from domestic or foreign difficulties by seeking victory in a nuclear war against the United States. But the prospects of such a victory can be readily imagined as influencing their judgment about the certainty of warning needed to trigger a pre-emptive strike. Again, it is not difficult to picture a situation in which the Soviet leaders, agitated by setbacks and eager to regain lost ground, might undertake some limited aggressive action, giving rise to Western counteractions that could be interpreted as warning of an intention to make a nuclear strike. In this connection, contrast Soviet nonintervention in Yugoslavia in 1948 with Soviet intervention in Hungary in 1956. In 1948 Stalin was the unchallenged dictator of the Soviet Union. His failure to prevent Tito's defection and his subsequent failure to force Yugoslavia back into the Soviet camp did not appreciably diminish his position at home. In 1956 Khrushchev could have been, and probably was, blamed for creating the conditions that led to the Hungarian revolution. Even his ruthless suppression of the revolution does not seem to have silenced the opposition to him within the Party. In 1948, either because of the established pattern of caution in foreign policy, or because of a sense of military inferiority, Stalin did not risk a general war by a direct invasion of Yugoslavia. He satisfied himself with the hope that "loyal" communists within the Yugoslav Party would overthrow Tito. In 1956 the Soviet leadership placed no such faith in the Hungarian communists and accepted whatever risk of general war Soviet intervention in Hungary entailed. Presumably they felt that greater Soviet military power reduced the risk of general war.

The contrast between 1948 and 1956 suggests that growing Soviet military strength, by increasing Soviet confidence, will encourage bolder Soviet political activities. Before Stalin's death Soviet expansionist tactics were always applied in areas bordering the Soviet bloc. Today, however, the Soviet Union has leapfrogged some allies of the West to establish close relations with countries like Egypt and Indonesia. The number of points at which friction with the West can take place has increased. Furthermore, failures in Soviet foreign policy threaten the domestic position of the leaders, and successes bolster it. We should not necessarily conclude, however, that Soviet aggressiveness and willingness to run risks are always greater under "collective leadership" than under an autocrat. In the present stage of collective rule, where a leader who is *primus inter pares* must listen to the advice of his associates, hasty judgments are less likely than they might be under a single dictator. Hence it is less likely that the Soviet leadership of today will rashly and falsely assume that they have a retaliation-proof striking capability or that they must initiate nuclear war in order to forestall an imaginary plan of the enemy's.

None of the above considerations goes far toward answering the question, Is the Soviet Union planning preventive war? They suggest, however, that the initiation of a "preventive" nuclear war by the Soviet Union will not be seriously considered by the Soviet leaders unless the Soviet Union's military strength promises to be able to destroy the enemy while limiting destruction in the Soviet Union to an acceptable level. They also suggest, to the extent that Soviet political and economic expansion abroad is unopposed and successful, that the political leadership within the Soviet Union will improve its position, so that the need for desperate foreign adventures to recover lost prestige will be correspondingly less.

No single factor is likely to bring about a Soviet decision to initiate war against the United States. Soviet prospects for peaceful expansion, the Soviet domestic situation, and the Soviet estimate of opponents' intentions will all enter into any such decision. Yet if all these factors are favorable to aggression, they cannot lead to a decision to attack except in the unlikely event that the Soviet Union has developed a military preeminence that the leaders are confident will limit damage to their country to an acceptable level. The Soviet leaders cannot count on achieving such pre-eminence as long as the United States and its allies continue their efforts to improve their military position.

In 1955 the Soviet Union was probably too weak to consider seriously a policy of seeking nuclear war with the United States, no matter how much advantage they could derive from surprise. Is it justifiable to conclude from the subsequent efforts of the Soviet Union to improve her military strength that she is planning to initiate a nuclear war in circumstances where surprise would be maximally assured—that is, preventively? It is far more likely that the Soviet Union is seeking a retaliation-proof capability in order to give herself freedom of action, should a wide variety of other circumstances favor a Soviet surprise attack.

So far we have been attempting, with little concrete evidence to go on, to discover the actual intentions of the Soviet leaders in relation to their policy of readiness to strike pre-emptively. It remains to examine the public statements that have been made about Soviet intentions. How has the new Soviet military doctrine been presented to audiences at home and abroad? The answer to this question, of course, can throw only a little indirect light on the problem of actual Soviet intentions.

In making their strategies effective, the Soviet leaders must indoctrinate their fighting men. A new strategy has to be presented in such a way that its weaknesses will be minimized and its strengths emphasized. For the sake of good morale a certain amount of distortion may have to be introduced. In this field of activity the Soviet leaders obviously enjoy an advantage over their democratic counterparts. Military leaders in the democracies must point to, sometimes even advertise, deficiencies in military posture in order to raise funds from elected representatives. They may even reveal aspects of future development that have deleterious consequences for service and civilian morale. In the Soviet Union, of course, deficiencies in the armed forces are discussed either in private or in a guarded way before the public. The morale of the Soviet armed forces is an important consideration in the official promulgation of strategy. The members of the armed forces want to believe, and are told, that they will not have to fight unless attacked, and that if attacked they will be victorious. These traditional ingredients of military indoctrination, designed for purposes of morale, are not easy to reconcile with the new official doctrine that striking first offers great if not crucial advantages to the attacker. The awkwardness is compounded by the requirement that the Soviet armed forces be ready to repulse a surprise nuclear attack, no matter how remote that contingency. To inculcate such readiness the importance of surprise attack cannot be minimized. The only way to harmonize all these requirements is to insist on the possibility of timely and unequivocal warning of an enemy attack. Then it is possible to argue with some consistency that surprise attack with nuclear weapons is very important, perhaps decisive, and that although the Soviet Union will fight only after being attacked she will be able to retaliate instantly, or to strike pre-emptively, so as to assure victory.

Foreign policy and military security obviously must affect the manner in which strategic formulas are presented in the open press. The Soviet Union never initiates an aggressive war; it fights only in self-defense. Soviet propaganda has been absolutely consistent although not always convincing on this point. Even the conquest of the Ukraine and the independent Caucasian states in 1920-1921 was carried out in the name of native self-determination. The Baltic states were absorbed "at their request." The Soviet war against Finland in 1939-1940 was "provoked by the Finns." In keeping with this picture of spotless virtue Soviet writers must insist that any future war will be precipitated by the capitalists, not by the socialist camp.

The difference between actual and professed Soviet intentions is well illustrated by General Kurasov's article, "On the Question of the Pre-emptive Blow." First Kurasov charges the West with planning "preventive" war, and denies that the Soviet Union plans "pre-emptive" war. He argues that the Soviet Union's policy has always been peaceful. She has reduced her armed forces, unilaterally ceased atomic weapons tests, and sought a meeting at the summit to dissolve international tensions. The Soviet Union cannot be complacent, however, because she has suffered in the past from surprise attacks. The enhanced importance of surprise in the nuclear age has been discussed by individual authors in the Soviet Union. Their theoretical statements on measures to frustrate surprise have been misinterpreted in the West "as a summons to pre-emptive war":

> The Soviet Union was never the first to start a war and in all cases has only taken up arms to defend itself after suffering the attack of the enemy.

> The ideas of "preventive war" and the dealing of a pre-emptive blow as a means of attack and of unleashing war are incompatible with the peaceful policy of the Soviet state. . . .

> The Soviet people cannot forget that imperialistic countries still exist whose ruling circles have not given up hopes for the annihilation of the socialist states. This forces the Soviet Union to strengthen its defensive capability in every way and constantly to maintain the armed forces in full fighting readiness to repel an attack of the imperialist aggressors at any moment. . . .

> But the Soviet Union has never threatened anyone with an attack, "preventive war," or dealing a pre-emptive blow. Always, beginning with the first days of the existence of the Soviet Union, the leaders of the Communist Party and of our state have said that, in the event of an attack upon us, an immediate retaliatory blow will be dealt to the aggressor.

> Naturally, the idea of dealing a retaliatory blow does not mean conducting only defensive actions. If any aggressor tried to make an attack upon us, the Soviet armed forces would conduct the most resolute offensive action against him.

> The great Lenin, foreseeing the possibility of an armed attack against our country because of the constant danger of war for us from world capitalism, showed that it was impossible to say we would only defend ourselves. "If we," he said, "in the face of constantly and actively hostile forces, should give the promise they propose, that we would never have recourse to certain actions which in the military

strategic sense could be considered offensive, then we would not only be fools but criminals too. . . ."

The Soviet armed forces must constantly improve their military readiness so that at any moment they can not only repel an aggressor's surprise attack against our country but can immediately deal him a retaliatory blow of the kind that will once and for all put an end to any and all attempts to disturb by armed force the ordained movement of the Soviet people to communism.[50]

In this article can be found all the themes suited to the various purposes that a public enunciation of strategy must serve. The Soviet Union is peaceful; the capitalists are hostile; the Soviet Union will never start a war; surprise with nuclear weapons is very important; Lenin said that it would be criminal to promise not to "have recourse to certain actions which in the military strategic sense could be considered offensive"; the Soviet Union must be vigilant and will repel a surprise attack; if attacked, she will win the ensuing war. These themes are considered suitable fare for both domestic and foreign audiences.

It is worth noting that General Kurasov lumps together the terms "preventive" and "pre-emptive," using them side by side more than once in a kind of jingle. He not only denies categorically that the Soviet Union is capable of initiating a preventive war; he also denies that it is Soviet policy to deal a pre-emptive blow. He defines neither term. It will be recalled, however, that Marshal Rotmistrov drew a clear distinction between the two kinds of attack and denied only that the Soviet Union would resort to the preventive kind. Evidently subtle or controversial distinctions are considered unsuitable for propaganda purposes. The easiest way out is to cut off discussion by denying the intention to initiate war under any circumstances whatsoever. Just as it is now Soviet official policy to be ready to deal a pre-emptive blow on receipt of timely and reliable warning of a planned enemy attack, so it is also official policy publicly to deny the existence of any such military doctrine.

That this denial is worthless as an indicator of Soviet in-

tentions we have tried to demonstrate by presenting evidence
to the opposite effect from the Soviet military press and official
statements. It is now time to examine the evidence of developing Soviet military posture to find out whether or not this
sustains our thesis that the strategy of pre-emption is now officially accepted in the Soviet Union.

NOTES

1. Editorial, "On Some Questions of Soviet Military Science," *Voennaia
   mysl'* *(Military Thought)*, No. 3, March, 1955, pp. 3-17.
2. C. L. Sulzberger, "Russia Deplores 'Challenge' by U.S.," *The New
   York Times,* April 18, 1947.
3. *Report of Joint Committee on Atomic Energy Created Pursuant to
   Public Law 585—Seventy-ninth Congress,* Report No. 1169, 81st
   Congress, First Session, October 13, 1949, p. 13.
4. Colonel G. A. Tokaev, *Stalin Means War,* London, 1951, pp. 91-122.
5. Colonel I. N. Nenakhov, "The Policy of the Communist Party in
   Strengthening the Active Defense of the Soviet Union," *Voennaia
   mysl',* No. 10, October, 1953, p. 16.
6. Major General N. Pukhovskii, "The Creative Character of Soviet
   Military Science," *Voennyi vestnik* *(Military Herald),* No. 1, January,
   1954, p. 18.
7. Marshal of the Soviet Union A. Vasilevskii, "On Guard over the
   Security of Our Soviet Motherland," *Red Star,* February 23, 1954.
8. Colonel S. Mazhorov and Colonel I. Tikhonov, "The Advanced Character of Soviet Military Science," *Red Star,* February 28, 1954.
9. Colonel A. Piatkin, "Some Questions of the Marxist-Leninist Science
   of War," *Voennaia mysl',* No. 3, March, 1954, p. 23 *et passim.*
10. Marshal of the Soviet Union A. Vasilevskii, "The Great Lesson of
    History," *Red Star,* May 7, 1954.
11. "On the Question of the Character of the Laws of Military Science,"
    Voennaia mysl', No. 11, November, 1954, p. 44.
12. Colonel V. Kargalov, Candidate in the Pedagogical Sciences, "Military
    Questions in the Decisions of the Communist Party," in *Marksizm-
    Leninizm o voine, armii i voennoi nauke* *(Marxism-Leninism on War,
    the Army, and Military Science),* Moscow, 1955, p. 20. The original
    appeared in *Red Star,* April 16, 1954. The manuscript of the book
    was delivered to the printer on October 8, 1954, and the galleys were
    ready for printing on February 3, 1955.
13. Major General N. Pukhovskii, "The Creative Character of Soviet
    Military Science," in *Marksizm-Leninizm o voine, armii i voennoi
    nauke,* Moscow, 1955, p. 100.
14. *Ibid.,* p. 107.
15. Colonel V. Vasilenko, "The Reactionary Essence and the Aggressive
    Character of Imperialistic Military Ideology," in *ibid.,* p. 213.
16. Marshal of Tank Forces P. Rotmistrov, "On the Role of Surprise in
    Contemporary War," *Voennaia mysl',* No. 2, February, 1955, p. 14.

17. *Ibid.,* p. 17.
18. *Ibid.,* p. 18.
19. *Ibid.,* pp. 18-19.
20. *Ibid.,* p. 20.
21. *Ibid.,* p. 21.
22. General of the Army V. Kurasov, "On the Question of the Pre-emptive Blow," *Red Star,* April 27, 1958.
23. Editorial, "On Some Questions of Soviet Military Science," *Voennaia mysl',* No. 3, March, 1955, p. 5.
24. Tank Marshal P. Rotmistrov, "For Creative Examination of the Questions of Soviet Military Science," *Red Star,* March 24, 1955.
25. Editorial, "The World-Historical Victory of the Soviet People," *Voennaia mysl',* No. 5, May, 1955, pp. 12, 13.
26. Colonel General P. Kurochkin, "The Victory of the Soviet Military Art in the Great Fatherland War," *Voennaia mysl',* No. 5, May, 1955, p. 18.
27. Marshal of the Soviet Union A. Vasilevskii, "The Great Victory of the Soviet People," *Izvestiia,* May 8, 1955.
28. Lieutenant General of Aviation P. Braiko, "Soviet Aviation in the Great Fatherland War," *Vestnik vozdushnogo flota (Herald of the Air Fleet),* No. 4, April, 1955, p. 19.
29. Editorial, "The Great Strength of the Leninist Idea of the Defense of the Socialist Government," *Vestnik vozdushnogo flota,* No. 4, April, 1955, p. 8.
30. Lieutenant General B. S. Shatilov, "An Important and Noble Theme," *Literaturnaia gazeta (Literary Gazette),* May 28, 1955.
31. Colonel General V. S. Popov, *Vneznapnost' i neozhidannost' v istorii voin (Surprise and the Unexpected in the History of War),* Moscow, 1955. The manuscript was delivered to the printer on November 1, 1954, and ready in galleys on June 10, 1955. Rotmistrov's review was an article entitled "Surprise in the History of Wars," *Voennyi vestnik,* No. 11, November, 1955, pp. 90-96.
32. Colonel General V. S. Popov, *Surprise and the Unexpected in the History of War,* Moscow, 1955, p. 31.
33. Tank Marshal P. Rotmistrov, "Surprise in the History of Wars," *Voennyi vestnik,* No. 11, November, 1955.
34. V. I. Skopin, *Militarizm,* Moscow, 1956, p. 431. (Manuscript delivered to the printer on July 25, 1956; in galleys on August 3, 1956.)
35. V. I. Skopin, *Militarizm,* 2d ed., corrected and expanded, Moscow, 1957, p. 503. (Manuscript delivered to the printer on July 5, 1957; in galleys on October 5, 1957.)
36. Editorial, "On Some Questions of Soviet Military Science," *Voennaia mysl',* March, 1955, pp. 7-8.
37. Tank Marshal P. Rotmistrov, "Surprise in the History of Wars," *Voennyi vestnik,* No. 11, November, 1955, p. 94.
38. Editorial, "Study the Experience of the Great Fatherland War Creatively," *Red Star,* May 6, 1955.
39. Marshal of the Soviet Union V. Sokolovskii, "The Tenth Anniversary of the World Famous Historical Victory," *Red Star,* May 8, 1955.

40. Lieutenant General V. S. Shatilov, "An Important and Noble Theme," *Literaturnaia gazeta,* May 28, 1955.
41. Editorial, "Glorious Anniversary," *Voennyi vestnik,* No. 4, April, 1956, p. 6.
42. Unsigned article, "The Great Victory of the Soviet People," *Red Star,* May 9, 1956. An unsigned article is more authoritative than a signed one, since presumably it has the sanction of the editors.
43. *Ibid.*
44. Unsigned article, "The Leadership of the Communist Party Is the Source of the Power of the Soviet State and Its Armed Forces," *Red Star,* July 19, 1956.
45. N. Talenskii, "On the Question of the Character of the Laws of Military Science," *Voennaia mysl',* No. 9, September, 1953, p. 38.
46. Editorial, "The World-Historical Victory of the Soviet People," *Voennaia mysl',* No. 8, May, 1955, p. 11.
47. "Secret Speech of Khrushchev Concerning the 'Cult of the Individual' Delivered at the Twentieth Congress of the Communist Party of the Soviet Union, February 25, 1956," in *The Anti-Stalin Campaign and International Communism: A Selection of Documents,* edited by the Russian Institute, Columbia University, New York, 1956, pp. 44, 45, 48.
48. Charles Andrew Willoughby, *Shanghai Conspiracy: The Sorge Spy Ring, Moscow, Shanghai, Tokyo, San Francisco, New York,* New York, 1952; Alexander Foote, *Handbook for Spies,* New York, 1949.
49. Editorial, "A Glorious Anniversary," *Voennyi vestnik,* No. 4, April, 1956, p. 6.
50. General of the Army V. Kurasov, "On the Question of the Pre-emptive Blow," *Red Star,* April 27, 1958.

CHAPTER SEVEN

THE CONDUCT OF A NUCLEAR WAR

The Soviet Union, like all other great powers, undoubtedly requires her Ministry of War to maintain an up-to-date series of war plans to meet various military contingencies. Such plans are periodically revised as the military strength and political goals of the major powers change. Less often they are altered to conform to new ideas about the nature of war. When, early in 1955, the Soviet leaders officially adopted the doctrine that the first blow could be decisive, it is more than probable that this led to a major revision of the plans for a large-scale nuclear war. To draw up satisfactory plans for such a war, the planners would need to know whether Soviet military doctrine emphasized primarily the possibility of recovery from a first blow (with the further possibility of going on to victory) or, on the other hand, the likelihood that the initial attack would determine the whole subsequent course of the war in the attacker's favor.

There is a good deal of evidence that Soviet plans for the conduct of a major war have undergone radical revision in recent years. An outline of present war plans emerges from various Soviet statements that while not numerous, are quite explicit. Moreover, there is a very extensive Soviet literature on the role of particular arms in the execution of the over-all plan for nuclear war.

At the Twentieth Party Congress, Marshal Zhukov's speech

set forth in general terms the revised Russian ideas on the conduct of war. Zhukov gave the highest official sanction to the prediction already adumbrated by lesser figures that nuclear, chemical, and bacteriological weapons would be widely employed in the war of the future. The existence of these new weapons, he said, did not reduce the decisive importance of the ground forces, but increased the importance of the air forces and active air defense. The air force, he concluded, was a most important means for ensuring the security of the Motherland. Never before had a high Soviet official assigned such importance to the air force.[1] The implication of Zhukov's remarks was unmistakable: delivery systems for nuclear weapons and defense against them were of the first importance.

Zhukov's thoughts were expanded and made explicit by General Krasil'nikov in an article written for an anthology on warfare published in 1956. Krasil'nikov, going farther than anybody else had to that time, asserted that a future war, if it came, could encompass not only Europe and Asia but also America and Africa, and consequently could "lose its former land character." The significance of aircraft and unmanned means of aerial attack and the significance of navies, especially submarines, had grown. Krasil'nikov emphasized, as do all Soviet writers, that air attack, though it had become terribly important, was not the be-all and the end-all of war. Its great importance, however, required the ability to strike a pre-emptive blow: "In order always to be ready to retaliate to possible enemy blows with even more destructive blows or *to frustrate the blows he is preparing* it is necessary to have a tremendous quantity of conventional weapons and weapons of mass destruction [author's italics]."[2] The new situation imposed the necessity to defend the entire territory of one's country from air attacks. The possibility of extensive damage to the rear through the action of aircraft made the initial period of the war more important than before. Surprise attack by a country better prepared for war than its victim had always given the attacker real strategic superiority, "at least during the first period of the war."[3]

Modern means of attack, Krasil'nikov continued, especially

aircraft, nuclear and chemical weapons, and airborne and mechanized troops, made it easier to carry out a surprise attack and also made "such a blow more dangerous than before." Surprise attack, widely employed in the Second World War, was now a typical device of warfare, and in preparing for war it had to be taken into account: "The seizure of the strategic initiative by the opponent is now fraught with exceptionally grave strategic and military-political consequences for the country suffering a surprise attack."[4]

One method of conducting a world war, continued the general, was to deliver a single massive blow in order to destroy the enemy's armed forces. Lightning war was the common name for this strategy. A second method was to destroy the opponent by a series of mighty blows. A third method was to concentrate the main forces on the destruction of the enemy's economy, cities, and political and administrative centers, and to combine this with decisive blows against his armed forces (that is, blows designed to finish off his already undermined forces). The first two were counterforce strategies; the third might be called the strategy of intensive and massive attrition.

Krasil'nikov then assessed the three strategies. The lightning war so frequently excoriated in Soviet military writing could, he admitted, bring victory after one or two blows, but only if the country or coalition so attacked was militarily weak and badly prepared for war. The examples selected by the Soviet writer—Poland in 1939, Belgium, Holland, and France in 1940—make it clear that he did not regard the Soviet Union as falling into the class of nations that could be beaten easily in a lightning war. The lightning war, he implied, could be successfully employed under modern conditions to knock a member out of a military coalition, and so to gain a very great strategic advantage, but not necessarily to win the war as a whole. An attempt to win the war by a single blow was doomed to failure against a strong coalition possessing great territory, modern military equipment, and good air defenses. The author expressed all this in a general frame of reference, so that he could have been talking about a Soviet attack on the United States, or an American attack on the Soviet Union.

Concentration of the attack against the deep rear was not considered by Krasil'nikov to be a winning strategy in itself, but an important contribution to the whole conduct of the war. He insisted that the only winning strategy was one adapted to an extended war with many campaigns, but emphasized at least as strongly the importance of the initial phase of the war. Mistakes in the early part of the war could lead to the loss of the war. The Soviet Union would not make such mistakes, implied Krasil'nikov. Thus he did away with an apparent inconsistency in his argument and left open the possibility of phases of nuclear war subsequent to the first.

Soviet military writers are obliged to make a special case of the defense of the Soviet Union whenever they are discussing a war initiated by another country. To say flatly that the opponent's surprise attack can win the war would be to surrender to pessimism and to undermine the morale of the armed forces. The Soviet position, therefore, does not minimize the problem of coping with an opponent's surprise attack, but holds out hope for a successful defense against it.

The following quotation from Krasil'nikov is the most detailed and explicit statement of the Soviet strategic plan for the first phase of a major war that has turned up in the research for this book:

The employment of modern means of conflict, allowing for the constantly growing range of aircraft, the further development of military equipment, and the complete motorization of the army, can give to military activities in the initial phase of the war a completely new character and an exceptional intensity. It is in this stage of the war that the most critical situations and special conditions of the armed conflict, determining the character of its later stages, can be created. The initial phase of the war can, in contemporary conditions, include one and often even two campaigns simultaneously conducted on different strategic fronts or in different theaters of military operations. The campaigns of the initial stage of the war are conducted in conditions differing from those in which the subsequent operations are conducted. [Among the conditioning factors] strategic surprise in starting the war is specially characteristic and it has a definite influence on the character of operations and on the mobilization of the country and the armed forces. The successful employment of strategic surprise in the initial phase of the war can lead to disruption of the opponent's existing plan for the strategic deployment of his main forces and to the possibility of a rapid piecemeal destruction of the troops concentrated by him. . . . An especially intense struggle to pre-empt the opponent and seize the strategic initiative will take place in the campaign of the initial phase of the war. The seizure of the initiative secures an opportunity to exploit the lack of readiness of the enemy's armed forces and to deal crushing destruction to the troops of his first strategic echelon. This is very important from the point of view of reducing his military economic resources and personnel contingents.

Especially characteristic of the initial campaigns, also, is an exceptionally intense struggle for the air, both on the front and over the territories of the contending countries and in the deep rear of these countries. Inasmuch as air forces have the greatest readiness for action and dispose of means for dealing powerful blows, campaigns will obviously be started by their active employment. In the campaign of the initial phase both sides will first seek to deal crushing destruction to the opponent's air forces, and his sources for the production of atomic weapons, and to seize mastery in the air.[5]

Krasil'nikov clearly believed that the first phase of the war was the most important, and that both sides would consequently try to seize the initiative. He divided the first phase into several major parts: the simultaneous destruction of the enemy's air forces, his stocks of nuclear weapons, the establishment of command of the air, and the disruption of the enemy's war plan: "Strategic surprise in starting the war" in this first phase could strongly affect the course of subsequent phases.

In March, 1957, Marshal Zhukov again expressed himself in general terms. Since atomic weapons would soon increasingly replace conventional weapons, the former "would inevitably be employed [in a future war] as the basic means of conflict. . . .

Atomic weapons . . . will be widely employed as organic weapons in the armies." One of the most important duties of the Soviet armed forces, especially the air force and active air defense, was to be "always ready to frustrate any attempt by the aggressor to accomplish a surprise attack upon our country."[6]

In June Marshal Zhukov made even more explicit the distinction between the first and subsequent phases of the war in a speech made in India when he said that

> in order not to be mistaken in the military strategic aspects, it is necessary to clarify the influence exerted on organization, tactics, and strategy by the new weapons and equipment which possibly will be employed both in the beginning and in the course of the war.[7]

As time passed, increasing emphasis was placed on the importance of forces-in-being deployed for immediate action, an obvious consequence of the doctrine that the first phase of nuclear war can be decisive. Colonel Petrov, in an article published in May, 1958, pointedly emphasized the importance of forces-in-being. His views are particularly interesting because they were offered as background material for students of doctrine in the armed forces.

Following the pattern established by Talenskii and Rotmistrov, Colonel Petrov stressed the importance of the first phase of a nuclear war without denying the importance of subsequent phases. He presented the successful defense of Soviet territory against enemy attack as a condition for the "speedy mobilization of the strategic reserves." By accepting the possibility of phases of the war subsequent to the first, he was remaining faithful to the new doctrine that the first phase of the war *could* but not necessarily *would* be decisive.

In his treatment of the forces-in-being, however, Colonel Petrov introduced a new note by restricting the definition of war potential in an unprecedented way. While recognizing that war potential had often been broadly defined as a combination of economic, political, and military factors, Petrov felt that a narrower definition would be more useful. "Since," he argued, "the fate of a war is directly determined by the fierce clash of the armed forces of the contending sides, war potential is understood to be only that portion of the potentialities which are incorporated into the country's armed forces themselves."[8] Forces-in-being now had the same importance that mobilizable potential once possessed. Consequently their readiness was of paramount importance. One's own forces "should be ready for the immediate conduct of military operations against the opponent's ground and air forces in case of a surprise attack."[9]

Although the fate of a war is determined by the fierce clash of the armed forces and although the most useful definition of war potential is forces-in-being, mobilization after the outbreak of hostilities and reserves are accorded great importance. The apparent inconsistency is resolved if we add that such mobilized reserves can only influence the outcome of a war if the forces-in-being are victorious at its outset. If the Soviet Union strikes first and destroys the bulk of the opponent's forces-in-being, the problem is relatively simple. If the opponent strikes the first blow, the Soviet forces-in-being must blunt that blow sufficiently to render it indecisive. Obviously the second task is immensely more difficult than the first, but Soviet military writers cannot admit that it is an impossible task. Hence Petrov's assignment of importance to both the first *and* subsequent phases of war. The novelty of his presentation is this: whereas formerly victory was to be won mainly by resources, arms, and troops mobilized after the outbreak of hostilities, now victory depends mainly on forces-in-being properly deployed to deal with (or perhaps deal) a surprise nuclear attack.

By examining the mission assigned to each arm of the Soviet forces, we can judge to what extent changes in the structure of these forces reflect the changes already traced in military doctrine. In doing so, however, we must remember that military forces have rarely been perfectly suited to the execution of the strategies favored at any particular time. Military thought may outpace military capability. The complexity of modern equipment, for example, brings long time lags between weapons design and operational readiness. The very pace of technological development tends to make much equipment obsolescent. On the other hand, technology may get ahead of military doctrine, as it did in the early history of nuclear weapons. It would be misleading, therefore, to draw conclusions about Soviet strategy from an examination of any individual weapon system, or even from a complex of such systems designed for a particular mission. We must keep in mind the whole picture, even while we are discussing isolated portions of it.

Before we look into what the Soviet military writers have asked of the several arms in nuclear warfare, we must pause to note the impact of the H-bomb on Soviet thinking. The H-bomb differed so greatly from the A-bomb that its development really constituted a second military revolution within a decade. Its very-much-greater blast effect; its lethal fall-out, which could persist for a long time and spread over great areas; and its relative lightness and compactness vastly increased the possible destructiveness of a nuclear war. It could be carried by many aircraft already operational in the Soviet and American air forces. It could be built into missile warheads, making the long-range guided missile far deadlier than had previously been thought possible. The fall-out effect of the H-bomb was especially important to the Russians because they had comforted themselves with the belief that their vast territory made them less vulnerable than other peoples to A-bombs. Even before the American tests of March, 1954, established the widespread fall-out effects of the H-bomb, some Russian thinkers were already arguing that atomic weapons had changed the whole character of war. The appearance of thermonuclear weapons certainly reinforced their arguments.

The results of the March tests of the H-bomb were quickly made known in the United States and the rest of the world and, by August, 1954, were published in the Soviet Union. For instance, a *Pravda* news story repeated some statements made by Drew Middleton in an article written for *Collier's* magazine. Middleton was quoted as saying that since from two to six H-bombs could destroy all of England, the question for the English people was not one of victory or defeat, but what small percentage of the population would survive.[10] The Soviet air force magazine described the three stages of the H-bomb reaction, its yield of ten megatons or more, and the secondary radiation at ground level, derived from wind-scattered fall-out. Despite the magnitude of its reported effects, the H-bomb was said to be a terror and propaganda weapon and not a tried means for the conduct of war.[11] This unconvincing conclusion, however, was excised from the second edition of a book in which this article was reprinted in 1955.[12]

It was soon admitted freely in the Soviet Union that the H-bomb had military utility. The question then arose of how best to deliver it to a target. Aside from manned bombers, the obvious delivery vehicle was the long-range missile, and the Soviet leaders must have been glad that they had not waited for the introduction of compact high-yield bombs before taking steps to develop what they now call the "decisive weapon."

The ballistic missile—when it becomes operational and has, in a satisfactory combination, accuracy, numbers, and reliability—will indeed be a formidable weapon of strategic surprise. As early as 1956, Major General Pokrovskii, who is prominent in military research and writing, was most enthusiastic about the ballistic missile on several counts. First, he considered that the accuracy of long-range missiles could be made greater than that of conventional artillery. The distance of the shell burst from its target is measured in hundredths of the range, sometimes in thousandths; a significantly smaller deviation could be expected with long-range missiles.[13] Pokrovskii, writing after the announcement of the launching of the first Soviet intercontinental ballistic missile, talked about a maximum deviation from the target of six to twelve miles. Maximum deviation is a vague term, and very probably deliberately vague.

Two other articles written about the same time gave roughly similar estimates of accuracy. A Doctor Kazakov, for example, gave 0.0002 of the distance traversed as the maximum possible error for intercontinental ballistic missiles armed with hydrogen-bomb warheads, when employed against military targets as large as cities. For a range of five thousand miles this would mean an accuracy of something like ten miles.[14] But a major general and professor in the most important technical academy of the air force, writing on September 14, talked in

terms of even greater accuracy, giving five or six miles as the
expected deviation from the target.[15] Whatever accuracy the
Russians privately expect of ballistic missiles, they are probably justified in their expectation that eventually the accuracy
of missiles will suffice for most purposes because of the great
areas destroyed by H-bombs. Pokrovskii had such confidence
in the accuracy and reliability of long-range, thermonuclear
missiles that he believed, "at least in principle," in the effectiveness of single firings.[16]

Despite the great problems of the attainment of accuracy,
the Russians view the missile as an important element in a
counterforce strategy because it is difficult to detect and inter-
cept in its brief flight. As the Russians themselves have pointed
out in a technical article on the subject, it will be enormously
difficult to detect the firing of ballistic missiles, even if certain
suggested devices sensitive to infrared radiation are fully developed. Detection may be technologically feasible, yet pro-
hibitively costly. Even if the firing of the ballistic missile
could be detected, very little time would remain to act on
this knowledge.[17] Before defending forces can take effective
countermeasures in fifteen or twenty minutes, the maximum
warning that could be hoped for, great technical advances must
take place.

Ballistic missiles are probably still too unreliable in performance for reliance on them alone to execute the counterforce
mission. There is a great likelihood that their very complex
equipment will fail to function altogether. This difficulty, however, may be overcome by assigning sufficient missiles to each
target to compensate for their unreliability. For a long time
to come the number adequate to compensate for unreliability
may be so large as to constitute an unacceptable cost. Although
the individual ballistic missile is seemingly such a blunder-
buss, in time it can be made a militarily effective weapon, and
it is certainly one that presents formidable problems to the
defense.

If the Soviet military planners were interested in these
weapons only for their value in deterring the United States,
they would surely accept missiles with errors four or five times

as large as the maximum actually designated as permissible in Soviet public writing. In a strike against the United States, errors of such magnitude might leave the American retaliatory force largely untouched. The Soviet accuracy requirements indicate that the ballistic missile is intended at least as much to strike actual military targets as to deter an enemy attack.

Another advantage of the ballistic missile stressed by Pokrovskii is the relative ease of constructing, dispersing, and camouflaging the launching platforms. They probably will be less difficult to conceal than airfields, as Pokrovskii insisted. One side will find it all the more difficult, therefore, to prevent missile launchings by the other.[18] Without international weapons inspection, the advantages of concealment would benefit mainly the Soviet Union, for few American installations where considerable numbers of people work can be kept secret. The Soviet Union is able to use methods to ensure secrecy that would not be permissible in the United States.

Missiles with thermonuclear warheads obviously do not have to be as accurate as conventional, high-explosive weapons. This was pointed out by the Commander-in-Chief of the Soviet Air Forces, Marshal of Aviation Vershinin, in a rare interview with the press. His published remarks provide a glimpse into the official Soviet estimate of the importance of the ballistic missile. The essential points are contained in the following excerpts:

> The modern destructive means for the conduct of wars do not require aiming aircraft or rockets precisely at a military base. It is no longer a matter of artillery duels or aerial bombing in the sense of the last war. Nevertheless bombers were frightful then too. . . . But the bombers and the terrible raids of the past can by no means be compared with what a future war would bring if some madman should begin it. Atomic and hydrogen weapons have appeared, as have various types of missiles with atomic and hydrogen warheads, including intercontinental ballistic missiles. These are weapons of terrible power.
>
> It is not appropriate to joke about such a serious matter, but friends who have been in England have told me of this

joke, now current in England. They say that the people in England are divided into optimists and pessimists. The pessimists believe that three hydrogen bombs exploded over the British Isles would be enough to knock them out completely. The optimists say this is not so; that not three but six bombs must be exploded. . . .

Now the expectation that America's remoteness will spare her military blows in the event of a new war is no longer tenable. In the age of jet technology and atomic energy, great distances will no longer play a decisive role. What was once inaccessible has now come within easy reach. The modern means for aerial attack, characterized by great speed and range, are capable of delivering blows to military targets anywhere on earth. Intercontinental ballistic missiles can deliver the most terrible weapon, the hydrogen bomb, instantly to the remotest regions of any continent on earth.

In present conditions, bombers are naturally still being built. The United States especially emphasizes this kind of weapon. But missiles now call into question the expediency of further developing bomber aircraft, since the former are more reliable and dependable. From the history of World War II we know how many bombers returned of those sent out on missions, and how many did not reach the target. It is almost out of the question for a missile not to reach the target. Modern anti-air defense is ineffective against these missiles.[19]

The implication of all this was unmistakable. The United States was now as vulnerable to attacks by the new Soviet missiles as the Soviet Union had been in recent years to attacks by American bombers from numerous, encircling bases. Vershinin said that manned bombers were not the ideal vehicles to carry nuclear weapons to the United States. Perhaps he meant, although obviously he could not say so, that the forward bases of SAC made American bombers a much greater threat to the Soviet Union than Russian bombers could be to the United States. Soviet ballistic missiles, however, he implied, deprived the United States of whatever advantage she might have enjoyed in manned bombers.

Although Soviet commentators carefully avoided committing themselves to a statement that the United States would take a long time to develop intercontinental ballistic missiles, they implied strongly that until this happened the Soviet Union would have a great over-all advantage.

A few days after the Vershinin interview, General Pokrovskii attributed to the ballistic missile an accuracy and destructive power that made it possible to destroy any strategic target on the earth's surface. In accordance with Soviet tradition, however, no weapon should be characterized as decisive in itself, so Pokrovskii added: "Without in any way denying the power of the intercontinental missile, even this weapon cannot be considered absolute and invincible."[20] This almost standard reservation was dropped in March, 1958, when Major General Talenskii said in so many words that the intercontinental ballistic missile was a decisive weapon. By this time there could be no doubt that Talenskii spoke for others beside himself:

> For the time being the Soviet Union has monopoly possession of the super-powerful intercontinental missile. . . . Yet the Soviet monopoly possession of *the decisive weapon of our time* has not given rise to a single aggressive feature in the foreign policy of the USSR. . . .*

> The Soviet Union employs the major advantages it has gained from possession of the *decisive modern weapon* to intensify its foreign-political efforts for lasting peace and security. . . .

> The military significance of having solved the problem of creating a powerful, super-long-range, ballistic missile, capable of entering cosmic space and hitting any designated point, is exceptionally great. It is not only a quantitative increase in the potentialities of military strategy; it

---

* The Soviet English-language version of the article where these passages appear renders the Russian word *reshaiushchii* as "ultimate," whereas here the standard rendering, "decisive," has been retained. Using "ultimate" obscures the significance of the abandonment of the old formula that no decisive weapons exist. For the official English version see Major General N. Talensky [sic], "Military Strategy and Foreign Policy," *International Affairs*, No. 3, 1958, pp. 26, 27.

is a qualitative leap which fundamentally changes the methods and forms of the armed conflict. The intercontinental ballistic missile changes military strategy and its potentialities to an immeasurably greater degree and much more rapidly than, for example, the appearance of firearms or of aircraft in the past [author's italics].[21]

It is difficult to exaggerate the importance of the epithet "decisive" when employed to characterize ballistic missiles. For more than a quarter of a century Soviet military discussions had branded as an "incorrect" tenet of "the aggressors" the notion that a single weapon could be decisive in war. Almost every mention of the blitzkrieg theory of war was coupled with a reference to the principle that no decisive weapon existed. For Talenskii to say that ballistic missiles were decisive weapons was to announce the lapse of an established law of war. In Marxian theory, laws of war like laws of society are not eternal but lose their force when one period of history gives way to another. Talenskii undoubtedly had just such an historical upheaval in mind, because he described the potentialities of military strategy as increasing qualitatively rather than quantitatively. In Marxian theory, which in this case borrows directly from Hegel, quantitative changes in the relation of social forces occur *within* an historical period; when the quantitative changes become so great as to constitute qualitative changes, a new epoch in history is marked. It is in the light of this communist dogma that one should interpret a statement, made by Chou En-lai on February 10, 1958, to the effect that the Soviet launching of two earth satellites constituted "a new turning point in the world situation."[22] That Chou En-lai's speech preceded Major General Talenskii's article suggests what one might have guessed in any case: Talenskii's announcement that the intercontinental ballistic missible was a decisive weapon reflected a party decision on the highest level.

Perhaps the Soviet leaders chose to express their full appreciation of the basic changes wrought in warfare by the advent of nuclear weapons at a point in weapons development when they had jumped ahead and acquired a monopoly, even if only a temporary one. Political and psychological considerations argue strongly in favor of this explanation, but other reasons of equal cogency can be suggested. These arise from the nature and capabilities of the ICBM. The intercontinental ballistic missile is the weapon of surprise *par excellence*. No other vehicle can deliver an H-bomb with such good chances of achieving surprise. At present the outlook for effective anti-missile missiles is not good; certainly no claims are made that they already exist. The intercontinental ballistic missile, as the Soviet writers reiterate, is only useful against fixed targets whose coordinates are known. Thus it is suitable for employment against airfields with their aircraft, missile bases with their missiles, naval bases with their ships, atomic centers, administrative centers, and industrial complexes. It is not suitable for firing at aircraft aloft or ships at sea. If it is to be used in a counterforce role, it must be used pre-emptively or preventively, unless it is to destroy only vacant airfields and naval bases.

The Russians, as we have seen, stress the ease with which missiles can be relocated and concealed. These characteristics greatly enhance the likelihood that numbers of these weapons would survive a surprise attack to retaliate against the opponent. This likelihood, in turn, is a deterrent against such a surprise attack. It seems that the Russians value the deterrent power of the ICBM, but consider it mainly as a weapon of surprise. Accuracy is not required for purposes of retaliation and deterrence, yet the Soviet military writers demand accuracy. Thus, it seems reasonable to believe that the Soviet ICBM system is now assigned essentially, although not exclusively, to a first-strike mission.

Manned bombers will obviously be important for some time to come. Soviet views on air bombing have changed a great deal in the past twenty years. Before World War II, the Soviet air force was essentially an adjunct of the army, designed mainly for infantry support, interdiction, and reconnaissance. During the war it was also employed to support partisan activity, which had no more been foreseen than the retreats of the Red Army. When the Russians analyzed the experience of aerial bombing in World War II, they decided that it had not contributed

much to the collapse of Germany. A different conclusion would
have left them at an admitted disadvantage, for the best bomber
until the end of the forties, the B-29, could be used by the
United States from forward bases to attack Russia, while the
Russian copy of this machine lacked the bases that would
enable it to reach the United States.

The Russians seem to have retained for quite a long time
their low estimate of the power of strategic bombing. They
failed to take certain feasible measures to reduce, if not eliminate, the American superiority in bomb-delivery systems. They
were backward, for example, in developing an aerial refueling
capability. The refueling of aircraft aloft was achieved on a
small scale more than twenty years ago. In the Soviet Union
experimental refueling took place as early as 1933. Sir Alan
Cobham's refueling system had been carefully described in the
technical literature before World War II. Not until 1955, however, did an article appear in the Soviet press describing aerial
refueling as an essential component of an intercontinental
bombing system, and not until 1957 did the Soviet Union
demonstrate a bomber refueling capability in practice.[23] Refueling in the air could not in itself have eliminated the American advantage in bomb-delivery capability, but it would have
helped a great deal. Refueled planes could fly further with
heavier loads. Even when the Soviet Union replaced her copies
of the B-29 with longer-range planes, refueling could have increased their effectiveness. The Russians may have been slow to
develop refueling for many reasons, but one of them was probably the persistent assumption that even a major war would not
involve Soviet bombing of the United States. It is tempting to
believe that the basic changes of 1955 in Soviet military thinking either stimulated or accelerated the rapid advances in refueling that took place in the next two years.

Other evidence of a more direct kind sustains the thesis
that the Soviet evaluation of strategic bombing changed radically some time in 1955. For example, in January, 1955, the
Soviet air force magazine carried an article on the effects of
atomic radiation that discussed atomic weapons largely in terms
of their tactical employment. Pointing out that aircraft were

the vehicles most suited for nuclear weapons, the writer envisaged the chief targets as troops in the field, naval vessels, industrial areas, and air fields. Since it was so difficult to hide atomic artillery in position or on the march, and since the accuracy of both guided and unguided missiles was poor (despite the difficulty of defense against them), aircraft would be the basic vehicles for atomic weapons. Accordingly, a prime purpose of bombing would be to deny the opponent the use of his airfields, so as to weaken the air support of his ground forces. In this scheme, atomic weapons would be used to interdict the enemy's airfields, and to influence the ground or naval battle. They were not strategic weapons to be used at long range against the enemy's forces or industry.[24]

Before long other opinions were finding public expression. There was a growing confidence that aircraft could carry bombs against targets in the deep rear, even thousands of miles away. One writer implied that American aircraft could successfully deliver weapons to the Soviet Union. He thought the B-36 too slow for that purpose, but admitted the superiority of the B-47, which he described as rapidly replacing the B-29 and B-50, and as able to carry a nine-ton bomb load at high speed over the rather short range of 3600 miles. The comparatively short range of the B-47, he continued, required SAC to introduce tankers.[25] By 1956 articles in the Soviet press completely accepted this possibility. An article in *Red Star* about pilotless aircraft with subsonic speeds estimated that they could accomplish long-range bombing missions quite successfully. These vehicles that, said the article, accomplished the very same tasks as ordinary aircraft, were designed to destroy great administrative and industrial centers, railroad junctions, seaports, bases, and areas where troops and military equipment were concentrated. The advantage of this sort of vehicle was its ability to operate in any weather and to take off even from mobile launching platforms. Pilotless aircraft could be guided in various ways, either by automatic pilot, which in the opinion of this writer curtailed accuracy, or by inertial guidance, preferable in very long flights. This writer, and doubtless other more important persons, now saw large-scale war in terms of long-range bombing.[26]

A month later an article in *Red Star* discussed the employment of air-to-surface guided missiles. These, it was said, would solve "the problem of accuracy in bombing from modern aircraft" and reduce the loss of bombers. Other bombs might be released at a ground distance of perhaps fifteen kilometers from the target, but a guided air-to-surface missile could be released hundreds of kilometers away. If these missiles had atomic warheads, the simplest automatic guidance system would suffice because the radius of destruction would exceed possible errors in finding the target. If ordinary warheads were used, the greater accuracy provided by a homing system would be needed.[27]

A year later there was no longer even a lingering doubt about the role of air power in future wars. Air power, it was frequently urged, should not be developed at the expense of other branches of the armed services. A balanced growth was needed. Evidently there was at least a possibility that the air force would absorb too much of the defense budget.

Together with missiles, it was said, aircraft now had the task of achieving the first surprise blow in the initial period of the war and disrupting the enemy's military and economic potential. They must also, in a broad sense, command the air: "Without the attainment of mastery of the air, the rapid seizure of the strategic initiative in the initial period of the war and the successful development of military activities on land and sea are unthinkable." As a consequence of the long range at which air power can operate, "the boundary between the front and the rear in hostile coalitions is obliterated, which makes it possible to subject important enemy strategic targets in other continents to powerful attacks. Missiles, as well as aircraft, will play a large role in this activity."[28]

As soon as the first artificial earth satellite was up, however, the official Soviet attitude became one of ostensible contempt for bombing aircraft, at least for those of the Western countries. Khrushchev told two British Members of Parliament that the era of the bomber was now past; bombing planes could be burned without further ado.[29] This remark was not reported in the Soviet Union. In talking to James Reston of *The New York Times,* Khrushchev referred to the obsolescence of aircraft in a much more restrained manner:

> A revolution of a certain kind is taking place at the present time. Military specialists believe that both bomber aircraft and fighters are in the twilight of their existence. The speed and ceiling of bombers is such that modern missiles can destroy them.[30]

Khrushchev could legitimately argue that missiles would sooner or later partially replace bombing aircraft, but his comments probably sprang from his eagerness to belittle the Western advantage in strategic-bombing capability, now that he had a plausible excuse for doing so. Khrushchev pushed the ballistic missile as far as it would go, and further, in an obvious effort to discredit the Western military posture:

> It should be plainly said that the time is not very far off when everyone will have to recognize that military bases on the territory of other countries no longer have the significance once assigned to them by some immoderately boastful generals and aggressively inclined statesmen of the Western powers. One must soberly and realistically assess the development of modern technology, as a result of which the situation has basically changed. By the creation of the intercontinental missile, the question of the possibility of delivering hydrogen bombs to any point on the earth's surface is solved. Distance is no longer a barrier. As far as military bases in Europe, Africa, and Asia are concerned, missiles have long existed which can be delivered to any part of these continents. I do not think it is a secret that we now have a collection of such missiles capable of accomplishing one or another operational or strategic mission. Let us not play hide and seek, but look squarely at the state of affairs. Can it really be supposed that the locations of military bases are known only to those who constructed them? And if the location of these bases is known, then modern missiles and other equipment can rapidly put them out of commission.[31]

Khrushchev was obviously exaggerating the speed with which ballistic missiles could replace aircraft, in order to gain the maximum propaganda advantage from the latest Soviet technological achievements. The Soviet air force commander, General Vershinin, had spoken only of the possibility of ceasing the development of bomber aircraft, not of stopping their production. Khrushchev himself took a more sober attitude when addressing professional audiences at home. In a short speech to graduates of the aircraft engineering schools, he left plenty of room for manned aircraft in the Soviet scheme of things:

> The modern means of warfare are very powerful. Now, as you know, the role of winged aircraft piloted by individuals is somewhat reduced; and jet aircraft and missiles are taking their place.

> Without denying existing weapons to ourselves, we should go forward to perfect all kinds of weapons and to master the new jet and missile technology . . . so as to be always ready to repulse an attack. . . .[32]

Two months later an article in the daily organ of the Soviet air forces declared that aircraft would continue to be important in joint operations with ground and naval forces, "but could also annihilate the opponent's strategic targets, in the interests both of the war as a whole and of particular campaigns." One passage was considerably at odds with Khrushchev's remarks about the obsolescence of manned aircraft:

> The logical process of the qualitative development of the modern means of air attack, especially intercontinental ballistic missiles and medium range missiles, does not mean . . . that aircraft have outlived their day and that missiles will completely replace them in the near future. The presence in the weapon systems of the air forces of jet bombers and supersonic fighters and of airborne missiles of the air-to-surface and air-to-air classes, and the [presence] of atomic and hydrogen weapons and other means of destruction, have significantly improved the battle potentialities of aircraft for the accomplishment of

varied missions. The newest means of radio contact, radar, cybernetics, guidance systems, and automatation free aircraft operations from the limits imposed by darkness and bad weather. The results already achieved in the development of aircraft and in the means of destruction employed by them, and also the ceaseless qualitative improvement of aircraft equipment, give a basis for supposing that aircraft will play a very important role in a future war.[33]

The writer of this passage then quoted Khrushchev's speech to the graduates of the aircraft engineering academy and concluded that there was no question of the "disappearance of aircraft as weapons [carriers] in the armed forces, but rather a question of the nature of their further development."[34] The continued development of jamming devices, air-to-surface missiles, and "over-the-shoulder" bombing was balancing improvements in antiaircraft measures; therefore aircraft would continue to play a very important role in future wars.

Here was a Soviet colonel directly contradicting the words of his commander-in-chief nine months previously. Evidently Vershinin—and Khrushchev—had been either hasty or insincere when they publicly minimized the manned bomber. The Soviet leaders, especially Khrushchev, seem to have been somewhat carried away by the excitement of the ballistic missile and to have "retired" the aircraft as a vehicle for nuclear weapons as soon as the first successful ICBM firings had occurred. Either they soon changed their minds, or they had never really believed what they said.

Aircraft possess still other important advantages over missiles that Soviet writers neglect: they can be recalled. As General Thomas S. Power, the Commander-in-Chief of the Strategic Air Command, explained in a press interview, "in the event of the real alert . . . our aircraft would be launched and their crews would be assigned predetermined targets. However, they would be launched under positive-control procedures which would insure that, if the emergency did not materialize, they would not proceed. . . . The positive control procedures insure that no SAC aircraft can pass beyond proper bounds far from the Soviet Union or its satellites without additional unequivocal orders that can come only from the President of the U.S."[35] This means that in a severe international crisis the nation with an efficient air force need not be trigger-happy. Without a flexible recall system for aircraft, and in all cases with missiles, only one of two decisions is possible: send or hold. The ability to recall aircraft gives more time for deciding whether an attack is really impending or not.

Whatever the missile was doing to the aircraft, there could be no doubt that it would further extend the usefulness of the submarine. The size and destructiveness of H-bombs made them adaptable as warheads for missiles that could be fired from submarines. If and when Russian submarines were extensively equipped with missiles carrying nuclear warheads, the Soviet Union would enter a new era in her naval history. Russia had always suffered to some extent from her limited access to the great oceans of the world. By the eighteenth century her coastal regions comprised four distinct areas, the Arctic, the Baltic, the Black Sea, and the Far East, of which the first three could easily be bottled up by a strong naval opponent. The Russian navy consisted of two, later three, separate forces that could not easily be brought together even in peacetime. Not unnaturally, therefore, naval warfare has played a relatively small role in Russian history. The United States, on the other hand, has been protected by oceans from any possible strong enemies. For nearly a century these oceans were commanded by the British navy. In effect this fact precluded any serious threat to the United States, except on the one occasion when Britain herself was hostile, that is, in the War of 1812. In 1814 British sea power made possible the burning of Washington and the assault on New Orleans. On the enclosed waters of the Great Lakes, however, the United States established complete mastery. After 1880 American naval strength grew rapidly, became much more flexible with the opening of the Panama Canal in 1916, and was able to carry the battle to distant enemy territories in two world wars.

With the advent of missiles that can be launched from the sea, the relative naval positions of the United States and Soviet Russia may be entering a period of change. Since the

Soviet Union's only long, exposed coast is in the Pacific area, where there are few cities of any importance, her largely land-locked geography makes her less vulnerable to attack from short- and medium-range seaborne missiles than the United States, most of whose cities lie within easy missile range of the Atlantic and Pacific coasts. The longer the range of the missiles employed on both sides, however, the smaller will be the advantage possessed by the Soviet Union in any exchange of sea-borne missiles.

The Soviet leaders are favored in this field by the circumstance that a fleet of several hundred long-range submarines was laid down in and after 1945 as a commerce-raiding and counter-troopship force. Opinions may differ on the utility of such a force in a future nuclear war, but it is obvious that the arming of some or all of the existing submarines with nuclear missiles can greatly extend their mission in such a war.

The Soviet military press, in its discussion of the possible role of submarines in a future war, leaves no doubt that Soviet naval officers appreciate the potentialities of missiles launched from submarines. In 1957 a Soviet admiral flatly stated that the appearance of the missile with a nuclear warhead, together with its supporting systems, had given navies a new strategic significance. The possibility had arisen of employing long-range missiles from submarines against administrative and industrial targets. This had created a requirement for underwater launching, and the admiral reported that the United States was already working on this problem. The fundamental needs were for an increase in the range, accuracy, and blast effect of missiles with nuclear warheads.[36]

Another naval writer claimed for naval forces the ability to strike surprise blows from great distances in the initial period of war, by using nuclear explosives and guided missiles. He described the strategic potential of naval forces in terms of what an opponent could do to the Soviet Union, and called for defensive fleet units to repulse attack by sea.[37]

A Major General Boltin took an army point of view in an article on military science written for the naval newspaper, *Soviet Fleet*. He stressed surprise in the initial stage of the war, but said nothing about submarines. Indeed he questioned the continued utility of capital ships when aircraft and missiles could deliver nuclear weapons.[38]

The development of systems for delivering nuclear weapons from a great distance has induced the Soviet Union to devote close attention to problems of air defense. Even in the Second World War, when they felt that aerial bombing could not do decisive damage, the Russians considered air defense worth an important investment. Before they had arrived at a clear idea of the role and value of nuclear weapons, the Russians elevated their estimate of the importance of bombing and invested considerable sums in warning systems against enemy bombers, an enterprise made easier by the open publication of American radar techniques. The development of jet interceptors was hastened by the purchase of British Rolls-Royce Nene engines. The Russians then made massive preparations for active air defense. But even these did not bespeak a true appreciation of the requirements for defense against nuclear bombing. To repel an attack by bomb-carrying aircraft, the Soviet Union needed all-weather interceptors, equipped with tracking and fire-control radar. Adequately equipped fighter planes were not introduced into the Soviet air force until the beginning of 1955. Surface-to-air missiles, also a vital component in any modern air-defense system, appeared at about the same time. Many fiscal and technical problems may have delayed the production of these defense weapons, but in the light of Soviet weapons theory and development in the period 1945-1953 it seems equally likely that the Russians lacked the sense of urgency that a fuller appreciation of the role and power of nuclear weapons later produced.

The Soviet press started to emphasize the tremendous importance of active air defense as late as the beginning of 1955, when readers were warned that not a single enemy plane must be allowed to get through the active defenses. The great destructive effects of nuclear weapons made this imperative. Here was a sharp contrast to the doctrine of World War II, under which active defenses were expected only to reduce the effects of localized bombing raids and to exact as high a toll as possible from the enemy bomber forces. In the nuclear age, however, a very few bombs could wipe out even the largest target, and it became almost pointless thereafter to shoot down the bombers that had done the damage. After a successful raid en masse, the destruction of the empty bombers could make little difference to the strategic picture. The only worth-while active air defense was one that could limit urban destruction to an acceptable level.

An examination of the present Soviet air-defense system reveals much about Soviet objectives and expectations in the event of war. Defensive posture is often a guide to strategic intentions. A system of defense may fulfill any one of several strategic purposes. A well-nigh-perfect defense system, for example, can serve as an effective deterrent to an opponent's attack. Theoretically, a perfect defense in the nuclear age is possible, through massive quantities of electronic detectors, interceptor aircraft, and surface-to-air missiles. In the real world, however, it is extremely unlikely that a perfect or near-perfect defense system can be created. At present defensive systems are far from capable of holding off large-scale nuclear attacks, especially by ballistic missiles. Practically speaking, there seem to be absolute limits to the efficiency of defensive systems.

The human element can never be entirely excluded, and the demands for good judgment on short notice may be too much for certain sectors of a defense system. Add to this what has been aptly called the fog of war and the low efficiency of operations during first hostilities and it becomes difficult to see how any active air-defense system could ward off all nuclear weapons. If the defense permits hydrogen bombs to get through in considerable numbers, its value becomes questionable. Planners of today are bound to ask themselves whether big expenditures on active defense are really worth while. In this connection, the point is that Soviet active air defense does make good sense in combination with Russia's pre-emptive doctrine for the initiation of war. In itself Soviet active air defense makes little sense as a deterrent to an enemy's first strike.

A necessarily imperfect defense of urban complexes is not

an important deterrent, but the defense of one's own striking force is the essence of deterrence, since an undefended striking force does not constitute a deterrent, but only a potential first strike force. Many components of air defense, of course, are important for the defense both of cities and of one's own striking forces. As it happens, Soviet active air defense is clearly intended to prevent or reduce damage to cities. Its purpose is not only to deter a possible opponent by protecting retaliatory capability, but also to conduct war successfully should it break out. But Soviet planners are bound to realize that active air defense could save neither the cities nor the retaliatory force if the attacker achieved strategic surprise. Little is gained from air defense if the enemy achieves strategic surprise. Only if the weight and effectiveness of the opponent's blow can be reduced by a pre-emptive attack does an active air-defense system, such as the Soviet Union has been developing, hold out promise. In that case, the whole burden of reducing losses from enemy missiles and aircraft would not be borne by the defenses. A pre-emptive blow that destroyed part of the enemy's striking force would thereby reduce his retaliatory capability to proportions that Soviet active air defense could cope with. If destruction to the Soviet Union were kept within these limits, the tremendous investment in active air defense would be justified.

Soviet writings on air defense reveal that late in 1954 a tentative step was taken toward the official conclusion that aerial bombing against targets in the rear could be of decisive significance. Colonel Fedorov, writing in *Red Star* in January, 1954, remarked that popular morale would be very important in a future war because of "numerous and destructive bombings by enemy aircraft."[39] The standard line had been to depreciate the importance of strategic bombing. In reworking his article for inclusion in a book, Fedorov added that the population "suffered great difficulties and deprivations" from bombing.[40] About the same time another military writer went somewhat further, declaring that direct action against the military potential of the opponent coupled with active defense of one's own strategic rear constituted a new branch of military art.[41]

After the doctrinal changes of February, 1955, the official

organs of the armed forces made it quite clear that the question of attacks on industrial objectives had acquired a major importance. In the words of an editorial in the air force magazine, the imperialists intended to begin war "by dealing blows with atomic and hydrogen weapons on vitally important targets in our country and the countries of the peoples' democracies in order to put the basic industrial facilities out of commission in a few days, to paralyze transportation, and to demoralize the population." This estimate of the opponent's strategy was made in connection with the public advocacy of the pre-emptive strategy, now put forward as the only way to deprive an aggressor of the advantages of surprise.[42]

Using atomic weapons, a few airplanes could cause serious damage to targets deep inside the country. Hence, "the slightest mistake of an antiaircraft unit in conditions of atomic warfare can lead to very serious consequences."[43]

In February, 1956, at the Twentieth Party Congress, Marshal Zhukov spoke of the real threat from air attack, especially by long-range rockets and jet aircraft, and then reassured his listeners with the statement that a great deal of work had been done to build up the active air defenses of the country:

> At the present time the air defense possesses modern, supersonic fighter planes, high quality antiaircraft artillery, antiaircraft rocket weapons, and other means for insuring antiair defense. . . . The task of the defense of the rear of the country has never been as urgent as it is under modern conditions. In the interest of security the Soviet people demand further efforts for the improvement and organization of local antiair defense and the appropriate preparation of the whole population. . . .[44]

The sense of urgency with which the program of air defense, both active and passive, was pursued is conveyed in the opening paragraph of an article in *Voennye znaniia* (*Military Knowledge*), a popular magazine:

> The armies of the imperialist states at the present time possess varied means of air attack which permit them to deliver blows against populated centers, industrial estab-

lishments, and engineering complexes of countries thousands of kilometers from their borders. . . . Even the most remote population centers in the hinterland of any state can be the object of an enemy air attack in existing conditions.[45]

As a consequence of this possibility, said an article in *Red Star* a few months later, a powerful air defense was required to protect not only troops but also targets in the rear. "Neglecting the demands of the military art," warned the writer, has "often led to very serious military destruction."[46]

The emphasis on active air defense continued and in 1957 the Soviet press became more specific about the means that would be employed against the kind of attack described above. In March Marshal Zhukov told an audience of crack troops that Soviet planners assumed their probable opponents to have an adequate number of nuclear weapons and the means to deliver them to Soviet territory: "This circumstance requires our armed forces, especially . . . the air forces, to be always in readiness to frustrate any aggressor's attempt to accomplish a surprise attack on our country."[47]

In 1957 the Soviet military press expected an air attack upon the Soviet Union to concentrate mainly on airfields and air installations. The United States, said one review of American published statements on the subject, planned to base her active air defense on the destruction of her opponent's bases and airfields with atomic weapons.[48] British and American military opinion, wrote a Soviet colonel in June, had maintained that the primary task in the initial period of the war was the establishment of strategic air supremacy by mass employment of nuclear weapons against the opponent's airfields.[49] This was the obvious rationale behind the desire to pre-empt, and it called for vigorous measures to safeguard the striking force. The best possible active defense against enemy aircraft and missiles, according to the Soviet press, must have many ramifications. A warning system should provide signals for the interception of both high- and low-flying vehicles. The destruction of enemy air vehicles could best be accomplished by a mixed system of supersonic fighter aircraft equipped with search radar, high quality antiaircraft artillery, and surface-to-air missiles.[50]

The "best possible" active defense system, however, does not, in Soviet eyes, dispense with the need for civil defenses. Soviet planners are fully aware of the blast and fall-out effects of nuclear weapons and undoubtedly realize the immense difficulty of saving a large part of the population by civil-defense measures. Theoretically, shelters can be so well built and equipped that millions could survive within them until the fall-out from nuclear weapons had dissipated of itself or had been mechanically removed. But the cost of a thoroughly effective system of this kind would probably be beyond the finances of even the richest country. A more modest system, however, will suffice to reduce greatly the effects of an attack whose weight has been cut down already by a pre-emptive blow, by active defenses, or by both.

The rate of progress of the Soviet civil-defense program is secret, but its character and effectiveness may be judged to some extent through a considerable body of literature prepared for training the population, all of whom must participate in civil defense. In 1954 the Soviet government inaugurated an extensive program of popular education in civil defense against nuclear weapons. Since that time literally millions of copies of elementary pamphlets on the subject have been distributed in all the main Soviet languages.[51] A recent pamphlet in the series[52] begins with a clear but somewhat subdued account of the effects of various kinds of weapons. A second section describes traditional civil-defense measures for dealing with fires; a third describes some simple shelters, protective clothing and equipment, and hygienic measures; a fourth gives the rules for behavior after an atomic alarm is sounded, what to do during the raid, the meaning of signs to be posted after it giving the level of radioactive contamination, and the standard first-aid measures for those hurt. The last section tells how to pass through and clean up contaminated areas.

The psychological and political effects of a nuclear attack are not touched on in the training manuals, but a recent book on Western "militarism" has been remarkably explicit about these effects. The militarists, says the author, count on the mental disturbances that nuclear attacks can produce in millions of people. The exhaustion of waiting for a nuclear attack, the fatiguing inconveniences of antiatomic defense, the hermetically sealed antiatomic clothing worn in heat, frost, dampness, and darkness, with the concomitant acceleration of breathing, perspiration, and bleeding of any slight wound will all contribute to the terrorization of the civilian population. The militarists also expect that the great fear of gradual radioactive contamination will be much multiplied by the delay with which the symptoms of radiation poisoning will appear. They expect to benefit from the intensification of alarming rumors and to foster these through their own propaganda. "Indubitably, such militaristic expectations can be justified in some cases," concludes the author, but these effects of atomic bombing will be more pronounced among the people of capitalist countries than among people with "full political awareness."[53]

The general tone in the literature about bombing effects is reassuring. A typical account declares that active air defense is reliable and assures its readers that, "with efficient and properly organized antiatomic [civil] defense of populated places and of industrial and economic targets, loss from atomic bombings can be kept to a minimum."[54] In an interview with an American newspaper correspondent Khrushchev argued that the Soviet Union would escape the worst effects of nuclear weapons because of her size: "We too, of course, will suffer great losses. But look at the vast spaces on our map and look at Germany, France and Britain. One does not have to be a strategist or a military man to see the difference."[55] When the American correspondent volunteered the statement that the United States had vast spaces, Khrushchev answered: "Not quite as vast, and it should be kept in mind that American cities, such as New York, Chicago, San Francisco and others, have a large concentration of industries. Our industries are much more widely dispersed."[56] Khrushchev then explained that the recent Soviet governmental reorganization would bring about greater dispersion of industry, although it was not designed primarily for that purpose.

In February, 1958, it was revealed that the first stage of the civil-defense education program had been completed. A ten-hour course on antiatomic measures inaugurated in 1955 had been attended by some 85 per cent of the whole Soviet population. In January, 1957, a twenty-two hour course was begun, which included material on defense against chemical and bacteriological as well as atomic weapons. This course, compulsory for the whole population, was scheduled for completion in the large cities by July, 1958, and in the smaller cities and rural areas by the end of 1958. References were also made to preparation of a third program of training to be completed by 1960.[57]

The Soviet civil-defense program, which one can reconstruct from training literature, is a rather modest one in relation to the destructiveness of thermonuclear weapons. If large-yield H-bombs should fall in the center of cities, the kinds of shelter depicted in the pamphlets would not be very helpful. If on the other hand the bombs should fall on airfields outside cities or leave some cities altogether untouched, the shelters would save many lives that otherwise would have been lost from blast or fallout. If the Soviet Union suffered extensive nuclear bombing, the measures advocated in the mass training programs would avail little. The Soviet civil-defense program seems to start from optimistic assumptions about the course of any war that might break out. That optimism is perhaps based on the belief that the Soviet Union, if faced with war, would be able to get in the pre-emptive strike to which her leaders are committed. In that event the present civil-defense program would have a valuable role to play in defending the Soviet Union against the expected retaliation. Even in this relatively limited role, civil defense is extremely expensive. One may assume that the Soviet leaders expect to get positive military dividends from the effort that they have invested in civil defense.

Nuclear weapons have transformed naval operations as much as other departments of warfare.[58] We have considered above the utility of missile-launching submarines. The submarine makes it possible to use missiles with less accuracy and shorter range than would be required of intercontinental weapons. The short flight time for missiles fired near the coast makes detection and counteraction more difficult. As the accuracy of missiles increases, the advantages of firing them from submarines rather than from land bases may be diminished, but submarines like other naval units will always possess the virtue of mobility. This is an important element in deterrence because no surprise attack can be expected to obviate retaliation by mobile and easily concealed units. We can expect that submarines will play at least as great a role in the Soviet posture as in the American, if only because of the large number of American cities within easy range of oceans.

The main strategic functions of naval forces in the past have been to keep the seas open for one's own commerce while denying their use to the enemy, and to transport men, weapons, and supplies to distant theaters of war with minimum loss by enemy action. Russian wars, both Tsarist and Soviet, have involved expansion overland into contiguous areas. Russian naval operations have mostly been confined to sheltered waters, have usually been undertaken reluctantly, and have been subordinate to land operations at all times. Even in coastal defense the Russian navy has made a poor showing. The Russians have never aspired, like the French, to first-rank power by sea as well as by land. Far from being able to attack island countries off the Eurasian land mass, the Russians were incapable even of denying the Straits of Tsushima to the Japanese supply ships in 1904-1905. Overseas expansion has always been a task beyond Soviet strength. This circumstance helps to explain Soviet reluctance to build aircraft carriers. Moreover, while World War II demonstrated that the aircraft carrier was a capital ship indispensable for command of the seas, ship-based aircraft did not then have sufficient range or size for effective bombing of the rear. Today's aircraft carriers, however, may serve as takeoff platforms for strategic bombers. Nevertheless, the Soviet Union is making no effort to build herself a carrier fleet. As we shall shortly see, the Soviet leaders are convinced that in the nuclear age particularly, large surface units are an unnecessary luxury.

Had war come before the Soviet Union acquired a significant arsenal of nuclear weapons, the Soviet strategy would have been to expel the United States and its allies from Europe and to prevent by commerce raiding the offshore buildup required for a landing on the continent. Russia's continuing naval weakness, combined with her temporary deficiency in nuclear weapons, made it impossible for her to carry the war to American shores. The United States, on the other hand, was strong in just those areas where the Soviet Union was weak. Her commitments to NATO were based on her command of the oceans, which gave her the ability to transport supplies and reinforcements to Europe. Her policies in the Far East required that she be strong in the Pacific as well as in the Atlantic and Mediterranean. In any war between the United States and the Soviet Union, therefore, it was obvious that the roles of the opposing navies would be as different as their compositions.

In the Soviet view the advent of nuclear weapons has made it harder for the United States to base her strategy on naval might and easier for the Soviet Union to frustrate the United States in the execution of that strategy. In late 1956 and early 1957 the Soviet press devoted detailed attention to the changes that nuclear weapons had produced in navies. The increasing vulnerability of naval forces, especially in groups, is the theme of the Soviet writers. In the Second World War, they say, surface warships were vulnerable chiefly to four kinds of weapons: first to naval or shore-based artillery; second to torpedoes; third to bombs dropped from ship- or shore-based aircraft; and fourth to mines. The appearance of nuclear weapons and the improvements in missiles, they continue, have seriously aggravated the problem of capital-ship survival. In past wars naval forces proceeded in groups and sought protection by throwing out a system of defenses against hostile aircraft, submarines, and capital ships. The most valuable ships were screened by other ships and by aircraft equipped with detection devices and various specialized weapons. Even with these elaborate measures, say Soviet writers, many capital ships were lost by the major fleets of the world in the last war.

Today the survival problem for surface ships is more difficult than ever before, because completely effective explosive charges can be dispatched from great distances, with the requirement for accuracy reduced because of the great blast effect of nuclear weapons. According to Soviet writers, it has become practically senseless to assemble task forces like those used in past wars. Concentrations of naval vessels are so vulnerable to the effects of nuclear explosions that vessels must proceed at great distances from one another, so great indeed that they are virtually proceeding as independent units. A modern naval force requires special radar ships far ahead of the capital ships to detect dangers from aircraft. A naval formation dispersed for nuclear warfare may be three hundred miles in diameter. Now that aircraft can launch guided missiles they can strike naval vessels from a great distance. The submarine menace to surface ships remains as great as ever. All this creates a dilemma for the defenders of naval vessels.

To sum up, Soviet writers say that naval task forces are a thing of the past, that capital ships are obsolete or obsolescent, and that much smaller vessels can execute naval tasks as well or better than the large ships of former wars.

From these premises it follows that the American fleet, with its many large surface vessels, is to a great extent obsolescent. The numerous submarines of the Soviet fleet are regarded as useful under present conditions, while the surface fleet is not large. In a future war, say the Soviet writers, their own ground troops will be fighting in areas contiguous with the Soviet Union, while the United States will have to fight in areas separated by oceans. Hence the increased vulnerability of fleets is a tremendous advantage to the Soviet Union.

Articles in the Soviet press point out the severe effects of German attrition on American and British shipping in the last war and insist that in a future war the United States will again be unable to avoid the need to supply her forces by water over great distances. These discussions leave little doubt that Soviet planners expect a much higher degree of success in submarine warfare than the Germans enjoyed.

The Soviet writers assert that landing operations will be much more difficult in future wars than in the past. Great naval forces, troop convoys, and even artificial harbors, like those concentrated to effect landings in the last world war will be extremely vulnerable to nuclear weapons. Landings across the sea must now be made by small units, dispersed over a great area. These units will have to depend for supply on single vessels. These requirements will tremendously complicate the task of landing forces of the size landed in Normandy in 1944. Nevertheless, the landing of small forces behind enemy lines flanked by the sea may sometimes be better effected by water than by air. While the Soviet writers think there may still be uses for the kind of leapfrog operation conducted along the Black Sea coast against the Germans, they consider very difficult the landing of large numbers in the face of nuclear weapons. They concede that the landing force derives some advantages from nuclear weapons. Nuclear air bursts over the point of landing can be used to clear the area without contaminating the ground. Simultaneous ground bursts on the enemy flanks and rear will restrict his movements while the bridgehead is being established. In general, however, the Soviet articles imply that landing operations across great distances will be almost impossible because both convoys and beach assemblies have become so vulnerable.

Before the Soviet leaders recognized the full power of nuclear weapons, they felt that the United States would have to come to the Soviet Union across the sea in order to win a war against her. They felt confident that their superiority in ground forces would either deter or frustrate such a strategy. Now the Russians are still confident that the American war strategy must fail, but for different reasons. Now they feel that nuclear weapons will give an edge to the Soviet cause by making it extraordinarily difficult, if not impossible, for American naval forces to transport large numbers of troops and great quantities of supplies to the continent of Europe.[59] The Soviet military leaders consider that the United States should be deterred from making war against the Soviet Union by a realization of her inability to bring the war to a successful conclusion by occupying the Soviet Union. The Soviet leaders are so convinced that occupation of the defeated side's territory must conclude a war that they rarely mention it. The few references to this concomitant of victory are usually presented as truisms. Here is an example from *Soviet Fleet:*

> With the appearance of weapons of mass destruction, the opinion began to be expressed in the American military press that landing operations were no longer necessary and that atomic bombardment of the opponent by air forces would determine the outcome of the war. However, the Pentagon leaders rapidly condemned such expressions of view and laid it down that, despite the existence of new kinds of weapons, troops occupying the opponent's territory would determine the outcome of war.[60]

To prove his point the writer of this passage described in great detail the various American landing exercises conducted in 1955 and 1956.

In many ways nuclear weapons have made much easier the attainment of one of the objectives of the Soviet postwar naval program, namely to prevent control by a superior naval power of the waters adjacent to the Soviet homeland. This the Soviet writers call "operational" command of the seas, as distinct from "strategic" command of the seas. As a naval captain expressed it in the pages of *Military Thought:*

> In modern conditions, when atomic weapons are employed, the possibility is increased of gaining operational command [of the seas] when strategic command is in the hands of the opponent. Skillful use of atomic weapons permits the rapid weakening of the opponent's fleet in a particular sector, the creation of a favorable relationship of forces, and, until the opponent is able by moving forces from other sectors to change this relationship, the attainment of the operational goals which were set.[61]

In the Soviet view, the advent of nuclear weapons has affected land warfare rather less than naval warfare. Considerable changes, however, have been taking place in the Soviet ground forces.

Despite some reductions, the ground forces far surpass those of any other major power in size and are perhaps even qualitatively superior. This large and well-equipped force represents a tremendous investment of resources, and its maintenance must continue to be a heavy charge on the Soviet budget. How is one to reconcile such a force with the Soviet doctrine that the first phase of war may be decisive?

Not until the Soviet Union acquired delivery vehicles of intercontinental range could she hope to win victory in the first phase of war. Until that time she could do no more in the first phase than deny victory to her opponents. The Soviet leaders decided that a nuclear strike could settle the outcome of war even before they had the ability to deliver a telling blow at the United States. Until their recent acquisition of this ability, they had to deter or win a war with the forces that they could bring to bear in Europe and Asia. The ability of the Soviet army to conquer Europe rapidly was a deterrent to the initiation of a war against the Soviet Union. For some years after 1945 the United States nuclear capability depended on overseas bases and her war policy has always been influenced by the wishes of her European allies. In these years the Soviet army could help to deter an outbreak of war, but it held out small promise of victory over a powerful opponent whose homeland lay outside the Eurasian land mass. The function of the Soviet ground forces as a deterrent to the initiation of war by the West—something Soviet Marxism maintains is always possible—would be a sufficient explanation of the tremendous investment in those forces. A second and historically important function of the ground forces has been to suppress domestic unrest, and Russian armies have been traditionally deployed for this purpose. Soviet leaders have continued this practice and have used Soviet troops in Hungary and elsewhere to maintain Russian hegemony. Moreover the Soviet army has so long been the senior service that it is probably able to procure a larger share of the national resources than military doctrine in itself would require. In spite of their prestige and importance, however, the Soviet ground forces have not been able, or have not cared, to prevent those military changes that owe their existence to nuclear weapons.

At first examination, strategic nuclear weapons seem to make large land armies obsolete, and it is true that ground forces would not be very important if either the Soviet Union or the United States were knocked out in the initial stages of a war by a first nuclear strike. But neither of these cases can be very interesting to the Soviet military planner, for they represent the simple extremes of a whole range of complicated problems that he must solve. It is obvious to him that a large ground army cannot help a country defeated by nuclear devastation and that a victory guaranteed by other means would dispense with the need for enormous ground forces. The more interesting cases for study are those where the outcome of the initial phase of war is less one-sided. The cautious military planner is bound to give most of his attention to the latter.

Consider first a war in which the Soviet Union has destroyed rather more of the United States striking force and urban wealth than she herself has lost. Neither side knows how much residual striking capacity the opponent possesses; both hope to destroy the enemy's striking capacity early and completely enough to preserve a worthwhile proportion of their urban areas and resources. The role of the ground forces in such a situation will depend on the current state of the art in nuclear weapons. Obviously, the benefit to the Soviet Union of a rapid advance of her ground forces across Europe would be greater at a time when the only accurate Western missiles were based in Europe. At a later stage in Western missile development the significance of Soviet army successes might be less.

It may be argued that the most efficient means of eliminating a missile capability in Western Europe, which could do strategic damage to the Soviet Union, would be to launch Soviet missiles of medium range from Eastern Europe against them. This would be no guarantee, however, against missiles from newly established sites in Western Europe. The only sure way to deal with such a threat would be to occupy Western Europe rapidly. Missiles, as Soviet writers have pointed out more than once, are primarily useful against fixed targets whose coordinates are known in advance. In eliminating mobile and camouflaged targets, as General Pokrovskii has pointed out, the best results can be obtained by ground forces.[62]

The Soviet Union could, as she has threatened to do, drop

enough H-bombs on smaller countries such as Denmark, Norway, and England to make military operations impossible, owing to extreme radioactive contamination. On the other hand, if she could take out enemy missile bases with her own missiles without creating too much radioactive fall-out and then secure the ground area, the industry and resources of the enemy would assist her in the task of domestic reconstruction. In any case, whether or not the Soviet leaders are optimistic about the outcome of a future war, if it happens they will want to occupy Western Europe speedily.

Whether or not nuclear weapons existed, the Soviet military leaders were bound to require the Soviet armies to reach the Channel quickly in the event of war. Nuclear weapons made this task both more urgent and more complex. In the early fifties many Western spokesmen insisted that NATO's possession of tactical nuclear weapons would outweigh the numerical superiority of the Soviet armed forces. The argument ran that the Soviet forces would have to concentrate in order to make advances against smaller forces armed with nuclear weapons. This very concentration would provide the best possible target for nuclear weapons. The Western reasoning seems to have impressed Soviet military planners, who in 1954 started a major program to familiarize all ranks with the effects of nuclear weapons. At the same time, or soon afterwards, they began to introduce nuclear weapons into the ground forces. While the Soviet Union advocated an international agreement to abolish nuclear weapons, she was introducing them rapidly into her army. By March, 1957, Zhukov frankly warned that, "in the event of a great military conflict, atomic weapons would inevitably be put into use as the basic means of destruction. . . ."[63]

Now that both the Soviet Union and the Western powers possess what have been called tactical nuclear weapons, the possibility of a Soviet advance in the face of opposition presents new problems for both sides. Both possess tactical nuclear weapons, but the Soviet side has more men. Can the Soviet Union use her numerical superiority to gain a rapid victory?

Where tactical nuclear weapons are employed, it will be advantageous, if not completely to avoid the traditional concentrations of force, at least to concentrate as briefly as possible. Mobility is obviously necessary, and to gain it the Soviet ground forces have to be motorized, mechanized, and airlifted to an unprecented extent. In the Second World War the Soviet army was deficient in the desired mobility, flexibility, and rapidity of decision largely because it possessed too few vehicles. Since 1945, but more markedly since 1953, the Soviet planners have striven for improved mobility. Even leaving aside nuclear weapons, which Marshal Zhukov has said will be an organic part of the Soviet army, the requirements for increased mobility have greatly increased the cost of the Soviet establishment.

In gaining such mobility, airborne forces are of obvious importance. In the Second World War airborne forces were, as a rule, lightly armed, and their reinforcement by air with heavier weapons was generally unreliable. Their operations were carried out, typically, among or near heavy troop concentrations. In raids of strategic importance, like those on the bridges of Nijmegen and Arnhem, the airborne troops could accomplish little or nothing unless the main front moved up to them. Without a junction of forces, the gains of the airborne units could be neither exploited nor held. Given the ponderous movements of the Soviet ground forces, it is not surprising that their airborne operations were generally not marked by success. Airborne partisans, however, accomplished much good work, because they were not dropped into areas of heavy enemy troop concentration. To summarize, in the Second World War airborne troops sometimes played an important role, but one that was always ancillary to the part played by ground troops. The one great exception to this rule was the German conquest of Crete.

Since the introduction of nuclear weapons in the Soviet army, increased emphasis has been put on lifting troops by air. A military parade in Moscow on the fortieth anniversary of the revolution displayed a new helicopter with greatly increased carrying capacity. When nuclear weapons are used in the field, the dangers of troop concentration may result in such a dispersion of the enemy ground forces that airborne operations are facilitated. Moreover, if the enemy tries to concentrate against airborne troops who are destroying his dispersed forces piecemeal, he risks losing them to the action of nuclear weapons. In addition to the many special tasks performed in World War II, airborne troops of the future may be used to put newly established enemy missile bases out of operation. Urban targets, too, may invite airborne attacks, since the defending troops may be kept outside cities in order to make the latter less attractive as targets for nuclear weapons. Thus, airborne forces can now exploit various new types of vulnerability arising from the dispersion imposed by nuclear weapons.

Airlift by helicopter is recommended by Soviet writers as an aid to mobility and is being adopted by the Soviet forces. Larger aircraft with vertical or near vertical takeoff capability will permit the use of makeshift airfields, and thereby greatly increase the speed with which a given force can be airlifted, or the size of force that can be moved in a given time. If roads are badly damaged, the ability to move across country will be especially advantageous, and the Soviet forces want vehicles that can move independent of roads and cross rivers without pausing. Even more than in World War II earth-moving machines will be needed in a nuclear war to construct and repair airfields and roads.

The Soviet ground forces, then, possess numerical superiority and aim for superior mass mobility. In the West it was once maintained that if both sides had tactical nuclear weapons the numerical superiority of one side would count for less than it formerly did. Those who put forward this view did not raise the question of how to prevent a growing relative advantage accruing to the initially larger force in conditions of mutual attrition. Moreover, if superior mobility were added to superior numbers, the larger army might well achieve a major breakthrough and then exploit it to the full. The breakthrough, of course, would depend on adequate quantities of the latest offensive weapons. One Soviet writer has recently expressed the idea that nuclear warfare will require more, not fewer, ground forces and that large reserves will therefore continue to be important.[64] Difficult as it is to foresee what a nuclear ground battle will be like, the Soviet planners have chosen to emphasize mobility, and they are able to muster many convincing arguments for doing so. They can learn from the Western press, too, that the American army of today is aiming in the same direction.

If and when the Soviet army is fully equipped and trained in accordance with present plans, it would be reckless to suppose, as some Westerners have done, that Soviet troops will display less initiative and skill than Western troops simply because their political system affords less scope to individuality than those of the United States or Western Europe. Russian discussions of training for a war of the future give a general impression of openmindedness and readiness to examine problems objectively. The following quotation from an article by a Soviet general is characteristic of Soviet writing on the subject:

> The appearance of weapons of mass destruction in the weapon systems of modern armies, the qualitative perfection of military equipment, and the complete mechanization and motorization of infantry have worked essential changes in the character of modern warfare. As never before, war has become a thing of rapid movement, demanding rapid reactions to a rapidly changing military situation. Naturally, in such situations, it is very important to be able to execute in the shortest time various changes of formation on the battlefield: advancing columns to deploy to pre-battle positions, forming up on a fighting line, attacking the enemy from the march, pursuing the opponent in vehicles, etc.
>
> The most characteristic means of action in the offensive is to attack from the march. It results in approaching the opponent in vehicles and by rapid march and deployment into battle positions, and finally in the attack itself. Given favorable circumstances, the attack can be carried out by the uninterrupted movement of the motorized infantry into battle deployment. When atomic weapons are employed, then in the interests of saving personnel and military equipment the troops will operate in a basically loose formation, and will gather together into a striking force only at the moment of attack. Thus the contemporary offensive battle can schematically be viewed as a series of

attacks from a moving position into the battle situation.
. . . Naturally in this situation a significant portion of the
infantry's time will be spent in vehicles. . . . Thus in the
modern battle, victory will go to the side which, other
things being equal, possesses the greatest mobility and
maneuverability. It would be erroneous to suppose that
the mechanization and motorization of the army automatically introduces these qualities into its action. No
matter how perfected the technical equipment of the
troops, high mobility and maneuverability can appear
fully only where personnel are accustomed to maneuver
in vehicles, are well trained, and have the necessary technical preparation.[65]

Concern with the mobility of troops when nuclear weapons
are employed on the battlefield is only one of the many consequences of the changed Soviet conception of war. The revised
Soviet understanding of the nature of war has demanded, right
down the line, revisions in the doctrine governing the Soviet
armed services.

*　　*　　*

The Soviet forces are expected to deter or to repel aggression, but these defensive functions derive from the ability of
the forces to wage offensive war successfully. The guiding
Soviet principle is readiness to fight any kind of war in the
most effective way, no matter what the relative likelihood of
the different kinds of war. The Soviet leaders and planners
have not succumbed to the kind of defeatism that argues that
the destruction will be so great as to make it pointless to
prosecute a major war in the most vigorous and effective way.
The basis of the Soviet doctrine is that war would be a calamity
indeed, but that its most awful consequences can be reduced by
the creation and thorough training of a differentiated force
ready for every contingency. The Soviet leaders believe further
that in some circumstances it might be desirable to strike an
initial nuclear blow, and they mean to have a military establishment suited to that end.

NOTES

1. "Speech of Comrade Zhukov," in *XXth Congress Report,* Vol. 1, pp. 480-482.
2. Lieutenant General S. Krasil'nikov, "On the Question of the Character of Contemporary Warfare," in *Marksizm i Leninizm o voine i armii, sbornik statei (Marxism-Leninism on War and the Army, A Collection of Articles),* Moscow, 1956, pp. 152-154. Prepared for galleys on November 28, 1956.
3. *Ibid.*
4. *Ibid.*
5. *Ibid.,* pp. 160, 161.
6. "The Speech of the Minister of Defense of the U.S.S.R. Marshal of the Soviet Union G. K. Zhukov, at the All-Army Meeting of Crack Troops on March 16, 1957," *Pravda,* March 20, 1957.
7. Zhukov speech in India, quoted by Major General B. Boltin, "The Role of Experience in the Development of Soviet Military Science," *Sovetskii flot (Soviet Fleet),* June 6, 1957. This is the only source that has been found for any part of the speech.
8. Colonel V. Petrov, "On the Essence of War Potential. An Aid to Students of the Marxist-Leninist Theory of War and the Army," *Sovetskaia aviatsiia (Soviet Aviation),* May 20, 1958.
9. *Ibid.*
10. "An American Magazine on Anglo-American Discords," *Pravda,* August 30, 1954.
11. M. Krementsov, "Atomnoe oruzhie" ("Atomic Weapons"), *Vestnik vozdushnogo flota (Herald of the Air Fleet),* No. 8, August, 1954, pp. 65-70.
12. M. Krementsov, "The Hydrogen Bomb," in *Atomnoe oruzhie (Atomic Weapons),* Moscow, 1955, pp. 219-228.
13. Major General G. I. Pokrovskii, *Nauka i tekhnika v sovermennykh voinakh (Science and Technology in Modern Wars),* Moscow, 1956, p. 50.
14. Comrade I. E. Kazakov, "How the Guidance of the Intercontinental Ballistic Missile Is Carried Out: An Interview with Doctor of Technical Sciences, Comrade I. E. Kazakov," *Sovetskaia aviatsiia,* August 31, 1957.
15. Major General V. A. Semenov, Professor in the M. E. Zhukovskii Military Aerial Engineering Academy, "The Development of Rocket Technology," *Sovetskaia Rossiia (Soviet Russia),* September 14, 1957.
16. Pokrovskii, *op. cit.,* p. 51.
17. Engineer Major V. Kriksunov, "The Problems of the Interception of Intercontinental Ballistic Missiles," *Sovetskaia aviatsiia,* April 25, 1957.
18. Pokrovskii, *op. cit.*
19. "On the Bellicose Statements of Some American, British, and West German Generals. Answers of the Commander-in-Chief of the Air Forces of the USSR, Marshal of Aviation K. A. Vershinin to Questions by the *Pravda* Correspondent," *Pravda,* September 8, 1957.

20. Professor, Doctor of Technical Sciences, and Major General of the Engineering Technical Services, G. I. Pokrovskii, "Intercontinental Missiles and Other Vehicles for Strategic Weapons," *Sovetskii patriot* (*Soviet Patriot*), September 11, 1957.

21. Major General N. Talenskii, "The Question of Military Strategy and Foreign Policy," *Mezhdunarodnaia zhizn'* (*International Life*), No. 3, 1958, pp. 34, 35.

22. Chou En-lai, "The Present International Situation and China's Foreign Policy," a speech delivered to the fifth session of the first National People's Congress, February 10, 1958. I am indebted to Alice Langley Hsieh for this reference.

23. Engineer Major Iu. Rumiantsev, "Refueling Aircraft in the Air," *Red Star*, May 31, 1955.

24. Candidate in Technical Sciences, Lieutenant Colonel of Engineers, I. Naumenko, "The Penetrating Radiation Accompanying an Atomic Explosion," *Vestnik vozdushnogo flota*, No. 1, January, 1955, p. 83; I. Naumenko, "The Penetrating Radiation Accompanying an Atomic Explosion," in *Atomnoe oruzhie*, 2d ed., Moscow, 1955, pp. 170-171. The sentence on the poor accuracy of guided and unguided missiles was eliminated from the version published in the book, *Atomic Weapons*.

25. Lieutenant Colonel of Engineers P. Safonov, "Airplanes: Carriers of Atomic Weapons and Their Employment (A Review of the Foreign Press)," in *Atomnoe oruzhie*, pp. 241-255.

26. Lieutenant Colonel of Engineers A. Baldov, Docent, Candidate in the Technical Sciences, "Pilotless Aircraft," *Red Star*, July 14, 1956.

27. Lieutenant Colonel of Engineers V. Glukhov, Candidate in the Technical Sciences, "Guided Missiles and Torpedoes," *Red Star*, August 16, 1956.

28. Colonel Iu. Pshenianik, Docent, Candidate in the Military Sciences, "On the Role of Aviation in Modern War," *Sovetskaia aviatsiia*, March 17, 1957.

29. "Khrushchev's Triumph," *Neue Zürcher Zeitung*, October 10, 1957.

30. "Answers to the Questions of the Chief Diplomatic Correspondent of the American Newspaper, *The New York Times*, J. Reston, October 7, 1957," *Pravda*, October 11, 1957.

31. "Answers to the Questions of the Correspondent of the Canadian Newspaper, *The Toronto Telegram*, P. Dempson," in N. S. Khrushchev, *Za prochnyi mir i mirnoe sosushchestvovanie* (*For a Lasting Peace and Peaceful Coexistence*), Moscow, 1958, p. 216.

32. "N. S. Khrushchev's Speech," *Vestnik vozdushnogo flota*, No. 4, April, 1958, p. 6.

33. Colonel A. Lapenin, "Aircraft in Modern War," *Sovetskaia aviatsiia*, June 3, 1958.

34. *Ibid.*

35. "H-bomb Flights Toward Russia?" *U.S. News & World Report*, June 6, 1958, p. 76.

36. Professor, Rear Admiral N. Pavlovich, "The Naval Art and the Development of the Military Equipment of the Fleet," *Sovetskii flot*, March 6, 1957.

37. Captain N. Nikolaev, "The Navy in the System of the Armed Forces of the U.S.S.R.," *Sovetskii flot,* May 29, 1957.

38. Major General E. Boltin, "The Role of Experience in the Development of Soviet Military Science," *Sovetskii flot,* June 6, 1957.

39. Colonel G. Fedorov, Candidate in the Philosophical Sciences, "Marxism-Leninism on War and the Army," Part 1, "The Origin and Essence of Wars," *Red Star,* January 6, 1954.

40. G. Fedorov, "The Origin and Essence of Wars," in *Marksizm-Leninizm o voine, armii i voennoi nauke, Sbornik statei* (*Marxism-Leninism on War, the Army, and Military Science, A Collection of Articles*), Moscow, 1955, p. 33. (Delivered to the printer on September 10, 1954; in galleys on February 3, 1955.)

41. Colonel O. Zakrezhevskii, "The Influence of the Development of the Means of Warfare upon the Military Art," in *Marksizm-Leninizm o voine, armii i voennoi nauke, Sbornik statei,* Moscow, 1955, p. 195.

42. Unsigned editorial, "The Great Strength of the Leninist Idea of the Defense of the Socialist Government," *Vestnik vozdushnogo flota,* No. 4, April, 1955, p. 8.

43. G. Starko, "The Atom Bomb and Its Military Employment," in *Atomnoe oruzhie,* Moscow, 1955, p. 203.

44. "The Speech of Comrade G. K. Zhukov," *XXth Congress Report,* pp. 481-483.

45. M. Kozin, "The Organization and Tasks of MPVO [The Ministry of Antiair Defense] in Residences," *Voennye znaniia* (*Military Knowledge*), No. 3, March, 1956, p. 18.

46. Guards Major General of Tanks V. Voronchenko, "On the Influence of the Development of Military Equipment on the Manner of the Conduct of War and Military Operations," *Red Star,* July 26, 1956.

47. Marshal of the Soviet Union G. K. Zhukov, "A Speech at the All-Army Meeting of Crack Troops, March 16, 1957," Moscow, 1957, pp. 12-13.

48. Lieutenant Colonel of Engineers B. Surikov, "The Development of Antiair Defense," *Red Star,* March 23, 1957.

49. Lieutenant Colonel of Engineers, Candidate in the Technical Sciences, M. Pavlov, "The Anti-atomic Defense of Airfields," *Sovetskaia aviatsiia,* June 5, 1957.

50. Deputy of the Supreme Soviet of the U.S.S.R., Thrice Hero of the Soviet Union, Major General of Aviation I. Kozhedub, "Always on Guard," *Sovetskaia aviatsiia,* February 17, 1957; Colonel Iu. Pshenianik, Docent, Candidate in the Military Sciences, "On the Role of Aviation in Modern War," *Sovetskaia aviatsiia,* March 17, 1957.

51. *Knizhnaia letopis'* (*Catalogue of Books*), the weekly organ of the publishing industry, lists all the editions. An early standard version, *Pamiatka naseleniiu po zashchite ot atomnogo oruzhiia* (*Popular Handbook for Defense against Atomic Weapons*), 1954, 32 pages, has not been available for this study.

52. *Pamiatka naeleniiu po zashchite ot atomnogo, khimicheskogo i bakteriologicheskogo oruzhiia* (*Popular Handbook for Defense against Atomic, Chemical and Bacteriological Weapons*), Moscow, 1957, 61 pages.

53. V. I. Skopin, *Militarizm (Militarism)*, Moscow, 1956, pp. 67, 68. The second edition, Moscow, 1957, contains substantially the same text on pp. 75, 76.

54. M. M. Gvozdev and V. A. Iakovkin, *Atomnoe oruzhie i protivo-atomnaia zashchita (Atomic Weapons and Antiatomic Defense)*, Moscow, 1956, p. 6.

55. "Interview with Henry Shapiro, Correspondent of the American United Press Agency, November 14, 1957," *Pravda*, November 19, 1957.

56. *Ibid.*

57. *Sovetskii patriot* for February 11, 12, and 13, 1958, contains the texts of speeches at the Moscow conference where these facts were announced.

58. The material on Soviet naval views is derived from the following Soviet sources: Captain of the Second Rank (Commander) A. Kvitnitskii, "The Arming of the American Navy with Guided Jet Missiles," *Red Star*, September 4, 1956; Admiral V. Platonov, "Modern Views on the Conduct of Military Operations at Sea," *Red Star*, December 16, 1956; Captain of the Second Rank (Commander) K. Romanov, "Landing Operations in the Plans of the American Admirals," *Sovetskii flot*, January 5, 1957; Admiral L. Vladmirskii, "Modern Naval Construction," *Red Star*, February 15, 1957; Professor, Rear Admiral N. Pavlovich, "The Naval Art and the Development of the Military Equipment of the Fleet," *Sovetskii flot*, March 6, 1957; Rear Admiral A. Kruchenykh, "On the Character of Modern Military Action at Sea," *Sovetskii flot*, March 23, 1957; Rear Admiral V. Andreev, "Sea and Ocean Communications in Modern War," *Red Star*, April 25, 1957; Captain N. Nikolaev, "The Navy in the System of the Armed Forces of the U.S.S.R.," *Sovetskii flot*, May 29, 1957; Captain N. Gordeev, "The Defense of Naval Bases in Modern Conditions," *Red Star*, May 27, 1957; Captain P. Zhelezniak, "Aerial Means of Search for Submarines," *Sovetskii flot*, June 8, 1957; Candidate in Naval Sciences, Vice Admiral A. Kruchenykh, "On the Influence of Rocket Weapons on Fleet Tactics," *Sovetskii flot*, November 15, 1957; Lieutenant Colonel of Engineers B. Surikov, "Anti-missile Defense of Ships," *Sovetskii flot*, January 7, 1958; Doctor of Technical Sciences and Captain of Engineers [Naval] G. Migirenko, "Explosions and the Defense of Ships," *Sovetskii flot*, February 15, 1958; Captain of Engineers [Naval] A. Kilesso, " 'The Achilles' Heel' of the Aircraft Carrier Fleet," *Sovetskii flot*, March 20, 1958.

59. Captain of the Second Rank (Commander) K. Romanov, "Landing Operations in the Plans of the American Admirals," *Sovetskii flot*, January 5, 1957.

60. *Ibid.*

61. Captain D. Shavtsov, "Command of the Sea," *Voennaia mysl'*, No. 7, July, 1955, p. 14.

62. Major General, Doctor of Technical Sciences, G. I. Pokrovskii, *Rol' nauki i tekhniki v sovremennoi voine (The Role of Science and Technology in Modern War)*, pamphlet, Moscow, 1957, p. 24.

63. "The Speech of the U.S.S.R. Minister of Defense, Marshal of the Soviet Union G. K. Zhukov," *Red Star*, March 20, 1957.

64. Colonel I. S. Baz', "Soviet Military Science on the Character of Modern War," *Voennyi vestnik (Military Herald)*, No. 6, June, 1958, pp. 19-29.
65. Hero of the Soviet Union, Major General of Tank Troops O. Losik, "The Important Condition for the High Mobility of Troops," *Red Star*, March 30, 1957.

INDEX

OTHER VOLUMES OF RAND RESEARCH

Air War and Emotional Stress: Psychological Studies of Bombing and Civilian Defense, by Irving L. Janis. New York, N. Y.: McGraw-Hill Book Company, Inc., 1951.

Approximations for Digital Computers, by Cecil Hastings, Jr. Princeton, N. J.: Princeton University Press, 1955.

Behind the Sputniks: A Survey of Soviet Space Science, by F. J. Krieger. Washington, D.C.: Public Affairs Press, 1958.

The Berlin Blockade: A Study in Cold War Politics, by W. Phillips Davison. Princeton, N. J.: Princeton University Press, 1958.

The Compleat Strategyst: Being a Primer on the Theory of Games of Strategy, by J. D. Williams. New York, N. Y.: McGraw-Hill Book Company, Inc., 1954.

Dynamic Programming, by Richard Bellman. Princeton, N. J.: Princeton University Press, 1957.

Efficiency in Government through Systems Analysis: with Emphasis on Water Resource Development, by Roland N. McKean. New York, N. Y.: John Wiley & Sons, Inc., 1958.

The French Economy and the State, by Warren C. Baum. Princeton, N. J.: Princeton University Press, 1958.

German Rearmament and Atomic War: The Views of German Military and Political Leaders, by Hans Speier. Evanston, Ill.: Row, Peterson & Company, 1957.

The House without Windows: France Selects a President, by Constantin Melnik and Nathan Leites. Evanston, Ill.: Row, Peterson & Company, 1958.

International Communication and Political Opinion: A Guide to the Literature, by Bruce Lannes Smith and Chitra M. Smith. Princeton, N. J.: Princeton University Press, 1956.

Introduction to the Theory of Games, by J. C. C. McKinsey. New York, N. Y.: McGraw-Hill Book Company, Inc., 1952.

Labor Productivity in Soviet and American Industry, by Walter Galenson. New York, N. Y.: Columbia University Press, 1955.

Linear Programming and Economic Analysis, by Robert Dorfman, Paul A. Samuelson, and Robert M. Solow. New York, N. Y.: McGraw-Hill Book Company, Inc., 1958.

A Million Random Digits with 100,000 Normal Deviates, by The RAND Corporation. Glencoe, Ill.: The Free Press, 1955.

Mobilizing Resources for War: The Economic Alternatives, by Tibor Scitovsky, Edward Shaw, and Lorie Tarshis. New York, N. Y.: McGraw-Hill Book Company, Inc., 1951.

The Operational Code of the Politburo, by Nathan Leites. New York, N. Y.: McGraw-Hill Book Company, Inc., 1951.

The Organizational Weapon: A Study of Bolshevik Strategy and Tactics, by Philip Selznick. New York, N. Y.: McGraw-Hill Book Company, Inc., 1952.

Propaganda Analysis: A Study of Inferences Made from Nazi Propaganda in World War II, by Alexander L. George. Evanston, Ill.: Row, Peterson & Company, 1959.

Psychosis and Civilization, by Herbert Goldhamer and Andrew W. Marshall. Glencoe, Ill.: The Free Press, 1949.

The Rise of Khrushchev, by Myron Rush. Washington, D.C.: Public Affairs Press, 1958.

Ritual of Liquidation: The Case of the Moscow Trials, by Nathan Leites and Elsa Bernaut. Glencoe, Ill.: The Free Press, 1954.

Smolensk under Soviet Rule, by Merle Fainsod. Cambridge, Mass.: Harvard University Press, 1958.

Soviet Attitudes Toward Authority: An Interdisciplinary Approach to Problems of Soviet Character, by Margaret Mead. New York, N. Y.: McGraw-Hill Book Company, Inc., 1951.

Soviet Military Doctrine, by Raymond L. Garthoff. Glencoe, Ill.: The Free Press, 1953.

Soviet National Income and Product in 1928, by Oleg Hoeffding. New York, N. Y.: Columbia University Press, 1954.

Soviet National Income and Product, 1940-1948, by Abram Bergson and Hans Heymann, Jr. New York, N. Y.: Columbia University Press, 1954.

Strategic Surrender: The Politics of Victory and Defeat, by Paul Kecskemeti. Stanford, Calif.: Stanford University Press, 1958.

A Study of Bolshevism, by Nathan Leites. Glencoe, Ill.: The Free Press, 1953.

Two Studies in Soviet Controls: Communism and the Russian Peasant, and Moscow in Crisis, by Herbert S. Dinerstein and Leon Gouré. Glencoe, Ill.: The Free Press, 1955.

Weight-Strength Analysis of Aircraft Structures, by F. R. Shanley. New York, N. Y.: McGraw-Hill Book Company, Inc., 1952.

West German Leadership and Foreign Policy, edited by Hans Speier and W. Phillips Davison. Evanston, Ill.: Row, Peterson & Company, 1957.